A FIELD GUIDE TO

MEDICINAL

PLANTS AND HERBS

THE PETERSON FIELD GUIDE SERIES®

A FIELD GUIDE TO

MEDICINAL PLANTS AND HERBS

OF EASTERN AND CENTRAL NORTH AMERICA

Second Edition

STEVEN FOSTER
AND JAMES A. DUKE

SPONSORED BY THE NATIONAL AUDUBON SOCIETY,
THE NATIONAL WILDLIFE FEDERATION, AND
THE ROGER TORY PETERSON INSTITUTE

HOUGHTON MIFFLIN COMPANY
BOSTON NEW YORK

For information about permission to reproduce selections from
this book, write to Permissions, Houghton Mifflin Company,
215 Park Avenue, New York, New York 10003

PETERSON FIELD GUIDES and PETERSON FIELD GUIDE SERIES
are registered trademarks of Houghton Mifflin Company.

Library of Congress Cataloging in Publication Data

Foster, Steven, date.
A field guide to medicinal plants and herbs of eastern and
central North America / Steven Foster and James A. Duke. — 2nd ed.
p. cm. — (Peterson Field Guide Series)
"Sponsored by the National Audubon Society, the National Wildlife Federa-
tion, and the Roger Tory Peterson Institute."
Rev. ed. of: Field guide to medicinal plants. 1990.
Includes bibliographical references (p.   ).
ISBN 978-0-395-98814-5
ISBN 0-395-98815-2 (cloth)
ISBN 0-395-98814-4 (pbk)
1. Medicinal plants — East (U.S.) Identification.   2. Medicinal
plants— Middle West Identification.   3. Medicinal plants — Canada,
Eastern Identification.   I. Duke, James A., 1929–   . II. Foster,
Steven, 1957– Field guide to medicinal plants.   III. Title.
IV. Title: Medicinal plants and herbs.
V. Series.
QK99.U6F68   1999
581.6'34'0973 —dc21   99-33189   CIP

Book design by Anne Chalmers
Typeface: Linotype-Hell Fairfield; Futura Condensed (Adobe)

Printed in China

SCP   20   19   18   17   16

PREFACE

Why a field guide to American medicinal herbs? Didn't the use of herbal medicine dissolve into obscurity after the Dark Ages? Aren't folk remedies just old wives' tales, and the stuff of witches' brew? The answer is an unequivocal no. The plant kingdom is a storehouse of active chemical compounds. Herbs—defined as any plant used for flavor, fragrant, or medicinal purposes—encompass at least 25 percent of known flowering plants, and yet less than 2 percent have been scientifically investigated for their medicinal potential. Over 40 percent of prescription drugs sold in the U.S. contain at least one ingredient derived from nature. As many as 25 percent of prescription drugs contain an ingredient derived from higher (flowering) plants. This statistic has not changed by plus or minus 1 percent since the 1950s. Periwinkle (*Catharanthus roseus or Vinca rosea*) is a common ornamental in the U.S., often planted as a ground cover outside homes or city high-rises. Few people who pass by the plant realize that preparations derived from Periwinkle are used in chemotherapy for leukemia and more than a dozen other types of cancer. Alkaloids derived from the fungus ergot, which grows on Rye Grass and Giant Cane are used as uterine-contracting drugs. The many cardiac glycosides from Foxglove (*Digitalis*), commonly planted as an ornamental flower, are used in a variety of products for the management of several phases of heart disease. The primary source of material for the biosynthesis of steroid hormones is the plant kingdom. The social, economic, and political impact of oral contraceptives alone illustrates the importance of this group of plant-derived drugs. The manufacture of progesterone was made commercially feasible by the use of chemicals from Mexican yams, which were then converted to progesterone. With all the advances of modern medicine there is still nothing to replace morphine, derived from the Opium Poppy, as a pain reliever for major trauma. However, there is an opium replacement on the horizon, a strong pain-relieving compound derived from a tropical frog. Nature, in its infinite chemical factory, endows animals with biological active compounds, as it does plants.

Since the first edition of *Medicinal Plants* was published in 1990, Paclitaxel (formerly known by its registered trademark name, Taxol) has emerged as an important new drug in chemotherapy for certain forms of ovarian and breast cancer. Paclitaxel, which is derived through a semi-synthetic process from the English Yew *(Taxus baccata)*, is expected to be approved in the future for other difficult to treat hard cell cancer types, and is expected to reach sales of $1 billion per year. The fact is, herbs —plant drugs—are a very important and integral part of modern medicine.

We believe that safer natural compounds could be found to replace the synthetic compounds that occur in about 75 percent of our prescription drugs, and that evolution has better equipped us to deal with rational doses of preparations from medicinal plants. But since it costs, in our litigious American society, more than $350 million to prove a new drug safe and efficacious, we may need to wait for the Japanese to develop these natural medicines for us. In the last decade, the Japanese held more than half of the new patents on natural products. Unfortunately, most American medicinal plants have yet to be thoroughly investigated in terms of pharmacology and chemistry, much less through clinical trials in humans. Those that have been extensively studied in recent years have mostly been probed by European or Asian researchers. Little work is performed on American medicinal plants by American researchers, while virtually all other industrialized, technologically advanced societies intensively investigate their native medicinal flora. Much scientific research has also been conducted in developing countries where traditional medicine systems, some thousands of years old, are still an integral part of health care systems. China and India are prime examples. Although these countries may be called "developing" in terms of their economic and technical systems, the more than 5,000-year-old traditions of Traditional Chinese Medicine, and of Ayurveda in India, represent highly developed medical systems that are constantly being vindicated and enhanced by modern research. Their experience and research is valuable to our study of American medical botany.

In modern medicine in the U.S., only single isolated chemical components are used in prescription drugs, rather than the complex mix of chemicals found in a single herb. This has more to do with the structure of our drug laws than scientific advancement.

To invest millions of dollars in proving a drug safe and effective, pharmaceutical companies are interested in substances that can be patented. Therefore, no drug company is going to spend hundreds of millions of dollars to prove Echinacea can reduce the length and severity of a cold, if Echinacea cannot be patented.

Nevertheless, herbs in their whole form, rather than just a single chemical derived from them, have come to play an important role in health care. Since the first edition of this book was published, interest in herbs on a worldwide basis has exploded. In the past decade alone, herb product sales in the U.S. have increased by an astonishing tenfold at the retail level. In the early 1990s herb products were relegated to the realm of health and natural food stores with an estimated $500 million in sales. Today herb products are sold wherever Americans shop for food or drugs — supermarkets, discount department stores, chain and independent pharmacies, and the Internet — and are advertised nationally on television. Even the conservative *Journal of the American Medical Association* devoted an entire issue (vol. 280, no. 18, November 11, 1998) to the subject of alternative medicine. Back issues of this journal had sold out by early 1999. Herb product sales in the U.S. are expected to top $5 billion by the year 2000! The use of herbs for health purposes has become part of the American mainstream.

What has contributed to this extraordinary explosion in interest in herbs? One major factor is consumer interest in herb products, which has sparked legislation to make herb products more widely available. In 1997, 60 million adult Americans spent an average of $54.00 per year on herb products to treat colds, burns, headaches, rashes, insomnia, PMS, depression, gastrointestinal problems, and menopause, among other conditions.

Another major factor is increased scientific interest in herbs, resulting in dozens of controlled clinical trials, the gold standard of scientific evidence. Head-to-head controlled clinical trials comparing conventional antidepressant drugs with St. John's Wort have shown that St. John's Wort preparations are just as effective and safer than prescription antidepressants for the treatment of mild to moderate forms of depression. St. John's Wort preparations outsell prescription antidepressants by as much as 20 to 1 in Germany. Saw Palmetto fruit extracts have been shown to be as effective and at least as safe as prescription drugs for the treatment of benign prostatic hyperplasia (BPH), a nonmalignant enlargement of the prostate affecting a majority of men over 50 years of age. An indigenous American medical plant, Saw Palmetto is approved for use in BPH in Germany, France, and Italy. In addition, high-quality herb products are much less expensive than prescription drugs. The European influence (or even invasion) is a crucial factor in the rise of herbal medicines in America.

Much modern research on herbal medicines or "phytomedicines" has been stimulated by European interest. A phytomedicine is an herb product that represents the totality of chemical constituents in an herb or plant part, rather than a single isolated chemical component. Phytotherapy, the practice of herbal medicine, is most highly developed in Germany, where over 70 percent of physicians prescribe herb products, and medical students are required to pass a section on phytomedicine in licensure exams.

Although estimates vary, herb product sales in Germany are said to be as high as $8 billion per year. In Germany, phytomedicine is not viewed as "alternative medicine." Rather, phytomedicines are part of the mainstream medical establishment. Herbal preparations are simply another tool, normally available to physicians, pharmacists, and, ultimately, the consumer.

The German regulatory system allows standard registration of herb products as drugs, if those herbs have been approved by the Commission E, an expert committee of the German Federal Institute for Drugs and Medical Devices (the equivalent of our Food and Drug Administration). The Commission E monographs are published in Germany's equivalent of the *Federal Register* and serve as the basis for regulating herb products in that country. While the system has its flaws and detractors, it is the best-developed regulatory system for herbal medicines in an industrialized Western nation. Some have contended that it should serve as a model for herbal product regulation in the U.S. Recently, an English translation of the complete German Commission E monographs has been published (see work by M. Blumenthal, 1998, in the bibliography).

A landmark legislative development in the U.S. has also fueled the shift of herb products from the niche market of health and natural food stores into the mass market. In 1994 Congress passed and the president signed into law the Dietary Supplement Health and Education Act of 1994. It is commonly known by its acronym, DSHEA. DSHEA clearly defined herb products as "dietary supplements," allowing companies to list a product's benefits on the label, recommending how the product affects the "structure and function" of the body. Statements on the label cannot directly imply prevention or treatment of a specific condition; if such claims are made, the manufacturer must notify the FDA, and the claim must carry the caveat, "This statement has not been evaluated by the Food and Drug Administration. This product is not intended to diagnose, treat, cure, or prevent any disease." The law also created an Office of Dietary Supplements within the National Institutes of Health, and the appointment of a Presidential Commission on Dietary Supplement Labels. Balanced, truthful, nonmisleading, scientifically based third-party literature can also be used to provide the consumer with legitimate information on the intended use of herbal products.

Regulations are still being developed from the broadly conceived DSHEA legislation. The system is far from perfect, but the net effect has been to stimulate enormous interest by consumers, health-care professionals, scientists, regulators, and lawmakers in the role that herbs play in benefiting health.

Since this book first appeared a decade ago, one intention has been to further an awareness of the need for plant conservation by recognizing the economic or beneficial history of plants that could provide potential future economic and medicinal benefits for humans. Conservation and preservation are necessary on both the micro and macro levels. European and Chinese medical botanists who go on collecting trips to U.S. fields and forests are struck by the abundance of our wild herbs, and they caution that we should conserve them. The demand for certain species of wild-harvested native American herbs, such as Echinacea species, Black Cohosh, and Saw Palmetto, has increased by tenfold in the past decade. Rational conservation efforts will be necessary. We should make an effort to conserve native medicinal plants that may provide treatment or cures for cancer, heart disease, warts, the common cold, or even AIDS. The notion that American fields and forests are an endless fountain of animal, plant, or mineral resources is a nineteenth-century idea, not appropriate to the dwindling natural resources of the twenty-first century.

Unfortunately, a number of medicinal plants are now being extirpated without regard to preservation and the continued ecological success of the species. While the Endangered Species Act and Lacey Act have helped regulate the harvest of a few medicinals, notably Ginseng, the public consciousness is still swayed more toward protecting animals than plants. Commenting on dramatic declines in Kansas populations of Echinacea (Purple Coneflower) in recent years, one frustrated researcher remarked that if Echinacea had fur and cute little black eyes, it could elicit a little attention!

We hope this volume will help the reader gain a deeper appreciation of the plants around us. By understanding the traditional medicinal uses of so many of our wildflowers, woody plants, and weeds, we will gain a deeper sense of our relationship to the natural world. Knowing that a wildflower was a folk remedy for cancer, and that that knowledge may eventually produce the lead that helps researchers develop a new cancer treatment, adds a new dimension, a human element to conservation. Enjoy, and be cautious.

Steven Foster and James A. Duke

ACKNOWLEDGMENTS

The authors would like to thank the Threshold Foundation for partial support of Steven Foster's work in 1987 through a grant to the Elixir Botanical Garden Project in Brixey, Missouri. A note of thanks to Vinnie McKinney, Sally Goodwin, Ella Alford, and Nancy Ward for support of the work. A special thanks to Les Eastman for encouragement and for tracking down photos and plants for the color plates. The authors deeply appreciate the help, support, and friendship of Mark Blumenthal and staff at the American Botanical Council, Dr. Ed Croom, Dr. Norman Farnsworth, Kelly Kindscher, Dr. Paul Lee, members of the Sabbathday Lake Shaker Community, and Dr. Varro Tyler. Michael Flannery and the staff of the Lloyd Library provided many useful and obscure research materials.

Peggy Duke and Jude Farar are thanked for their behind-the-scenes contributions, without which this work could not have materialized. Additional support was provided by Ellen Gibbs, Sara Miller, Colin Foster, and Abbey Foster. A special thanks to Barbara Garsoe, childhood next-door neighbor, who helped instill Steven Foster's love of nature by leading a junior Audubon club.

Professor Yue Chongxi, at the Institute of Chinese Materia Medica, Academy of Traditional Chinese Medicine, Beijing, and Dr. Shiu Ying Hu, at Arnold Arboretum, Harvard University, are gratefully acknowledged for information they provided on Chinese uses of closely related plant species of China and North America.

Steven Foster would like to acknowledge the staff of Steven Foster Group, Inc., for their assistance on the book, including Mary-Pat Boian, Ellen Gibbs, and Kim Seymour. A special thanks to Josie Moore for scanning the photographs used in the book, and to Jonathan Marshall for overseeing all computer-related tasks. Leanna K. Potts deserves special thanks for steadfast work on indexes and life lists.

The authors are grateful for the fine work and gentle prodding of Harry Foster, Barry Estabrook, Dorothy Henderson, and Lisa White. Thanks to the rest of the staff of Houghton Mifflin for all the thankless details associated with book production.

Much thanks goes to botanists and photographers who submitted photos for the book, including Alan Detrick, Doug Elliott, Harry Ellis, Craig C. Freeman, Pamela Harper, Carl Hunter, Stephen L. Timme, and Martin Wall.

Credit must also be given to the dozens of botanists, medical botanists, pharmacognosists, toxicologists, ethnobotanists, physicians, and researchers in all disciplines touching upon medicinal plants for their hundreds of published works, which have been frequently and repeatedly consulted. If this book cited references in the style of a scientific publication, the bibliography would be half the length of the book. A few of the most pertinent works for further references are listed on pp. 362–64.

Tribute must be paid to the 1,100 to 5,000 generations of Native Americans whose experience and evolution with the indigenous medicinal flora ultimately made this book, and a scant two centuries of literature, possible.

Finally, Steven Foster would like to thank his parents, Herb and Hope Foster, for all they have given, and dedicate his work on this volume to them.

CONTENTS

A FIELD GUIDE TO
MEDICINAL
PLANTS AND HERBS

How to Use This Book

This book is not a prescriptor, just a field guide to medicinal plants of the eastern and central portion of the North American continent. The purpose of this guide is to help you to identify these plants safely and accurately, and to help you avoid similar-looking plants that could be dangerous or even fatally poisonous.

General Organization

SPECIES COVERED: There are more than 800 species of plants growing in the eastern U.S. that can be documented as having at least some medicinal use. This book includes 500 of the more significant medicinal plant species of the eastern U.S. with important historical uses, present use, or future potential. We have not attempted to cover all of the alien plants found here that are used medicinally in their native lands. For example, of the hundreds of ornamentals originating from east Asia in American horticulture, more than 1,000 species can be documented as being used in Traditional Chinese Medicine. Nearly all common weeds naturalized from Europe have been used as medicinal plants in their native lands. We have included many naturalized weeds, but not all of them.

AREA COVERED: This field guide covers all states east of, but excluding, Colorado, Montana, and New Mexico. It does not fully cover the southern half of Florida or the southern and western halves of Texas. Adjacent regions of Canadian provinces are included. Toward the southern, western, and extreme northern extensions of the range, our coverage is less comprehensive.

BOTANICAL AND MEDICAL TERMS: Since this book is intended as a guide for the layperson, we have used as few technical terms as possible. Nevertheless, the use of some specific terms relative to plant identification or the medicinal use of plants has been inevitable. We define those terms in the Glossary. Although we have defined terms relative to medicinal effects, we have not attempted to define each disease, condition, or ailment included in this book. We have kept disease terminology as simple as possible. For further explanations, should they be necessary, the reader is referred to any good English dictionary or medical dictionary.

ILLUSTRATIONS: All photos are by Steven Foster except where noted otherwise. Photographs have been taken over a period of 25 years. Most photographs were taken with various Nikon camera bodies and Nikkor lens, particularly the Micro-Nikkor series. Most photographs were taken with Fuji Velvia or Kodachrome 64 film.

IDENTIFYING PLANTS

Plants are arranged by visual features, based on flower color, number of petals, habitat, leaf arrangement, and so on. These obvious similarities help the reader to thumb quickly through the pages and find an illustration that corresponds with a plant in hand. Once you have matched a plant with an illustration, read all details in the descriptive text, making sure that all characteristics — key italicized details, range, habitat, flowering time, color, and the flower or leaf structure (see headings at top of pages facing the plates) — correspond. Never, never ingest a plant that has not been positively identified. (Read the sections on warnings on p. 10.)

The first part of the book covers wildflowers, which are arranged by flower color (white, yellow, orange, pink to red, blue-violet, green) and other visual similarities. Please note that there is tremendous variation in flower color in the plant world. If a plant may have white or blue flowers, for example, we have attempted to include the plant in both sections of this guide, usually depicted by a photograph only in the section with typical flower color. Your interpretation of "pink to red" may be viewed as "violet to blue" by others. Be aware of these subtle differences. Flowering shrubs, trees, and woody vines are in separate sections following the wildflowers. Flowering woody plants are generally not included in the wildflower section. Ferns and related plants follow the woody plant section. Last is a section on grasses or grasslike plants.

COMMON NAMES: One or two common names are listed at the beginning of each entry. Though some plants have only one common name, others may have many. Common names of wildflowers generally conform to those used in Peterson and McKinney's *A Field Guide to Wildflowers*. Sometimes, in an herbal context, a plant is better known by another common name. In these instances we have used the most commonly known name for the herb. For trees, shrubs, vines, grasses, and ferns, we have used the names we believe are best known.

PART USED: The plant part(s) used for medicinal purposes are listed in boldface type opposite the common name. In descriptions of woody plants, the word "bark" almost always refers to the inner bark of the tree or shrub, not the rough outer layer. Slippery Elm, for example, has a rough, corky outer bark that is not known to be of medicinal use, though it is often sold as Slippery Elm bark. The tawny white, fibrous, highly mucilaginous (slippery) inner bark can easily be stripped from the branches once the outer bark has been rasped away. Please see the section on "Conservation and Harvesting" (p. 7) for general guidelines on harvesting various plant parts.

SCIENTIFIC NAMES: Beneath the common name is the scientific or botanical name by which the plant is generally known (in our opinion). Scientific names are not set in stone. Although changes in scientific names are annoying, sometimes they must be made according to valid new information developed by botanists with a special interest in taxonomic relationships. Many plant guides in the Peterson Field Guide Series have relied on the eighth edition of *Gray's Manual of Botany* (Fernald, 1950), but we have not used it as the final word. Nearly 50 years have passed since its most recent revision, and many changes in nomenclature have since occurred. The second edition of Gleason and Cronquist's *Manual of Vascular Plants of Northeastern United States and Adjacent Canada* (New York Botanical Garden, 1991) and *A Synonymized Checklist of the Vascular Flora of the United States, Canada, and Greenland,* second edition by John Kartesz (1994), have been used as sources of new or changed scientific names. Where questions have arisen over the correct botanical name or attributed author of the name, we have used the United States Department of Agriculture's Integrated Taxonomic Information System (www.plants.usda.gov/plantproj/itis/itis_query.html) as the final arbiter. We have provided synonyms in brackets beneath the main botanical name to reflect alternate or obsolete scientific names that are often encountered in recent botanical manuals, popular field guides, and herbals. The synonyms also reflect the many taxonomic changes since the first edition of this guide was published in 1990.

The scientific name is followed by an abbreviation of the name of the botanist, or "species author," who named the plant. This is a useful reference tool for taxonomists and can be a flag for the layperson as well. For example, many old American herbals list the scientific name of the Slippery Elm as *Ulmus fulva* Michx., but all modern botanical works cite this elm as *Ulmus rubra* Muhl. "Michx." is the abbreviation for the name of the French botanist Andre Michaux (1746–1802), who assigned the name *Ulmus fulva* to this species. "Muhl." is the abbreviation for Gotthilf Henry Ernest Muhlenberg (1753–1815), who first proposed the name *Ulmus rubra.* Muhlenberg's *Ulmus rubra* has priority over Michaux's *Ulmus fulva,* according to the rules of the International Code of Botanical Nomenclature, and *Ulmus rubra* thus becomes the name used by botanists everywhere. Research on medicinal plants requires delving into historical literature, thus it is useful to have the "author citation" as a reference to the scientific name. It is a point of comparison that may help you verify which species is being discussed.

FAMILY NAMES: The scientific name is followed by the common name for the family. Technical names for plant families have not been included.

DESCRIPTION: A brief description of the plant follows. The descriptions are based primarily on visual characteristics, though we have sometimes included scent as an identifying feature. We regret that scratch-and-sniff features cannot be included in the text. The description begins with the growth habit of the plant (annual, perennial, twining vine, tree, shrub, and so on) and height. Characteristic details for leaves, flowers, or fruits follow. Key identifying features of each plant are in italics.

The earliest blooming date given is usually the time when the flowering period begins in the South. Blooming time in more northerly areas often begins a month or more later. Though the blooming date may be listed as "Apr.–June," the plant may only bloom for two weeks in any particular location. Take Goldenseal (*Hydrastis canadensis*), for example. Blooming time is listed as Apr.–May. In northern Arkansas the plant usually blooms around the first week of May. The flowers last only three to five days.

DISTRIBUTION: Under the heading "Where found" the habitat in which the plant grows is listed. It is also indicated whether the plant is an introduced alien or is native to the U.S. Many alien (non-native) plants are now naturalized or adventive—well established on their own without being cultivated. Many plants in this category often are still cultivated in herb, kitchen, or flower gardens; others are best known as weeds. Habitat is followed by the plant's range in Canada and the eastern and central U.S. Each plant's range is given from northeast to southeast and from southwest to northwest.

Although many wild plants are common and widespread, others are rare and should not be overcollected. Cautions about plants that are protected by law, or those which should be protected, are also included in this section.

This section presents a brief discussion of some of the more significant medicinal uses of a plant. Historic or folk uses are described first, generally starting with known uses of the plants by native peoples of North America. In most cases we have chosen to use the term "American Indian," rather than list native groups by their traditional "tribe" names. We sometimes list medicinal uses in India or cite work by Indian researchers, so this helps to avoid confusion. Readers are referred to Daniel Moerman's excellent work *Native American Ethnobotany* (1998) or Dr. Moerman's Web site (www.umd.umich.edu/cgi-bin/herb/) and Jim Duke's *Handbook of Northeastern Indian Medicinal Plants* (1986) or Dr. Duke's Web site (www.ars-grin.gov/duke/). The original references cited in these works and their bibliographies have been consulted for detailed accounts of uses of native plants by specific indigenous groups of people.

The discussion often covers American Indian usage, folk usage by settlers of the North American continent over the past 400 years, historical usage by medical practitioners, and vindication of medicinal uses as suggested by presence of specific chemical components or chemical groups, pharmacological studies (mostly with animals), and, if available, clinical studies or clinical applications.

Often in our discussion we have included notes on the experience of Chinese practitioners with a closely related plant species. For more than 200 years, botanists have recognized striking similarities between the floras of eastern Asia and eastern North America. Most plants involved in this pattern of "disjunctions" in plant geography are thought to be remnants of an ancient forest that covered the Northern Hemisphere more than 70 million years ago. Because many of the more than 140 genera that share ranges in eastern Asia and eastern North America are important medicinal plants on one continent or the other, the Chinese experience is relevant to North American species, and vice versa. Some plants included in this classical pattern of plant disjunctions are the various species of Ginseng (in the genus *Panax*), Witch-hazel *(Hamamelis)*, Sassafras, Mayapple *(Podophyllum)*, Magnolia, Sweetgum *(Liquidambar)*, Spicebush *(Lindera)*, and dozens of other plant groups included in this book.

In a historical context, we occasionally mention a concept known as the "doctrine of signatures." This refers to an ancient idea that if a plant part was shaped like, or in some other way resembled, a human organ or disease characteristic, then that plant was useful for that particular organ or ailment. With its 3-lobed leaves, Liverleaf (as herbalists referred to the *Hepatica* species) was thought to be useful in treating liver disease. If held to light, the leaves of Common St. John's Wort (*Hypericum perforatum*) appear to have numerous holes pricked through the surface. The resemblance between these holes and the pores in human skin led some people to believe that preparations made from the leaves of this plant were useful for healing cuts. Using this doctrine, one might assume that kidney beans were good for the kidneys, or that the leaves of Broad-leaved Arrowhead (*Sagittaria latifolia*) would be useful for wounds caused by the head of an arrow. This concept has no scientific basis, though uses conceived centuries ago have persisted and may even have been corroborated by scientific evidence.

Following American Indian, European, or folk use by other indigenous groups, we include information on the current status of the plant. In many cases, pharmacological studies on individual chemical components or extract of a plant or plant part confirm ethnobotanical uses. Controlled clinical studies have been conducted in the last decade on the benefits or preparations of such herbs as St. John's Wort, Chamomile, Saw Palmetto, Echinacea, and others. In many instances, these herbs are actually approved for therapeutic use in various countries, notably Germany. If a plant is approved today for therapeutic use in a country, we have included notations reflecting that fact. For German material, we have primarily relied on the English translation of the regulatory text of the German government, Mark Blumenthal's *The Complete German Commission E Monographs: Therapeutic Guide to Herbal Medicines* (American Botanical Council and Integrative Medicine, 1998). We also relied heavily on Jim Duke's data (www.ars-grin.gov/duke/).

PREPARATIONS: In the "Uses" section we discuss ways in which each plant has traditionally or historically been used. In most instances we have chosen to use the word "tea" to refer to both infusions and decoctions. A simple *infusion* is made by soaking an herb (usually the leaf or flower) in hot water for 10 to 20 minutes. A cold infusion may be made by soaking the plant material in cold water for a relatively long period of time (varying from 2 hours to overnight), or simply letting the hot infusion sit until it is cool.

A *decoction* is made by simmering the plant material—usually the root, bark, or seed—under low heat. As a general rule of thumb, the word "infusion" is reserved for leaves and flower material, and "decoction" for roots, barks, or seeds. Check the plant part used to determine whether a tea should be simmered or "decocted" or simply "infused," based on whether it is made from the bark, root, leaves, flowers, and so on.

The term *wash* is often used for the external application of a cooled "tea." A wash is usually applied to the skin over the affected area.

Poultice is another commonly used term for an external application of herbs. A poultice is typically a moist paste made from the plant material, beaten to pulp in a mortar and pestle or with some other instrument if the herbs are fresh, or soaked in warm water if the herbs are dried. The poultice is spread over the affected area. Since some plants, such as Comfrey or Mullein, have leaves with irritating hairs that may adversely affect the skin, a layer of thin cloth such as muslin may be applied to the skin, with the herb material placed on top of the cloth.

A *tincture* is a plant extract dissolved in alcohol. Most tinctures are made with dilute alcohol (100 proof or 50 percent ethanol, 50 percent distilled water). Traditionally a tincture is made simply by soaking a certain percentage of plant material (often 20 percent by weight to the menstruum, or solvent) in the alcohol and water for a period of about two weeks, shaking the material daily, then straining the liquid through cheesecloth or filter paper before bottling. Tinctures are also made by a process known as percolation, in which the menstruum is poured through the plant material, which has been finely ground and then placed in a funnel-shaped container with a receptacle at the bottom to catch the herb-fortified liquid.

DOSAGE: Since this book is intended to help the reader identify medicinal plants and appreciate their traditional uses, and not to serve as a prescriptor, we have not included dosage except in historical context. See cautions regarding individual sensitivity below.

WARNINGS: Last but not least, we include warnings. *Please be sure to read the warnings under each species account before handling the plant,* even for identification purposes: some plants can cause a painful skin rash. Some medicinal plants are very similar to and can be easily confused with a poisonous plant, with unpleasant or even fatal results. *Never eat or taste any part of a wild plant, or use it in any medicinal preparation, unless you are certain of its identification and safety, and that the dosage is correct, and that the plant has been properly prepared.*

CONSERVATION AND HARVESTING

If you intend to harvest a plant or plant part, you must observe certain rules and values after you have properly and positively identified it.

(1) If the plant is unusual or rare in your area, leave it be. Contact your local Audubon Society, native plant societies, botanical

gardens, or state conservation agencies for a list of rare or threatened plants in the immediate vicinity. Often plants that are common in one state may be rare in another. Pale Purple Coneflower (*Echinacea pallida*) is common in eastern Kansas, but it is very rare in western North Carolina at the eastern extreme of its range. The plant might be judiciously harvested in Kansas, but in North Carolina it should be left alone. Other plants, like Pink or Yellow Lady's-slippers, were historically valuable as medicinal plants, but should be left alone wherever they occur. Once you dig the root, the plant is no more. These wild orchids are difficult to propagate and cultivate. Once much more abundant in the wild, they have been historically extirpated as a medicinal plant and are currently overexploited as plants for wildflower gardens. We believe their sale should be banned, where appropriate, or carefully regulated. (Account books from the 1860s reveal that one company alone was selling more than 300 pounds of dried Lady's-slipper root a month.) It takes dozens of plants to get one pound of dried root. Although a number of orchids have traditionally been used in folk medicine, none is abundant enough for harvest.

In China, only a handful of wild-harvested Ginseng roots are dug each year. The Oriental Ginseng has been valued as a medicinal plant for more than 2,000 years. It has been virtually exterminated from the wild in China. One wild root of Oriental Ginseng can sell for as much as $20,000 on the Hong Kong market. Wild American Ginseng, by comparison, has only been traded as a commodity for a mere 200 years. Tons of wild-harvested American Ginseng are shipped to Oriental markets each year. How long will our plant populations be able to sustain themselves?

Goldenseal (*Hydrastis canadensis*) is one of the best-selling herbs in domestic health food markets. In recent years, supply shortages caused by alleged heavy harvesting of wild populations could threaten the plant's future. Like American Ginseng, Goldenseal is now monitored in international trade through the provisions of an international treaty, the Convention for International Trade in Endangered Species(CITES). Cultivation efforts are under way for Goldenseal. We strongly encourage the cultivation—rather than harvesting in the wild—of all native medicinal plants that enter commerce.

(2) Never collect all of the specimens of a plant in an area. One fear in publishing a volume such as this is that the interest in harvesting medicinal herbs for profit will outweigh the necessity of conservation. Take only what you need and no more than 10 percent of the individuals in a given population. If you harvest an entire population of most herbs, you will do so only once. Careful

consideration and attention to detail are necessary for identification, harvest, usage, and conservation.

(3) Find out who owns the property where you intend to harvest a medicinal plant and obtain permission to harvest it before going on the property. In Missouri and other areas, state law prohibits the harvest of plant material without the permission of the landowner. Along roadsides, the owner is often the state itself.

(4) Harvest the plant at the correct time of year. Most herbs in which the leaves or whole herb (flowers, leaves, and stem) are used are harvested just before or just as the plant comes into flower. The amount and nature of the biologically active chemical components in a plant varies in quantity and quality according to the stage of the plant's growth, and even the time of day when it is harvested. Flowers are best harvested as they reach their peak bloom. As a general rule, it is best to harvest leaf and aboveground plant materials before noon on a sunny day, after the dew has dried off the leaves. Seeds should be harvested only when fully ripened, but before they have dispersed.

Roots are usually harvested when the plant is dormant. It is generally better to harvest most roots in autumn rather than spring. In spring, wet weather results in higher moisture content in the roots, which makes them more difficult to dry. Autumn-harvested roots should be dug after the plant's seeds have matured. Federal law prohibits Ginseng from being harvested until after the fruits have ripened. Unfortunately, the practice of harvesting Ginseng roots before the seeds have had a chance to develop is still common. Such practices should be discouraged. Goldenseal is often harvested in the spring, as the plant emerges from the ground and begins flowering, but it should be harvested only after it sets seed in late summer. Roots, generally speaking, should not be harvested when the leaves and stem are still growing, in order to avoid affecting both the quality of the plant material and the plant's ability to set seeds.

(5) If you are harvesting bark, always take it from the lateral branches—do not strip it from the main trunk. Harvest only from one side of the branch. Avoid girdling the branches. Bark serves as a protective covering for the plant. The rough outer bark consists mainly of corky cellular tissue that later develops wood cells, especially on the inner surface. The inner bark—the part usually gathered for medicinal purposes—consists mainly of long wood cells, often forming fibers of great strength and toughness. Bark is most easily removed when the sap rises, in spring to early summer. Of course, the bark is the tree's lifeline, from its roots to its top. Complete girdling (stripping a complete circle of bark around the trunk or branches) will usually kill a tree.

We cautiously advise our readers that this field guide is just that —a key to the recognition of medicinal plants. Perhaps we have been overly careful in our warnings, but in fact there are people who are allergic to any given species of plant. All food plants, like medicinal plants, contain greater or lesser amounts of minerals, vitamins, carcinogens, anticarcinogens, oxidants and antioxidants, enzyme-agonists and enzyme antagonists, toxins and antitoxins, and other biologically active compounds.

In our caution we have mentioned that dozens of these plants can cause contact dermatitis, although we have handled most of the species treated in this book and have experienced dermatitis only from Stinging Nettles and Poison Ivy. Further, we suspect that the pollen of most species, if gathered and forcibly inserted in the nostrils, would induce sneezing and perhaps even allergic rhinitis in some people. And, of course, all plants included in this book contain substances that are poisonous in excess. Dosage and proper preparation are very important. Everyone should be cautious about ingesting any new material, food or medicine. The reaction of one individual may differ from that of another.

Unfortunately, some very innocuous medicinal plants, like Wild Carrot (Queen Anne's Lace), can closely resemble some very poisonous plants, like Poison Hemlock. And some of the Angelicas and Skirret might be confused with poisonous Waterhemlock. We would not trust all botanists, much less all amateurs, to identify them accurately. Even professional botanists have died after misidentifying mushrooms or plants in the unrelated Parsley family. In spring it is easy to grab a wild iris among the new cattail shoots. Results might not be fatal, but unpleasant. One elderly couple confused Foxglove for Comfrey, and died shortly thereafter. Father or Mother Nature is not benign: He or She has produced some of our deadliest poisons. If you are imprudent, you may ingest some of Nature's lethal compounds.

In spite of these perils, we lose fewer people to herbal accidents (fewer than 10 per year) than we do to iatrogenic (hospital or doctor-induced accidents) or intentional ingestion of narcotics derived from plants (6,000 deaths a year in America), alcohol (100,000 deaths a year), or the smoking of the Indian gift, tobacco (300,000 deaths a year).

Basil, Comfrey, and Sassafras are some herbs that have come under fire for containing potential carcinogens. An article published in *Science* (Ames et. al., "Ranking Possible Carcinogenic Hazards," 17 Apr. 1987, vol. 236, pp. 271–280) puts these carcinogens in proper perspective. A cup of Comfrey leaf tea was stated to be about 1/100 as carcinogenic for its symphytine as a can of beer was for its ethanol. A gram of basil was 1/28 as carcinogenic for its estragole as the beer was for its ethanol. A sassafras root beer, now banned by our FDA, was 1/14 as carcinogenic for its safrole as the can of beer for its ethanol.

We cannot agree with herbalists who say that herbal medicine has no side effects. Probably all natural and synthetic compounds, good and bad, are biologically active in many ways in addition to the one we wish to harness in medication. Moreover, any medicine—herbal, natural, or synthetic—can be toxic in overdoses. We again remind our readers that this field guide is a key to the recognition of medicinal plants, not a prescriptor. Only your doctor or other health care professional who is licensed to do so can prescribe an herb for you. We cannot and do not prescribe herbal medication.

Symbols:

☠ = **Poisonous**. Dangerous or deadly to ingest, or perhaps even to touch.

⚠ = **Caution**. See warning in text.

🜨 = Known to cause **allergic reactions** in some individuals.

🖐 = Known to cause **dermatitis** in some individuals.

⚗ = Used in **modern medicine** in the U.S.

SPECIES
ACCOUNTS

MISCELLANEOUS SHOWY FLOWERS

PRICKLY POPPY
Argemone albiflora Hornem.

Stem juice, seeds, leaves
Poppy Family

Bluish green herb; 2–3 ft. *Yellow* (or white) *juice. Thistlelike* leaves and stems with *sharp bristles.* Flowers with 4–6 petals at least 2 in. wide; May–Sept. **WHERE FOUND:** Waste places; scattered. Introduced. Conn. to Fla.; Texas to Mo., Ill. **USES:** Seed tea is emetic, purgative, demulcent. Plant infusion used for jaundice, skin ailments, colds, colic, wounds. Externally, used for headaches. Folk remedy for cancers, itching, and scabies. **WARNING:** Contains **toxic** alkaloids. Seed oil causes glaucoma and edema.

TURTLEHEAD, BALMONY
Chelone glabra L.

Leaves
Figwort Family

Smooth perennial; 2–3 ft. Stem somewhat 4-angled. Leaves lance-shaped to oval, toothed. Flowers white to pink, swollen; in tight clusters atop plant; July–Oct. *Flowers* 2-*lipped;* with swollen, strongly arching *upper lip* (resembling a turtle's head, hence the name). **WHERE FOUND:** Moist soils. Nfld. to Ga.; Mo. to Minn., Ont. **USES:** American Indians used tea of flowering tops to treat worms, also as a contraceptive to prevent pregnancy. Leaf tea said to stimulate appetite; also a folk remedy for worms, fever, jaundice; laxative. Used by nineteenth-century physicians for dyspepsia, liver diseases, fevers, and inflammation. Ointment used

(Left) *Prickly Poppy* (Argemone albiflora) *in flower. Note the thistlelike leaves and spiny capsules.* (Above) *Turtlehead, Balmony* (Chelone glabra) *in flower. Note the strongly arching upper lip.*

for piles, inflamed breasts, painful ulcers, herpes. Contains a bitter resin.

LILY-OF-THE-VALLEY
Convallaria majalis L.

Root, flowers
Lily Family

Perennial, spreading by root runners; 4–8 in. Leaves 2–3; basal, oblong-ovate, entire (not toothed); *veins parallel; connecting veins obvious when held to light.* Flowers bell-shaped, white; May–June. **WHERE FOUND:** Europe. Widely escaped from cultivation. **USES:** Tea of flowers and roots traditionally used in valvular heart disease (Digitalis substitute), fevers; diuretic, heart tonic, sedative, emetic. Root ointment, folk remedy for burns, to prevent scar tissue. Russians use for epilepsy. Approved in Germany for the treatment of mild cardiac insufficiency, to economize cardiac efficiency, and to improve tone of the veins. **WARNING:** Potentially **toxic.** Use only under a physician's supervision. Although widely prescribed in Germany, it is seldom used in the U.S. Can interact with other drugs; is not administered in conjunction with other cardiac drugs. Leaves can be a mild skin irritant.

Lily-of-the-valley (Convallaria majalis) *is more often found in gardens than in wild habitats.*

Dutchman's-breeches (Dicentra cucullaria) *flowers each have 2 inflated, "pantlike" spurs.*

DUTCHMAN'S-BREECHES
Dicentra cucullaria (L.) Bernh.

Leaves, root
Bleeding-heart Family

Perennial; 5–9 in. Leaves much dissected. Flowers white, yellow-tipped; appearing upside-down on an arching stalk; Apr.–May. *Each flower has 2 inflated, "pantlike" spurs.* **WHERE FOUND:** Rich woods. Se. Canada to Ga. mountains; Ark., Okla. to N.D. **USES:** Iroquois used leaf ointment to make athletes' legs more limber. Among the Menomini, it was the most important love charm, thrown by a suitor at his potential mate. If the root was nibbled, it was believed one's breath would attract a woman, even against her will. Leaf poultice a folk medicine for skin ailments. Root tea is diuretic; promotes sweating. Contains alkaloid with CNS-depressant activity; used for paralysis and tremors. **WARNING:** Potentially poisonous; may also cause skin rash.

MISCELLANEOUS AQUATIC PLANTS

WILD CALLA, WATER-ARUM
Calla palustris L.

Root
Arum Family

Note the shining oval, heart-shaped leaves, to 6 in. long. Flower a *white spathe* clasping a golden, *clublike* spadix; May–Aug. **WHERE FOUND:** Circumpolar. Ponds, mud. Nfld. to N.J.; Ind., Wisc., Minn. to Alaska. **USES:** American Indians used dried-root tea for flu, shortness of breath, bleeding; poultice on swellings and

(Above) *Wild Calla* (Calla palustris L.). *Photo by Pamela Harper.* (Right) *Buckbean or bogbean, found in wet habitats, has cloverlike leaves. Photo by Martin Wall.*

snakebites. **WARNING:** Raw plant contains calcium oxalate; can burn and irritate skin, and mucous membranes, if taken internally.

BUCKBEAN, BOGBEAN
Menyanthes trifoliata L.

Root, leaves
Gentian Family

⚠ Note the *cloverlike* leaves arising from the root. Flowers 5-parted, white to pinkish, on a naked raceme; Apr.–July. *Petals with fuzzy beards.* **WHERE FOUND:** Bogs, shallow water. Canada south to Md., W. Va.; Ohio, Ind. to Ill. **USES:** Dried-leaf or -root tea traditionally a digestive tonic; used for fevers, rheumatism, liver ailments, dropsy, worms, skin diseases; astringent; stops bleeding. Science confirms phenolic acids may be responsible for bile-secreting, digestive tonic, and bitter qualities. Use of leaf approved in Germany for treatment of dyspeptic discomfort and loss of appetite. Stimulates flow of saliva and gastric juices. **WARNING:** Fresh plant causes vomiting.

FRAGRANT WATER-LILY
Nymphaea odorata Ait.

Roots
Water-lily Family

⚠ Aquatic perennial with large, round, floating leaves; leaf notched at base. Flowers white, to 5 in. across; sweetly fragrant; June–Sept. **WHERE FOUND:** Ponds, slow waters. Nfld. to Fla.; Texas to Neb. **USES:** The large, spongy, fleshy roots were traditionally used by American Indians, particularly for lung ailments; root tea for coughs, tuberculosis, inflamed glands, mouth sores; stops bleeding; poulticed root for swellings. In folk tradition, a mixture of root and lemon juice was used to remove freckles and pimples. Root tea is drunk for bowel complaints, primarily as an astringent and antiseptic for chronic diarrhea. **WARNING:** Large doses may be toxic.

LIZARD'S-TAIL, WATER-DRAGON
Saururus cernuus L.

Root, leaves
Lizard-tail Family

Perennial; 2–5 ft. Leaves large, asymmetrically *heart-shaped*. Flowers tiny, white, on a showy, *nodding "tail"*; May–Sept. **WHERE FOUND:** Shallow water, swamps, R.I. to Fla., Texas to Minn. **USES:** American Indians used root poultice for wounds, inflamed breasts (the plant is also known as "Breastweed"), and inflammations. Tea of whole plant used as a wash for general illness, rheumatism; internally for stomach ailments. Contains several novel compounds with sedative effects. Subject of considerable chemical and pharmacological research in the 1990s. **RELATED SPECIES:** Asian counterpart, *S. chinensis,* is also used to relieve inflammation in Traditional Chinese Medicine; strongly anti-inflammatory. It, too, contains novel sedative compounds.

Fragrant Water-lily (Nymphaea odorata) *is usually found in ponds or lakes.*

Lizard's-tail, Water-dragon (Saururus cernuus) *produces a tail-like spike of flowers, nodding when mature.*

AQUATIC PLANTS; 3 PETALS

WATER-PLANTAIN
Dried leaves, root

Alisma subcordatum Raf.   Arrowhead Family

[*Alisma plantago-aquatica* var. *parviflorum* (Pursh) Farw.]

Erect or drooping (in deep water) perennial, 1–3 ft. in flower. Long-stemmed, nearly heart-shaped leaves. Flowers tiny (less than ⅛ in. long), in whorls on branched stalks; June–Sept. Petals same length as sepals. **WHERE FOUND:** Shallow water or mud. N.J. to Ga.; west to Texas, Neb. **USES:** Tea diuretic; used for "gravel" (kidney stones), urinary diseases. Fresh leaves rubefacient—they redden and irritate skin. American Indians used root poultice for bruises, swellings, wounds. An 1899 article by a California physician reported on the use of the root tincture (alcohol extract), mixed with equal parts water and glycerin, as a local application to nostrils to treat "nasal catarrh." **RELATED SPECIES:** The root of the closely related *A. plantago-aquatica* is used in China as a diuretic for dysuria, edema, distention, diarrhea, and other ailments. Chinese studies verify the plant's diuretic action. In laboratory experiments with animals, the herb lowers blood pressure, reduces blood glucose levels, and inhibits the storage of fat in the liver.

Four species of Water-plantain (Alisma sp.) occur in our range, distinguished by technical factors.

Common Water-plantain (Alisma triviale) produces tiny white flowers. Photo by Stephen Lee Timme.

There are about 30 species of sagittaria found in North America. Note the arrow-shaped leaves.

COMMON WATER-PLANTAIN

Alisma triviale Pursh
[*Alisma plantago-aquatica* var. *brevipes* (Greene)]

Root
Arrowhead Family

Similar to above species, but leaves are mostly oval, though the base is often slightly heart-shaped. Flowers larger, to ¼ in. June–Sept. Panicle often with fewer branches. **WHERE FOUND:** Shallow water, ditches. N.S. to Md.; Neb. to Minn. and beyond. **USES:** American Indians used root tea for lung ailments, lame back, and kidney ailments.

BROAD-LEAVED ARROWHEAD

Sagittaria latifolia Wild.

Roots, leaves
Arrowhead Family

Aquatic perennial. Leaves *arrow-shaped; lobes half as long to as long as* main part of leaf. Flowers white; petals 3, rounded; filaments of stamens smooth. Flowers June–Sept. The bracts beneath the flowers are blunt-tipped, thin, and papery. The beak of the mature fruit (achene) projects at a right angle from the main part of the fruit. **WHERE FOUND:** Ponds, lakes. Throughout our area. Technical details separate the more than 15 species in our range. There are more than 30 species in N. America. **USES:** American Indians used the edible tubers in tea for indigestion; poulticed them for wounds and sores. Leaf tea was used for rheumatism and to wash babies with fever. Leaves were poulticed to stop milk production. Roots were eaten like potatoes. **WARNING:** Arrowheads (not necessarily this species) *may* cause dermatitis. Do not confuse with Wild Calla or Water-arum (*Calla palustris*); see p. 17.

YUCCAS OR PLANTS WITH YUCCA-LIKE LEAVES

RATTLESNAKE-MASTER

Eryngium yuccifolium Michx.

Root
Parsley Family

Perennial with bluish cast; 1½–4 ft. Leaves mostly basal (reduced on stem), yucca-like (hence the species name), parallel-veined, spiny-edged. Flowers white to whitish green, tiny, covered by bristly bracts; in tight heads to 1 in. across; Sept–Nov. **WHERE FOUND:** Prairies, dry soil. S. Conn. to Fla.; Texas to Kans., Minn. **USES:** American Indians used root as poultice for snakebites, toothaches, bladder trouble; for coughs, neuralgia; also an emetic. Traditionally, root tincture was used as a diuretic; also for female reproductive disorders, gleet, gonorrhea, piles, and rheumatism. Chewing the root increases saliva flow. **WARNING:** Do not confuse with False Aloe or Rattlesnake-master (*Manfreda virginica*, p. 117), which may produce strongly irritating latex. **RELATED SPECIES:** *Eryngium aquaticum* (not shown) has linear leaves and is found in marshes and bogs.

Rattlesnake-master (Eryngium yuccifolium) has bristly, light green leaves that superficially re-semble those of yucca.

Flowers of the Adam's Needle Yucca (Yucca filamentosa) grow on smooth-branched stalks.

Flowers of the Soapweed Yucca (Yucca glauca) grow on a single stalk. Upward of 30 species of Yucca occur in North America, most in the desert Southwest. Two species are found in the eastern U.S.

YUCCA, ADAM'S NEEDLE
Yucca filamentosa L.

Roots
Lily Family

⚠ Perennial; to 9 ft. in flower. Leaves in a rosette; stiff, spine-tipped, oblong to lance-shaped, with *fraying, twisted threads on margins.* Flowers whitish green bells on *smooth,* branched stalks; June–Sept. **WHERE FOUND:** Sandy soils. S. N.J. to Ga. Cultivated elsewhere. **USES:** American Indians used root in salves or poultices for sores, skin diseases, and sprains. Pounded roots were put in water to stupefy corralled fish so they would float to the surface for easy harvest. Plant yields a strong fiber. Fruits used as food by some people. Saponins in roots of yucca species possess long-lasting soaping action and have been used in soaps and shampoos. **WARNING:** Root compound (saponins) are **toxic** to lower life forms.

YUCCA, SOAPWEED
Yucca glauca Nutt.

Roots
Lily Family

⚠ Blue-green perennial; 2–4 ft. Leaves in a rosette; stiff, swordlike; rounded on back, *margins rolled in.* Flowers whitish bells; May–July. **WHERE FOUND:** Dry soils. Iowa to Texas; Mo. to N.D. **USES:** American Indians poulticed root on inflammations, used it to stop bleeding; also in steam bath for sprains and broken limbs; hair wash for dandruff and baldness. Leaf juice used to make poison arrows. Antifungal, antitumor, and antiarthritic activity have been suggested by research. Water extracts have shown antitumor activity against B16 melanoma in mice. One human clinical study suggests that saponin extracts of yucca root were effective in the treatment of arthritis, but the findings have been disputed. **WARNING:** Same as for *Yucca filamentosa.*

SHOWY BELLS OR TRUMPETS

FIELD BINDWEED
Convolvulus arvensis L.

Leaf, root, flowers
Morning-glory Family

Creeping vine. Leaves arrow-shaped; *lobes sharp, not blunt;* 1–2 in. Flowers white (or pink), to 1 in.; June–Sept. **WHERE FOUND:** Fields, waste places. Most of our area. Alien (Europe). **USES:** American Indians used cold leaf tea as a wash on spider bites; internally to reduce profuse menstrual flow. In European folk use, flower, leaf, and root teas considered laxative. Flower tea used for fevers, wounds. Root most active—strongly purgative.

HEDGE BINDWEED
Calystegia sepium ssp. *sepium* (L.) R. Br.
[*Convolvulus sepium* L.]

Root
Morning-glory Family

Trailing vine with white or pink, morning-glory-type flowers; May–Sept. Leaves arrow-shaped with *blunt lobes at base.* **WHERE**

Field Bindweed (Convolvulus arvensis) *has arrow-shaped leaves with sharp lobes. Photo by Stephen Lee Timme.*

Hedge bindweed (Calystegia sepium ssp. sepium) *has arrow-shaped leaves with blunt lobes.*

FOUND: Thickets, roadsides. Most of our area. **USES:** Root historically used as a purgative; substitute for the Mexican jalap (*Ipomoea purga*). Traditionally used for jaundice, gallbladder ailments; thought to increase bile flow into intestines.

JIMSONWEED
Datura stramonium L.

Leaves, root, seed
Nightshade Family

Annual; 2–5 ft. Leaves coarse-toothed. Flowers white to pale violet; 3–5 in., trumpet-shaped; May–Sept. Seedpods spiny, chambered. **WHERE FOUND:** Waste places. Throughout our area. **USES:** Whole plant contains atropine, scopolamine, and other alkaloids; used in eye diseases (atropine dilates pupils); causes dry mouth, depresses bladder muscles, impedes action of parasympathetic nerves, used in Parkinson's disease; also contains scopolamine, used in patches behind ear for vertigo. Leaves were once smoked as an antispasmodic for asthma. Folk cancer remedy. **WARNING: Violently toxic.** Causes severe hallucinations. Many fatalities recorded. Those who collect this plant may end up with swollen eyelids.

WILD POTATO-VINE
Ipomoea pandurata (L.) G. F. W. Mey.

Root, whole plant
Morning-glory Family

Twining or climbing, often purple-stemmed vine with a very large tuberous root. Leaves *heart-shaped*. Flowers large (2–3 in.), white with pink stripes from center; June–Sept. **WHERE FOUND:** Dry soils.

(Left) *Jimsonweed* (Datura stramonium) *is one of our most toxic wildflowers. Photo by Doug Elliott.* (Above) *Wild Potato-vine* (Ipomoea pandurata) *produces heart-shaped leaves.*

Conn. to Fla.; Texas, Mo., Kans. to Mich. **USES:** American Indians poulticed root for rheumatism, "hard tumors." Root tea used as a diuretic, laxative, and expectorant, for coughs, asthma, beginning stages of tuberculosis; "blood purifier"; powdered plant used in tea for headaches, indigestion.

MISCELLANEOUS NONWOODY VINES

VIRGIN'S BOWER   **Whole flowering plant**
Clematis virginiana L.   Buttercup Family
    Clambering vine. Leaves divided into 3 *sharp-toothed leaflets.* Flowers white, with 4 *petal-like sepals;* in clusters; July–Sept. Feathery plumes attached to seeds. **WHERE FOUND:** Rich thickets, wood edges. N.S. to Ga., La., e. Kan. north to Canada. **USES:** Liniment once used by physicians for skin eruptions, itching; weak leaf tea used for insomnia, nervous headaches, nervous twitching, and uterine diseases. **WARNING: Toxic.** Highly irritating to skin and mucous membranes. Ingestion may cause bloody vomiting, severe diarrhea, and convulsions.

WILD CUCUMBER, BALSAM-APPLE   **Root**
Echinocystis lobata (Michx.) Torr. & Gray   Cucumber Family
    Climbing vine with tendrils. Leaves *maple-shaped; 5-lobed,* toothed along edges. Flowers 6-*petaled,* in clusters of leaf axils; June–Oct. Fruits *solitary,* egg-shaped; fleshy, covered with weak

Virgin's Bower (Clematis virginiana), *usually blooming in late summer, is easily seen from a distance because of its abundant display of flowers.*

Wild Cucumber (Echinocystis lobata) *in flower.*

Passion-flower (Passiflora incarnata) *is one of the few temperate species of this mainly tropical plant group. Usually violet-blue, rarely completely white. The egg-shaped edible fruits contain a delicious pulp. If stepped on, they "pop," hence the name Maypop.*

bristles. **WHERE FOUND**: Thickets. N.B. to Fla.; Texas to Minn. **USES**: American Indians used the extremely bitter root tea as a bitter tonic for stomach troubles, kidney ailments, rheumatism, chills, fevers, and obstructed menses. Also used in love potions and as a general tonic. Pulverized root poulticed for headaches. **WARNING**: Do not confuse this plant with *Momordica balsamina* L., a tropical member of the Cucumber family also known as Balsam-apple. Its root is purgative and considered toxic. The two plants have been confused in the literature because authors did not carefully compare scientific names of "balsam-apples." Both, as members of the Cucumber family, may contain cucurbitacins, which are extremely active as antitumor and cytotoxic agents at levels of less than one part per million.

PASSION-FLOWER, MAYPOP
Whole flowering plant

Passiflora incarnata L.
Passion-flower Family

⚠ Climbing vine, to 30 ft.; tendrils *springlike.* Leaves *cleft,* with 2–3 slightly toothed lobes. Flowers large, showy, unique, whitish to purplish, with *numerous threads* radiating from center; July–Oct. Fruits fleshy, egg-shaped. **WHERE FOUND:** Sandy soil. Pa. to Fla.; e. Texas to s. Mo. **USES:** American Indians poulticed root for boils, cuts, earaches, and inflammation. Traditionally used as an antispasmodic, and as a sedative for neuralgia, epilepsy, restlessness, painful menses, insomnia, and tension headaches. Research shows extracts are mildly sedative, slightly reduce blood pressure, increase respiratory rate, and decrease motor activity. Fruits edible, delicious. **WARNING:** Potentially harmful in large amounts.

WHITE ORCHIDS

DOWNY RATTLESNAKE-PLANTAIN
Root, leaves

Goodyera pubescens (Willd.) R. Br. ex Ait. f.
Orchid Family

Perennial; to 16 in. (in flower). Leaves essentially basal, oval, with *white veins in a checkered pattern,* and white spreading hairs. Whitish flowers on a *dense, woolly raceme.* July–Sept. **WHERE FOUND:** Woods. Me. to Fla.; Ala., Ark., Mo. to w. Que. Rare—do not harvest. **USES:** The distinctive bluish green leaves with prominent white veins in a "rattlesnake" pattern earned this plant its common name, as well as did the use of the root for snakebites, based on the doctrine of signatures (see p. 5). American Indians used root tea for pleurisy, snakebites; leaf tea taken (with whiskey) to improve appetite, treat colds, kidney ailments, "blood tonic,"

Downy Rattlesnake-plantain (Goodyera pubescens) *blooms in late summer. The leaves are easy to distinguish in this orchid's wooded habitat.*

Nodding Ladies' Tresses (Spiranthes sp.) *have a distinct double-spiraling flower spike. Most orchids are relatively rare and should not be harvested. Some are protected by law.*

toothaches. Externally, leaf poultice used to "cool" burns, treat skin ulcers. Physicians once used fresh leaves steeped in milk as poultice for tuberculous swelling of lymph nodes (scrofula). Fresh leaves were applied every 3 hours, while the patient drank a tea of the leaves at the same time. **REMARKS:** Of historical interest only. Too scarce to harvest.

NODDING LADIES' TRESSES

Whole plant

Spiranthes cernua (L.) L. C. Rich.　　　　　　　　Orchid Family

　　Delicate, fleshy-rooted orchid; 4–20 in. Basal leaves are firm, thick, pale green; leaves much reduced on flowering stalk. Tiny, white, *downward-arching* flowers in a double spiral; Aug.–Nov. **WHERE FOUND:** Bogs, meadows. Most of our area. **USES:** American Indians used plant tea as a diuretic for urinary disorders, venereal disease, and as a wash to strengthen weak infants. **RELATED SPECIES:** Other N. American, European, and S. American species have also been used as a diuretic and aphrodisiac.

PINK LADY'S-SLIPPER, MOCCASIN-FLOWER, AMERICAN VALERIAN

Root

Cypripedium acaule Ait.　　　　　　　　　　Orchid Family

　　Usually pink; *rarely white* in some individual plants or populations. Perennial; 6–15 in. Leaves 2, *basal.* Flower a strongly veined pouch with a *deep furrow;* May–June. **WHERE FOUND:** Acid woods. Nfld. to Ga.; Ala., Tenn. to Minn. Too rare to harvest. **USES:** This plant, called American Valerian, was widely used in nineteenth-century America as a sedative for nervous headaches, hysteria, insomnia, nervous irritability, mental depression from sexual abuse, and menstrual irregularities accompanied by despondency (PMS?). Active compounds are not water-soluble. The Pink Lady's-slipper was considered a substitute for the more commonly used Yellow Lady's-slipper (p. 108). Both were harvested in significant tonnage in the nineteenth century, contributing to scarcity in the twentieth century. Orchids often have swollen, ball-shaped tubers, suggesting testicles; these roots are widely regarded as aphrodisiacs, perhaps reflecting the doctrine of signatures (see p. 5). **WARNING:** May cause dermatitis.

LOW-GROWING, CREEPING EVERGREENS

BEARBERRY, UVA-URSI

Leaves

Arctostaphylos uva-ursi (L.) Spreng.　　　　　　Heath Family

　　Trailing shrub; bark fine-hairy. Leaves *shiny-leathery, spatula-shaped.* Flowers white, urn-shaped; May–July. Fruit is a dry red berry. **WHERE FOUND:** Sandy soil, by rocks. Arctic to n. U.S. A trailing shrub found in sandy soils and near exposed rock from the Arctic south to the northern tier of American states. **USES:** Dried-leaf tea diuretic, strongly astringent; urinary-tract antiseptic for cystitis (when urine is alkaline, achieved by adding a teaspoonful of baking soda to a glass of water), nephritis, urethritis, kidney stones, and gallstones. In Germany, bearberry is approved as a urinary antiseptic. Also used in bronchitis, gonorrhea, diarrhea, and to stop

Bearberry (Arctostaphylos uva-ursi).

Trailing arbutus (Epigaea repens) *has oval leathery leaves. Photo by Martin Wall.*

bleeding. Leaves contain more than a dozen anti-inflammatory and antiseptic compounds. **WARNING:** Contains arbutin, which hydrolyzes to the **toxic** urinary antiseptic hydroquinone; therefore, use is limited to less than one week in German herbal practice. Leaves are also high in tannins (up to 8 percent).

TRAILING ARBUTUS, MAYFLOWER
Leaves

Epigaea repens L.   Heath Family

Trailing perennial; to 6 in. Leaves *oval, leathery*. Flowers in clusters, white (or pink), tubular, 5-lobed. March–May. **WHERE FOUND:** Open, sandy woods. Nfld. to Fla.; Miss., Tenn., Ohio to Mich. Protected in some states. **USES:** American Indians used leaf tea for kidney disorders, stomachaches, "blood purifier." Leaf tea a folk remedy for bladder, urethra, and kidney disorders, "gravel" (kidney stones). Shakers sold this plant as "gravel-plant." **WARNING:** Contains arbutin; although it is effective as a urinary antiseptic, it hydrolyzes to hydroquinone, which is **toxic.**

WINTERGREEN, TEABERRY
Leaves

Gaultheria procumbens L.   Heath Family

Wintergreen-scented; to 6 in. Leaves oval, glossy. Flowers waxy, *drooping bells*; July–Aug. Fruit a dry red berry. **WHERE FOUND:** Woods, openings. Canada to Ga.; Ala. to Wisc., Minn. **USES:** Wintergreen refers to the evergreen nature of the leaves, but to most minds it has become associated with a specific flavor produced by the compound methyl salicylate. This plant and Black Birch were once commercial sources of wintergreen flavor, now largely replaced by synthetic methyl salicylate. Traditionally, leaf tea used

(Above) *The leaves of the Winter-green* (Gaultheria procumbens) *have a strong wintergreen fragrance.* (Right) *Partridgeberry* (Mitchella repens) *produces bearded white petals.*

for colds, headaches, stomachaches, fevers, kidney ailments; externally, wash for rheumatism, sore muscles, lumbago. Essential oil (methyl salicylate) in leaves is synthetically produced for "wintergreen" flavor. The chemical behind the aroma, methyl salicylate, with anti-inflammatory and painkilling activities, has recently been shown to enable plants to communicate with one another. Experimentally analgesic, carminative, anti-inflammatory, antiseptic. In experiments, small amounts have delayed the onset of tumors. **WARNING:** Essential oil is **highly toxic;** absorbed through skin, harms liver and kidneys.

PARTRIDGEBERRY, SQUAW-VINE
Mitchella repens L.

Leaves

Madder Family

Leaves opposite; rounded. Flowers white (or pink); 4-parted, terminal, *paired;* May–July. Fruit is a single dry red berry lasting over the winter. **WHERE FOUND:** Woods. Nfld. to Fla.; Texas to Minn. **USES:** Historically, dried- or fresh-leaf or berry tea was used for delayed, irregular, or painful menses and childbirth pain; astringent used for piles, dysentery, diuretic. Externally, used as a wash for swellings, hives, arthritis, rheumatism, and sore nipples, for which it was highly esteemed. The plant is still collected and sold in the herb trade. Also called "squaw-vine" because the leaves have historically been used for menstrual difficulties.

CURIOUS FLESHY PLANTS WITH SPECIAL-IZED GROWTH HABITS

ROUND-LEAVED SUNDEW
Drosera rotundifolia L.

WHOLE PLANT
Sundew Family

⚠ An insectivorous (insect-eating) denizen of bogs, the Sundew has unusual leaves that are barely 2 in. tall. The reddish leaves are covered with hairs exuding a sticky, dewlike secretion that catches and holds unwary insects. Once the insect is captured, the Sundew's leaves fold over it to digest it. Small perennial; 2–9 in. Leaves tiny, to ½ in. across; rounded, blade mostly wider than long; *covered with reddish, glandular-tipped hairs exuding sticky "dewdrops."* Flowers white or pinkish, on a 1-sided raceme, opening 1 at a time; June–Aug. **WHERE FOUND:** Wet acid soil, bogs. Nfld. to Fla.; Ill., Minn. **USES:** The leaves of Sundew have traditionally been used for lung ailments, perhaps reflecting the concept of the doctrine of signatures. Since the plant somewhat resembles the bronchioles of the lungs, it was used for lung ailments. Traditionally, tea or tincture used for dry, spasmodic coughs, asthma, arteriosclerosis, and chronic bronchitis; also as an aphrodisiac; poultice or plant juice used on corns and warts. Europeans regard the extracts and tinctures as antitussive and spasmolytic. Contains plumbagin, which is immuno-stimulating in small doses; antibacterial, antifungal, and antiviral. Exudates from the leaves have been used to treat warts. **REMARKS:** Conservation concerns have arisen over the harvesting of the herb for use in European herbal medicine.

INDIAN-PIPE
Monotropa uniflora L.

Whole plant, root
Indian-pipe Family

Once called Ice Plant because it resembles frozen jelly and "melts" when handled. Also called Bird's Nest, in reference to the shape of the entangled root fibers. The species name *uniflora* means "one flower," referring to the single flower atop each stalk. Saprophytic perennial, without chlorophyll; 6–8 in. *Whole plant translucent white.* Scalelike leaves nearly absent. Flower *a single nodding bell;* June–Oct. **WHERE FOUND:** Woods. Much of our area. Too scarce to harvest. **USES:** American Indians used plant juice for inflamed eyes, bunions, warts; drank tea for aches and pains due to colds. Root tea used for convulsions, fits, epilepsy; sedative. Physicians once used tea as antispasmodic, nervine, sedative for restlessness, pains, nervous irritability. As a folk remedy for sore eyes, the plant was soaked in rose water, then a cloth was soaked in the mixture and applied to the eyes. Water extracts are bactericidal. **WARNING:** Safety undetermined; possibly **toxic**—contains several glycosides.

The Round-leaved Sundew (Drosera rotundifolia) is usually found in acidic bog habitats.

Indian-pipe (Monotropa uniflora) lacks chlorophyll and is easy to recognize by its single flower.

GIANT BIRD'S NEST

Stems, fruits

Pterospora andromeda Nutt.   Wintergreen Family

Parasitic perennial; 1–4 ft. Covered with clammy hairs. Stalk purple-brown, leafless; base scaled. Flowers small, drooping urns; June–Sept. **WHERE FOUND:** Pine woods. Local. P.E.I. to Vt., N.Y.;

Giant Bird's Nest (Pterospora andromeda) has a reddish stem as flowers mature.

Giant Bird's Nest (P. andromeda). Note the clammy hairs. Photo by Craig C. Freeman.

west to Wisc., B.C. Rocky Mts.; south to Mexico. **USES:** American Indians used a cold tea made from the pounded stems and fruits to treat bleeding from the lungs; dry powder used as a snuff for nosebleeds; astringent and hemostatic.

3–6 PETALS; LEAVES ONION-SCENTED

WILD LEEK, RAMP   **Leaves, root**
Allium tricoccum Ait.   Lily Family
Perennial; 6–18 in. Leaves 2–3, smooth, to 2¼ in. wide; fleshy, strongly onion- or leek-scented; leaves wither before whitish to creamy yellow flowers bloom. Flowers June–July. **WHERE FOUND:** Rich moist woods. Localized, but often in abundant populations. N.B. south to Ga. mountains, west through Tenn., Ill., Iowa. **USES:** Cherokees ate leaves for colds, croup, and as spring tonic. Warm juice of leaves and bulbs used for earaches. Strong root decoction emetic. Similar to but less potent than Garlic. The wide range of effects attributed to Garlic (see below) probably accrue to Ramp or Wild Leek as well.

GARLIC   **Bulb**
Allium sativum L.   Lily Family
To 3 ft. Leaves extend *almost to middle of stem.* Note the 2- to 4-in.-long *narrow, papery green spathe* around flowers. **WHERE FOUND:** Fields, roadsides. Alien. Planted and occasionally escaped from cultivation. N.Y. to Tenn., Ky., Mo.; north to Ind. Garlic has evolved through cultivation by humans over 7,000 years. Believed to have originated in the Asian steppes, Garlic's existence is entirely dependent on humans. It is not found in a wild state except when escaped from cultivation. **USES:** Peeled cloves have been eaten or made into tea, syrup, or tincture to treat colds, fevers, coughs, earaches, bronchitis, shortness of breath, sinus congestion, headaches, stomachaches, high blood pressure, arteriosclerosis, diarrhea, dysentery, gout, and rheumatism. For external uses, end of Garlic clove is cut, then juice is applied to ringworm, acne (see warning below); folk cancer remedy. Cough syrup traditionally made by simmering 10 Garlic cloves in 1 pint of milk, adding honey to taste; syrup taken in 1-tablespoon doses as needed. In China, Garlic is used for digestive difficulties, diarrhea, dysentery, colds, whooping cough, pinworms, old ulcers, swellings, and snakebites. Experimentally, it lowers blood pressure and serum cholesterol; antibacterial, antifungal, diuretic. Clinical studies suggest efficacy in gastrointestinal disorders, hypertension, heart ailments, and arteriosclerosis. According to demographic studies, Garlic is thought responsible for the low inci-

Wild Leek, Ramp (Allium tricoc-cum) *is abundant in local popula-tions. Photo by Doug Elliot.*

Garlic (Allium sativum) *produces white flowers.*

Allium sativum. *The familiar bulbs of garlic don't produce their char-acteristic odor (or health benefits) until cut or crushed, which causes a chemical reaction.*

dence of arteriosclerosis in parts of Italy and Spain where Garlic consumption is heavy. Allicin, the substance responsible for Garlic's characteristic odor, is thought to be responsible for some of the plant's pharmacological qualities. Allicin is a chemical byproduct of an enzymatic reaction produced when garlic is cut or crushed. In experiments with mice, Garlic extracts had an inhibitory effect on cancer cells. Garlic has been the subject of more than 2,500 scientific studies over the past 25 years, including more than 18 clinical studies that involved more than 3,000 patients and evaluated Garlic's effects in lowering blood lipids (cholesterol). Results are mixed, but generally positive. **WARNING:** The essential oil extracted from the bulbs is extremely concentrated and can be irritating.

3–6 PETALS, IN STARS OF TUBES

FALSE SOLOMON'S-SEAL   **ROOT, LEAVES**
Maianthemum racemosum spp. *racemosum* (L.) Link   Lily Family
[*Smilacina racemosa* (L.) Desf.]

Perennial; 1–2 ft. Zigzag stem arched. Leaves oval. Flowers in terminal clusters; May–July. *Stamens longer than petals.* **WHERE FOUND:** Rich woods. N.S. to Ga.; Ala., Ark. to Mich. and westward. **USES:** American Indians used root tea for constipation, rheumatism, stomach tonic, "female tonic"; root smoke inhaled for insanity, and to quiet a crying child. Leaf tea used as a contraceptive and

The flowers of False Solomon's-seal (Maianthemum racemosum) *grow in terminal clusters. Photo by Stephen Lee Timme. The flowers of Solomon's-seal* (Polygonatum biflorum) *droop from leaf axils.*

False Lily-of-the-valley, Canada Mayflower (Maianthemum canadense) *in a wooded habitat.* Colic-root, Stargrass (Aletris farinosa). *Note the mealy texture of flowers.*

for coughs; externally, for bleeding, rashes, and itch. Herbalists used to induce sweating and urination; "blood purifier."

SOLOMON'S-SEAL   Root
Polygonatum biflorum (Walt.) Ell.   Lily Family

Perennial; 1–3 ft. Leaves oval to elliptical; alternate. Flowers tubular, *drooping in pairs (or three) from leaf axils;* May–June. **WHERE FOUND:** Rich woods. Conn. to Fla.; Texas, Neb. to Mich. **USES:** American Indians used root tea for indigestion, profuse menstruation, lung ailments, "general debility"; also to promote sound sleep, treat coughs; laxative; fresh root poulticed (or root tea used externally as a wash) for sharp pains, cuts, bruises, sores, and carbuncles. Root tea a folk remedy for piles, rheumatism, arthritis, lung ailments, and skin irritations. Contains saponins. Considered anti-inflammatory and astringent.

FALSE LILY-OF-THE-VALLEY, CANADA MAYFLOWER   Root, whole flowering plant
Maianthemum canadense Desf.   Lily Family

Perennial, often forming large colonies. 3–6 in. Usually 2 leaves; base strongly cleft (heart-shaped). Tiny, 4-pointed flowers; Apr.–July. Berries whitish, turning pinkish; speckled. **WHERE FOUND:** Woods. Lab. to Ga. mountains; Tenn. to Iowa, Man. **USES:** American Indians used plant tea for headaches and to "keep kidneys open during pregnancy." Also used as a gargle for sore throats.

Root used as a good luck charm to win games. Folk expectorant for coughs; soothing to sore throats.

COLIC-ROOT, STARGRASS   Root
Aletris farinosa L.   Lily Family
Perennial; 1½–3 ft. Leaves in a basal rosette, lance-shaped. Flowers white, tubular, tightly hugging a tall, leafless stalk; May–Aug. Flowers *swollen at base; surface mealy*. **WHERE FOUND:** Dry or moist peat, sand. S. Me. to Fla.; west to Texas; north to Wisc., Mich. **USES:** Root decoction used as bitter tonic for indigestion. Promotes appetite; also used for diarrhea, rheumatism, and jaundice. Used for colic, but small doses may cause hypogastric colic. Tincture once used for rheumatism. Contains diosgenin, which has both anti-inflammatory and estrogenic properties.

4 PETALS; LEAVES TOOTHED, 6 IN. LONG OR LESS

SHEPHERD'S PURSE   Whole plant in fruit
Capsella bursa-pastoris (L.) Medik.   Mustard Family
Annual; 4–23 in. Basal leaves in rosette, *dandelion-like*. Stem leaves small, clasping. Flowers tiny. Seedpods *heart-shaped*. (Pods of *C. rubella,* once a separate species, now treated as synonymous with *C. bursa-pastoris,* have concave sides.) **WHERE FOUND:** Waste places. Throughout our area. Alien (Europe). **USES:** Dried- or fresh-herb tea (made from seeds and leaves) stops bleeding, allays profuse menstrual bleeding; diuretic. Has proven uterine-contracting properties; traditionally used during childbirth. Dried herb a useful styptic against hemorrhage. Tea also used for diarrhea, dysentery; also externally, as a wash for bruises. Sciences confirms anti-inflammatory, diuretic, and anti-ulcer activity; decreases blood pressure in laboratory animals. Both water and methanolic extracts accelerate blood coagulation. Above-ground parts (in fruit) approved in Germany for symptomatic treatment of excessive or irregular menstrual bleeding and to stop nosebleeds; externally to allay bleeding from injuries. **WARNING:** Seeds are known to cause rare cases of blistering of skin.

TOOTHWORT, TOOTHACHE ROOT, PEPPER ROOT   Root
Cardamine diphylla (Michx.) Wood   Mustard Family
[*Dentaria diphylla* Michx.]
Perennial; 6–14 in., with creeping rootstock. Stem leaves in opposite pairs; leaves divided into 3 *toothed leaflets,* the middle one largest. Flowers 4-petaled, in terminal clusters; Apr.–June. **WHERE FOUND:** Moist woods. Ont. to S.C. mountains, Ky., Minn. **USES:** Root

Shepherd's Purse (Capsella bursa-pastoris). *Note the small white flowers and purse-shaped seed-pods.*

Toothwort (Cardamine diphylla). *One of our earliest wildflowers, usually white or pale pink.*

peppery; used as a folk remedy for toothaches. American Indians chewed root for colds; poulticed root for headaches. Root tea gargled for sore throats, hoarseness, and to clear throat.

POOR-MAN'S-PEPPER, PEPPERGRASS   **Seedpods, leaves**
Lepidium virginicum L.   Mustard Family

Smooth or minutely hairy annual or biennial; 6–24 in. Leaves lance-shaped, sharp-toothed; *stalked at base.* Flowers white, inconspicuous; May–Nov. Petals *as long as or longer than* sepals. Seedpods roundish. **WHERE FOUND:** Waste places. Throughout our area. **USES:** American Indians used bruised fresh-plant or -leaf tea for Poison Ivy rash, scurvy; used as a substitute for Shepherd's Purse. Leaves poulticed on chest for croup. **WARNING:** Application may cause skin irritation, blisters.

WATERCRESS   **Leaves**
Rorippa nasturtium-aquaticum (L.) Hayek   Mustard Family
[*Nasturtium officinale* Ait. f.]

Watercress, well known for its edible, mustardlike leaves, forms large colonies in cool running water. It begins its life cycle in early spring. Creeping perennial; 4–36 in. Mustard-flavored leaves di-

(Left) *Poor-man's-pepper, Pepper-grass* (Lepidium virginicum).
(*Above*) *Watercress* (Rorippa nasturtium-aquaticum).

vided into 3–9 leaflets, or strongly divided. Tiny flowers; March–June. **WHERE FOUND:** Widespread in cool running water. **USES:** Fresh leaves are high in vitamins A and C and iodine when harvested before flowering. Traditionally used as a diuretic, "blood purifier"; also used for lethargy, rheumatism, heart trouble, bronchitis, scurvy, and goiter. Leaf extracts are used clinically in India to correct vitamin deficiency. Approved in Germany for treatment of inflammation of the respiratory tract. **WARNING:** Do not harvest leaves from polluted waters. Poisoning has resulted from eating leaves from polluted waters in which the plant has absorbed heavy metals and toxins.

4-PETALED FLOWERS; LEAVES VARIOUS

HORSERADISH   **Root**
Armoracia rusticana P. G. Gaertn., B. Mey. & Scherb
[*A. lapthifolia* Gilib.]   Mustard Family
⚠ Large-rooted herb; 1–4 ft. Leaves large, broad, lance-shaped (sometimes jagged); *long-stalked*. Leaves much reduced on flowering stalks. Flowers white, tiny, 4-petaled; May–July. Pods tiny, egg-shaped. **WHERE FOUND:** Moist fields. Throughout. Alien (Europe), persists after cultivation. **USES:** Root used as a condiment. Root tea weakly diuretic, antiseptic, and expectorant; used for bronchitis, coughs, bronchial catarrh, calculus (dental plaque).

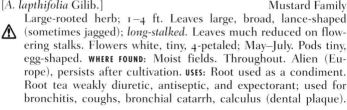

(Left) *Horseradish* (Armoracia rusticana) *is often found near gardens or old fields.* (Above) *Bunchberry* (Cornus canadensis) *blankets the floors of northern forests.*

Root poultice used for rheumatism, respiratory congestion. Few things are better at opening the sinuses than too large a bite of pungent horseradish sauce. Science confirms plant is antibiotic against gram-negative and gram-positive bacteria, pathogenic fungi. Experimentally, it has antitumor activity, as science has come to expect from the Mustard family. In Germany, the root is approved for treatment of inflammation of the respiratory tract and supportive treatment of urinary tract infections. Externally, preparations of root approved to treat lung congestion and minor muscle aches. **WARNING:** Large amounts may irritate digestive system. Plant tops are a **fatal poison** to livestock. External use may cause skin blisters.

The slender stems of Cleavers (Galium aparine) *are mixed among the swordlike leaves of a Crested Dwarf Iris.*

BUNCHBERRY

Leaves, roots

Cornus canadensis L.   Dogwood Family

Perennial; 3–8 in. Leaves in *whorls of 6.* Flowers white, in clusters; surrounded by *4 showy, petal-like bracts;* May–July. Fruits scarlet. **WHERE FOUND:** Cool woods. Northern N. America south to W. Va. mountains, also in n. Calif. **USES:** American Indians used leaf tea for aches and pains, kidney and lung ailments, coughs, fevers, and as an eyewash. Root tea was used for infant colic. Root and leaves used in tea for "fits." Fruits eaten as a snack food; gathered and stored for winter use.

CLEAVERS

Whole plant

Galium aparine L.   Madder Family

Weak-stemmed, often drooping annual; 1–2 ft. Stem *raspy,* with prominent prickles. Leaves lance-shaped; *usually 8, in whorls.* Inconspicuous whitish flowers on stalks from leaf axils; Apr.–Sept. **WHERE FOUND:** Thickets. Throughout our area. Alien. **USES:** Herbal tea traditionally used as a diuretic, "blood purifier"; used for bladder and kidney inflammation, dropsy, "gravel" (kidney stones), fevers. Juice of fresh herb used for scurvy. Herb tea used internally and externally as a folk cancer remedy. Juice contains citric acid, reported to have antitumor activity. Experimentally, extracts are hypotensive (lower blood pressure). Also contains asperuloside, which is anti-inflammatory. **WARNING:** Juice may cause contact dermatitis.

5 PETALS; 3-PARTED LEAVES

GOLDTHREAD, CANKER ROOT

Root

Coptis trifolia (L.) Salib.   Buttercup Family
[*Coptis groenlandica* (Oeder) Fern.]

Mat-forming perennial; to 3 in., with *bright yellow, threadlike roots.* Leaves shiny, evergreen, resembling miniature strawberry leaves. Flowers with 5 white showy sepals; May–July. **WHERE FOUND:** Cool forests. Canada to N.C. mountains; Tenn. north to n. Ohio, Ind., Iowa. **USES:** Root is highly astringent, chewed for canker sores; tea used for jaundice. Contains berberine, which has many properties, including anti-inflammatory and antibacterial effects. Root traditionally used for dyspepsia, thrush, alcoholism, nausea, conjunctivitis, jaundice, nausea, sore throat, stomach cramps, and other uses. Widely used in nineteenth-century America. Today it is seldom used and rarely present in the herb trade, probably because the root is literally a thread, hence difficult to harvest in quantity. Chinese species of *Coptis* have entered the American market as a substitute for Goldenseal.

WOOD STRAWBERRY
Leaves, root
Fragaria vesca L.
Rose Family
Perennial, with runners. 3–6 in. Leaves *pointed*, not rounded, at tip. Flowers white; calyx lobes spreading or recurved. Flowers May–Aug. Fruits with *seeds on surface*. **WHERE FOUND:** Woods. Canada to Va.; Mo. to N.D. Alien (Europe). **USES:** American Indians used root tea for stomach ailments, jaundice, profuse menses. In European folk medicine, leaf tea used as a "blood purifier" and as a diuretic for "gravel" (kidney stones). Tea also used as an external wash on sunburn. Root tea diuretic. Root used as "chewing stick" (toothbrush). Strawberries (both wild and domesticated) are rich in anticancer ellagitannins.

COMMON OR VIRGINIA STRAWBERRY
Leaves, root
Fragaria virginiana Duchesne
Rose Family
Generally larger than Wood Strawberry (above); leaves more rounded, seeds embedded in fruits. **WHERE FOUND:** Fields, openings. Most of our area. Native. **USES:** American Indians and early settlers used leaf tea as a nerve tonic. Also used to treat bladder and kidney ailments, jaundice, scurvy, diarrhea, stomachaches, gout. Considered slightly astringent. Fresh-leaf tea used for sore throats. Berries eaten for scurvy, gout. Root tea traditionally used to treat gonorrhea, stomach and lung ailments, irregular menses; diuretic.

BOWMAN'S ROOT, INDIAN PHYSIC
Whole plant
Porteranthus trifoliatus (L.) Britt.
Rose Family
[*Gillenia trifoliata* (L.) Moench.]
Smooth, slender perennial, 2–3 ft. Leaves alternate; divided into 3 nearly stalkless, sharp, unequal, toothed leaflets. Flowers terminal, in a loose panicle; May–July. Flowers white with a reddish tinge; petals scraggly. **WHERE FOUND:** Rich woods. Ont. to Ga.; Ala. to Mich. **USES:** Traditionally, plant tea is strongly laxative and emetic; minute doses used for indigestion, colds, asthma, hepatitis. Poultice or wash used for rheumatism, bee stings, swellings. **RELATED SPECIES:** Not shown, *P. stipulatus* (Muhl.) Britt. (*G. stipulata* [Muhl. ex Willd.] Nutt.) has prominent leaflike stipules and is used similarly. **WARNING:** Potentially **toxic.**

(Left) *Goldthread, Canker Root* (Coptis trifolia). (Above) *Seeds grow on the surface of the fruit of the Wood Strawberry* (Fragaria vesca).

Common or Virginia Strawberry (Fragaria virginiana). *Seeds are embedded in the fruits.*

Bowman's Root, Indian Physic (Porteranthus trifoliatus) *has long, twisted petals. Photo by Martin Wall.*

CANADA ANEMONE

Roots, leaves

Anemone canadensis L.
Buttercup Family

⚠ Perennial; 1–2 ft. Basal leaves on long stalks. Stem leaves stalk-less, *tightly hugging stem*. Leaves deeply divided with 5–7 lobes. Flowers white. "Petals" (actually 5 showy sepals) 1–1¼ in. long; May–July. **WHERE FOUND:** Damp meadows. N.S. south through New England to W. Va.; west to Ill., Mo., Kans.; B.C. south to N.M. **USES:** Astringent, styptic. American Indians used root or leaf tea (as a wash or poultice) for wounds, sores, nosebleeds. Eyewash used for twitching and to cure cross-eyes. The root was chewed to clear the throat before singing. Among certain Plains Indian groups, the root was highly esteemed as an external medicine for many ailments, and mystical qualities were attributed to the plant. **WARNING:** Probably all our anemones contain the caustic irritants so prevalent in the Buttercup family.

PASQUEFLOWER

Whole plant

Pulsatilla patens ssp. *patens* (L.) P. Mill.
[*Anemone patens* L.]
Buttercup Family

☠ Perennial; 2–16 in. *Silky* leaves arising from root. Leaves *dissected into linear segments*. Showy flowers, 1–1¼ in. wide; "petals" (sepals) purple or white, in a *cup-shaped receptacle*; March–June. Seeds with *feathery plumes*. **WHERE FOUND:** Moist meadows, prairies, woods. Iowa to Colo.; north to Wash., Alaska. **USES:** Minute doses diluted in water have been used internally in homeopathic practice for eye ailments, skin eruptions, rheumatism, leukorrhea, obstructed menses, bronchitis, coughs, asthma. **WARNING:** Poisonous. Extremely irritating.

THIMBLEWEED

Roots, seeds

Anemone virginiana L.
Buttercup Family

Perennial; 2–4 ft. Leaves *strongly veined*, with distinct stalks (not sessile). Flowers 2 or more, with greenish white, petal-like sepals (no true petals). Flowers late Apr.–Aug. Fruit thimblelike. Seeds covered in *cottony fluff*. **WHERE FOUND:** Dry, open woods. Me. to Ga.; Ark. to Kans.; north to S.D. **USES:** Expectorant, astringent, emetic. American Indians used root decoction for whooping cough, tuberculosis, diarrhea. Root poulticed for boils. In order to revive an unconscious patient, the smoke of the seeds was blown into the nostrils. To divine the truth about acts of a "crooked wife," the roots were placed under her pillow, to induce dreams.

Canada Anemone (Anemone canadensis) *has stalkless leaves that tightly hug the stem. Photo by Stephen Lee Timme.*

Pasqueflower (Pulsatilla patens) *typically has pale violet or white petals.*

Thimbleweed (Anemone virginiana) *has strongly veined leaves with distinct stalks. Most Anemone species and many members of the Buttercup family contain irritating compounds. Photo by Stephen Lee Timme.*

MISCELLANEOUS FLOWERS WITH 5 PETALS

BUCKWHEAT
Leaves, seeds

Fagopyrum esculentum Moench.   Buckwheat Family

Annual; 1–4 ft.; stems weak, somewhat succulent. Leaves broadly triangular to arrow-shaped, to 3 in. long. Flowers white or pink, small, loosely crowded together in drooping terminal inflorescence; May–Sept. Fruits are the familiar triangular buckwheat of commerce, a smooth, shining achene; July–Oct. **WHERE FOUND:** Near cultivated ground. Alien. Escapes from cultivation. Occasional throughout. **USES:** Tea of the leaves used to treat erysipelas. Poultice of the powdered seeds used in buttermilk as an English folk remedy to stimulate milk flow. Plant is high in rutin, which reduces capillary fragility. In European traditions, the herb has been used to treat venous and capillary problems, as it increases tone of veins, and is taken to prevent hardening of the arteries. A recent controlled clinical study evaluated a buckwheat herb tea in the treatment of chronic venous insufficiency; results were that it reduced edema (water retention), improved blood flow through the femoral vein, and enhanced capillary resistance.

COMMON NIGHTSHADE
Leaves, berries

Solanum nigrum L.   Nightshade Family

Perennial; 1–2¼ ft. Leaves broadly triangular, irregularly toothed. ⚠ Flowers are white stars with *protruding yellow stamens*; petals

(Left) *Buckwheat* (Fagopyrum esculentum) *is a weak-stemmed, white-flowered annual.* (Above) *Buckwheat* (F. esculentum). *Its fruits are the buckwheat of commerce.*

(Left) *Hairy Nightshade* (Solanum sarrachoides) *has hairy rather than smooth leaves as in* S. nigrum. (Above) *Viola species often used generically, rather than by the specific species.*

curved back; May–Sept. Fruits are black berries. **WHERE FOUND:** Waste places. N.S. to Fla.; local westward. Alien (Europe). **USES:** Externally, leaf-juice preparations have been used as a folk remedy for tumors, cancer. Berries formerly used as a diuretic; used for eye diseases, fever, rabies. Extracts used in tea in India, China, Europe, Japan, Africa, etc. **WARNING:** Some varieties contain solanine, steroids; deaths have been reported from use. In India, some varieties are eaten as vegetables, but similar varieties may be **violently toxic.**

CANADA VIOLET
Root, leaves

Viola canadensis L.
Violet Family

Slightly hairy to smooth perennial; to 10 in. Leaves oval to heart-shaped. Flowers white; Apr.–July. Petals yellowish at base, becoming violet-tinged at base, especially when older. **WHERE FOUND:** Mostly in northern deciduous woods. N.H. to S.C. mountains, Iowa to N.D. **USES:** American Indians used root tea for pain in bladder region. Root and leaves traditionally used to induce vomiting; poulticed for skin abrasions, boils.

CHICKWEED
Whole plant

Stellaria media (L.) Villars
Pink Family

Annual or biennial prostrate weed; 6–15 in. Leaves oval, smooth (*long leafstalks hairy*). Flowers small, white; March–Sept. Petals 2-parted, shorter than sepals. **WHERE FOUND:** Waste places. Throughout our area. Alien. **USES:** Tea of this common Eurasian herb is tra-

(Above) *Chickweed* (Stellaria media). *One of our most common annual weeds.* (Right) *Foamflower* (Tiarella cordifolia). *Its leaves superficially resemble maple leaves. Photo by Martin Wall.*

ditionally used as a cooling demulcent and expectorant to relieve coughs; also used externally for skin diseases and to allay itching, anti-inflammatory. Science has not confirmed folk use. Still much used. Said to curb obesity.

FOAMFLOWER
Tiarella cordifolia L.

Leaves, root
Saxifrage Family

Perennial; 6–12 in. Leaves *maplelike*. Flowers white; 5 petals (with claws), stamens long; Apr.–May. **WHERE FOUND:** Rich woods. N.B. to N.C., S.C., and Ga. mountains; Tenn. mountains to Mich. **USES:** American Indians used leaf tea as a mouthwash for "white-coated tongue," mouth sores, and eye ailments; considered tonic diuretic. Root tea once used as a diuretic; used for diarrhea; poulticed on wounds. High tannin content may explain traditional uses.

NODDING WAXY FLOWERS WITH 5 PETALS

SPOTTED PIPSISSEWA
Chimaphila maculata (L.) Pursh

Leaves
Wintergreen Family

Perennial; 4–10 in. Leaves lance-shaped, in whorls, *midrib broadly white-marked*. Flowers whitish pink, drooping, waxy; June–Aug. **WHERE FOUND:** Rich woods. Me. to Ga.; Ala., Tenn. to Mich. **USES:** Substitute for *C. umbellata* (below). **WARNING:** Said to be a skin irritant.

PIPSISSEWA   **Leaves**
Chimaphila umbellata (L.) Nutt.   Wintergreen Family
⚠   Perennial; 6–12 in. Leaves in *whorls;* lance-shaped, toothed,
shiny. Flowers whitish pink, with a ring of red anthers; drooping,
waxy; June–Aug. **WHERE FOUND:** Dry woods. N.S. to Ga.; Ohio to
Minn. **USES:** American Indians used leaf tea for backaches, coughs,
bladder inflammations, stomachaches, kidney ailments; "blood
purifier," diuretic, astringent, drops used for sore eyes. Leaves
were smoked as a tobacco substitute. Physicians formerly used
leaf tea for bladder stones, kidney inflammation (nephritis), prostatitis, and related ailments. Science confirms diuretic, tonic, astringent, urinary antiseptic, and antibacterial activity. Loaded
with biologically active compounds—arbutin, sitosterol, ursolic
acid. Chimaphilin, found in the leaves, has antiseptic, anti-yeast,
antibacterial, and blood-thinning activities. The constituents may
be responsible for inducing skin irritation. Ursolic acid proves to
be one of those "miracle aspirin" compounds, the so-called COX-
2 inhibitors. **WARNING:** Leaves poulticed on skin may induce redness, blisters, and peeling. Arbutin hydrolyzes to the **toxic** urinary
antiseptic hydroquinone.

SHINLEAF (NOT SHOWN)   **Whole plant**
Pyrola elliptica Nutt.   Wintergreen Family
Perennial; 5–10 in. Leaves in a basal rosette; leaves thin, elliptical; top rounded, blade usually longer than stem. Flowers greenish white; style curving. June–Aug. **WHERE FOUND:** Dry to rich woods.
P.E.I. to Md., W. Va.; Neb. and across Canada to Alaska. **USES:**
American Indians used tea of whole plant to treat epileptic
seizures in babies; leaf tea was gargled for sore throats, canker
sores; leaf poulticed for tumors, sores, and cuts. Root tea used as
a tonic.

ROUND-LEAVED PYROLA   **Leaves**
Pyrola americana Sweet   Wintergreen Family
[*Pyrola rotundifolia* L. var. *americana* (Sweet) Fern.]
Like Shinleaf but *larger;* leaves more rounded, shinier, thicker,
and more leathery. Leaf *stems as long as blades.* **WHERE FOUND:**
Woods, bogs. Nfld. to N.C. mountains; west to Minn., S.D. **USES:**
Formerly used by physicians as an astringent for skin eruptions,
sore throat or mouth, diuretic for urinary infections; antispasmodic for epilepsy, nervous disorders; leaves poulticed on boils,
carbuncles, swelling, painful tumors. Bruised plant used as a
styptic. Contains arbutin, a proven diuretic and antibacterial
agent that breaks down into **toxic** hydroquinone when metabo-
lized. Arbutin is found in many members of the Heath family.

Spotted Pipsissewa (Chimaphila maculata) *has dark green leaves with distinct white veins.*

Pipsissewa (Chimaphila umbellata) *produces waxy flowers.*

(Above) A Pipsissewa (C. umbellata) *flower.* (Right) Round-leaved Pyrola (Pyrola americana) *was used for urinary infections, like many herbaceous Wintergreen family members. Photo by Martin Wall.*

FLOWERS WITH 6–9 PETALS; UMBRELLA-LIKE LEAVES

UMBRELLA-LEAF **Root**
Diphylleia cymosa Michx. Barberry Family
Smooth perennial; 8–36 in. 2 leaves on a stout stalk. Leaves *cleft, umbrella-like; each division with 5–7 toothed lobes.* Flowers white, in clusters; May–Aug. **WHERE FOUND:** Rich woods (rare). Mountains. Va. to Ga. Too rare to harvest. **USES:** A related Chinese species (see below) is used in Traditional Chinese Medicine, but the scarcity and narrow range of the American species probably have limited the interest in medicinal use of this plant. The Cherokees used the root tea of Umbrella-leaf to induce sweating. It was considered diuretic, antiseptic, and useful for smallpox. Physicians thought its effects might be similar to those of Mayapple (see below). **WARNING:** Probably **toxic. RELATED SPECIES:** A closely related Chinese species, *D. sinensis* (not shown), contains the toxic anticancer compound podophyllotoxin. In Traditional Chinese Medicine *D. sinensis* is used for coughs, malaria, cancerous sores, snakebites, and jaundice, and is considered antiseptic. Historical and modern uses of *D. sinensis* indicate parallels in chemistry and use with Mayapple.

TWINLEAF **Whole plant, root**
Jeffersonia diphylla (L.) Pers. Barberry Family
Perennial; 8–16 in. Leaf broadly rounded in outline, but with 2 *distinct sinuses (notches).* Flowers white, 8-petaled; Apr.–May. **WHERE FOUND:** Rich woods. W. N.Y. to Md., W. Va., Va., N.C.; Tenn., Ky. to Wisc. Too rare to harvest. **USES:** American Indians used root tea for cramps, spasms, nervous excitability, diarrhea; diuretic for "gravel" (kidney stones), dropsy, urinary infections, gargle for sore throats; externally, used as a wash for rheumatism, sores, ulcers, inflammation, and cancerous sores. **WARNING:** Probably **toxic.**

MAYAPPLE, AMERICAN MANDRAKE **Root**
Podophyllum peltatum L. Mayapple Family
Perennial; 12–18 in. Leaves smooth, paired, *umbrella-like; distinctive.* A single waxy white flower, to 1 in. across, *droops from crotch of leaves;* Apr.–June. Fruit is globe-shaped to egg-shaped, about 2 in. long; edible but relished by rodents who collect as soon as ripe, robbing humans of a wild food. July–Aug. **WHERE FOUND:** Woods, clearings. S. Me. to Fla.; Texas to Minn. **USES:** American Indians and early settlers used roots as a strong purgative, "liver cleanser," emetic, worm expellent; for jaundice, constipation, hepatitis, fevers, and syphilis. Resin from root, podophyllin

---

Umbrella-leaf (Diphylleia cymosa) *has distinctly cleft leaves with 5–7 lobes. Seldom used because of scarcity and a relatively limited range. Photo by Doug Elliot.*

(highly allergenic), used to treat venereal warts. Extract active against herpes, influenza, and vaccinia viruses. Podophyllotoxin, an important lignan from the root, has anti-cancer and antimalarial activity. Two semisynthetic derivatives, etoposide and teniposide, are used in chemotherapy against several cancer types. Sales of the two compounds exceed $200 million per year. Etoposide is used in combination with other compounds for testicular cancers and as a primary treatment for small-cell lung cancer. Also for various forms of leukemia. Teniposide is used to fight certain childhood leukemias. Fruits edible. **WARNING:** Tiny amounts of root or leaves are **poisonous.** Powdered root and resin can cause skin and eye problems.

Twinleaf (Jeffersonia diphylla) *has winglike leaves. Photo by Alan Detrick.*

Twinleaf (J. diphylla). *Note the distinct seed capsule. Photo by Alan Detrick.*

(Above) *Mayapple* (Podophyllum peltatum) *grows in large patches in a variety of habitats.* (Right) *Note the flowers beneath leaves in fork of stem.*

LOW, SHOWY SPRING FLOWERS WITH 6–10 PETALS

WINDFLOWER, RUE ANEMONE
Root

Anemonella thalictroides (L.) Spach
Buttercup Family

[*Thalictrum thalictroides* (L.) Boivin.]

 Delicate perennial; 4–8 in. Leaves in *whorls*; small, *3-lobed*. Flowers white (or pink), with 5–11 "petals" (sepals); March–May. **WHERE FOUND:** Rich woods. Me. to Fla.; Ark. and e. Okla. to Minn. **USES:** American Indians used root tea for diarrhea and vomiting. Tuberous roots considered edible. Historically, root preparation used by physicians as an experimental application to treat piles. **WARNING:** Possibly **toxic.**

BLOODROOT
Root

Sanguinaria canadensis L.
Poppy Family

 Perennial; 6–12 in. Juice is *orange.* Leaves distinctly round-lobed. Flowers white, to 2 in., with 8–10 petals; flowers appear before or with leaves; March–June. **WHERE FOUND:** Rich woods. N.S. to Fla., e. Texas to Man. **USES:** The blood-red fresh root was used in minute doses as an appetite stimulant, in larger doses as an arterial sedative. Formerly, root was used as an ingredient in cough medicines. American Indians used root tea for rheumatism, asthma, bronchitis, lung ailments, laryngitis, fevers; also as an emetic. Root juice

(Above) *Windflower, Rue Anemone* (Anemonella thalictroides) *is a common spring wildflower.* (Right) *Bloodroot* (Sanguinaria canadensis) *flowers appear before trees grow leaves in spring.*

(Left) *Bloodroot* (S. canadensis) *leaves are distinctly lobed.* (Above) *Bloodroot* (S. canadensis) *gets its name from the blood-red color of the roots.*

is applied to warts, also used as a dye and as a decorative skin stain. A bachelor of the Ponca tribe would rub a piece of the root as a love charm on the palm of his hand, then scheme to shake hands with the woman he desired to marry. After shaking hands,

The Sharp-lobed Hepatica (Hepatica nobilis) has pointed leaf tips.

The Sharp-lobed Hepatica (H. nobilis) has white to violet flowers.

The leaves of the Round-lobed Hepatica (Hepatica americana) have rounded tips.

the girl would be found willing to marry him in 5–6 days. Experimentally, the alkaloid sanguinarine has shown antiseptic, anesthetic, and anticancer activity. It is used commercially as a plaque-inhibiting agent in toothpaste, mouthwashes, and rinses. Ingestion of the root can cause a positive opiate test in urinalysis. **WARNING: Toxic. Do not ingest.** Jim Duke has experienced tunnel vision from nibbling the root. Sanguinarine said to cause glaucoma.

SHARP-LOBED HEPATICA, LIVERLEAF   **Leaves**
Hepatica nobilis var. *acuta* (Pursh) Steyermark   Buttercup Family
[*Hepatica acutiloba* DC.]

Flowers usually bluish lavender or pinkish, though often whitish. Feb.–early June. See p. 198 and color plate.

ROUND-LOBED HEPATICA   **Leaves**
Hepatica nobilis var. *obtusa* (Pursh) Steyermark   Buttercup Family
[*Hepatica americana* (DC.) Ker.]

Similar to Sharp-lobed Hepatica, but leaf lobes are *rounded*. Flowers are often white; March–June. **WHERE FOUND:** Dry woods. N.S. to Ga., Ala.; Mo. to Man. **USES:** Same as for *H. acutiloba* (see above). See p. 198.

FLOWERS IN SINGLE, GLOBE-SHAPED CLUS-TERS; FRUITS RED

RED BANEBERRY **Root**
Actaea rubra (Ait.) Willd. Buttercup Family

 Perennial; 2–3 ft. Similar to White Baneberry (see p. 60), though the flowerhead is rounder, and the berries are *red* and on less stout stalks. Fruits; July–Oct. **WHERE FOUND:** Rich woods. S. Canada to n. N.J., W. Va.; west through Ohio and Iowa to S.D., Colo., Utah, and Ore. **USES:** American Indians used root tea for menstrual irregularity, postpartum pains, and as a purgative after childbirth; also used to treat coughs and colds. **WARNING:** Plant is **poisonous—** may cause vomiting, gastroenteritis, irregular breathing, and delirium.

GOLDENSEAL **Root**
Hydrastis canadensis L. Buttercup Family

Hairy perennial; 6–12 in. Usually 2 leaves on a forked branch; one leaf larger than the other; each is rounded with 5–7 *lobes; double-toothed.* Flowers are single with greenish white stamens in clusters; Apr.–May. Berries like those of raspberry. **WHERE FOUND:** Rich woods. Vt. to Ga.; Ala., Ark. to Minn. Goldenseal is becoming less common in our eastern deciduous forests because of overcollection, hence it is now monitored in international trade. **USES:** Root traditionally used in tea or tincture to treat inflamed

(Above) *Red baneberry* (Actaea rubra) *produces fleshy red fruits.*
(Right) *Goldenseal* (Hydrastis canadensis) *flowers bloom for shorter than one week.*

mucous membranes of mouth, throat, digestive system, uterus; also used for jaundice, bronchitis, pharyngitis, gonorrhea. Tea (wash) a folk remedy for eye infections. Until the 1980s, components of the root were used commercially in eyewash preparations. Contains berberine, an antibacterial agent that increases bile secretion and acts as an anticonvulsant. Experimentally, berberine lowers blood pressure and acts as mild sedative. The root also contains the alkaloids hydrastine and canadine. Recent research suggests a synergistic action of the major alkaloids in reducing muscle-spasm activity. When any single alkaloid was removed from the mix, the effect was greatly lessened. A 1998 study suggests that Goldenseal may help fight drug-resistant tuberculosis, one of today's most lethal infectious bacterial diseases. **WARNING:** Avoid during pregnancy. Based on the plot of a 1900 novel, *Stringtown on the Pike,* by the pharmacist John Uri Lloyd, Goldenseal's popularity is in part stimulated by the notion that it masks detection of illicit drugs in urinalysis. This has prompted drug-testing labs to test for Goldenseal in the urine. Scientists have disproved rumor that Goldenseal masks morphine in urine tests.

AMERICAN GINSENG
Panax quinquefolius L.

Root

Ginseng Family

Perennial; 1–2 ft. Root fleshy, sometimes resembling human form. Leaves *palmately divided* into 4–5 (occasionally 3–7) sharp-toothed, oblong-lance-shaped leaflets. Flowers whitish, in *round umbels;* June–July. Fruits are 2-*seeded red berries.* The rhizome at the top of the root, often referred to as the neck, reveals annual scars left by the year's leaf stem. The age of the root, which affects quality and price, is determined by counting the leaf scars. Only roots five years old or older are desirable (active components—ginsenosides—increase significantly between the fourth and fifth year of growth). **WHERE FOUND:** Rich woods. Me. to Ga.; Okla. to Minn. Wild root is becoming increasingly scarce due to dramatic price increases in the 1990s. Interstate commerce of the root is regulated by the federal government. It is unethical (and illegal) to harvest the roots before the red berries ripen and set seed; this occurs in late summer or early autumn. In a 5-year transplant population, Duke found that approximately 10 percent of plants did not emerge above ground each growing season, but remained dormant. **USES:** Root considered demulcent, tonic. Research suggests it may increase mental efficiency and physical performance and aid in adapting to high or low temperatures and stress (when taken over an extended period). Ginseng's effect is called "adaptogenic"—tending to return the body to normal while

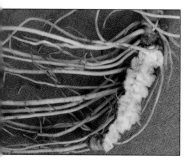

(Above) *Goldenseal* (H. canadensis) *gets its name from the bright golden color of the rhizome.* (Right) *It produces insipid red fruit that resembles raspberries.*

The bright red berries of American Ginseng appear in late summer.

American Ginseng's root is one of the highest-priced products from American forests.

increasing resistance to adverse influences on the body. Ginseng has long been considered an aphrodisiac. A recent study explains this effect via nitric oxide release in the corpus cavernosum. May also possess cancer-preventative activity. In Germany, Asian ginseng (*Panax ginseng* C. A. Meyer) is approved as a tonic in times of fatigue, debility, declining work capacity and concentration, and during convalescence. **WARNING:** Some caution required; large doses are said to raise blood pressure, though this has been disputed.

FLOWERS IN RADIATING CLUSTERS; RIPE FRUITS NOT RED

WHITE BANEBERRY, DOLL'S EYES
Actaea pachypoda L.
[*Actaea alba* auct. non (L.) P. Mill.]

Root
Buttercup Family

Perennial; 1–2 ft. Leaves twice-divided; leaflets oblong, sharp-toothed. Flowers in oblong clusters on *thick red stalks.* Fleshy *white berries with a dark dot at tip;* July–Oct. The dark dot at the tip of the white berry earns this plant the common name Doll's Eyes. **WHERE FOUND:** Rich woods. S. Canada to Ga., La.; Okla. to Minn. **USES:** Menomini used small amounts of root tea to relieve pain of childbirth, and headaches due to eye strain. Once used for coughs, menstrual irregularities, colds, and chronic constipation; thought to be beneficial to circulation. **WARNING: Poisonous.** All parts may cause severe gastrointestinal inflammation and skin blisters.

INDIAN HEMP
Apocynum cannabinum L.

Root, stems, berries, latex
Dogbane Family

Shrublike; 1–2 ft. Leaves (except lowermost ones) with definite stalks, to ¼ in. long. Flowers terminal, whitish green, bell-like, 5-sided; June–Aug. Seedpods paired; 4–8 in. long. **WHERE FOUND:** Much of our area and beyond. **USES:** Used as in *A. androsaemifolium* (p. 172); also, stems used for fiber, cordage. Milky sap is a folk remedy for venereal warts. American Indians used berries and root in weak teas for heart ailments; diuretic. **WARNING: Poisonous.** Contains toxic cardioactive (heart-affecting) glycosides. Cymarin and apocymarin have shown antitumor activity; the latter also raises blood pressure.

FOUR-LEAVED MILKWEED
Asclepias quadrifolia Jacq.

Root
Milkweed Family

Flowers white or pinkish. Leaves *in whorls* of 4. See p. 175.

White Baneberry (Actaea pachypoda) *produces distinct white, dry, fleshy fruit.*

The common name "Doll's Eyes" derives from the black spots on the fruits.

(Left) *Indian Hemp* (Apocynum cannabinum) *flowers in late summer.* (Above) *Four-leaved Milkweed has four leaves in a whorl. Photo by Stephen Lee Timme.*

VIRGINIA WATERLEAF
Hydrophyllum virginianum L.
Flowers whitish to violet. See p. 200.

Whole plant
Waterleaf Family

DWARF GINSENG
Panax trifolius L.

Leaves, root
Ginseng Family

    Globe-rooted perennial; 2–8 in. Leaves divided into 3 (occasionally 5) *toothed, oblong to lance-shaped* leaflets. Flowers white to

(Left) *Virginia Waterleaf* (Hydrophyllum virginianum) *has white to violet flowers.* (Above) *Dwarf Ginseng* (Panax trifolius) *is a seldom-used Ginseng.*

yellow (or pinkish), in small umbels; Apr.–May. Fruits green or yellow. **WHERE FOUND:** Rich woods. N.S. to Pa., Ga. mountains, Ind., Iowa to Minn. In a transplant experiment, Duke has confirmed that plants may have male flowers one year and female flowers the next year and vice versa. **USES:** American Indians used tea of the whole plant for colic, indigestion, gout, hepatitis, hives, rheumatism, and tuberculosis; root chewed for headaches, short breath, fainting, nervous debility. Little used or researched. Above ground for only 2 months.

TINY FLOWERS IN GLOBE-SHAPED CLUSTERS OR PANICLES; ARALIAS; MOSTLY HERBACEOUS

HAIRY SARSAPARILLA
Aralia hispida Vent.

Root, leaves
Ginseng Family

Shrubby; 1–3 ft. Foul-smelling. Stem with *sharp, stiff bristles.* Leaves twice-compound; leaflets oval, cut-toothed. Small greenish white flowers in *globe-shaped umbels*; June–Aug. Fruits are dark, foul-smelling berries. **WHERE FOUND:** Sandy open woods. E. Canada, New England south to Va., W. Va., west to Ill., Minn. **USES:** Leaf tea promotes sweating. Bark (root bark especially) diuretic, "tonic"; allays kidney irritation and associated lower back pain, increases secretions in dropsy and edema.

(Left) *Hairy Sarsaparilla* (Aralia hispida) *occurs in dry woods.* (Right) *Wild Sarsaparilla* (Aralia nudicaulis) *is one of the most common understory plants in New England forests.*

WILD SARSAPARILLA   Root
Aralia nudicaulis L.   Ginseng Family

Smooth perennial; to 2 ft. Leaves twice-divided; each of the 3 divisions has 3–5 toothed, oval leaflets. Flowers in a single umber on a separate stalk, *below leaves*; May–July. Root is long-running, horizontal, fleshy. **WHERE FOUND:** Moist woods. Nfld. to Ga.; west to n. Mo., Ill., N.D. to Colo. and Idaho. **USES:** American Indians used the pleasant-flavored root tea as a beverage, "blood purifier," tonic; used for lassitude, general debility, stomachaches, and coughs. Externally, the fresh root was poulticed on sores, burns, itching, ulcers, boils, and carbuncles; also used to reduce swelling and cure infections. In folk tradition, root tea or tincture was used as a diuretic and "blood purifier"; promotes sweating; used for stomachaches, fevers, coughs. Root poultice used for wounds, ulcers, boils, carbuncles, swelling, infection, rheumatism. Former substitute for true (tropical *Smilax*) sarsaparilla. This plant was widely used in "tonic" and "blood purifier" patent medicines of the late nineteenth century.

SPIKENARD   Root
Aralia racemosa L.   Ginseng Family

Perennial; 3–5 ft. Stem *smooth; dark green or reddish.* Leaves compound, with 6–21 toothed, *weakly heart-shaped* leaflets. Flowers whitish, in small umbels on branching racemes;

Spikenard (Aralia racemosa) *occurs in rich, wooded habitats.*

June–Aug. Root *spicy-aromatic.* **WHERE FOUND:** Rich woods. Que. to Ga.; west to Kans.; north to Minn. **USES:** Same as for *A. nudicaulis* (above); also used for coughs, asthma, lung ailments, and rheumatism, syphilis, and kidney troubles. Formerly used in cough syrups. Root tea widely used by American Indians for menstrual irregularities, for lung ailments accompanied by coughs, and to improve the flavor of other medicines. Externally, root poulticed on boils, infections, swellings, and wounds. Contains saponins, possibly with expectorant action.

FLOWERS IN LONG, SLENDER, TAPERING CLUSTERS

BLACK COHOSH   **Root**
Cimicifuga racemosa (L.) Nutt.   Buttercup Family
[*Actaea racemosa* L.]

Perennial; 3–8 ft. Leaves thrice-divided; sharply toothed; *terminal leaflet 3-lobed, middle lobe largest.* Flowers white, *in very long spikes;* May–Sept. *Tufts of stamens conspicuous.* **WHERE FOUND:** Rich woods. S. Ont. to Ga.; Ark., Mo. to Wisc. Greatly increased modern use could pressure wild populations. **USES:** Used by American Indian groups for menstrual irregularities and to aid childbirth; in nineteenth-century America the root tincture was widely used as an anti-inflammatory for rheumatism; also used for bronchitis, chorea, fevers, nervous disorders, lumbago, snakebites, and menstrual irregularities. Research has confirmed that Black Cohosh reduces levels of a hormone associated with hot flashes; also hypoglycemic, sedative, and anti-inflammatory activity. Emerging as one of the most important American medicinal plants for the twenty-first century, at least ten clinical studies have confirmed that extracts from the root are useful in the treatment of

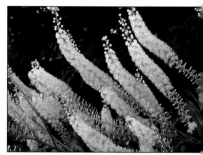

(Left, Above, Below) *Black Cohosh* (Cimicifuga racemosa) *leaves are difficult to distinguish from those of Baneberry. Its root is emerging as one of the most important medicinal plants in treating menopause. Root preparations have been prescribed by German gynecologists since the mid-1950s.*

menopausal symptoms, particularly hot flashes. It is approved in Germany for treatment of premenstrual symptoms, painful or difficult menstruation, and to reduce severity of menopausal symptoms. Prescribed by European gynecologists for more than 40 years; more than 2 million patients use this plant. **WARNING:** Avoid during pregnancy.

POKEWEED, POKE
Phytolacca americana L.

Root, fruits, leaves
Pokeweed Family

Coarse, large-rooted perennial; 5–10 ft. *Stem often red* at base. Leaves large, entire (toothless), oval. Flowers with greenish white, petal-like sepals, July–Sept. Fruits *purple-black,* in droop-

(Left) *Pokeweed, Poke* (Phytolacca americana) *is usually considered poisonous.* (Above) *Pokeweed's fruits are purple-black, in drooping clusters.*

ing clusters; Aug–Nov. **WHERE FOUND:** Waste places. Much of our area (except N.D., S.D.). **USES:** American Indians used berry tea for rheumatism, arthritis, dysentery, berries poulticed on sore breasts. Old-timers in the Ozarks still eat one pokeberry a year as a preventative or to treat arthritis. Root poulticed for rheumatism, neuralgic pains, bruises; wash used for sprains, swellings; leaf preparations once used as an expectorant, emetic, cathartic; poulticed for bleeding, pimples, blackheads. Folk uses similar. Plant contains a highly toxic Pokeweed antiviral mitogen, being investigated for anticancer and anti-HIV potential. **WARNING: All parts are poisonous,** though leaves are eaten as a spring green, after cooking through 2 changes of water. (Do not confuse with American White Hellebore, *Veratrum viride*, pp. 118 and 236, which is highly toxic.) Plant juice of Pokeweed can cause dermatitis, even damage chromosomes.

LIZARD'S-TAIL WATER-DRAGON   **Root, leaves**
Saururus cernuus L.   Lizard-tail Family
    Aquatic or wet-ground-loving perennial. See p. 18.

CULVER'S-ROOT   **Root**
Leptandra virginica (L.) Nutt.   Figwort Family
[*Veronicastrum virginicum* (L.) Farw.]
    Perennial; 2–5 ft. Leaves lance-shaped, toothed; in *whorls of 3–7*.
⚠ Flowers tiny white (or purple) tubes with 2 projecting stamens;

The root of Culver's-root (Leptandra virginica) was formerly used as a strong laxative. Some botanists have noted population declines attributed to over-harvest.

on showy spikes; June–Sept. **WHERE FOUND:** Moist fields. Mass. to Fla.; e. Texas to Man. **USES:** American Indians used root tea as a strong laxative, to induce sweating, to stimulate liver, to induce vomiting; diuretic. Used similarly by physicians. **WARNING:** Traditionally, *dried* root is used; *fresh* root violently laxative. Potentially **toxic**.

FLOWERS IN UMBRELLA-LIKE CLUSTERS (UMBELS); 5 TINY PETALS; LEAVES FINELY DISSECTED

CARAWAY
Carum carvi L.

Seeds
Parsley Family

 Smooth biennial; 1–2 ft. Stem hollow. Leaves finely divided, *carrotlike*. Flowers tiny, white (or pink); May–July. Seeds slightly curved, ribbed, caraway-scented. **WHERE FOUND:** Fields. Scattered throughout our area; absent from South. Alien. **USES:** Seed tea carminative, expectorant. Relieves gas in digestive system, soothing to upset stomach; also used for coughs, pleurisy. Thought to relieve menstrual pain, promote milk secretion. Externally, used as a wash for rheumatism. Oil is antibacterial. Caraway seed, the seed on most rye breads in this country, is one of the best sources of limonene, with potential for preventing and treating breast cancer. Use of seeds is approved in Germany for mild spasms of the gastrointestinal tract accompanied by bloating and a feeling of fullness. **WARNING:** Young leaves are very similar to those of Fool's Parsley and Poison Hemlock. To identify Fool's Parsley, see *A Field Guide to Wildflowers*, p. 48.

Caraway (Carum carvi) fruits have a familiar caraway fragrance. Well known as a culinary herb whose fruit (seeds) are used to flavor breads and baked goods. It is less well known as a medicinal plant.

POISON HEMLOCK
Conium maculatum L.

Poison—Identify to avoid
Parsley Family

Branched perennial; 2–6 ft. Stems hollow, grooved, *purple-spotted.* Leaves *carrotlike,* but in overall outline are more like an equilateral triangle, and with more divisions. Leaves *ill-scented when bruised.* Leafstalks *hairless.* Flowers white, in umbels; May–Aug. **WHERE FOUND:** Waste ground. Most of our area. Alien. **USES:** Whole plant a traditional folk cancer remedy, narcotic, sedative, anal-

Poison Hemlock (Conium maculatum) has spotted stems. It is highly toxic.

Poison Hemlock (C. maculatum) with white umbels. It is highly toxic.

Queen Anne's Lace (Daucus carota) *has a purple floret in the center of the umbel.*

Valerian (Valeriana officinalis) *has white to pale lavender flowers. It is widely naturalized in the Northeast.*

gesic, spasmolytic, anti-aphrodisiac. **WARNING: Deadly poison. Ingestion can be lethal. Contact can cause dermatitis. Juice is highly toxic.** Young Poison Hemlock plant closely resembles the western Osha root.

QUEEN ANNE'S LACE, WILD CARROT
Root, seeds

Daucus carota L.
Parsley Family

Bristly stemmed biennial; 2–4 ft. Leaves finely dissected. Flowers in a *flat cluster*, with 1 small *deep purple floret* at center; 3-forked bracts beneath; Apr.–Oct. **WHERE FOUND:** Waste places, roadsides. Throughout our area. Alien (Europe). **USES:** Root tea traditionally used as a diuretic, to prevent and eliminate *urinary* stones and *worms*. Science confirms its bactericidal, diuretic, hypotensive, and worm-expelling properties. Seeds a folk "morning after" contraceptive. Experiments with mice indicate that seed extracts may be useful in preventing implantation of fertilized egg. (Not recommended for such use.) Recent studies indicate a cancer-preventative effect associated with the root, and anticancer activity is attributed to components in the seeds. **WARNING:** May cause dermatitis and blisters. Proper identification is essential so that it is not mistaken for one of the deadly poisonous members of the Carrot family (*Umbelliferae*), such as Poison Hemlock.

VALERIAN
Valeriana officinalis L.
See p. 160.

See p. 160.

Root
Valerian Family

UMBRELLA-LIKE CLUSTERS; STEMS PUR-PLISH OR PURPLE-TINGED; LEAF SEGMENTS NOT FERNLIKE

ANGELICA
Angelica atropurpurea L.

Leaves, root, seeds
Parsley Family

Smooth biennial; stem is *smooth purple or purple-tinged*, hence the species name *atropurpurea* (dark purple); 4–9 ft. Leaves with 3 leaflets, each *divided again 3–5 times*. Upper leafstalks have *inflated* sheaths. Flowers in large, semiround heads, June–Aug. **WHERE FOUND:** Rich, wet soil. Nfld. to Del., W. Va.; Ill. to Wisc. **USES:** Leaf tea used for stomachaches, indigestion, gas, anorexia, obstructed menses, fevers, colds, colic, flu, coughs, neuralgia, rheumatism. Roots, seeds strongest; leaves weaker. Stimulates secretion of gastric juices and alleviates smooth-muscle spasms. **WARNING:** Contains furcoumarins, which can cause photosensitivity. Because it grows in the same habitat as the Poison Hemlock, and the untrained botanical collector may confuse the two, harvest should be avoided unless positively identified by a trained botanist. **RELATED SPECIES:** Other Angelicas, including *A. sinensis* and *A. dahurica*, are famous Chinese drugs for "female ailments." The European *A. archangelica,* sometimes naturalized in eastern North America, reportedly contains 15 calcium blockers, one as potent as the synthetic verapamil, used for the treatment of angina. Root approved in Germany for treatment of loss of appetite, stomach discomfort due to mild gastrointestinal tract spasms, flatulence, and a feeling of fullness in the abdomen.

WATER-HEMLOCK
Cicuta maculata L.

Poison—Identify to avoid
Parsley Family

Biennial; 1–7 ft. *Stems smooth; purple-streaked or -spotted.* Leaves divided 2–3 times; leaflets lance-shaped, coarsely toothed. Flowers in loose umbels; May–Sept. *Strong odor.* **WHERE FOUND:** Wet meadows, swamps. Most of our area. **USES:** Too lethal for use; contains compounds similar to those found in Poison Hemlock (below). **WARNING: Highly poisonous.** Do not confuse with harmless members of the Parsley family.

Angelica (Angelica atropurpurea) *has dark purple stems.*

Water-hemlock (Cicuta maculata) *occurs in wet habitats.*

POISON HEMLOCK
Conium maculatum L.

Poison—Identify to avoid
Parsley Family

Stems *purple-spotted*. **WARNING: Deadly poison.** Ingestion can be lethal. Contact can cause dermatitis. See p. 68.

COW-PARSNIP
Heracleum maximum Bartr.
[*Heracleum lanatum* Michx.]

Root, leaves, tops
Parsley Family

Large, woolly, strong-smelling biennial or perennial; to 6–9 ft. Leaves divided into 3 *maplelike segments*; sheath *inflated*. Umbels large: 6–12 in. across; flowers with notched petals; May–Aug. **WHERE FOUND:** Moist soils. Nfld. to Ga. mountains; west to Mo., Kans., N.D., and westward. **USES:** Root tea was widely used by American Indians for colic, cramps, headaches, sore throats, colds, coughs, flu; externally poulticed on sores, bruises swellings, rheumatic joints, boils. In folk use, root tea was used for indigestion, gas, asthma, epilepsy. Powdered root (1 teaspoon per day over a long period) was taken, with a strong tea of the leaves and tops, for epilepsy. Root contains psoralen, which is being researched and tested in the treatment of psoriasis, leukemia, and AIDS. **WARNING:** Foliage is **poisonous** to livestock; roots contain phototoxic compounds, including psoralen. Acrid sap can

Cow-parsnip (Heracleum maximum) *is one of our largest Parsley family members.*

cause blisters on contact. The authors know an herbalist who badly blistered his forearms and wrists after handling the plant.

FLOWERS IN UNEVEN OR SPARSE UMBELS; LEAVES PARTED AND TOOTHED

SWEET CICELY   **Root**
Osmorhiza claytonii (Michx.) C. B. Clarke   Parsley Family
⚠ Soft-hairy perennial; 1–3 ft. Root rank-tasting. Leaves fernlike; thrice-compound. Flowers tiny, white; May–June. **WHERE FOUND:** Moist woods. N.S. to N.C. mountains; Ala., Ark. to Sask. **USES:** American Indians chewed the root or gargled root tea for sore throats; poulticed root on boils, cuts, sores, wounds; tea a wash for sore red eyes, drunk for coughs. **WARNING:** Do not confuse with Poison Hemlock (*Conium*). See p. 68.

SWEET CICELY, ANISE ROOT   **Root**
Osmorhiza longistylis (Torr.) DC.   Parsley Family
⚠ A relative of *O. claytonii*, but stouter and nearly smooth; distribution more western. Root *very sweet, aromatic, fleshy.* **WHERE FOUND:** Ont. to N.C.; Okla. to N.D. **USES:** American Indians used root tea for general debility, panacea; tonic for upset stomach, parturition (childbirth); root poulticed on boils, wounds; root tea an eyewash. In folk medicine, used as an expectorant, tonic for coughs, stomachaches. Root eaten or soaked in brandy. **WARNING:** Do not confuse with Poison Hemlock (*Conium*). See p. 68.

(Above) *Sweet Cicely* (Osmorhiza claytonii). *Photo by Stephen Lee Timme.* (Right) *Sweet Cicely, Anise Root* (Osmorhiza longistylis). *Photo by Martin Wall.*

BLACK OR CANADIAN SANICLE
Leaves, root
Sanicula canadensis L.   Parsley Family

Biennial; to 36 in. Leaves long-stalked; palmate, with 3–5 *leaflets* that are double-toothed or deeply incised; upper leaves reduced, becoming bract pairs. Flowers whitish, in uneven umbels; May–July. Fruits grow on a small but distinct stalk. **WHERE FOUND:** Dry woods, openings. S. N.H. to Fla.; Texas to Neb. **USES:** American Indians used the powdered root as a heart remedy; to stimulate menses; abortive. Leaves, which contain allantoin, were poulticed for bruises, inflammation.

BLACK SANICLE OR SNAKEROOT
Root
Sanicula marilandica L.   Parsley Family

Perennial; 1–4 ft. Leaves palmate, with 5–7 *leaflets*; 2 of the leaflets are deeply cleft, suggesting 7 leaflets. Flowers whitish, in uneven umbels with leaflike bracts beneath; Apr.–July. *Prickled fruits sessile (without stalks); base of bristles bulbous.* **WHERE FOUND:** Thickets, shores. N.S. to Fla.; Mo. to e. Kans., N.D. **USES:** The thick rhizome (root) was used by American Indians in tea for menstrual irregularities, pain, kidney ailments, rheumatism, fevers; root also poulticed on snakebites.

(Above) *Canadian Sanicle* (Sanicula canadensis). *Photo by Stephen Lee Timme.* (Right) *Black Sanicle or Snakeroot* (Sanicula marilandica). *Photo by Martin Wall.*

FLOWERS WITH 5 "PETALS," IN FLAT-TOPPED CLUSTERS

YARROW

Achillea millefolium L.

Whole plant in flower
Composite Family

Soft, fragrant perennial; 1–3 ft. Leaves lacy, *finely dissected.* Flowers white (less frequently pink), in flat clusters; May–Oct. Each tiny flowerhead has 5 petal-like rays that are usually slightly wider than long; each ray has 3 teeth at tip. **WHERE FOUND:** Fields, roadsides. Throughout. **USES:** One of the chief uses is as a vulnerary—an agent to stop bleeding of wounds. The Latin name *Achillea* honors Achilles, and legend states that he used a poultice of Yarrow flowers to stop the bleeding of his wounded soldiers in battle. Herbal tea (made from dried flowering plant) used for colds, fevers, anorexia, indigestion, gastric inflammations, and internal bleeding. Fresh herb a styptic poultice. Expectorant, analgesic, and sweat-inducing qualities of some components may provide relief from cold and flu symptoms. Used similarly by native cultures throughout the Northern Hemisphere. Experimentally, extracts are hemostatic and anti-inflammatory. Contains more than 100 biologically active compounds, including more than a dozen anti-inflammatory compounds. **WARNING:** May cause dermatitis. Large or frequent doses taken over a long period may be potentially harmful. Contains thujone, a toxic compound.

(Left) *Yarrow* (Achillea mille-folium) *is a common weed in fields and waste places.* (Above) *Yarrow* (A. millefolium). *Note the finely dissected leaves.*

FLOWERING SPURGE
Leaves, root
Euphorbia corollata L.   Spurge Family

Deep-rooted, milky-juiced, smooth-stemmed perennial; 1–3 ft. Leaves without stalks, *oval to linear*. Flowers white, in many forked umbels, rising from *whorl of reduced leaves*. Note the 5 "petals" (actually bracts) surrounding flowers. Flowers June–Aug. **WHERE FOUND:** Fields, roadsides. Ont., N.Y. to Fla.; Texas to Minn. **USES:** American Indians used leaf tea for diabetes; root tea as a strong laxative, emetic, for pinworms, rheumatism; root poultice used for snakebites. **WARNING:** Extremely strong laxative. Juice may cause blistering.

TALL CINQUEFOIL
Whole plant, root
Potentilla arguta Pursh   Rose Family

Erect, *glandular-hairy* perennial; 1–3 ft. Pinnate leaves at base of stem divided into 7–11 oval, sharp-toothed leaflets, downy beneath; minute, leaflike "follicles" often present between alternating leaflets. Flowers white to cream, 5-petaled; June–Aug. **WHERE FOUND:** Rocky soils, prairies. N.B. to Ind., Mo., Okla.; west to Ore., Alaska. **USES:** As with yellow-flowered members of the genus (and the Rose family in general), the whole plant or root, in tea or as a poultice, stops bleeding (astringent to capillaries); used for cuts, wounds, diarrhea, dysentery. Use probably due to content of tannins. **RELATED SPECIES:** In Germany, the herb is used to treat mild

(Above) *Flowering Spurge* (Euphorbia corollata). *Its stems produce a milky juice.* (Right) *Tall Cinquefoil* (Potentilla arguta), *with a showy ring of stamens. Photo by Craig C. Freeman.*

cases of excessive menstrual bleeding, diarrhea, and mild inflammations of the throat and mouth.

SMALL WHITISH FLOWERS IN LEAF AXILS; PARASITIC OR SEMIPARASITIC PLANTS

DODDER | **Whole plant**
Cuscuta species | Morning-glory Family

Parasitic, chlorophyll-lacking, leafless annuals; leaves replaced by a few scales. *Stems yellow or orange.* **WHERE FOUND:** Low ground. Most of our area. Dodders clamber over other growth and cause serious damage as annual weeds. **USES:** Stems used by Cherokees as a poultice for bruises. **WARNING:** Dodders are called love vines and "vegetable spaghetti" but are not generally considered edible. **RELATED SPECIES:** About 15 species in our area, distinguished by flowers and fruit details. (1) **Common Dodder** (*C. gronovii* Willd.) has *small*, whitish, *waxy, 5-lobed* flowers in loose or crowded clusters. (2) In China, the stems of other *Cuscuta* species are used in lotions for inflamed eyes. The Chinese value the seeds of dodders for urinary tract ailments. The tea of **Chinese Dodder** (*C. chinensis*) has demonstrated anti-inflammatory, cholinergic, and CNS-depressant activity. **WARNING:** Some parasitic flowering plants take up toxins from their hosts.

EYEBRIGHT

Whole plant

Euphrasia stricta D. Wolff ex J. F. Lehm.

Figwort Family

[Euphrasia officinalis L.]

⚠ Slender, semiparasitic (root is attached to grasses) annual; 4–8 in. Leaves tiny, bristle-toothed. Flowers June–Sept. *3 lower lobes notched*, with purple lines. Highly variable. **WHERE FOUND:** This complex plant group comprises more than 170 named species (mostly European) that are distinguished by botanists on minute technical details, though herbalists treat the group as a single herb. Dry or moist fields, roadsides, waste places. Subarctic south to Que., Me., Mass., N.Y. **USES:** Tea astringent. A folk remedy (wash or poulticed) for eye ailments with mucous discharge; coughs, hoarseness, earaches, headaches with congestion. The small flowers, which look like eyes, evoke the medieval doctrine of signatures, suggesting use for eye ailments. Poorly researched, *Euphrasia* species contain anti-inflammatory and antibacterial compounds, perhaps providing a basis for traditional use. **WARNING:** Experimentally, may induce side effects, including dim vision. Avoid use without physician's advice. **RELATED SPECIES:** Other *Euphrasia* species have been used similarly.

Dodder (Cuscuta *sp.) is a yellow, chlorophyll-lacking parasite that entangles other plants.*

Eyebright (Euphrasia officinalis) *is a low-growing plant of the far north.*

SEA MILKWORT (NOT SHOWN)   **Root**
Glaux maritima L.   Primrose Family
   Light-colored, fleshy perennial; 2–12 in. Leaves opposite, without stalks; oval. Flowers solitary, whitish to pink, 5-parted, in axils just above leaves; June–July. **WHERE FOUND:** Sandy shores, salt marshes; mostly coastal. Que. south to Va. **USES:** American Indians ate the boiled roots to induce sleep.

SQUARE-STEMMED AROMATIC HERBS (MINTS); FLOWERS IN AXILS OR TERMINAL

LEMON BALM, MELISSA   **Leaves**
Melissa officinalis L.   Mint Family
   Perennial; 1–2 ft. Leaves opposite; oval, round-toothed; *strongly lemon-scented*. Flowers whitish, inconspicuous, in whorls; May–Aug. **WHERE FOUND:** Barnyards, old house sites, open woods. Scattered over much of our area. Commonly grown in herb gardens. Alien (Europe). **USES:** Dried- or fresh-leaf tea is a folk remedy for fevers, painful menstruation, headaches, colds, insomnia; mild sedative, carminative; leaves poulticed for sores, tumors, insect bites. Experimentally, hot water extracts have been shown strongly antiviral for Newcastle disease, herpes, mumps. Strong extracts (200:1) sold in ointments in Europe to treat cold sores and genital herpes. This use is backed by clinical studies. In Germany, Lemon Balm preparations are approved for treatment of sleeplessness caused by nervous conditions and digestive tract spasms. Like extracts of Rosemary and Sage, Lemon Balm extracts slow the breakdown of acetylcholine, a messenger compound deficient in brain-cell cultures of Alzheimer's disease patients. Contains at least 8 antiviral compounds (against herpes), 8 sedative compounds, and 12 anti-inflammatory components. Leaves also have antibacterial, antihistaminic, antispasmodic, and antioxidant activity.

WILD MINT   **Leaves**
Mentha canadensis L.   Mint Family
[listed as *Mentha arvensis* L. in older texts]
   Perennial; 6–25 in. Fine, backward-bending hairs, at least on stem angles. Flowers tiny, whitish or pale lilac; in small axillary clusters; June–Oct. **WHERE FOUND:** Damp soil. Canada, n. U.S. Our only native mint plant; a highly variable species. **USES:** American Indians used leaf tea for colds, fevers, sore throats, gas, colic, indigestion, headaches, diarrhea; in short, same medicinal uses as for Peppermint and Spearmint in Western folk medicine.

(Above) *Lemon Balm, Melissa* (Melissa officinalis) *is easily distinguished by its lemon-scented leaves.* (Right) *Wild Mint* (Mentha canadensis) *occurs in moist habitats.*

WHITE HORSEMINT
Leaves

Monarda bradburiana Beck
Mint Family

Perennial; 1–2 ft.; leaves with peppery scent, ovate to broad-ovate; ¾–2 in. broad, 2–3¼ in. long, sharp-toothed. Flowers in terminal head, white or rose with prominent purple dots; upper lip of flower cottony-hairy; upper flower lip about equal length of corolla tube; May–June. **WHERE FOUND:** Rocky wooded hills. Ind. to s. Ala., west to Texas and se. Kans. Our earliest blooming *Monarda* species. **USES:** Leaf tea used for fevers, upset stomach, digestive gas; cold and cough remedy; pleasant beverage tea. Probably the least used *Monarda*. **RELATED SPECIES:** Occasionally treated as synonymous with *Monarda russeliana* Nutt. but it has smaller, narrower leaves; upper lip of corolla is not beaded at tip, among other differences.

HOARY MOUNTAIN MINT
Leaves

Pycnanthemum incanum (L.) Michx.
Mint Family

Perennial; 2–6 ft. Leaves oval to lance-shaped, *stalked, toothed; hoary beneath (upper ones white-haired on both sides).* Flowers pale lilac; July–Sept. Calyx lobes apparently 2-lobed; lobes lance-shaped. **WHERE FOUND:** Dry thickets. N.H. to Fla., north to Tenn., s. Ill. **USES:** Leaf tea once used for fevers, colds, coughs, colic, stomach cramps; said to induce sweating, relieve gas. American Indians poulticed leaves for headaches; washed inflamed penis with tea.

White Horsemint (Monarda brad-buriana) *occurs in woodlands.*

Hoary Mountain Mint (Pycnan-themum incanum). *Photo by Stephen Lee Timme.*

VIRGINIA MOUNTAIN MINT (NOT SHOWN)   **Leaves, root**
Pycnanthemum virginianum (L.) Pers.   Mint Family
    Perennial; 2–4 ft. Leaves lance-shaped, *without stalks; base rounded.* Flowers whitish lilac, in dense terminal clusters; July–Sept. **WHERE FOUND:** Dry thickets. Me. to N.C.; Mo., e. Kans. to N.D. **USES:** Same as for *P. incanum* (above), also used for amenorrhea, dysmenorrhea. Other Mountain Mints are used similarly. American Indians took the powdered root to treat stoppage of menstrual periods, interpreted to mean that it was used as an early-term abortifacient. Flowers and buds used to flavor meats and soups.

SQUARE-STEMMED PLANTS; LEAVES OPPO-SITE; WEAK OR RANK SCENTS; MINT FAMILY

AMERICAN BUGLEWEED,
CUT-LEAVED WATER HOREHOUND   **Whole plant**
Lycopus americanus Muhl.   Mint Family
    The most abundant of the more than 7 species in our range. Perennial; 1–2 ft. Grows from edible, whitish, screwlike horizontal root. Leaves deeply cut; *lower ones suggest oak leaves.* Flowers in whorls of leaf axils; June–Sept. Stamens protruding; calyx lobes sharply pointed, longer than mature nutlets. **WHERE FOUND:** Wet places. Throughout our area. **USES:** Thought to be the same as for *L. virginicus* (below). **REMARKS:** The bugleweeds (*Lycopus* species) are known as water horehounds in some books. Like the true Horehound (*Marrubium vulgare,* below), these plants have been used as a folk remedy for coughs.

American Bugleweed (Lycopus americanus) *is our most common bugleweed.*

Bugleweed (Lycopus virginicus) *and other species are distinguished by technical characteristics. Most species are used interchangeably.*

BUGLEWEED

Whole plant

Lycopus virginicus L.

Mint Family

Perennial; 6–40 in. Leaves lance-shaped, *strongly toothed;* lower ones with long, narrow bases. Flowers *in axils,* with broadly triangular calyx lobes, shorter than nutlets; July–Oct. **WHERE FOUND:** Wet places. N.S. to Ga., Ark. to Okla., Neb. to Minn. **USES:** Traditionally, used as a mild sedative, astringent; especially for heart diseases, chronic lung ailments, coughs, fast pulse, thyroid disease, diabetes. Bugleweed has a long history of empirical use for a variety of conditions, including treatment of heart palpitations, goiter, hyperthyroidism, and Graves' disease. Science has confirmed the potential value of this plant in treating hyperthyroidism. Bugleweed extracts inhibit iodine metabolism and thyroxine release in the thyroid. Biological effects caused by Graves' disease can be reduced by Bugleweed extracts. Leaf extracts are considered more active than the root. Approved in Germany for use in cases of thyroid hypofunction and thyroid enlargement (without functional disorders). **WARNING:** In rare cases, Bugleweed has been found to enlarge the thyroid. If therapy is discontinued, symptoms may return.

HOREHOUND

Leaves

Marrubium vulgare L.

Mint Family

White-woolly, rank-scented perennial; 12–20 in. Leaves round-oval; toothed, *strongly wrinkled*. Flowers in whorls; May–Sept. White calyx with 10 bristly, curved teeth. **WHERE FOUND:** Waste places; escaped. Scattered over much of our area. Alien. A European native common in pastures and often cultivated in herb gardens. **USES:** The malodorous, bitter leaves are a well-known ingredient in cough syrups and throat lozenges, especially in Europe. Bitter-tasting herb is a famous folk remedy as a bitter stomachic to stimulate digestion and an expectorant primarily used to break up phlegm, relieve coughs, soothe sore throats, and relieve bronchitis and other upper-respiratory ailments. Also used for stomach and gallbladder disorders, jaundice, hepatitis; fresh leaves poulticed on cuts, wounds. Experimentally, marrubiin is an expectorant and increases liver bile flow. Volatile oil is an expectorant, acts as a vasodilator. An alcoholic extract has been confirmed to help reduce pain and reduce muscle spasms of the gastrointestinal tract. In Germany, Horehound preparations are approved for supportive treatment of coughs and colds and as a digestive aid and appetite stimulant. **WARNING:** Plant juice may cause dermatitis.

Horehound (Marrubium vulgare) *with wrinkled gray-green leaves.*

Catnip (Nepeta cataria). *Catnip is well known for the response it elicits in cats.*

CATNIP

Leaves, flowering tops

Nepeta cataria L. — Mint Family

Perennial; 12–24 in. Leaves *stalked*, ovate; *strongly toothed*. Flowers in crowded clusters; June–Sept. Flowers whitish, purple-dotted; *calyx soft-hairy.* **WHERE FOUND:** Much of our area. Alien. **USES:** Tea made from leaves and flowering tops is a folk remedy for bronchitis, colds, diarrhea, fevers, chicken pox, colic, headaches, irregular menses; said to induce sleep, promote sweating, alleviate restlessness in children; leaves chewed for toothaches. Experimentally, nepetalactone, a mild sedative compound in Catnip, also possesses herbicidal and insect-repellent properties. Best known as a feline euphoric, Catnip produces the "Catnip response," which includes sniffing, licking, chewing, head-shaking, rolling, and rubbing, affecting not only house cats but large cats as well. This phenomenon is the result of an inherited autosomal dominant gene, absent in about one-third of cats. Similar effects are not experienced by humans.

DELICATE TINY FLOWERS LESS THAN ¼ IN. LONG, IN DENSE SPIKES

NARROW-LEAVED PLANTAIN

Leaves, seeds

Plantago lanceolata L. — Plantain Family

Annual; 10–23 in. Leaves *lance-shaped; 3-ribbed*. Flowers tiny, whitish, in a *short cylindrical* head on a grooved stalk; Apr.–Nov. **WHERE FOUND:** Waste places. Throughout our area. Alien weed. **USES:** Traditionally, leaf tea used for coughs, diarrhea, dysentery, bloody urine. Science confirms bronchodilation action; used in Europe for bronchitis and bronchial spasms due to colds. Approved in Germany for treatment of catarrh of the upper respiratory tract and inflamed mucous membranes of the mouth and throat. Leaves applied to blisters, sores, ulcers, swelling, insect stings; also used for earaches, eye ailments; thought to reduce heat and pain of inflammation. Science has vindicated utility in healing sores, with mild antibiotic and anti-inflammatory. The mucilage from any plantain seed may lower cholesterol levels. **WARNING:** Some plantains may cause rare instances of contact dermatitis. **RELATED SPECIES:** *P. asiatica* is used clinically in China to reduce blood pressure (50 percent success rate). Seeds of *P. ovata* and *P. psyllium* (not shown) are widely used in bulk laxatives; also reduce rate of coronary ailments.

COMMON PLANTAIN

Leaves, seeds

Plantago major L. — Plantain Family

Perennial; 6–18 in. Leaves *broad-oval; wavy-margined* or toothed, ribbed; stalk is grooved. Flowers in a slender, elongate head;

Narrow-leaved Plantain (Plantago lanceolata) *has spikes of tiny white flowers.*

Narrow-leaved Plantain (P. lanceolata) *is named for its narrow-ribbed leaves.*

(Above) *Common Plantain* (Plantago major) *often grows on lawns.* (Right) *Seneca Snakeroot* (Polygala senega).

May–Oct. **WHERE FOUND:** Waste places. Throughout our area. Alien. **USES:** Same as for *P. lanceolata* (above). Prominent folk cancer remedy in Latin America. Used widely in folk medicine throughout the world. Confirmed antimicrobial; stimulates healing process.

SENECA SNAKEROOT

Root

Polygala senega L.   Milkwort Family

Perennial; 6–18 in. Leaves alternate; lance-shaped, small. Small, pea-like, white flowers in a terminal spike; May–July. **WHERE FOUND:** Rocky woods. N.B. to Ga.; Ark. to S.D. **USES:** American Indians used root tea as emetic, expectorant, cathartic, diuretic, antispasmodic, sweat inducer; used to regulate menses, also for cold, croup, pleurisy, rheumatism, heart troubles, convulsions, coughs; poulticed root for swellings. Historically, root tea used similarly, also in pneumonia, chronic bronchitis, asthma; thought to "relax respiratory mucous membranes." Research suggests use for pulmonary conditions. Occurrence of methyl salicylate (see Wintergreen, p. 30) in root suggests a rationale behind use of this plant's root to relieve pain, rheumatism, etc. Roots of this N. America native are more widely used in modern Japan and Germany than in the U.S. The root is approved in Germany as an expectorant for treatment of inflammation of the upper respiratory tract.

DEVIL'S-BIT

Root

Chamaelirium luteum (L.) Gray   Lily Family

Flowers whitish at first, then turning yellow. See p. 118.

CLUSTERS OF PEA-LIKE FLOWERS; 3 LEAFLETS

ROUND-HEADED BUSH-CLOVER

Root, stem, whole plant

Lespedeza capitata Michx.   Pea Family

Perennial; 2–5 ft. Leaves cloverlike, with 3 lance-shaped leaflets. Flowers creamy white (base pink), in crowded, bristly heads; July–Sept. **WHERE FOUND:** Dry fields. New England to Fla.; Texas to Minn. **USES:** Moxa (burning sticks) were used by American Indians to treat neuralgia and rheumatism. Small pieces of dried stem were moistened with saliva on one end, then stuck to the skin, lit, and allowed to burn the skin. Plant extract of disputed utility in chronic kidney disease. Experimentally, extract has demonstrated antitumor activity against Walker-256 carcinosarcoma, and is reportedly effective in lowering blood cholesterol levels. Also thought to lower blood levels of nitrogen compounds in persons with high nitrogen levels in urine. Contains several biologically

Round-headed Bush-clover (Lespedeza capitata) *is common in prairie habitats. Photo by Stephen Lee Timme.*

White Sweet-clover (Melilotus alba) *is an abundant late-summer roadside weed.*

active compounds. Pharmaceutical preparations are manufactured in Europe from this plant.

WHITE SWEET-CLOVER
Flowering plant

Melilotus alba Medik.
Pea Family

Biennial; 1–9 ft. Leaves cloverlike; leaflets elongate, slightly toothed. Small, white, pea-like flowers in long, tapering spikes; Apr.–Oct. **WHERE FOUND:** Roadsides. Throughout our area. Alien (Europe). **USES:** Dried flowering plant once used in ointments for external ulcers. In animal studies, components lowered blood pressure. **WARNING:** Coumarins in this clover may decrease blood clotting.

WHITE CLOVER
Whole plant, flowers

Trifolium repens L.
Pea Family

Perennial; 4–10 in. Leaves 3-parted, often with "V" marks. Flowers stalked, white (often pink-tinged); in round heads; Apr.–Sept. **WHERE FOUND:** Fields, lawns. Throughout our area. Alien (Europe). **USES:** American Indians adopted leaf tea for colds, coughs, fevers, and leukorrhea. In European folk medicine, flower tea is used for

White Clover (Trifolium repens) *is very common across the U.S.*

rheumatism and gout. Like Red Clover, and probably most clovers, White Clover contains the estrogenic isoflavone genistein, with a multitude of activities, including cancer-preventative and antioxidant activity.

STIFF-STEMMED LEGUMES WITH 15 OR MORE LEAFLETS

PRAIRIE MIMOSA
Leaves, seeds
Desmanthus illinoensis (Michx.) MacM. ex B. L. Robins. & Fern.
Pea Family

Smooth-stemmed, erect perennial; 1–4 ft. Leaves twice-divided; 20–30 tiny *leaflets.* Flowers greenish white, in globular heads. June–Aug. Pods curved, in loose *globular heads.* **WHERE FOUND:** Prairies, fields. Ohio to Ala.; Texas, Colo. to N.D. **USES:** Pawnees used leaf tea as a wash for itching. A single report states that a Paiute Indian placed 5 seeds in the eye at night (washed out in morning) for chronic conjunctivitis. The leaves are reportedly high in protein.

WILD LICORICE
Root, leaves
Glycyrrhiza lepidota (Nutt.) Pursh
Pea Family

Shrubby perennial; 5–9 ft. Leaves compound; 15–19 *leaflets,* oblong to lance-shaped, *glandular-dotted* (use lens). Flowers whitish, on short spikes. Fruits oblong, with *curved prickles;* June–Aug. **WHERE FOUND:** Prairies, fields. W. Ont. to Texas, Mo. west to Wash. **USES:** American Indians applied a poultice of leaves infused in hot water to ears to treat earaches. The fresh root was chewed to treat toothaches. Root tea was used to reduce fevers in children. **RELATED SPECIES:** This American species is similar to the Eurasian **Licorice Root** (*G. glabra*) and the Chinese species (*G. uralensis*), both extensively used in European and Asian herbal medicine. Sweet to musty-flavored roots of these related species

Prairie Mimosa (Desmanthus illinoensis) *with white flowers. Its fruits turn brown in twisted clusters. Photo by Craig C. Freeman.*

Wild Licorice (Glycyrrhiza lepidota) *produces spiny seedpods.*

were traditionally used for soothing irritated mucous membranes, inflamed stomach, ulcers, asthma, bronchitis, coughs, bladder infections. *G. glabra* and *G. uralensis* have been extensively investigated; considered estrogenic, anti-inflammatory, anti-allergenic, anticonvulsive, and antibacterial. Approved in Germany for the supportive treatment of gastric and duodenal ulcers and for congestion of the upper respiratory tract. Chinese studies indicate antitussive effects of these plants are equal to and longer-lasting than those of codeine. Clinically useful against gastric and duodenal ulcers, bronchial asthma, coughs. Licorice root is one of the most extensively used drugs in Chinese herbal prescriptions. In combinations, the Chinese believe that it helps to detoxify potentially poisonous drugs, weakening their effects. Our Wild Licorice (little studied) contains up to 6 percent of the active component glycyrrhizin. **WARNING:** Wild Licorice can raise blood pressure. May cause water retention and hypertension, a result of sodium retention and potassium loss. Avoid use in cases of hypertension. In Germany, use is limited to 4 to 6 weeks.

COMPOSITES IN FLAT-TOPPED CLUSTERS; LEAVES NOT FINELY DIVIDED

BONESET, THOROUGHWORT
Leaves

Eupatorium perfoliatum L.   Composite Family

⚠ Perennial; 1–4 ft. Leaves *perfoliate, wrinkled,* easily distinguished at any stage of growth by its perfoliate leaves (stem appears to pass through the joined opposite leaves), which resemble an elongated diamond shape. Flowers white to pale purple, in flat clusters; July–Oct. **WHERE FOUND:** Moist ground, thickets. N.S. to Fla.; La., Texas to N.D. **USES:** The leaves were used to treat "break-bone fever" (dengue fever), characterized by severe aching down to the bones. This is how the name Boneset originated. A common home remedy of nineteenth-century America, extensively employed by American Indians and early settlers. Widely used, reportedly with success, during flu epidemics in nineteenth and early twentieth century. Leaf tea once used to induce sweating in fevers, flu, and colds; also used for malaria, rheumatism, muscular pains, spasms, pneumonia, pleurisy, gout, etc. Leaves poulticed onto tumors. German research suggests nonspecific immune-system-stimulating properties, perhaps vindicating historical use in flu epidemics. Plant extract weakly anti-inflammatory. **WARNING:** Emetic and laxative in large doses. May contain controversial and potentially liver-harming pyrrolizidine alkaloids.

(Left) *Boneset, Thoroughwort* (Eupatorium perfoliatum) *was an important medicinal plant used by colonial Americans.* (Above) *White Snakeroot* (Ageratina altissima, *formerly* Eupatorium rugosum), *the culprit of "milk sickness."*

(Left) *Wild Quinine* (Parthenium integrifolium) *is common in prairie habitats.* (Above) *Wild Quinine* (P. integrifolium). *The cut root* (left) *resembles that of Pale Purple Coneflower* (Echinacea pallida), *right; hence, it is a common Echinacea adulterant.*

WHITE SNAKEROOT
Root, leaves

Ageratina altissima var. *altissima* (L.) King & H. E. Robins.
[*Eupatorium rugosum* Houtt.]   Composite Family

 Variable perennial; 2–5 ft. Leaves opposite, on slender stalks; somewhat heart-shaped, toothed. Flowers white, in branched clusters; July–Oct. **WHERE FOUND:** Thickets. Que. to Ga.; Texas to Sask. **USES:** American Indians used root tea for ague, diarrhea, painful urination fevers, "gravel" (kidney stones); poultice for snakebites. Smoke of burning herb used to revive unconscious patients. **WARNING:** "Milk sickness," with weakness and nausea, may result from consuming the milk of cows that have grazed on this plant. Milk sickness claimed thousands of lives on the western frontier of the U.S. in the early 1800s, including Abraham Lincoln's mother, who died of the disease when Lincoln was seven years old. Symptoms of milk sickness include prostration, severe vomiting, tremors, liver failure, constipation, delirium, and death. The disease is rarely encountered today.

WILD QUININE
Root, leaves, tops

Parthenium integrifolium L.   Composite Family

Large-rooted perennial; 2–5 ft. Large, oval, lance-shaped leaves, to 1 ft. *long;* rough, blunt-toothed. Flowerheads to ¼ in. wide;

white, in loose umbels; May–July. **WHERE FOUND:** Prairies, rock outcrops, roadsides. Mass. to Ga.; e. Texas to Minn. **USES:** Catawbas poulticed fresh leaves on burns. Flowering tops were once used for "intermittent fevers" (like malaria). Root used as a diuretic for kidney and bladder ailments, gonorrhea. One study suggests Wild Quinine may stimulate the immune system. Common adulterant—historically and in modern times—to Purple Coneflower (*Echinacea purpurea*, p. 227). **WARNING:** May cause dermatitis or allergies.

FLOWERHEADS LONG, CYLINDRICAL; COMPOSITES WITH WEEDY GROWTH HABITS

PALE INDIAN PLANTAIN
Leaves

Arnoglossum atriplicifolium (L.) H. E. Robins.

[*Cacalia atriplicifolia* L.]
Composite Family

Large perennial; 4–9 ft. Stems smooth or slightly striated. Leaves broadly rounded to triangular, with irregular rounded teeth; glaucous beneath, *palmately veined*. Flowers in flat clusters; July–Sept. Each tubular head has 5 flowers, apparently without rays (petals minute). **WHERE FOUND:** Dry woods, openings. N.J. to

Pale Indian Plantain (Arnoglossum atriplicifolium).

Pilewort, Fireweed (Erechtities hieracifolia). *Photo by Craig C. Freeman.*

Ga.; Okla., Neb. to Mich., Minn. **USES:** American Indians used the leaves as a poultice for cancers, cuts, and bruises, and to draw out blood or poisonous material. **RELATED SPECIES:** *Arnoglossum muehlenbergii* (Schultz-Bip.) H. E. Robins; [*Cacalia muhlenbergii* (Schultz-Bip.) Fern.] (not shown) is similar, but its leaves are green on both sides; stems grooved.

PILEWORT, FIREWEED
Whole plant
Erechtites hieracifolia (L.) Raf. Composite Family
Annual; 1–9 ft. Leaves lance-shaped to oblong, 2–8 in. long; toothed, often lacerated. Flowers white, with no rays; flowers are enveloped in a *swollen group of leafy bracts.* **WHERE FOUND:** Thickets, burns, waste places. Me. to Fla.; Texas, Okla., S.D. to Minn. **USES:** Tea or tincture of whole plant formerly used as an astringent and tonic in mucous-tissue ailments of lungs, bowels, stomach; also used externally for muscular rheumatism, sciatica. Used in diarrhea, cystitis, dropsy, etc. Neglected by scientific investigators.

WHITE LETTUCE, RATTLESNAKE ROOT
Whole plant
Prenanthes alba L. Composite Family
Perennial; 2–5 ft. Stem smooth, purple, with whitish bloom. Leaves triangular or deeply lobed; toothed. Flowers white, in *drooping clusters;* July–Sept. "Seed" (technically fruit) fuzz a *deep rust color.* **WHERE FOUND:** Rich woods, thickets. Me. to Ga.; Mo. to N.D. **USES:** American Indians put powdered root in food to stimulate milk flow after childbirth. Root tea used as a wash for "weakness." Stem latex used as a diuretic in "female" diseases; boiled in milk, taken internally for snakebites. Leaves poulticed on snakebites. Roots poulticed on dog bites and snakebites. Tea drunk for dysentery.

White Lettuce, Rattlesnake Root
(Prenanthes alba). *Note the drooping flowers.*

HORSEWEED, CANADA FLEABANE

Whole plant

Conyza canadensis (L.) Cronq.
[*Erigeron canadensis* L.]

Composite Family

> *Bristly* annual or biennial weed; 1–7 ft. Leaves numerous, lance-shaped. Flowers greenish white. See p. 237.

WOOLLY PLANTS; EVERLASTING FLOWER CLUSTERS

PEARLY EVERLASTING

Whole plant

Anaphalis margaritacea (L.) Benth. & Hook. f.

Composite Family

> Perennial; 1–3 ft. Highly variable. Stem and leaf undersides *cottony*. Leaves linear; gray-green above. Flowers in a cluster of globular heads; July–Sept. Heads with several rows of *white, dry, petal-like* bracts (male flowers have yellow tufts in center). **WHERE FOUND:** Dry soil, fields. Nfld. to N.C.; Calif. to Alaska. **USES:** Expectorant, astringent, anodyne, sedative. Used for diarrhea, dysentery. American Indians used tea for colds, bronchial coughs, and throat infections. Poultice used for rheumatism, burns, sores, bruises, and swellings. Leaves smoked for throat and lung ailments.

PLANTAIN-LEAVED PUSSYTOES

Whole plant

Antennaria plantaginifolia (L.) Hook

Composite Family

> Highly variable, *woolly-stemmed* perennial; 3–16 in. Basal leaves spoon-shaped, *silky*, with 3–5 *nerves* (veins); more woolly on lower

(Above) *The flowers of Pearly Everlasting* (Anaphalis margaritacea) *remain intact after drying.* (Right) *Plantain-leaved Pussytoes. Historically most species of pussytoes are used interchangeably.*

Sweet Everlasting, Rabbit Tobacco (Pseudognaphalium obtusifolium). Leaves and flowers were formerly smoked, hence the name Rabbit Tobacco. Photo by Martin Wall.

surface than above. Stem leaves small, lance-shaped. Flowers white in several flowerheads; Apr.–June. **WHERE FOUND:** Dry woods, fields. Me. to Ga.; Okla. to N.D. **USES:** Boiled in milk, this plant was a folk remedy for diarrhea, dysentery. Tea drunk for lung ailments. Leaves poulticed on bruises, sprains, boils, and swellings. One of the multitude of snakebite remedies. **RELATED SPECIES:** (1) **Field Pussytoes** (*A. neglecta,* not shown) is smaller, and its leaves have 1 prominent nerve or midvein. (2) **Solitary Pussytoes** (*A. solitaria,* not shown) differs from *A. plantaginifolia* in that it has only 1 flowerhead.

SWEET EVERLASTING, RABBIT TOBACCO　　　**Leaves**
Pseudognaphalium obtusifolium ssp. *obtusifolium*(L.) Hilliard & Burtt
[*Gnaphalium obtusifolium* L.]　　　　　　　Composite Family
　　Soft-hairy biennial; 1–2 ft. Leaves alternate, lance-shaped, without stalks. Flowers dirty white *globular heads* in *spreading* clusters; July–Nov. Flowerheads enclosed by dry, petal-like bracts. **WHERE FOUND:** Dry soil, fields. Much of our area. **USES:** Leaves and flowers (chewed or in tea) trad itionally used for sore throats, pneumonia, colds, fevers, upset stomach, abdominal cramps, asthma, flu, coughs, rheumatism, leukorrhea, bowel disorders, mouth ulcers, hemorrhage, tumors; mild nerve sedative, diuretic, and antispasmodic. Fresh juice considered aphrodisiac.

DAISYLIKE FLOWERS

MAYWEED, DOG FENNEL　　　　　　　　**Whole plant**
Anthemis cotula L.　　　　　　　　　　　Composite Family
　　Bad-smelling annual; 8–20 in. Leaves finely (thrice-) dissected. Flowers white; May–Nov. Disk flowers studded with *stiff chaff.* **WHERE FOUND:** Waste places. Throughout our area. Alien. **USES:** Tea

Mayweed, Dog Fennel (Anthemis cotula). *Photo by Stephen Lee Timme.*

Eclipta (Eclipta prostrata) *is a common tropical weed.*

used to induce sweating, vomiting; astringent, diuretic. Used for fevers, colds, diarrhea, dropsy, rheumatism, obstructed menses, and headaches. Leaves rubbed on insect stings. **WARNING:** Touching or ingesting plant may cause allergies.

CHICORY   **Roots, leaves**
Cichorium intybus L.   Composite Family
  Flowers usually blue (rarely white or pink). See also p. 223.

ECLIPTA   **Whole plant**
Eclipta prostrata (L.) L. [*Eclipta alba* (L.) Hassk.]   Composite Family
  Annual; up to 1 ¼ ft. tall, with rough hairs; stems weak, rooting at nodes. Leaves linear to lanceolate, apparently entire, but with a few marginal teeth; up to 4 in. long, with or without leafstalks. Flowers in terminal or axillary small heads, with white ray flowers, small, to less than ⅜ in. across; July–Oct. **WHERE FOUND:** Waste places, cultivated fields, damp, sandy soils. Alien. Native to New World tropics. Throughout our range. Mostly absent north of Mass. **USES:** Used in Traditional Chinese Medicine for bleeding, both internal and external, dysentery, premature gray hairs, bleeding gums, loosening of teeth. In India, the leaves are used as a

tonic to treat liver and spleen disease; considered to be cooling. Plant juice used for jaundice and catarrh in infants; rubbed on gums for toothaches; applied externally with oil to relieve headaches. Also used to treat abscesses and snakebites. A study found that it neutralized the venom of the South American rattlesnake (*Crotalus durissus terrificus*) in the laboratory. Science confirms antibacterial, anticandidal, astringent, and anti-inflammatory and immuno-stimulating activity.

OX-EYE DAISY
Whole plant, roots
Leucanthemum vulgare Lam.
Composite Family
[*Chrysanthemum leucanthemum* L.]

Familiar white daisy of roadsides; perennial; 1–3 ft. tall. Leaves more or less cleft, lobed, or toothed; reduced above, lance- to spatula-shaped at base. Flowers have white petals and yellow centers, 2 in. across; May–Sept. **WHERE FOUND:** Fields, roadsides, waste places. Throughout. Alien from Europe. Very common weed. **USES:** In European traditions, used as a tonic, antispasmodic (in whooping cough), to regulate menses, induce vomiting; diuretic; astringent. Root formerly used to reduce night sweats; flowers used in

Ox-eye Daisy (Leucanthemum vulgare) *is a widely naturalized weed across the U.S.*

German Chamomile (Matricaria recutita) *has hollow flower receptacles.*

tea as an antispasmodic. American Indians adopted tea for fever, spring tonic; externally, a wash for chapped hands; eyewash. Effects considered similar to those of Chamomile. Contains anti-inflammatory and spasm-relieving components. **WARNING:** May cause contact dermatitis or cross-allergic reactions with other Composite family members.

GERMAN, HUNGARIAN, OR WILD CHAMOMILE   Flowers
Matricaria recutita L.   Composite Family
[*Chamomilla recutita* (L.) Rauschert, *Matricaria chamomilla* L.]

Smooth, *apple-scented* annual; 6–24 in. Leaves *finely divided.* Flowers daisylike, ¾ in. across; receptacle hollow within. Flowers May–Oct. **WHERE FOUND:** Locally abundant. Much of our area. Alien. **USES:** In Germany, Chamomile's reputation as a medicinal herb is reflected in its name, which translates into "capable of anything." Dried flowers make a famous beverage tea, traditionally used for colic, diarrhea, insomnia, indigestion, gout, sciatica, headaches, colds, fevers, flu, cramps, and arthritis. Flowers also a folk cancer remedy. Experimentally, essential oil is antifungal, antibacterial, anodyne, antispasmodic, anti-inflammatory, and anti-allergenic. One component in the leaves, apigenin, has been shown to have anti-anxiety and sedative activity. Essential oil contains at least two dozen different compounds with anti-inflammatory action, which may work in concert with one another to reduce inflammation. Approved in Germany for internal use to treat inflammation or spasms of the gastrointestinal tract and inflammation of the respiratory tract. Externally, approved for inflammatory conditions of the mouth and gums or bacterial-induced skin diseases. **WARNING:** Ragweed allergy sufferers may react to Chamomile, too.

FEVERFEW   Leaves
Tanacetum parthenium (L.) Shultz-Bip.   Composite Family
[*Chrysanthemum parthenium* (L.) Bernh.]

Bushy perennial; 1–3 ft. Leaves *pinnately divided into ovate divisions;* coarsely toothed. Flowers daisylike (but smaller), with a *large disk* and *stubby white rays;* June–Sept. **WHERE FOUND:** Roadsides, waste places. Alien native to the Balkan Peninsula; escaped from cultivation in N. and S. America, most of Europe. Widely grown as a garden ornamental and in herb gardens. Highly variable both in looks and chemistry. Some chemical types contain the active constituent parthenolide, one of several closely related compounds with anti-migraine potential. **USES:** Tea of whole plant a folk remedy for arthritis, colds, fevers, cramps, worms; regulates

Feverfew (Tanacetum parthenium) *is commonly grown as an ornamental.*

menses; sedative. Proven effective (1–4 fresh leaves chewed per day) as a preventative (reducing number, duration, and time between) of migraine attacks. British studies suggest that Feverfew can prevent 70 percent of migraines. Now backed by five clinical studies (four positive, one negative). One study revealed that Feverfew can profoundly reduce pain intensity and typical symptoms associated with migraine attacks. Approved in Canada and England for use against migraines. Also shown to be antiseptic, anti-inflammatory. **WARNING:** May cause dermatitis or allergic reactions. Mouth sores common.

SWEETFLAG, CALAMUS
Acorus americanus (Raf.) Raf.
[*Acorus calamus* L., *Acorus calamus* var. *americanus* (Raf.) H. D. Wulff.]

Rootstock
Arum Family

Strongly aromatic, colony-forming perennial; 1–4 ft. *Root jointed.* *Cattail-like leaves*, with a *vertical midrib.* Flowers tightly packed on a fingerlike spadix, jutting *at an angle* from leaflike stalk; May–Aug. **WHERE FOUND:** Pond edges, wet fields. Most of our area. Often found in depressions of pastures, pond edges, ditches, and moist meadows, this member of the Arum family, with grasslike leaves, produces fleshy rhizomes that form large clumps. It is the aromatic rhizomes that are used in traditional medicine. The fingerlike flowerheads, which grow about one-third up the stem, are usually found on a low percentage of plants in a given population. **USES:** Dried-root tea (or chewed root) used as aromatic bitter for gas, stomachaches, indigestion, heartburn, fevers, colds, and coughs; antispasmodic, anticonvulsant, and CNS-depressant. In India, used as an aphrodisiac. American Indians nibbled root for stomach ailments, to assuage thirst, and as a stimulant on long journeys. German studies show that for maximum efficacy and safety against spasms, diploid American strains, devoid of beta-asarone, should be used. Oils devoid of beta-asarone showed spasmolytic properties comparable to those of standard antihistaminic drugs. Controlled dosage of root helped lower serum cholesterol levels in rabbit studies. **WARNING:** Some strains said to contain the carcinogen beta-asarone. Vapors from roots repel some insects.

ASPARAGUS
Asparagus officinalis L.

Root, shoots, seeds
Lily Family

Perennial; 6 ft. or more. Leaves *finely fernlike* (actually branches functioning as leaves). Flowers seldom noticed. Fruits reddish. June. **WHERE FOUND:** Garden escape. Throughout our area. Alien. **USES:** Spring shoots a popular vegetable. Asian Indians report asparagine (in shoots) is a good diuretic in dropsy and gout. Japanese report green asparagus aids protein conversion into amino acids. Has been suggested as a food to treat gout, as asparagus contains at least ten anti-inflammatory minerals or compounds. Roots considered diuretic, laxative (due to fiber content), induce sweating. Chinese report roots can lower blood pressure. Seeds possess antibiotic activity. Use of root is approved in Germany as a diuretic for irrigation therapy in the treatment of uri-

Sweetflag, Calamus (Acorus amer-icanus) with aromatic, grasslike leaves.

Asparagus (Asparagus officinalis) is fernlike as it matures.

Asparagus (A. officinalis) is best known by its edible spring shoots.

Yellow-eyed Grass (Xyris carolini-ana). Photo by Carl Hunter.

nary tract inflammation; also to prevent kidney stones. **WARNING:** May cause rare contact dermatitis or allergic skin reactions.

YELLOW-EYED GRASS Root
Xyris caroliniana Walt. Lily Family

Perennial; 6–36 in., in flower. Leaves *grasslike*, about ⅛ in. wide, ⅓ as long as flower scape. Flowers yellow, 3-petaled, above a *cone-like head* of leathery scales. Differs from about 15 other species in our range in that flower stalks are 2-ribbed, opposite, sheathed. Flowers June–Sept. Seeds 13-ribbed. Variable. **WHERE FOUND:** Moist, sandy soil. Cen. Me. to Fla.; La. to Wisc. **USES:** American Indians used root tea for diarrhea.

CUPLIKE FLOWERS (AT LEAST WHEN YOUNG)

MARSH-MARIGOLD, COWSLIP Root, leaves
Caltha palustris L. Buttercup Family

Aquatic perennial with a *succulent, hollow* stem. Leaves glossy, *heart- or kidney-shaped.* Flowers like a large buttercup (to 1½ in. wide); deep yellow, with 5–9 "petals" (actually sepals); Apr.–June. **WHERE FOUND:** Swamps, wet ditches. Most of our area. **USES:** Root tea induces sweating; emetic, expectorant. Leaf tea diuretic, laxative. Ojibwas mixed tea with maple sugar to make a cough syrup that was popular with colonists. Syrup used as a folk antidote to snake venom. Contains anemonin and protoanemonin, both with marginal antitumor activity. **WARNING:** All parts may irritate and blister skin or mucous membranes. Sniffing bruised stems induces sneezing. Intoxication has resulted from the use of the raw leaves in salads or using the raw flower buds as substitutes for capers. Do not confuse with American White or False Hellebore, which is toxic (see p. 118).

SPATTERDOCK, YELLOW POND LILY Root
Nuphar lutea (L.) Sm. Water-lily Family
[*Nuphar luteum* (L.) Sibthorp and Smith]

Aquatic perennial. Leaves round-oval; *base V-notched;* leaves submersed or erect above water. Flowers yellow, cuplike; stigma disk-like; May–Sept. **WHERE FOUND:** Ponds, slow-moving water. Canada south to S.C.; west to Ill., Iowa. **USES:** American Indians used root tea for "sexual irritability," blood diseases, chills with fever, heart trouble; poulticed on swellings, inflammations, wounds, contusions, boils. Elsewhere, roots used for gum, skin, and stomach inflammations. A folk remedy for impotence; rhizome contains

(Left) *Marsh-marigold, Cowslip* (Caltha palustris) *has yellow, buttercup-like flowers. Photo by Alan Detrick.* (Above) *Spatterdock, Yellow Pond Lily* (Nuphar *sp.*). *Yellow Pond Lilies have cup-shaped yellow flowers. Historically, species were used interchangeably.*

steroids. Alkaloids reportedly hypotensive, antispasmodic, cardioactive, tonic; vasoconstrictor. Like many other species, this plant contains antagonistic alkaloids, one hypotensive, one hypertensive. Can the human body select the one it needs? WARNING: Large doses of root potentially **toxic.**

PRICKLY-PEAR CACTUS   **Pads, fruits**
Opuntia humifusa (Raf.) Raf.   Cactus Family

Cactus; to 1 ft. Jointed pads have tufts of bristles, usually sharp-spined. Large, showy yellow flowers; May–Aug. WHERE FOUND: Dry soils. Mass. to Fla.; Texas to Minn. Our most common eastern cactus. USES: American Indians poulticed peeled pads on wounds, applied juice of fruits to warts, and drank pad tea for lung ailments. In folk medicine, peeled pads poulticed for rheumatism, juice used for "gravel" (kidney stones), baked pads used for gout, chronic ulcers, and wounds. RELATED SPECIES: *Opuntia ficus-indica* (L.) P. Mill. has been the subject of a number of Mexican clinical trials exploring its potential to help non-insulin-dependent diabetics. The results have been mixed. An Israeli research group found the dried flowers useful in reducing the urgency to urinate in cases of benign prostatic hyperplasia.

(Left, Above) *Prickly-pear Cactus* (Opuntia humifusa) *has beautiful yellow-orange flowers and produces edible fruits.*

4-PETALED FLOWERS IN TERMINAL CLUSTERS; MUSTARDS

WINTER CRESS
Barbarea vulgaris Ait.

Leaves
Mustard Family

Highly variable, smooth-stemmed mustard; 1–2 ft. Lower leaves with 4–8 lateral, *earlike* lobes; uppermost leaves *clasping, cut, toothed.* Flowers deep yellow; Apr.–Aug. Seedpods (silique) mostly erect, *short-beaked;* fruit stalks more slender than the pods. **WHERE FOUND:** Wet fields. Ont. to S.C.; Ark., Okla. to Ill. Alien. **USES:** Cherokees ate greens as a "blood purifier." The leaf tea was taken once every half hour to suppress coughs. Tea thought to stimulate appetite; diuretic, used

Winter Cress (Barbarea vulgaris). *Note the earlike lobes on lower leaves.*

against scurvy. Europeans poulticed leaves on wounds. **WARNING:** Although this plant has been described as an edible wild food, studies indicate it may cause kidney malfunctions. Internal use should be avoided.

BLACK MUSTARD
Brassica nigra (L.) Koch

Seed, leaves, oil
Mustard Family

Annual; 2–3 ft. Lower leaves bristly, coarsely lobed; upper leaves *lance-shaped, with no hairs.* Flowers yellow; June–Oct. Pods *hug stem.* **WHERE FOUND:** Waste places. Throughout our area. Alien. **USES:** Leaves and seeds irritant, emetic. Leaf poultice used for rheumatism, chilblains, toothaches, headaches. Seeds eaten as a tonic and appetite stimulant, for fevers, croup, asthma, bronchial conditions. Ground seeds used as a snuff for headaches. Leafy Brassica species have emerged as important subjects in the study of cancer prevention. Contains compounds shown to have strong anticancer activity and may prevent (even at relatively small levels) breast and colon cancers. Works in part by encouraging the self-destruction of cancer-damaged cells, and also by increasing intracellular glutathione. **WARNING:** Allyl isothiocyanate (responsible for mustard flavor) is a strong irritant. May blister skin. Eating large quantities may cause red, burnlike skin blotches that occasionally develop into ulcers.

(Above) *Black Mustard* (Brassica nigra). (Right) *The seeds of Black Mustard* (B. nigra).

FIELD OR WILD MUSTARD (NOT SHOWN)

Seeds

Brassica rapa L.   Mustard Family

Succulent, gray-green annual herb; 24–32 in. Lower leaves sparsely toothed or divided. Differs from other *Brassica* species in that the upper leaves *clasp the stem*, with *earlike lobes*. Flowers pale yellow; June–Oct. Pods erect, slender-beaked. **WHERE FOUND:** Fields. Throughout our area. Alien (Eurasia). **USES:** Crushed ripe seeds poulticed on burns. Like some other Mustard family members, it contains factors that the National Cancer Institute has suggested may prevent certain cancers. Leafy vegetables of many wild and cultivated *Brassicas* (cabbage, cauliflower, broccoli, collards, kale, kohlrabi, mustard, rape, turnips) are rich in vitamins A and C, fiber, and isothiocyanates, all cited by the National Cancer Institute as having some cancer-preventing activity.

FLOWERS WITH 4 PETALS

CELANDINE

Stem juice, roots, leaves

Chelidonium majus L.   Poppy Family

Smooth-stemmed biennial; 1–2 ft. Stems brittle; yellow juice within. Leaves divided, *round-toothed or lobed*. Flowers yellow, 4-petaled; to ¾ in. across; Apr.–Aug. Seedpods *smooth, linear, 2-valved*. **WHERE FOUND:** Waste places. Much of our area. Alien (Europe). **USES:** Fresh stem juice a folk remedy (used externally) for warts, eczema, ringworm, corns. The root juice is bright orange. A folk medicine of N. America, Europe, and China. Root tincture once used by physicians for inflammations, hemorrhoids; taken internally for jaundice, lung ailments, diuresis. Fresh leaves once used for amenorrhea, poulticed for wounds. Folk cancer remedy in China. Mentioned as a potential cancer remedy in the *Journal of the American Medical Association* as early as 1897, Celandine contains at least 4 antitumor compounds, including chelerythrine, citric acid, coptisine, and sanguinarine. Ukrain, a semisynthetic version of chelionine, causes regression of tumors. Approved in Germany for treatment of discomfort caused by spasms of bile ducts and the gastrointestinal tract. In experiments has shown blood pressure–lowering activity. **WARNING: Toxic.** Stem juice highly irritating, allergenic; may cause paralysis.

ST. ANDREW'S CROSS

Root, leaves

Hypericum hypericoides (L.) Crantz.   St. John's Wort Family

Variable, smooth subshrub (somewhat woody); 1–2½ ft. Leaves linear-oblong; in pairs. Flowers terminal, solitary, with 4 sepals; 1 pair of sepals large and leaflike, the other pair tiny or lacking; narrow yellow petals form a cross. Flowers July–Aug. **WHERE FOUND:**

(Left) *Celandine* (Chelidonium majus) *produces yellow sap in its leaves and stems.* (Above) *St. Andrew's Cross* (Hypericum hypericoides). *Note the four petals in a cross pattern. Photo by Doug Elliot.*

Sandy soil. Mass. to Fla.; e. Texas to Ill. **USES:** American Indians chewed the root for snakebites; root tea used for colic, fevers, pain, toothaches, diarrhea, dysentery; externally, as a wash for ulcerated breasts. Leaf tea used for bladder and kidney ailments, skin problems, and children's diarrhea. Like St. John's Wort, in laboratory experiments St. Andrew's Cross has shown some potential against HIV-infected cells. **WARNING:** May cause photodermatitis (see *H. perforatum*, p. 128).

COMMON EVENING-PRIMROSE
Seeds, root, leaves
Oenothera biennis L. Evening-primrose Family

Biennial; 1–8 ft. Leaves numerous, lance-shaped. Flowers yellow, with 4 broad petals, June–Sept. *Sepals drooping, stigma X-shaped.* Flowers bloom after sunset, unfolding before the eyes of those who watch them open, hence the common name. **WHERE FOUND:** Roadsides, fields. Throughout our area. **USES:** American Indians used root tea for obesity, bowel pains; poulticed root for piles, bruises; rubbed root on muscles to give athletes strength. Recent research suggests seed oil may be useful for atopic eczema, allergy-induced eczema, asthma, migraines, inflammations, premenstrual syndrome, breast problems, metabolic disorders, diabetes, arthritis, and alcoholism. Backed by more than 120 scientific studies. Research has demonstrated that extracts of this plant can alleviate imbalances and abnormalities of essential fatty acids in prostaglandin production. Evening-primrose oil is a natu-

Common Evening-primrose (Oenothera biennis) *commonly blooms in the evening and on overcast days.*

Celandine Poppy (Stylophorum diphyllum) *occurs in rich woods, blooming in early spring.*

ral source of gamma-linolenic acid. Approved in Britain for treatment of atopic eczema, premenstrual syndrome, and prostatitis.

CELANDINE POPPY
Leaves

Stylophorum diphyllum (Michx.) Nutt.   Poppy Family

Perennial herb; to 20 in. tall, with saffron-colored juice in stems and leaves. Leaves mostly basal, deeply lobed into 5–7 segments, with obtuse lobes or toothed margins; one pair of smaller leaves on stem. Flowers yellow, to 2 in. across; late March–May. **WHERE FOUND:** Rich, moist woods. Pa. south to Tenn., west to Ark.; north to Mich. and Wisc. **USES:** Suggested as an antispasmodic by nineteenth-century physicians. Tincture used externally for skin eruptions and hemorrhoids. Internally it was used for liver and spleen afflictions. Historically, the root has also been found as an adulterant to Goldenseal. **WARNING:** Considered potentially poisonous. **RELATED SPECIES:** The only other species, *Stylophorum lasiocarpum* (Oliver) Fedder and *S. sutchuense* (Franch.) Fedder, both occur in eastern Asia, where they are considered obscure medicinal plants, of interest because of their alkaloids.

YELLOW OR YELLOWISH ORCHIDS

ADAM-AND-EVE ROOT, PUTTY ROOT
Root

Aplectrum hyemale (Muhl. ex Willd.) Torr.   Orchid Family

Perennial; 10–16 in. Large single leaf with *distinct pleats* (folds) or often white lines; leaf lasts through winter, shrivels before plant flowers. Flowers yellowish to greenish white; *lips purple, crinkle-edged*; May–June. **WHERE FOUND:** Rich woods. Que., Vt. to

Adam-and-eve Root (Aplectrum hyemale). *Note the red-tinged petals. Photo by Martin Wall.*

Spotted Coralroot (Corallorrhiza maculata) *lacks chlorophyll.*

Ga.; west to Ark., e. Kans., s. Minn. Leave it be! Too rare to harvest. **USES:** American Indians poulticed roots on boils. Root tea formerly used for bronchial troubles.

SPOTTED CORALROOT   **Root**
Corallorrhiza maculata (Raf.) Raf.   Orchid Family
   Brownish—*no chlorophyll*; 8–20 in.; stalk *sheathed*, leafless.
   Flowers grayish yellow to dull purple, with purple-red spots;
   July–Aug. **WHERE FOUND:** On leaf mold, in woods. Nfld. to N.C.;
   Ohio, S.D., and westward. Five species (apparently used interchangeably) occur in our area. **USES:** Folk remedy for colds, "breaking fevers"; induces profuse sweating, which reduces temperature. Root tea also used for bronchial irritation, coughs. American Indians used root tea as a blood "strengthener."

LARGE YELLOW LADY'S-SLIPPER,
AMERICAN VALERIAN   **Root**
Cypripedium pubescens Willd.   Orchid Family
[*Cypripedium calceolus* var. *pubescens* (Willd.) Correll]
   Variable, mostly hairy perennial; 8–36 in. Leaves broadly lance-shaped; *alternate* on stem. Flowers yellow, often purple-streaked;

Large Yellow Lady's-slipper (Cypripedium pubescens) *is one of our most striking orchids. Photo by Alan Detrick.*

May–July. **WHERE FOUND:** Rich woods, bogs. Nfld. to Ga.; Mo., Kans. to Minn. Too rare to harvest. Yellow Lady's-slippers were probably once more common, but heavy harvesting for medicinal use in the last century decreased populations. **USES:** Lady's-slippers, called American Valerian, were widely used in nineteenth-century America as a sedative for nervous headaches, hysteria, insomnia, nervous irritability, mental depression from sexual abuse, and menstrual irregularities accompanied by despondency (PMS?). Active compounds not water-soluble. **WARNING:** All Lady's-slippers may cause dermatitis. **RELATED SPECIES:** (1) *Cypripedium parviflorum* Salisb. (*C. calceolus* var. *parviflora* [Salisb.]Fern.), not shown, is a smaller plant (to 8 in.) with a more northerly range. The petals are usually more twisted and burgundy-purple to light brown. It is only slightly hairy compared to its larger relative. (2) The **Pink Lady's-slipper** (*C. acaule,* p. 29) was considered a substitute for the more commonly used Yellow Lady's-slipper; its properties were considered analogous.

FLOWERS WITH 5 PETALS; LOW-GROWING PLANTS

CREEPING WOOD-SORREL
Oxalis corniculata L.

Leaves
Wood-sorrel Family

Creeping perennial; 6–10 in. Leaves cloverlike, with large, brownish stipules. Flowers yellow; Apr. to frost. Seedpods *deflexed.* **WHERE FOUND:** Waste places. Throughout. Alien. **USES:** Sour, acidic leaves were once chewed for nausea, mouth sores, sore throats. Fresh leaves were poulticed on cancers, old sores, ulcers. Leaf tea used for fevers, urinary infections, and scurvy. **WARNING:** Large doses may cause oxalate poisoning.

(Above) *Creeping Wood-sorrel* (Oxalis corniculata) *produces yellow flowers and cloverlike leaves.* (Right) *Purslane* (Portulaca oleracea), *with red stems and succulent leaves.*

PURSLANE
Leaves
Portulaca oleracea L.
Purslane Family

Prostrate, *smooth*, fleshy annual; to 1 ft. Stems often reddish and forking. Leaves spatula-shaped, *fleshy*. Flowers tiny, yellowish; in leaf rosettes; June–Nov. **WHERE FOUND:** Waste ground. Throughout our area. Alien. **USES:** American Indians adopted the plant as a poultice for burns, juice for earaches, tea for headaches, stomachaches. Plant juice said to alleviate caterpillar stings; used in Europe (as poultice) for inflammation, sores, eczema, abscesses, pruritus, and painful urination (strangury). Reportedly hypotensive and diuretic. Leaves best known as a wild edible; very nutritious. This palatable powerhouse is a very good source of omega-3 fatty acids, especially alpha-linolenic acid, and beta-carotene, vitamin C, alpha-tocopherol, magnesium, and potassium. Also reportedly contains dopa and noradrenalin (norepinephrine). This neurohormone reduces hemorrhage at the tissue level, perhaps accounting for use in Traditional Chinese Medicine to stop postpartum bleeding. Considered a good antioxidant and has antibiotic activity.

DWARF CINQUEFOIL
Whole plant
Potentilla canadensis L.
Rose Family

Prostrate perennial, on cylindrical rhizomes; 2–10 in. Leaves palmate; leaflets rounded, *sharply toothed above middle,* strongly

(Left) *Dwarf Cinquefoil* (Potentilla canadensis). *Most cinquefoils are used interchangeably for astringent properties. Photo by Martin Wall.* (Right) *Indian strawberry* (Duchesnea indica), *with a strawberry-like appearance, produces insipid red fruits.*

wedge-shaped at base. Flowers yellow with 5 rounded petals; March–June. **WHERE FOUND:** Fields, woods. N.S. to S.C.; Mo. to Minn. **USES:** American Indians used tea of pounded roots to treat diarrhea; considered astringent. Other cinquefoils are considered astringent as well. As with many astringent Rose family members, tannins may explain many of the activities.

INDIAN STRAWBERRY
Whole plant, flowers
Duchesnea indica (Andr.) Focke
Rose Family

Small, creeping perennial; to 6 in. Leaves *strawberry-like*. Flowers yellow; 3-toothed bracts *longer than petals and sepals*. Flowers Apr.–July. *Strawberry-like* fruit insipid. **WHERE FOUND:** Yards, waste places. Most of our area. Asian alien. **USES:** In Asia, whole-plant poultice or wash (astringent) used for abscesses, boils, burns, insect stings, eczema, ringworm, rheumatism, traumatic injuries. Whole-plant tea used for laryngitis, coughs, lung ailments. Flower tea traditionally used to stimulate blood circulation.

FLOWERS IN AXILS, WITH 5 PETALS OR PARTS; LEAVES ALTERNATE

VELVET LEAF Leaves, roots, seeds

Abutilon theophrasti Medik. Mallow Family

Annual; 3–6 ft. *Entire plant velvety.* Leaves heart-shaped, *large* (4–10 in. long), irregularly toothed. *Single* yellow flowers, each 1–1 ¼ in. across, in leaf axils; June–Nov. Fruit sections beaked. **WHERE FOUND:** Waste places. Throughout our area. Alien (India). **USES:** Chinese use 1 ounce dried leaf in tea for dysentery, fevers; poultice for ulcers. Dried root used in tea for dysentery and urinary incontinence. Seed powder diuretic; eaten for dysentery, stomachaches. CNS-depressant in mice experiments.

FROSTWEED Whole plant, root

Helianthemum canadense (L.) Michx. Rockrose Family

Like that of the American Dittany, the roots of this perennial sometimes form "volcanoes" of ice, hence the name Frostweed. Perennial; 6–20 in. Leaves alternate, lance-shaped, *toothless,* green on upper surface; basal leaves absent. First flower *solitary,* yellow, 5-petaled, with many stamens; later flowers without petals, few stamens. Flowers May–June. **WHERE FOUND:** Dry, sandy

Velvet Leaf (Abutilon theophrasti). *Photo by Stephen Lee Timme.* *Frostweed* (Helianthemum spp.) *Photo by Carl Hunter.*

soil, rocky woods. Que., s. Me. to N.C.; Tenn. to Ill., Minn. **USES:** American Indians used leaf tea for kidney ailments, sore throats; "strengthening" medicine. Patients were covered by a blanket "tent" to hold steam; feet soaked in hot tea for arthritis, muscular swellings, and rheumatism. Historically, physicians once used a strong tea for scrofula (tuberculous swelling of lymph nodes), for which it was reported to produce astonishing cures; also diarrhea, dysentery, and syphilis. Externally, used as a wash for skin diseases such as prurigo, and eye infections; gargled for throat infections. Leaves poulticed on "scrofulous tumors and ulcers."

CLAMMY GROUND-CHERRY

Physalis heterophylla Nees.

Leaves, root, seeds
Nightshade Family

Perennial; 1–3 ft. Stem sticky-hairy; upper part of stem with slender, soft, wide-spreading hairs. Leaves oval, coarsely toothed; *base rounded*, with *few teeth*. Flowers bell-like, greenish yellow with a brownish center; June–Sept. Fruit enclosed in a papery bladder. **WHERE FOUND:** Dry clearings. N.S. to Fla.; Texas to Minn. The most abundant of about 12 highly variable species in our range. **USES:** American Indians used tea of leaves and roots for headaches; wash for burns, scalds; in herbal compounds to induce vomiting for bad stomachaches; root and leaves poulticed for wounds. Seed of this and other *Physalis* species are considered useful for difficult urination, fevers, inflammation, various urinary disorders. Plant compounds are being researched for antitumor activity. **WARNING:** Potentially **toxic.**

(Above) *Clammy Ground-cherry* (Physalis missouriensis). *Note the hairy flower stalks.* (Right) *The inflated pod of Chinese-lantern* (Physalis alkekengi), *a commonly cultivated perennial.*

NODDING, BELL-LIKE, 6-PARTED FLOWERS;LEAVES BASAL OR IN WHORLS

CLINTONIA, BLUEBEARD LILY
Leaf, root

Clintonia borealis (Ait.) Raf.   Lily Family

Perennial; 4–12 in. Leaves basal; leathery, shiny, entire (not toothed). Flowers bell-like, on a leafless stalk; yellow (or greenish); May–July. Berries blue. **WHERE FOUND:** Cool woods. Nfld. to Ga. mountains; west to Wisc., Minn. **USES:** American Indians poulticed fresh leaves on burns, old sores, bruises, infections, rabid-dog bites; drank tea of plant for heart medicine, diabetes; root used to aid labor in childbirth. Root contains anti-inflammatory and estrogenic diosgenin, from which progesterone, testosterone, and other hormones can be made in the laboratory.

TROUT-LILY
Leaves, root

Erythronium americanum Ker-Gawl.   Lily Family

Perennial; to 1 ft., with 1–2 *mottled,* lance-shaped leaves. Flowers lily-like, yellow; March–May. *Petals strongly curved back.* **WHERE FOUND:** Moist woods, often in colonies. N.S. to Ga.; Ark., Okla. to Minn. **USES:** American Indians used root tea for fevers; leaf poul-

Clintonia (Clintonia borealis) *produces blue-black berries. Photo by Martin Wall.*

Trout-lily (Erythronium americanum) *produces yellow flowers and mottled leaves.*

(Above) *White Trout-lily* (Erythronium albidum) *is used interchangeably with* E. americanum, *a species with white flowers.* (Right) *Indian Cucumber* (Medeola virginiana) *has stem leaves in whorls beneath flowers. Photo by Martin Wall.*

tice for hard-to-heal ulcers and scrofula. Iroquois women ate raw leaves to prevent conception. Root poultice was used to draw out splinters, reduce swelling. Fresh and recently dried leaves and roots were considered emetic, expectorant. Externally, leaves are considered softening to skin tissue, though they may cause immediate allergic reactions. Water extracts are active against gram-positive and gram-negative bacteria. **RELATED SPECIES:** In **White Trout-lily** (*E. albidum* Nutt.), flowers are white, leaves seldom mottled. It is found from Ont. to Ga.; Ky., Ark., Okla. to Minn. Used similarly. Components of *E. grandiflorum* Pursh (not shown), a plant that grows in western N. America, have been shown to be slightly antimutagenic.

INDIAN CUCUMBER
Root, leaves, fruit
Medeola virginiana L.
Lily Family

Perennial; 1–3 ft. Leaves *oval*; 6–10, in *1 or 2 whorls* (plants with only 1 whorl usually do not flower). Flowers yellow, *drooping*; stamens red to purplish, petals and sepals curved back. Flowers Apr.–June. **WHERE FOUND:** Rich, moist wooded slopes. N.S. to Fla.; Ala., La. north to Minn. **USES:** Cucumber-flavored root is crisp, edible; American Indians chewed root and spit it on hook to make fish bite. Leaf and berry tea administered to babies with convulsions. Root tea once used as a diuretic for dropsy.

NODDING, BELL-LIKE, 6-PARTED FLOWERS; LEAVES PERFOLIATE OR SESSILE; BELL-WORTS

LARGE BELLWORT
Uvularia grandiflora Sm.

Root, plant
Lily Family

Perennial; 6–20 in. Solitary or growing in small stands. Leaves oval to lance-shaped, *not glaucous;* clasping or perfoliate; *white-downy beneath.* Leaves have a wilted appearance. Flower a yellow-orange drooping bell, petals *smooth* within, twisted. Flowers Apr.–June. **WHERE FOUND:** Rich woods. S. Que. to Ga. mountains; Ark. to e. Kans., e. N.D. **USES:** American Indians used the root tea as a wash for rheumatic pains; in fat as an ointment for sore muscles and tendons, rheumatism, and backaches. Plant poulticed to relieve toothaches and swellings. Root tea once used for stomach and lung ailments.

PERFOLIATE BELLWORT
Uvularia perfoliata L.

Root
Lily Family

Perennial, forming colonies; 6–18 in. Leaves long-oval; *smooth beneath.* Stem perfoliate—*appears to pass through leaf.* Flowers

Large Bellwort (Uvularia grandi-flora) *leaves have a wilted appearance.*

Perfoliate Bellwort (Uvularia per-foliata). *Note that the stem punctures the leaves. Photo by Martin Wall.*

Wild Oats (Uvularia sessilifolia).
Leaves do not surround stem.
Should not be confused with the
grasses Avena satira *or* A. fatua,
also called Wild Oats.

yellow-orange bells; petals rough-granular on inner surface. Flowers Apr.–June. **WHERE FOUND:** Thin woods. S. Vt. to Fla.; La. to Ont. **USES:** American Indians used root tea as a cough medicine and for sore mouth, sore throat, inflamed gums, and snakebites. Formerly used as a substitute for Large Yellow Lady's-slipper (see p. 108); in tea or ointment for herpes, sore ears, mouth sores, mild cases of erysipelas (acute local skin inflammation and swelling).

WILD OATS   Roots
Uvularia sessilifolia L.   Lily Family
Perennial; 6–12 in. Leaves sessile, *not surrounding stems* as in above species; glaucous beneath. Stem *forked* about ⅔ of way up from the ground. Flowers pale, straw-colored bells; May–June. **WHERE FOUND:** Alluvial woods, thickets. N.B. to Ga.; Ala. to Ark., north to N.D. **USES:** American Indians used the root tea to treat diarrhea and as a "blood purifier"; taken internally to aid in healing broken bones. Poulticed for boils and broken bones. Root a folk medicine for sore throats and mouth sores; said to be mucilaginous (slimy) and somewhat acrid-tasting when fresh.

MANY 6-PARTED FLOWERS, IN A SPIKE OR PANICLE

FALSE ALOE, RATTLESNAKE-MASTER   Root
Manfreda virginica (L.) Salisb. ex Rose   Amaryllis Family
[*Agave virginica* L.]
Leaves *radiating from root*; lance-shaped, smooth, *fleshy* (mottled purple in form *tigrina*); to 16 in. long. Flowers greenish white to yellow, tubular, fragrant at night. Flowers 6-parted, scattered in a *loose spike on a 3- to 6-ft. stalk*; June–July. **WHERE FOUND:** Dry soils. Ohio, N.C., W. Va. to Fla.; west to Texas; north to s. Ill. **USES:** American Indians used diuretic root tea for dropsy. Wash used for snakebites. Root nibbled for severe diarrhea, worms; laxative.

False Aloe, Rattlesnake-master (Manfreda virginica) produces succulent leaves.

Devil's-bit (Chamaelirium luteum). *Photo by Martin Wall.*

Like species of *Agave,* this plant might be used as a source for steroid synthesis. **WARNING:** May produce a strongly irritating latex. Do not confuse with another plant called Rattlesnake-master (*Eryngium yuccifolium,* p. 22).

DEVIL'S-BIT   **Root**
Chamaelirium luteum (L.) Gray   Lily Family

Perennial; to 3 ft. (in flower). Leaves smooth, oblong, in basal rosettes. *Male and female flowers on separate plants.* Flowers yellowish, *in crowded spikes* (usually drooping at tip); May–July. **WHERE FOUND:** Rich woods. W. Mass., N.Y. to Fla.; Ark. to. Ill., Mich. **USES:** Small doses of powdered root used for colic, stomach ailments, appetite stimulant, indigestion, and to expel worms. Root tea said to be a uterine tonic. Used for a wide variety of ailments associated with male and female reproductive organs. **WARNING:** Avoid during pregnancy.

AMERICAN WHITE OR FALSE HELLEBORE   **Root**
Veratrum viride Ait.   Lily Family

Perennial; 2–8 ft. Leaves large, broadly oval; *strongly ribbed.* Flowers yellowish, turning dull green; small, *star-shaped,* in a many-flowered panicle; Apr.–July. **WHERE FOUND:** Wet wood edges,

American White or False Helle-bore (Veratrum viride) *produces strongly pleated leaves. In early spring, the large, broad, pleated leaves are seen in wet woods.*

swamps. New England to Ga. mountains; Tenn. to Wisc. **USES:** Historically valued as an analgesic for pain, epilepsy, convulsions, pneumonia, heart sedative; weak tea used for sore throat, tonsillitis. Used in pharmaceutical drugs to slow heart rate, lower blood pressure; also for arteriosclerosis and forms of nephritis. Components of the plant (alkaloids) are known to slow heart rate, reduce systolic and diastolic pressure, and stimulate peripheral blood flow to the kidneys, liver, and extremities. Powdered root used in insecticides. **WARNING: All parts, especially the root, are highly or fatally toxic.** Leaves have been mistaken for Pokeweed (see p. 65) or Marsh-marigold (p. 101) and eaten. Too dangerous for use. Even handling the plant is dangerous, as the alkaloids can be absorbed through the skin.

FLOWERS IRREGULAR, LIPPED, TUBULAR

GOLDEN CORYDALIS
Whole plant, root
Corydalis aurea Willd.
Bleeding-heart Family
Perennial; 6–16 in. Leaves finely dissected. Flowers yellow, ½ in. long, with a *blunt spur* at back; upper petal toothed, *without a wing.* Other yellow *Corydalis* species in our area have a projecting wing on the top petal. Flowers March–May. **WHERE FOUND:** Sandy, rocky soils, open woods. Canada to N.Y., W. Va. mountains; west to Ill., Mo. **USES:** American Indians used tea for painful menstruation, backaches, diarrhea, bronchitis, heart diseases, sore throats, stomachaches; inhaled fumes of burning roots for headaches. Historically, physicians used tea for menstrual irregularities, dysentery, diarrhea, recent syphilitic nodes, and related afflictions. **RELATED SPECIES:** Roots of several Chinese *Corydalis* species are used for menstrual irregularities, pain, and hemorrhage. Chinese

Corydalis micrantha—*one of ten or more North American species. Most Corydalis species bloom before foliage of trees.*

Yellow Jewelweed (Impatiens pallida). *Its leaves are used to treat Poison Ivy rash. In most areas, it is much less common than Jewelweed* I. capensis.

studies show that alkaloids from the genus work as muscle relaxants, painkillers; inhibit gastric secretions, suggesting usefulness against ulcers. **WARNING:** *Corydalis* species are potentially toxic in moderate doses.

YELLOW JEWELWEED, PALE TOUCH-ME-NOT

Leaves, stem juice

Impatiens pallida Nutt.　　　　　　　Touch-me-not Family

Annual; 3–5 ft. Similar to Spotted Touch-me-not (*I. capensis*, p. 154) but flowers are *yellow,* spurs are shorter. Seedpods explode when touched. **WHERE FOUND:** Wet, shady, limey soils. Nfld. to Ga. mountains; Ark. to Kans. **USES:** Crushed leaves are poulticed on recent Poison Ivy rash.

BUTTER-AND-EGGS

Whole plant

Linaria vulgaris P. Mill.　　　　　　　Figwort Family

Perennial; 1–3 ft. Many lance-shaped leaves. Flowers are yellow, *orange-marked; snapdragon-like, with drooping spurs;* June–Oct. The snapdragon-like flowers appear in two shades of yellow, hence the name Butter-and-Eggs. **WHERE FOUND:** Waste places. Throughout our area. Alien. **USES:** In folk medicine, leaf tea used as a laxative, strong diuretic; for dropsy, jaundice, enteritis with drowsiness, skin diseases, piles. Ointment made from flowers used for piles, skin eruptions. A "tea" made in milk has been used as an insecticide. Science confirms diuretic and fever-reducing activities.

(Above) *Butter-and-eggs* (Linaria vulgaris) *has bicolored flowers.* (Right) *The leaves of Lousewort, Wood Betony* (Pedicularis canadensis) *are fernlike and persist through summer.*

LOUSEWORT, WOOD BETONY

Root, leaves

Pedicularis canadensis L.   Figwort Family

Perennial; 5–10 in. Leaves mostly basal; lance-shaped, deeply incised. Flowers *hooded*, like miniature snapdragons; yellow, reddish (or both), in tight terminal clusters; Apr.–June. **WHERE FOUND:** Open woods. Que., Me. to Fla.; Texas to Man. and westward. **USES:** American Indians used root tea for stomachaches, diarrhea, anemia, and heart trouble; also in cough medicines; poulticed for swellings, tumors, sore muscles. Finely grated roots were secretly added to food as an alleged aphrodisiac. Not currently studied.

5 OR MORE PETALS; LEAVES COMPOUND OR STRONGLY DIVIDED

SMALL-FLOWERED AGRIMONY

Whole plant

Agrimonia parviflora Ait.   Rose Family

Perennial; 3–6 ft. Stem hairy. Leaves divided; main stem leaves with 11–19 *unequal* leaflets. Leaflets smooth above, hairy below; strongly serrated, 1–3 in. long. Tiny yellow flowers, *in slender, branched wands*; July–Sept. **WHERE FOUND:** Damp thickets, in clumps. W. Conn., N.Y. to Fla., e. Texas north to Neb., s. Ont. **USES:** Herbal tea (made from whole plant) astringent, stops bleeding; used for wounds, diarrhea, inflammation of gallbladder, urinary incontinence, jaundice, and gout. Thought to "strengthen" blood and aid food assimilation. Gargled for mouth ulcers, throat

Small-flowered Agrimony (Agrimonia parviflora). *Most agrimony
species used similarly for astringent properties.*

Small-flowered Agrimony (A. parviflora). *Its main stem leaves produce 11–19 uneven leaflets.*

inflammation. **RELATED SPECIES:** *Agrimonia eupatoria* (European
alien) is used similarly; in France it is drunk as much for its flavor
as for its medicinal virtues. Tea of the European species is believed to be helpful in diarrhea, blood disorders, fevers, gout, hepatitis, pimples, sore throats, and even worms. In studies with
mice, the European species *A. pilosa* has shown antitumor activity. In Germany it is approved for use in the treatment of mild diarrhea and inflammations of the throat and mouth; used externally for mild skin inflammations.

GOAT'S BEARD   **Root**
Aruncus dioicus (Walter) Fem.   Rose Family
Shrublike; 4–6 ft. Leaves mainly basal; divided into large, serrated, oval leaflets. Tiny, yellowish white flowers, *crowded in
spikes on a pyramidal plume;* March–May. **WHERE FOUND:** Rich
woods, stream banks. Ky. to Ga.; west to Okla.; north to Iowa.
USES: Cherokees poulticed pounded root on bee stings. Root tea
used to allay bleeding after childbirth and to reduce profuse urination. Tea also used externally, to bathe swollen feet.

Goat's Beard (Aruncus dioicus) occurs in wooded habitats.

Buttercups (Ranunculus spp.) are considered potentially toxic.

COMMON OR TALL BUTTERCUP
Root, leaves

Ranunculus acris L.
Buttercup Family

⚠ Erect annual or perennial; 2–3 ft. Leaves palmately divided into 5–7 *stalkless, lance-shaped, toothed segments.* Flowers shiny; golden yellow within, lighter outside; May–Sept. Fruits flat, *smooth, with distinct margins.* **WHERE FOUND:** Fields. Throughout our area, but mostly absent from prairies. Alien (Europe). **USES:** Fresh leaves historically used as external rubefacient in rheumatism, arthritis, neuralgia. American Indians poulticed root for boils, abscesses. Action based on irritating affected part. **WARNING:** Extremely acrid, causing intense pain and burning of mouth, mucous membranes; blisters skin. **Avoid use.** Similar warning applies to other buttercups and many other plants in the Buttercup family.

FLOWERS IN UMBRELLA-LIKE CLUSTERS (UMBELS)

DILL
Leaves, seeds

Anethum graveolens L.
Parsley Family

⚠ Smooth, branched annual; often glaucous; 2–4 ft. Leaves finely dissected into linear segments *with characteristic fragrance of dill* (the flavoring for dill pickles). Flowers in umbel, with 30–40 spreading rays, to 6 in. Individual flowers yellowish; June–Sept. Fruits half as wide as long, to ⅜ in. long, also with *characteristic dill fragrance;* Aug.–Oct. **WHERE FOUND:** Garden soils. Occasional throughout the U.S. Alien from s. Europe. **USES:** Dill leaves are typically used for flavoring; considered digestive, carminative; a folk medicine for conditions of the gastrointestinal and urinary tract; reduces spasms. Contains numerous bioactive compounds.

Dill (Anethum graveolens) *produces leaves with the distinct fragrance of dill.*

Fennel (Foeniculum vulgare) *produces anise-scented leaves.*

Seed (fruit) formerly widely used as a carminative and stomachic. Considered antispasmodic and antibacterial. Approved in Germany as a tea for dyspepsia. **WARNING:** Proper identification essential. Do not confuse with fatally toxic Parsley family members.

FENNEL   **Seeds**
Foeniculum vulgare P. Mill.   Parsley Family
    Smooth herb; 4–7 ft. *Strongly anise-* or *licorice-scented.* Leaves *threadlike.* Yellowish flowers in flat umbels; June–Sept. **WHERE FOUND:** Roadsides. Conn. to Fla.; Neb. to Mich. *Very* common weed in California. Alien (Europe). Several different types of Fennel, including annual, biennial, and perennial varieties varying in form and leaf color, are grown in gardens for food, flavoring, and ornamental and medicinal use. **USES:** Seeds (actually fruits) or tea taken to relieve gas, infant colic, stimulate milk flow. Reportedly diuretic, expectorant, carminative, laxative; soothing to stomach; used to improve the flavor of other medicines. Seeds have been shown to increase gastrointestinal motility, and to increase expectorant action from the lungs by 12 percent. Boiled water extracts of leaves were shown to produce a reduction in arterial blood

pressure without reducing heart rate or respiratory rate. Seeds eaten in Middle East to increase milk secretion, promote menstruation, and increase libido. Powdered seeds poulticed in China for snakebites. Experimentally, seed oil relieves spasms of smooth muscles, kills bacteria, removes hookworms. Fennel seed is our best source of anethole, used commercially as "licorice" (actually anise) flavor. Seeds approved in Germany for treatment of gastrointestinal fullness and spasms, catarrh of the upper respiratory tract. Seed extracts stimulate gastrointestinal motility. **WARNING:** Fennel or its seed oil may cause rare contact dermatitis. Ingestion of oil may cause vomiting, seizures, and pulmonary edema.

WILD PARSNIP · Root
Pastinaca sativa L. · Parsley Family

Biennial; 2–5 ft. Stalk *deeply grooved* (ribbed). Leaves in stout rosette in first year, divided into 5–15 stalkless, toothed, oval leaflets. Tiny golden flowers with 5 petals, in umbels, May–Oct. **WHERE FOUND:** Roadsides, waste places. Much of our area. Alien. **USES:** American Indians used roots to treat sharp pains, tea in small amounts for "female" disorders; poulticed roots on inflam-

Wild Parsnip (Pastinaca sativa).
Note its deeply grooved stalk.
Photo by Stephen Lee Timme.

Golden Alexanders (Zizia aurea)
occurs in dry habitats.

mations, sores. **WARNING:** May cause photodermatitis due to xanthotoxin, which is used to treat psoriasis and vitiligo. Avoid contact and exposure to sunlight.

GOLDEN ALEXANDERS **Root**
Zizia aurea (L.) W. D. J. Koch Parsley Family

Smooth *perennial*; 1–3 ft. Leaves thin; all *twice-compound* with 35 leaflets or divisions, divided again; leaflets *finely sharp-toothed.* Tiny yellow flowers in an umber with 6–20 rays; Apr.–June. **WHERE FOUND:** Dry woods, rocky outcrops. New England to Ga.; Texas to Sask. **USES:** American Indians used root tea for fevers. Historically, the plant has been referred to as a vulnerary (agent used to heal wounds) and a sleep inducer; it was also used for syphilis. **WARNING:** Possibly **toxic**—eating a whole root has caused violent vomiting, which itself was believed to mitigate further adverse reaction. Amateurs fooling with plants in the Parsley family are playing herbal roulette.

IRREGULAR 2-LIPPED FLOWERS; MINT FAMILY

YELLOW GIANT HYSSOP **Leaves**
Agastache nepetoides (L.) O. Ktze. Mint Family

Perennial; 3–5 ft. Seems *square,* mostly smooth; branching above. Leaves opposite; narrowly ovate to lance-shaped, saw-toothed. Flowers yellow to whitish, in dense, usually continuous spikes; July–Sept. **WHERE FOUND:** Rocky, wooded hillsides, wood edges. S. Que. to Va.; ne. Texas, e. Okla. to S.D., Minn. **USES:** American Indians used the leaves in a compound mixture to apply to Poison Ivy rash. **REMARKS:** The name *nepetoides* refers to the plant's resemblance to *Nepeta* (Catnip).

STONEROOT, HORSE-BALM **Roots, leaves**
Collinsonia canadensis L. Mint Family

Branching, square-stemmed perennial herb; 2–4 ft. Leaves large, oval, coarsely toothed. Root hard, broader than long. Flowers greenish yellow, *lower lip fringed, stamen strongly protruding*; lemonlike scent; July–Sept. **WHERE FOUND:** Rich woods. Ont., Vt. to Fla.; Mo. to Wisc. **USES:** Folk uses include leaf poultice for burns, bruises, wounds, sores, sprains; root tea for piles, laryngitis, indigestion, diarrhea, dysentery, dropsy, kidney and bladder ailments. Contains alkaloids; strongly diuretic, useful in cystitis. Roots contain more than 13,000 parts per million of rosmarinic acid, the same antioxidant (preservative) found in Rosemary. Studies also report diuretic, stomachic, and tonic effects. **WARNING:** Minute doses of fresh leaves may cause vomiting.

Yellow Giant Hyssop (Agastache nepetoides) *produces small yellow flowers.*

The flower petals of Stoneroot, Horse-balm (Collinsonia canadensis) *are fringed.*

HORSEMINT
Monarda punctata L.

Leaves
Mint Family

Strongly aromatic biennial or short-lived perennial; 1–4 ft. Leaves lance-shaped. Flowers like gaping mouths; yellowish, purple-dot-ted; in tiered whorls, *with yellowish to lilac bracts beneath;* July–Oct. **WHERE FOUND:** Dry soils. L.I. to Fla.; La., Texas Ark., Kans. **USES:** American Indians used leaf tea for colds, fevers, flu, stomach cramps, coughs, catarrhs, bowel ailments. Historically, doctors used this mint as a carminative, stimulant, digestive, and

Horsemint (Monarda punctata) *produces a thyme-like scent and yellow flowers with violet spots.*

diuretic, and to regulate menses. Oil high in thymol; antiseptic, expels worms. Thymol, now manufactured synthetically, was once commercially derived from thyme (*Thymus* species). During World War I, commercial thyme fields were destroyed in Europe and Horsemint was grown in the U.S. as a substitute source of thymol.

MISCELLANEOUS FLOWERS WITH 5 PETALS

COMMON ST. JOHN'S WORT
Hypericum perforatum L.

Leaves, flowers
St. John's Wort Family

Perennial; 1–3 ft. Leaves oblong, dotted with translucent glands. Flowers yellow, stamens in a bushy cluster, 5 petals with *black dots* on *margins*. Flowers June–Sept. **WHERE FOUND:** Fields, roadsides. Throughout. Alien (Europe). **USES:** St. John's Wort has emerged as the best-known herbal treatment for mild to moderate forms of depression. Reportedly outselling the conventional antidepressant Prozac by as much as 20 to 1 in Germany, it is approved in that country for treatment of depression. More than 20 controlled clinical trials have confirmed its safety and effectiveness. St. John's Wort brings us a great example of synergy

Common St. John's Wort (Hypericum perforatum). *Note the black dots on flower margins.*

Common St. John's Wort (H. perforatum), *a frequent roadside herb.*

Whorled Loosestrife (Lysimachia quadrifolia) *produces yellow flowers that are often spotted or streaked with red. Photo by Martin Wall.*

of different chemical compounds; several compounds are believed to contribute different mechanisms to help relieve depression. Its compounds regulate brain levels of such important compounds as dopamine, interleukins, melatonin, monoamine-oxidases, and serotonin. It has been shown to be a selective serotonin re-uptake inhibitor.

Fresh flowers in tea, tincture, or olive oil were once a popular domestic medicine for treatment of external ulcers, wounds (especially those with severed nerve tissue), sores, cuts, and bruises. Tea is a folk remedy for bladder ailments, depression, dysentery, diarrhea, worms. Experimentally, antidepressant, sedative, anti-inflammatory, and antibacterial. Contains the biologically active compounds choline, pectin, rutin, sitosterol, hypericin, pseudo-hypericin, and hyperforin. Studies in the 1980s found that hypericin and pseudohypericin have potent anti-retroviral activity, without serious side effects. Being researched for AIDS treatment. **WARNING:** Taken internally or externally, hypericin may cause photodermatitis (skin burns) on sensitive skin that is exposed to light. As an antidepressant, it is used only for mild to moderate forms of depression, not severe forms.

WHORLED LOOSESTRIFE
Lysimachia quadrifolia L.

Leaves, root
Primrose Family

Delicate perennial; 1–3 ft. Leaves in *whorls of 4* (3–6). Flowers *yellow; red-dotted or -streaked;* from leaf axils; May–Aug. **WHERE FOUND:** Calcareous bogs, moist thickets. Me. to Va., Ga.; Ill. to Wisc. **USES:** American Indians used plant tea for "female ailments," kidney trouble, bowel complaints; root tea emetic.

COMMON MULLEIN   **Leaves, flowering tops**
Verbascum thapsus L.   Figwort Family

⚠ Biennial; 1–8 ft. in flower; produces a rosette of large, fuzzy, gray-green leaves the first year, and an attractive spike of light yellow flowers the second year. Leaves are large, broadly oval, *very hairy (flannel-like); hairs branching.* Flowers yellow, in tight, long spikes; July–Sept. **WHERE FOUND**: Poor soils. Common throughout our area. Alien. A roadside weed naturalized from Europe, it also grows in sandpits and gravel pits; it seems to thrive in the poorest of soils. **USES**: Traditionally, leaf and flower tea expectorant, demulcent, antispasmodic, diuretic, for chest colds, asthma, bronchitis, coughs, kidney infections; leaves poulticed for ulcers, tumors, piles; flowers soaked in olive or mineral oil are used as earache drops. In Europe, flowers are preferred over leaves; both are used in European cough remedies. Leaves high in mucilage, soothing to inflamed mucous membranes; experimentally, strongly anti-inflammatory. Science confirms mild expectorant and antiviral activity against herpes simplex and influenza viruses. Contains verbascoside, which has antiseptic, antitumor, antibacterial, and immunosuppressant activity. In Germany the flowers are approved as an expectorant in inflammations of the upper respira-

Common Mullein (Verbascum thapsus). *Its yellow flowers appear in its second year.*

The leaves of Common Mullein (V. thapsus) *are large, gray, and fuzzy.*

tory tract. Asian Indians used the stalk for cramps, fevers, and migraine. The seed is a narcotic fish poison. **WARNING:** The leaves contain rotenone and coumarin, neither of which is viewed with great favor by the FDA. Hairs may irritate skin.

PEA-LIKE FLOWERS; 3 LEAFLETS

CREAM WILD INDIGO
Baptisia bracteata var. *leucophaea* (Nutt.) Kartesz & Gandhi
[*Baptisia leucophaea* Nutt.]

Seeds, roots, leaves

Pea Family

Hairy, bushy perennial; 10–30 in. Leaves with 3 spatula-shaped leaflets. Flowers *cream-yellow,* on showy lateral drooping racemes, with *large leaflike bracts beneath*; Apr.–June. **WHERE FOUND:** Dry soils. Ark., Texas, Neb. to Minn. **USES:** Ointment of seed powder mixed in buffalo fat was applied to stomach for colic (by Pawnees). Root tea formerly used for typhoid and scarlet fever; leaf tea in "mercurial salivation"; used externally on cuts and wounds (astringent). Recent research suggests immune-system stimulant activity. **WARNING:** Potentially **toxic.**

WILD INDIGO
Baptisia tinctoria (L.) R. Br.

Root

Pea Family

Smooth, *blue-glaucous* perennial; 1–3 ft. Leaves narrowly cloverlike, nearly stalkless. Flowers yellow, few, on numerous racemes on upper branchlets; May–Sept. **WHERE FOUND:** Dry open woods, clearings. Va. to Fla.; less common from s. Me. to Ind., se. Minn. **USES:** American Indians used the root tea as an emetic and purgative; cold tea to stop vomiting. A poultice of the root was used for toothaches, to allay inflammation; wash used for cuts, wounds,

Cream Wild Indigo's (Baptisia bracteata) *flowers spread laterally.*

Wild Indigo (Baptisia tinctoria) *has small yellow pea-like flowers.*

Yellow Sweet-clover (Melilotus officinalis) *commonly grows along roadsides.*

bruises, and sprains. Historically, fresh-root tea was considered laxative, astringent, antiseptic. Used for typhus and scarlet fever; gargled for sore throats. Tea used as a wash for leg, arm, and stomach cramps, wounds. Said to stimulate bile secretion. Root poultice for gangrenous ulcers. German studies have shown the extract stimulates the immune system. **WARNING:** Large or frequent doses are potentially harmful.

YELLOW SWEET-CLOVER
Melilotus officinalis (L.) Lam.

Flowering plant
Pea Family

Straggly biennial; 2–6 ft. Leaves in cloverlike arrangement; leaflets narrow, elongate, slightly toothed. Flowers small, yellow, pea-like, in long, tapering spikes; *fragrant when crushed*; Apr.–Oct. **WHERE FOUND:** Roadsides. Throughout our area. Alien (Europe). **USES:** Dried flowering plant traditionally used in tea for neuralgic headaches, painful urination, nervous stomach, colic, diarrhea with flatulence, painful menstruation with lameness and cold sensation, aching muscles; poulticed for inflammation, ulcers, wounds, rheumatism; smoked for asthma. Recent clinical trials support use in cyclic mastalgia. Tea of leaves used to treat varicose veins. **WARNING:** Moldy hay causes uncontrollable bleeding in cattle due to coumarins. Science has developed compounds like warfarin from such coumarins to prevent blood-clotting in rodents.

LEGUMES (PEA FAMILY); MANY LEAFLETS

WILD SENNA
Senna marilandica (L.) Link [*Cassia marilandica* L.]

Leaves, seedpods
Pea Family

Erect perennial; 3–6 ft. Leaves compound, with 4–8 pairs of elliptical leaflets. Note *rounded gland at base of leafstalk.* Yellow flowers in loose clusters at leaf axils; July–Aug. Seedpods with

(Left) *Wild Senna* (Senna marilandica) *produces a rounded gland at base of leafstalk.* (Above) *Related to* Chamaecrista nictitans *(5 anthers per flower, petals of unequal length),* C. fasciulata, *pictured here, used similarly, has 10 anthers per flower, with petals of equal length.*

joints twice as wide as they are long. **WHERE FOUND:** Dry thickets. Pa. to Fla.; Kans. to Iowa. **USES:** Powdered leaves or tea given as a strong laxative, also for fevers. One teaspoon of ground Coriander seeds was added to leaf tea to prevent griping (cramps); tea of pods milder, slower-acting. Laxatives made from Alexandrian Senna (*C. senna*, Africa) and Indian Senna (*C. angustifolia*, India) are found in every pharmacy.

WILD SENSITIVE-PLANT	**Roots**
Chamaecrista nictitans var. *nictitans* (L.) Moench	Pea Family
[*Cassia nictitans* L.]	

Perennial; 6–15 in. Leaves *fold when touched.* Leaflets in 6–15 pairs. Flowers yellow, small (¼ in. long), with 5 stamens; July–Sept. **WHERE FOUND:** Sandy soil. Mass., N.Y. to Fla.; Texas, Kans., Mo. to Ohio. **USES:** Cherokees used root tea with other plants to relieve fatigue. **RELATED SPECIES:** *C. fasciculata* has been used similarly.

SICKLEPOD, COFFEEWEED	**Leaves, seeds**
Senna obtusifolia (L.) Irwin & Barneby	Pea Family
[*Cassia obtusifolia* L.]	

Annual; to 3 ft. Leaflets in 3 pairs; obovate; tip rounded, often with an abrupt point. Note cylindrical gland between 2 lowermost

(Left) *Sicklepod, Coffeeweed* (Senna obtusifolia) *has sickle-shaped seedpods.* (Above) *Goat's Rue* (Tephrosia virginiana) *has pale yellow and red blooms.*

leaflets. Flowers July–Sept. Pods to 9 in. long, curved. **WHERE FOUND:** Waste places. Pa., Ky., Mo. and southward. **USES:** Pesticides have been developed to eradicate this weed from midwestern corn fields. Both a food and medicinal plant. Seed tea used for headaches, fatigue, and stomachaches. In North Africa, nomadic tribes use the leaves to make a fermented protein paste. Seeds of *S. tora* (see below) are roasted as a coffee substitute, eaten during famine. Chinese use seeds of *S. tora* for boils (internal and external), eye diseases. Fruit tea used for headaches, hepatitis, herpes, and arthritis. **RELATED SPECIES:** *S. obtusifolia* is considered distinct from and synonymous with *S. tora*. Taxonomy is confused. *S. tora* has foul-smelling leaves that are used for leprosy, psoriasis, and ringworm.

GOAT'S RUE
Root, leaves

Tephrosia virginiana (L.) Pers.
Pea Family

Silky-hairy perennial; 1–2 ft. Leaves pinnate; 17–29 leaflets. Flowers *bicolored*—yellow base, pink wings; May–Aug. Legume (seedpod) hairy. **WHERE FOUND:** Prairies, sandy soil. N.H. to Fla.; Texas to Man. **USES:** American Indians used root tea to make children muscular and strong; cold tea used for male potency, and to treat tuberculosis, coughs, bladder problems; leaves put in shoes to treat rheumatism. Root reportedly used as fish poison; vermicidal, insecticidal, purgative. Experimentally, plant has shown anti-cancer *and* cancer-causing potential. **WARNING:** May cause contact dermatitis. Contains the insecticide rotenone. Seeds **toxic.**

THISTLES AND OTHER COMPOSITES WITH FERNLIKE LEAVES OR LACERATED UPPER LEAVES

SPANISH NEEDLES, SOAPBUSH NEEDLES   **Leaves**
Bidens bipinnata L.   Composite Family

Square-stemmed annual; 1–3 ft. Leaves *strongly dissected*, fernlike. Flowers yellow, rays absent. Aug.–Oct. Elongate seeds ("needles") in spreading clusters; each seed topped with 2–4 barbs. **WHERE FOUND:** Waste places, sandy soil. Mass., N.Y. to Fla.; Texas to Kans. **USES:** Cherokees used leaf tea as a worm expellent. Leaves were chewed for sore throats. Plant juice once used for eardrops and as a styptic. **WARNING:** May be an irritant. **RELATED SPECIES:** A related species has CNS-depressant and blood sugar–lowering activity.

BLESSED THISTLE   **Whole plant**
Cnicus benedictus L.   Composite Family

 Hairy annual herb; 10–30 in. Both leaves and stems hairy. Stems 5-sided. Leaves *broadest at base;* lacerated, spiny-toothed. Flowers yellow *with a large leafy bract beneath;* Apr.–Sept. Reddish, spinelike projections surround yellow tufts of flowers. **WHERE FOUND:** Roadsides, waste places. Local. Alien. **USES:** Weak tea (2 teaspoons to 1 cup of water) of dried flowering plant traditionally used in Europe to stimulate sweating, appetite, milk production; diuretic. Folk reputation as remedy for boils, indigestion, colds, deafness, gout, headaches, migraines, suppressed menses, chilblains, jaundice, and ringworm. Experimentally, it increases gastric and bile secretions; antibacterial, anti-inflammatory. Contains two lig-

Spanish Needles, Soapbush Needles (Bidens bipinnata). *Photo by Stephen Lee Timme.*

Blessed Thistle (Cnicus benedictus) *produces spider web–like hairs in the flowers.*

Golden Ragwort, Squaw-weed (Senecio aureus) *produces heart-shaped leaves at the base and divided leaves on stem. Blooms very early.*

nans, arctigenin and tracheologenin, that have been experimentally useful against retroviruses. These compounds are also found in Burdock. Highly bitter principles in the leaf, such as cnicin, stimulate secretion of gastric juices and saliva, and are responsible for Blessed Thistle's use as an appetite stimulant. Approved in Germany for treatment of loss of appetite and dyspeptic discomfort. Seeds have served as emergency oil seeds. **WARNING:** Large doses may cause irritation, vomiting.

GOLDEN RAGWORT, SQUAW-WEED
Leaves, roots
Senecio aureus L.   Composite Family

Perennial; 2–4 ft. Has 2 leaf types, unlike other *Senecio* species in our range—basal leaves *heart-shaped, rounded*; upper leaves lance-shaped, incised. Highly variable. This early spring wildflower, often growing in clumps among exposed rocks in streams, is easily distinguished from other *Senecio* species by the heart-shaped leaves at the base of the plant. Flowers yellow, in flat-topped clusters; late March–July. **WHERE FOUND:** Stream banks, moist soil, swamps. Most of our area. **USES:** Root and leaf tea traditionally used by American Indians, settlers, and herbalists to treat delayed and irregular menses, leukorrhea, and childbirth complications; also used for lung ailments, dysentery, difficult urination. Its traditional use in treating a variety of female diseases led to its common name, Squaw-weed. **WARNING:** Many ragworts (*Senecio* species) contain **highly** toxic pyrrolizidine alkaloids.

COMPOSITES WITH PROMINENT OVERLAPPING BRACTS

Gumweed, Rosinweed (Grindelia *squarrosa) produces gummy flow-erheads.*

GUMWEED, ROSINWEED
Leaves, flowers

Grindelia squarrosa (Pursh) Dunal — Composite Family

Highly variable; 1–3 ft. Leaves *strongly aromatic,* mostly serrate, linear-oblong; mostly clasping. Flowers yellow, with *very gummy braces;* bract tips recurved; July–Sept. **WHERE FOUND:** Prairies, road-sides. Prairie states; spreading locally eastward. **USES:** Plant tea tra-ditionally used for asthma, coughs, kidney ailments, bronchitis. Tea of flowering tops used for colic, stomachaches. Externally, a leaf poultice or wash was used for sores, skin eruptions, wounds. This and other *Grindelia* species have been used in folk remedies for cancers of the spleen and stomach, burns, colds, fever, gonor-rhea, pneumonia, rashes, rheumatism, smallpox, and tuberculo-sis. Said to be sedative, spasmolytic, and antibacterial. Herb ap-proved in Germany for treatment of catarrhs of the upper respiratory tract. **RELATED SPECIES:** *G. lanceolata* Nutt. differs in that the individual bracts surrounding the flowerhead are spreading rather than strongly curved back, among other technical details. Its general range is more eastern than that of *G. squarrosa.* For all practical historical medicinal purposes, both plants were used in-terchangeably.

ELECAMPANE
Roots, leaves, flowers

Inula helenium L. — Composite Family

Perennial; 4–8 ft. Leaves large, burdock-like, but narrower and *woolly beneath;* upper leaves reduced. Flowers yellow, *large—to 4 in. across; rays slender;* July–Sept. Broad bracts beneath flower-head. **WHERE FOUND:** Fields, roadsides. Locally established. Alien. **USES:** Root tea (½ ounce to 1 pint water) a folk remedy for pneumo-nia, whooping cough, asthma, bronchitis, upset stomach, diar-

(Above) *Elecampane* (Inula hele-nium) *produces large yellow flow-ers with narrow rays.* (Right) *Ele-campane* (I. helenium) *produces large burdock-like leaves.*

rhea, worms; used in China for certain cancers. Wash used for fa-cial neuralgia, sciatica. Experimentally, tea strongly sedative to mice; antispasmodic, expectorant, worm expellent, anti-inflam-matory, antibacterial, and fungicidal. In studies of mice, the root infusion (tea) had pronounced sedative effects. Contains alanto-lactone, which is a better wormer than santonin and less toxic. In small doses it lowers blood-sugar levels, but in larger doses it raises blood sugar, at least in experimental animals. Roots contain 20 to 44 percent inulin, a dietary fiber that is recently recom-mended for leaky gut syndrome. **WARNING:** Contains **toxic** sesquiterpene lactones, notably alantolactone, which can irritate mucous membranes. This compound attaches to skin proteins, causing sensitization and contact allergic dermatitis. Because risks outweigh benefits, use is not recommended in Germany.

GOLDENRODS AND BUTTONLIKE COMPOSITES

PINEAPPLE-WEED   **Leaves, flowers**
Matricaria discoidea DC.   Composite Family
[*Matricaria matricarioides* (Less.) Porter]
    Pineapple-scented annual; 4–16 in. Leaves *finely dissected; seg-ments linear.* Flowers tiny, without rays; yellow "button" is a ray-less composite flower. May–Oct. **WHERE FOUND:** Waste places, road-sides. Throughout our area. Alien. **USES:** Traditionally, plant tea

(Left) *Pineapple-weed* (Matricaria discoidea) *often grows in poor dry soils, even in cracks of pavement.* (Above) *Canada Goldenrod* (Solidago canadensis). *Our most common goldenrod.*

used for stomachaches, flatulence, colds, menstrual cramps; wash used externally, for sores, itching. **WARNING:** Some individuals may be allergic to this plant.

CANADA GOLDENROD
Solidago canadensis L.

Roots, flowers
Composite Family

Our most common goldenrod. 1–5 ft. Stem smooth at base, hairy below lower flower branches. Leaves many; lance-shaped, 3-veined, sharp-toothed. Flowers in a broad, triangular panicle; July–Sept. **WHERE FOUND:** Fields, roadsides. Most of our area. **USES:** American Indians used root for burns; flower tea for fevers, snakebites; crushed flowers were chewed for sore throats. Contains quercetin, a compound reportedly useful in treating hemorrhagic nephritis. Seeds eaten as survival food. Leaf extracts are diuretic and mildly antispasmodic. Like the European *Solidago virgaurea* L., the leaves of Canada Goldenrod are approved in Germany for use as a diuretic in treatment of inflammatory diseases of the lower urinary tract. Also used in irrigation therapy to both prevent and treat urinary and kidney gravel. **WARNING:** Causes allergies, though most allergies attributed to goldenrods are due to Ragweed pollen.

SWEET GOLDENROD
Solidago odora Ait.

Leaves
Composite Family

Anise-scented perennial; 2–5 ft. Leaves lance-shaped, not toothed

Sweet Goldenrod (Solidago odora). *Leaves, when crushed, emit a pleasant, tarragon-like fragrance.*

Common Tansy (Tanacetum vulgare). *Leaves are fernlike, flowers are yellow buttons.*

 (but tiny prickles catch skin when rubbed backward along edge of leaf). Flowers on 1 side of branch; July–Oct. **WHERE FOUND:** Dry, open woods. S. N.H. to Fla.; Texas to Okla., Mo. **USES:** Leaf tea pleasant-tasting. Formerly used as a digestive stimulant, diaphoretic, diuretic, mild astringent; for colic, to regulate menses, stomach cramps, colds, coughs, fevers, dysentery, diarrhea, measles; externally, a wash for rheumatism, neuralgia, headaches. **WARNING:** May cause allergic reactions.

COMMON TANSY   **Whole plant**
Tanacetum vulgare L.   Composite Family

Strong-scented perennial; 1–4 ft. Leaves *fernlike.* Flowers to ½ in., in flat terminal clusters. June–Sept. **WHERE FOUND:** Roadsides, fields. Scattered throughout our area. Alien (Europe). **USES:** Traditionally, weak cold leaf tea was used for dyspepsia, flatulence, jaundice, worms, suppressed menses, weak kidneys; externally, as a wash for swelling, tumors, inflammations; spray or inhalant of tea for sore throats. Experiments have confirmed that Tansy is antispasmodic and antiseptic. Leaves insecticidal. **WARNING:** Oil is **lethal**— ½ ounce can kill in 2–4 hours. May cause dermatitis.

DAISYLIKE FLOWERS, BLACK-EYED SUSANS

GARDEN COREOPSIS, TICKSEED
Coreopsis tinctoria Nutt.

Whole plant
Composite Family

Smooth-stemmed annual; 2–4 ft. Leaves divided into slender segments. Flowers yellow; *base of rays brown*; June–Sept. **WHERE FOUND:** Moist fields. Minn. to Texas. Garden escape westward. **USES:** American Indians used root tea for diarrhea and as an emetic.

SNEEZEWEED
Helenium autumnale L.

Disk florets, leaves
Composite Family

Perennial; 2–5 ft. Winged, angled stems. Leaves lance-shaped to ovate-oblong, coarsely toothed. Flowers yellow; *disk globular; rays wedge-shaped, 3-toothed*; July–Nov. **WHERE FOUND:** Rich thickets, wet fields. Que. to Fla. and westward. **USES:** American Indians used powdered dried disk florets as a snuff for head colds and catarrh, or drank tea for "catarrh of stomach." Powdered leaves induce sneezing. Flower tea used to treat intestinal worms. Folk remedy for fevers. Helenalin, a lactone found in this and other species of *Helenium*, has shown significant antitumor activity in the cancer-screening program of the National Cancer Institute. **WARNING: Poisonous** to cattle. May cause contact dermatitis. Helenalin is poisonous to fishes and worms as well as to insects.

(Left) *Garden Coreopsis* (Coreopsis tinctoria) *produces bicolored flowers.* (Above) *Sneezeweed* (Helenium autumnale) *produces winged, angled stems.*

BLACK-EYED SUSAN

Root

Rudbeckia hirta L.

Composite Family

Biennial or short-lived perennial; 1–3 ft. Leaves lance-shaped to oblong, *bristly-hairy.* Flowers yellow, daisylike, with 8–21 rays around a deep brown center; June–Oct. **WHERE FOUND:** Fields, roadsides, waste places. Most of our area. **USES:** American Indians used root tea for worms, colds; external wash for sores, snakebites, swelling; root juice for earaches. Like Echinacea, the Black-eyed Susan has been found to have immuno-stimulant activity. **WARNING:** Contact sensitivity to the plant has been reported.

GREEN-HEADED CONEFLOWER

Root, flowers, leaves

Rudbeckia laciniata L.

Composite Family

Large, branched perennial; 3–12 ft. Leaves deeply divided into 3–5 sharp-toothed lobes. Flowers yellow; rays drooping, disk *greenish yellow;* June–Sept. **WHERE FOUND:** Moist, rich thickets. Throughout our area and beyond. **USES:** American Indians used root tea (with Blue Cohosh, p. 223) for indigestion. Flower poultice (with Blue Giant or Anise-Hyssop, p. 213, and a Goldenrod species) applied to burns. Cooked spring greens were eaten for "good health." Was once sold as a balsamic diuretic and tonic, recommended for urinary catarrh.

Black-eyed Susan (Rudbeckia hirta). *Note its prominent dark center.*

Green-headed Coneflower (Rudbeckia laciniata). *Photo by Pamela Harper.*

TALL PLANTS WITH DANDELION-LIKE FLOWERS

WILD LETTUCE
Lactuca canadensis L.

Leaves, sap
Composite Family

Biennial; usually over 30 in. tall. Stem smooth, branched, with whitish film. Highly variable. Leaves lance-shaped, wavy-margined to deeply lobed. Flowers in panicles of yellow, dandelion-like heads; July–Sept. **WHERE FOUND:** Thickets. Most of our area. **USES:** American Indians used plant tea as a nerve tonic, sedative, pain reliever. Milky latex from stem used for warts, pimples, Poison Ivy rash, and other skin irritations. Used similarly by settlers. The milky juices of this and other lettuces, wild and "tame," have been used to make the so-called lettuce opium ("head lettuce"), which has been openly sold as a sedative in the U.S. We suspect it might make a better substitute for rubber than for opium or chicle. **WARNING:** This species and other *Lactuca*s may cause dermatitis or internal poisoning.

PRICKLY LETTUCE
Lactuca serriola L. [*Lactuca scariola* L.]

Leaves, sap
Composite Family

Annual or biennial; 2–7 ft. Leaves oblong to lance-shaped or dandelion-like but *prickly;* margins with weak spines. Flowers yellow,

Wild Lettuce (Lactuca canadensis) *produces dandelion-like flowers. Leaf margins lack prickles.*

The leaves of Prickly Lettuce (Lactuca serriola) *have prickly margins.*

Field Sow-thistle (Sonchus arvensis) *is a common garden weed.*

dandelion-like. July–Oct. **WHERE FOUND:** Waste places. Much of our area. Alien (Europe). **USES:** American Indians used leaf tea to stimulate milk flow; diuretic. Also used like other wild lettuces. **WARNING:** May cause dermatitis or internal poisoning.

FIELD SOW-THISTLE
Sonchus arvensis L.

Root, sap, leaves
Composite Family

Perennial; 1½–4 ft. Leaves divided, dandelion-like; base *heart-shaped*, clasping; *weak-spined*. Flowers dandelion-like; July–Oct. Bracts often glandular-hairy. **WHERE FOUND:** Fields, waste places. Nfld. to Del.; Mo. to N.D., Alaska. Alien (Europe). **USES:** American Indians used leaf tea to calm nerves; wash for caked breasts. Asian Indians use the root in tea for asthma, bronchitis, cough, and whooping cough; leaves (poultice or wash) for swellings; latex (juice) for severe eye inflammations. In Europe, leaves are poulticed as an anti-inflammatory. Folk tumor remedy. Young shoots are eaten as a salad or potherb.

SMALL PLANTS WITH DANDELION-LIKE FLOWERS

RATTLESNAKE-WEED
Hieracium venosum L.

Leaves, root
Composite Family

Perennial; 1–2 ft. Leaves oblong to lance-shaped at base, veins *strongly purple-red*. Flowers small, yellow, dandelion-like, on branching stalks; May–Oct. **WHERE FOUND:** Open woods, clearings. Much of our area. **USES:** Powdered leaves and roots were considered astringent, expectorant. Tea used for hemorrhages, the spitting up of blood, diarrhea, and coughs. One of numerous snakebite remedies. Juice in fresh leaves used as folk medicine (external) for warts.

The leaves of Rattlesnake-weed (Hieracium venosum) *have prominent veins. Photo by Martin Wall.*

DANDELION
Taraxacum officinale G. H. Weber ex Wiggers

Roots, leaves

Composite Family

Familiar weed; 2–18 in. Flowering stalk hollow, with milky juice. Leaves jagged-cut. Flowers yellow; March–Sept. and sporadically throughout the year. Bracts reflexed. **WHERE FOUND:** Lawns, fields, waste places. Throughout our area. **USES:** Fresh-root tea traditionally used for liver, gallbladder, kidney, and bladder ailments, diuretic (not indicated when inflammation is present). Also used as a tonic for weak or impaired digestion, constipation. Dried root thought to be weaker, often roasted as coffee substitute. Dried-leaf tea a folk laxative. Experimentally the root is hypoglycemic, a weak antibiotic against yeast infections (*Candida albicans*), and stimulates flow of bile and weight loss. Folkloric use in cystitis and other inflammations is explained by a large number of anti-inflammatory compounds in the leaves and root. All plant parts have served as food. Leaves and flowers are rich in vitamins A and C. Dandelion leaf approved in Germany for treatment of loss of appetite and dyspepsia with a feeling of fullness and flatulence. The root is approved for treatment of bile flow disturbances, as a diuretic, to stimulate appetite, and to treat dyspepsia. **WARNING:** Contact dermatitis reported from handling the plant, probably caused by latex in stems and leaves.

(Above, Right, Left) *The Dandelion's* (Taraxacum officinale) *flowers are familiar to all. Its leaves are eaten as a green and used in medicine. The seed head is a familiar sight on lawns (even the day after mowing).*

COLT'S FOOT

Leaves, flowers

Tussilago farfara L.

Composite Family

⚠ Perennial; 4–8 in. Leaves rounded, slightly lobed, toothed; base strongly heart-shaped. Flowers *appear before* leaves. March–Apr.. Flowers yellow *with many slender rays,* on a *reddish-scaled* stalk. **WHERE FOUND:** Fields. N.S. to N.J.; Ohio to Minn. Alien. **USES:** Leaf and flower tea traditionally used as a demulcent and expectorant for sore throats, coughs, asthma, bronchitis, lung congestion. One of Europe's mostly popular cough remedies; dried leaves smoked for coughs and asthma. Smoke is believed to impede impulse of fibers of parasympathetic nerves and to act as an antihistamine. Research indicates that leaf mucilage soothes inflamed

(Left, Above) *Colt's Foot* (Tussilago farfara) *flowers appear before leaves in early spring, sometimes sprouting through snow. The leaves appear after the flowers.*

mucous membranes and that leaves have spasmolytic activity. Leaf is approved in Germany for treatment of cough and hoarseness, inflammation of the respiratory tract, and mild inflammation of the mouth or throat. **WARNING:** Contains traces of liver-affecting pyrrolizidine alkaloids; potentially toxic in large doses. In Germany, use is limited to 4 to 6 weeks per year, except under advice of a physician.

PLANTS WITH SUNFLOWER-LIKE FLOWERS

SUNFLOWER
Whole plant
Helianthus annuus L.   Composite Family

Annual; 6–10 ft. Leaves mostly alternate, rough-hairy, broadly heart- or spade-shaped. Flowers orange-yellow; disk flat; July–Oct. **WHERE FOUND:** Prairies, roadsides. Minn. to Texas; escaped elsewhere. Wild parent of our domesticated sunflower. **USES:** American Indians used flower tea for lung ailments, malaria. Leaf tea taken for high fevers; astringent; poultice on snakebites and spider bites. Seeds and leaves said to be diuretic, expectorant. **WARNING:** Pollen or plant extracts may cause allergic reactions.

JERUSALEM ARTICHOKE
Tubers, stalks, flowers
Helianthus tuberosus L.   Composite Family

Hairy, tuber-bearing perennial; 5–10 ft. Leaves oval, thick, hard; sandpapery above, 3-nerved; leafstalk winged. Yellow flowers;

Sunflower (Helianthus annuus) *is an annual with familiar flowers.*

Jerusalem Artichoke (Helianthus tuberosus) *produces edible tubers.*

Aug.–Oct. **WHERE FOUND:** Thickets, fields. Throughout our area. **USES:** American Indians drank leaf and stalk tea or ate flowers to treat rheumatism. Folk use has suggested that the edible tubers, which contain inulin, may aid in treating diabetes. Inulin also used for leaky gut syndrome. Like those of beans, the roots are known to induce intestinal gas.

COMPASS-PLANT   **Root, leaves, resin**
Silphium laciniatum L.   Composite Family

 Perennial; 3–10 ft. Leaves large, *deeply divided, rough-hairy; aromatic.* Flowers yellow, with few rays; July–Sept. **WHERE FOUND:** Prairies, glades. Mich. to Ark., Texas, Okla. to N.D. **USES:** American Indians used root tea as a general tonic for debility; worm expellent. Leaf tea emetic, once used for coughs, lung ailments, asthma. Resin said to be diuretic. Root tea used for coughs, asthma, gonorrhea. **WARNING:** Of unknown toxicity.

CUP-PLANT   **Root**
Silphium perfoliatum L.   Composite Family

 Square-stemmed perennial; 3–8 ft. Upper leaves united at base, *forming a cup.* Flowers like small sunflowers; July–Sept. **WHERE FOUND:** Rich, moist thickets. Ont. to Ga., Okla. to S.D. **USES:** Ameri-

Compass-plant (Silphium lacinia-tum) *produces showy yellow flow-ers on long stalks.*

Compass-plant (S. laciniatum) *leaf edges follow the sun, hence the name Compass-plant.*

Cup-plant (Silphium perfoliatum) *produces strongly perfoliate leaves that are cup-shaped at the stem.*

The leaves of Prairie-dock (Sil-phium terebinthinaceum) *emit a turpentine odor when crushed.*

can Indians used root tea for lung bleeding, back or chest pain, profuse menstruation, and to induce vomiting; inhaled smoke for head colds, neuralgia, and rheumatism. Historically, root tea was used for enlarged spleen, fevers, internal bruises, debility, liver ailments, and ulcers. **WARNING:** Of unknown toxicity.

PRAIRIE-DOCK
Root

Silphium terebinthinaceum Jacq.
Composite Family

 Perennial; 2–9 ft. Leaves *huge,* heart-shaped, *odor of turpentine when crushed.* Flowers like small sunflowers; Aug.–Oct. **WHERE FOUND:** Prairies, glades. Ont. to Tenn.; Mo. to Ohio, Ind. **USES:** Same as for *S. laciniatum* (above). **WARNING:** Potentially **toxic.**

BLACKBERRY LILY
Root

Belamcanda chinensis (L.) DC.
Iris Family

Though called a lily, the Blackberry Lily is actually an Iris family member. Perennial; 1–2 ft. Leaves swordlike. Flowers in cymes, *orange, mottled with purple or brownish marks*; each flower lasts only one day; May–August. Fruits are 3-lobed capsules, splitting to reveal black fleshy seeds (hence the name Blackberry Lily). **WHERE FOUND:** Pastures, roadsides, ditches. Alien from E. Asia, introduced into Europe in the 1730s. Conn. south to Ga.; west to Texas, Neb. Widely grown as a perennial garden flower. **USES:** Roots used in Traditional Chinese Medicine in prescriptions for sore throats, cough, asthma, wheezing, bronchitis. Externally, poulticed for sprains, boils, contusions, rheumatism; folk cancer remedy for breast cancer. Science confirms blood pressure–lowering, antifungal, antibacterial, and antiviral activity. **WARNING:** Usually used under medical supervision in China. Avoid during pregnancy. Contains toxic iridoid components, including belamcandin and iridin.

DAYLILY
Root, flower buds

Hemerocallis fulva L.
Lily Family

Perennial; 3–6 ft. Leaves in clumps, *swordlike*. Flowers *face upward or outward, not downward*; striped in middle, petals curved back. Large, showy flowers; May–July. **WHERE FOUND:** Escaped from

(Left, Above) *Blackberry Lily* (Belamcanda chinensis). *Note the overlapping, iris-like leaves. Its fruits superficially resemble blackberries.*

Daylily (Hemerocallis fulva) *is a commonly naturalized lily from eastern Asia.*

gardens. Grows near abandoned houses and gardens throughout. Alien (Asia). A familiar garden perennial from Eastern Asia, Daylily has become widely naturalized in the U.S. and is now thought to be more common in the wild in North America than in its native China. **USES:** The roots and young shoots are an ancient medicinal of Traditional Chinese Medicine, used for more than 2,000 years for mastitis, breast cancer, and a variety of other ailments. In China, the root tea is used as a diuretic in turbid urine, edema; to treat poor or difficult urination, jaundice, nosebleeds, leukorrhea, uterine bleeding; poultice for mastitis. A folk cancer remedy for breast cancer. Experimentally, Chinese studies indicate that root extracts are antibacterial, useful against blood flukes (parasites), and diuretic. The edible flower buds are used for diuretic and astringent properties in jaundice and to "relieve oppression and heat in the chest"; poulticed for piles. **WARNING:** The roots and young leaf shoots are considered potentially **toxic.** Chinese reports indicate that the toxin accumulates in the system and can adversely affect the eyes, even causing blindness in some cases. Chinese studies hint that the roots may also contain the carcinogen and teratogen colchicine, which, though poisonous, has long been used in the treatment of acute gout crises. Foragers beware.

CANADA LILY   Root
Lilium canadense L.   Lily Family
Perennial; 2–5 ft. Leaves lance-shaped, usually in whorls. *Nodding* yellow, orange, or reddish flowers; spotted, bell-shaped; July–Aug. **WHERE FOUND:** Moist meadows, openings. Se. Canada. to e. Md., Va. mountains, N.C., Ga., Fla.; Ala. to Ky. **USES:** American Indians used root tea for stomach ailments, irregular menses, dysentery, rheumatism; root poultice used externally, for snakebites.

(Above) *Canada Lily* (Lilium canadense) *is a tall plant with bell-like, hanging flowers.* (Right) *Wood Lily* (Lilium philadelphicum) *produces upturned, spotted flowers.*

WOOD LILY
Root, flowers

Lilium philadelphicum L.
Lily Family

Perennial, 1–3 ft. Leaves in whorls. Flowers bright orange, *upturned, spotted;* June–July. **WHERE FOUND:** Acid woods, openings, clearings. Me. to W. Va., Ga. mountains, north to Ky., Ont. **USES:** American Indians used root tea for stomach disorders, coughs, consumption, fevers; to expel placenta; externally, for swelling, bruises, wounds, sores. Flowers poulticed for spider bites.

MISCELLANEOUS ORANGE-RED FLOWERS

COLUMBINE
Roots, seeds, whole plant

Aquilegia canadensis L.
Buttercup Family

Perennial; 1–2 ft. Leaves divided in 3's. Flowers drooping, bell-like, with 5 *spurlike appendages at top;* Apr.–July. **WHERE FOUND:** Moist, rich woods. S. Canada southward. Throughout our area. **USES:** Astringent, diuretic, anodyne. American Indians used minute amounts of crushed seeds for headaches, "love charm" (uses related?), fevers. Seeds rubbed into hair to control lice. Root chewed or weak tea for diarrhea, stomach troubles, diuretic. Root tea for uterine bleeding. **WARNING:** Potentially **poisonous.**

(Left) *Columbine* (Aquilegia canadensis). *Note the 5 spurlike appendages atop the flower.* (Above) *Butterflyweed, Pleurisy-root* (Asclepias tuberosa) *produces striking orange blossoms.*

BUTTERFLYWEED, PLEURISY-ROOT   Root
Asclepias tuberosa L.   Milkweed Family

Perennial; 1–3 ft. Stem *without milky juice*. Leaves *lance-shaped*. ⚠ Flowers showy orange (rarely yellow); May–Sept. **WHERE FOUND:** Dry roadsides, prairies. S. N.H. to Fla.; Texas, Kans., Minn. **USES:** Tea or tincture of large, tuberous root once widely used for lung inflammations (pleurisy), asthma, and bronchitis; anodyne, laxative, diuretic, expectorant. Root poultice used for bruises, swellings, rheumatism, and lameness. **WARNING:** Potentially **toxic** in large quantities.

JEWELWEED, SPOTTED TOUCH-ME-NOT   Leaves, juice
Impatiens capensis Meerb.   Touch-me-not Family

Smooth annual; 3–5 ft. Leaves oval, toothed; lower ones opposite, upper ones alternate. Flowers pendantlike, *with red spots*; June–Sept. **WHERE FOUND:** Wet, shady soil. Most of our area. **USES:** Crushed leaves are poulticed on recent Poison Ivy rash—a well-known folk remedy. Mucilaginous stem juice, harvested before flowering, also applied to rash. A 1957 study by a physician found it effective (in 2–3 days) in treating 108 of 115 patients. Some people swear by the leaf tea as a Poison Ivy rash preventative; others rub on frozen tea (in the form of ice cubes) as a remedy. Poultice a folk remedy for bruises, burns, cuts, eczema, insect bites, sores, sprains, warts, ringworm. A component in the leaves, lawsone, explains reported antihistamine and anti-inflammatory activities.

(Above) *Jewelweed* (Impatiens capensis) *is commonly used to prevent and treat Poison Ivy rash.*
(*Right*) *Hoary Puccoon* (Lithospermum canescens) *produces yellow to orange flowers.*

HOARY PUCCOON
Whole flowering plant

Lithospermum canescens (Michx.) Lehm.   Forget-me-not Family

Perennial, with *very fine, soft white hairs*; 4–18 in. Leaves alternate, lance-shaped. Flowers orange to yellow; Apr.–June. Flowers 5-petaled, in curled or flat clusters; stamens concealed in tube. **WHERE FOUND:** Dry soils, prairies. S. Ont. to Ga., Miss.; Texas to Sask. **USES:** American Indians used leaf tea (as a wash) for fevers accompanied by spasms. Wash rubbed on persons thought to be near convulsions. Some species of *Lithospermum* have been used for thyroid problems and as a contraceptive.

PLANTS WITH 3 "PARTS"

WILD GINGER
Root

Asarum canadense L.   Birthwort Family

⚠ Creeping perennial. Leaves *strongly heart-shaped*. Flowers maroon, *urn-shaped*, with 3 "petals" (actually sepals); between crotch of leaves; Apr.–May. Root strongly aromatic. **WHERE FOUND:** Rich woods. Canada to S.C., Ala., Okla. north to N.D. **USES:** American Indians highly valued root tea for indigestion, coughs, colds, heart conditions, "female ailments," throat ailments, nervous conditions, and cramps. Relieves gas, promotes sweating; expectorant; used for fevers, colds, sore throats. Contains the antitumor compound aristolochic acid. However, like so many compounds, it is reported to both cause and "cure" cancer.

(Above) *Wild Ginger* (Asarum canadense). *Flowers are at ground level.* (Right) *Pink Lady's-slipper* (Cypripedium acaule) *is common in the Northeast.*

Historically, a frontier ginger substitute. WARNING: Aristolochic acid is considered an insidious toxin, inducing mutations.

PINK LADY'S-SLIPPER   Root
Cypripedium acaule Ait.   Orchid Family

Perennial orchid; 6–15 in. Leaves 2; *basal.* Flower pink (rarely white), strongly veined; pouch with a deep furrow; May–June. WHERE FOUND: Acid woods. Nfld. to Ga.; Ala., Tenn. to Minn. Too rare to harvest. USES: Called American Valerian. Widely used in the nineteenth century as a sedative for nervous headaches, hysteria, insomnia, and "female" diseases. See Yellow Lady's-slipper (p. 108). WARNING: May cause dermatitis.

INDIAN PAINTBRUSH, PAINTED CUP   Flower
Castilleja coccinea (L.) K. Spreng.   Snapdragon Family

Annual; to 2 ft. Leaves in basal rosettes. Flowers with *3-lobed, scarlet-tipped bracts* (rarely yellow); Apr.–July. WHERE FOUND: Meadows, prairies. S. N.H. to Fla.; Texas, Okla. to s. Man. USES: American Indians used weak flower tea for rheumatism, "female diseases"; also as a secret love charm in food, and as a poison, "to destroy your enemies." WARNING: Potentially **toxic.**

Indian Paintbrush (Castilleja coccinea) flowers are typically orange-red and occasionally pale yellow.

Indian Paintbrush, Painted Cup (Castilleja coccinea) in its prairie habitat.

RED TRILLIUM, WAKEROBIN, BETHROOT

Root, whole plant

Trillium erectum L.   Lily Family

Perennial; 6–16 in. Leaves triangular-oval; 3, *in a single whorl.* Flowers dull red (to white), with 3 triangular petals and sepals; Apr.–June. **WHERE FOUND:** Rich woods. N.S. to Ga. mountains, Fla.; Tenn. to Mich., Ont. **USES:** The root was traditionally used as an aid in childbirth, hence the name "Bethroot" (a corruption of "birth root"). American Indians used root tea for menstrual disorders, to induce childbirth, to aid in labor; for "change of life" (menopause), uterine astringent, aphrodisiac (root contains steroids). Used for coughs and bowel troubles.

Red Trillium (Trillium erectum) *produces dull red flowers.*

Whole plant poulticed for tumors, inflammation, and ulcers. Historically, physicians used root tea as above, and for hemorrhages, asthma, difficult breathing, chronic lung disorders; externally, for snakebites, stings, skin irritations. A tea of equal parts of Bugleweed (*Lycopus virginicus*, p. 81) and Bethroot was once used for diabetes.

MISCELLANEOUS PLANTS WITH PINK OR RED FLOWERS

NODDING WILD ONION
Allium cernuum Roth

Bulb, whole plant
Lily Family

Perennial; 1–2 ft. Leaves soft, flat. Stem *arching* at top. Flowers pink-white; July–Aug. **WHERE FOUND:** Open woods, rocky soil. N.Y. to Ga.; west to Texas; west from Mich., Minn. to B.C. **USES:** Cherokees used slender bulbs for colds, colic, croup, and fevers. After a dose of Horsemint (*Monarda punctata*) tea, the juice of this wild onion was taken for "gravel" (kidney stones) and dropsy. Poultice of plant applied to chest for respiratory ailments. Effects probably similar to, but weaker than those of Garlic (see p. 34).

Nodding Wild Onion (Allium cernuum). Note the nodding flowerheads.

Cypress-vine (Ipomoea quamoclit) produces scarlet flowers.

CYPRESS-VINE Herb

Ipomoea quamoclit L. Morning-glory Family

Slender, smooth, weak-stemmed, twining annual. Vine to 15 ft. long. Leaves broadly oval overall, pinnately divided into many narrow, linear segments. Flowers 1 to several, scarlet, funnel-shaped, to 1¾ in. long. July–Sept. **WHERE FOUND:** Fields and waste places. Alien. Tropical America. Cultivated as an ornamental and occasionally naturalized, especially in South. **USES:** A South American folk medicine for pain-relieving and purgative effects. Externally applied to carbuncles, snakebites, sores, and piles. In India the leaves are eaten as a potherb. In Australia it has been used as a purgative and snakebite remedy. **WARNING:** Leaves contain potentially toxic hydrocyanic acid.

FEVERWORT, COFFEE PLANT Root, leaves

Triosteum perfoliatum L. Honeysuckle Family

Perennial; 2–4½ ft. Leaves opposite; *connected around stem* (perfoliate). Flowers greenish to dull purple, in leaf axils; 5 *prominent sepals*; May–July. Fruit bright red to orange. **WHERE FOUND:** Moist woods. Mass. to Ga., Ala., Okla. to Minn. **USES:** American Indians

Feverwort, Coffee Plant (Triosteum perfoliatum) *produces small red flowers in leaf axils. Photo by Doug Elliot.*

Valerian (Valeriana officinalis) *flowers vary from white to pink.*

used the root tea for irregular to profuse menses, constipation, urinary disorders; cold tea for bad colds and sore throats. Root poulticed for snakebites, sores, and felons. Leaf tea taken to induce sweating. Historically, root was used by physicians for headaches, colic, vomiting, diarrhea, and indigestion. Diuretic for chronic rheumatism. In large doses it is cathartic and emetic. Seeds used as coffee substitute.

VALERIAN   Root
Valeriana officinalis L.   Valerian Family
Perennial; 4–5 ft. Leaves strongly divided, *pinnate*; lower ones toothed. Tiny, pale pink to whitish flowers, in tight clusters; June–July. **WHERE FOUND:** Escaped, along roadsides, especially in ne. U.S. Que., Me. to N.J., Pa.; Ohio to Minn. Alien (from Europe). **USES:** A well-known herbal calmative, antispasmodic, nerve tonic; used for hypochondria, nervous headaches, irritability, mild spasmodic affections, depression, despondency, insomnia. Research has confirmed that teas, tinctures, and/or extracts of this plant are CNS-depressant, antispasmodic, and sedative when agitation is present, but also a stimulant in fatigue; antibacterial, antidiuretic, liver-protective. Valerian is a leading over-the-counter tranquilizer and sleep aid in Europe. Ten controlled clinical studies have been published on Valerian preparations; a recent study found it worked best as a sleep aid over a period of a month rather than on a single-dose basis. Approved in Germany for use as a sedative, in sleep-inducing preparations for nervous restlessness, and to aid in falling asleep. Cats are said to be attracted to the scent of the root as they are to Catnip. In eighteenth-century apothecaries, the quality of Valerian root was determined by the way in which cats reacted to it. According to folklore, the root repels rats. **RELATED SPECIES:** *Valeriana sitchensis* (not shown), native to the w. U.S., is thought to have higher levels of valepotriates, thus stronger medicinal activity.

MISCELLANEOUS PLANTS OF BOGS AND SWAMPS

WATER OR PURPLE AVENS   Root
Geum rivale L.   Rose Family
Perennial; 1–2 ft. Basal leaves much divided, leaflets toothed, *outermost one largest*; stem leaves divided into 3 *parts*. Nodding, dull reddish (rarely yellow) globular flowers, mostly in 3's; May–Aug. Fruits hooked. **WHERE FOUND:** Bogs, moist ground. Lab. to W. Va. Minn. west to B.C. **USES:** Powdered root was once used as astringent for hemorrhage, fevers, diarrhea, dysentery, indiges-

Water or Purple Avens (Geum rivale) *is often found in wooded bog habitats.*

Swamp Pink (Helonias bullata) *is too rare to harvest. Photo by Alan Detrick.*

tion, leukorrhea. **RELATED SPECIES:** In China and Japan, a tea of the whole plant of *Geum japonicum* is used as a diuretic and as an astringent to treat coughs and the spitting up of blood. The root and leaves of *G. japonicum* are used as a poultice or wash for skin diseases and boils. Possesses proven antiviral activity, probably due to tannins. Other *Geums* are used similarly.

SWAMP PINK   **Too rare for harvest**
Helonias bullata L.   Lily Family
    Perennial; 1–3 ft. Leaves spatula- or lance-shaped, in an evergreen rosette. Flowers vibrant pink, in a tight, egg-shaped cluster, borne on a tall, hollow stem; Apr.–July. **WHERE FOUND:** Swamps, bogs. Coastal plain from N.Y., N.J. to Va., n. Ga. to Pa. mountains. Rare —should not be harvested at all. **USES:** Confused in the literature with Devil's-bit (*Chamaelirium luteum*, p. 118).

PITCHER-PLANT   **Leaves, root**
Sarracenia purpurea L.   Pitcher-plant Family
    The tubular, "pitcher-shaped" leaves have evolved to capture and digest insects. The "pitchers," often containing water, have smooth surfaces, making it difficult for insects to crawl out.

Pitcher-plant (Sarracenia purpurea) *produces distinctive
pitcherlike leaves.*

Pitcher-plant (S. purpurea) *flowers range from green to reddish in
color.*

Downward-pointing hairs at the top of the pitcher further prevent
insects from escaping. Once the insect drowns, the leaves secrete
enzymes that digest soft body parts, obtaining nutrients that are
otherwise unavailable in its habitat. Unique perennial; 8–24 in.
Leaves red-veined, *pitcherlike*. Flowers dull red or greenish, nodding, with a *large flat pistil*; May–July. **WHERE FOUND:** Peat or sphag-
num bogs, savannas, and wet meadows. Nfld. to Fla., Ohio to
Minn.; scattered elsewhere. May be a threatened species; best
left undisturbed in the wild. **USES:** American Indians used root to
treat smallpox, lung and liver ailments, spitting up of blood; childbirth aid; diuretic. Dried-leaf tea used for fevers, chills, and shak-
iness. Historically, physicians considered the herb to be a stimulating tonic, diuretic, and laxative. The plant was thought to be a
preventive for smallpox—it was used in an effort to modify the
disease and shorten its duration, but it was believed to be ineffec-
tive by those who tried it. European physicians researched the
plant as a possible smallpox cure in the nineteenth century, but
without success. Medicinal merit neither proved nor disproved.

MISCELLANEOUS SHOWY FLOWERS; WET SOILS

QUEEN-OF-THE-PRAIRIE   Root
Filipendula rubra (Hill) B. L. Robins.   Rose Family
Smooth perennial; 2–8 ft. Leaves deeply divided; *segments inter-
rupted.* Flowers pink-red, *in spreading terminal clusters*;
June–Aug. **WHERE FOUND:** Moist meadows, bogs. Pa. to Ga.; west to
Iowa; north to Mich. Rare in southern extensions of range. **USES:**

Queen-of-the-prairie (Filipendula rubra). *Photo by Pamela Harper.*

Fox Indians (Wisc.) used the root for heart trouble and in "love potions." Because of its high tannin content, the root was valued as a folk medicine for its astringent properties in diarrhea, dysentery, and to stop bleeding. Like the European **Queen-of-the-Meadow** or **Meadowsweet,** *Spirea (Filipendula) ulmaria,* this plant probably contains chemical forerunners of aspirin. Salicin, the popular analgesic derived from poplars and willows, probably decomposes in the digestive tract to salicylic acid, a compound first isolated from Meadowsweet flower buds in 1839. The semisynthetic acetyl-salicylic acid (aspirin) is said to have fewer side effects than the natural compound from which it is derived. Still, nonsteroidal anti-inflammatory drugs, including aspirin, account for 10,000–20,000 deaths per year. Probably all medicines, natural and synthetic, have side effects.

SWAMP ROSE-MALLOW   Leaves, root
Hibiscus moscheutos L.   Mallow Family
   Musky-scented perennial; 5–7 ft. Lower leaves often 3-lobed; median leaves lance-shaped. Flowers to 8 in. across; white, with a *purple-red center;* June–Sept. **WHERE FOUND:** Marshes. Md. to Fla.; Ala. to Ind. **USES:** Abounds in mucilage. Leaves and roots of this plant, like those of related species and genera, used as demulcent and emollient in dysentery and lung and urinary ailments.

CARDINAL FLOWER   Root, leaves
Lobelia cardinalis L.   Bluebell Family
   Many consider this one of our most showy wildflowers. The vibrant scarlet flower spikes flag its presence along stream or pond edges in late summer. Perennial; 2–3 ft. Leaves oval to lance-

Swamp Rose-mallow (Hibiscus moscheutos) *produces pink flowers with a darker center.*

Cardinal Flower (Lobelia cardinalis) *is one of the showiest wildflowers.*

shaped, toothed. Flowers scarlet (rarely white), in brilliant spikes; July–Sept. **WHERE FOUND:** Moist soil, stream banks. N.B. to Fla.; Texas to Minn. **USES:** American Indians used root tea for stomachaches, syphilis, typhoid, worms; ingredient of "love potions." Leaf tea used for colds, croup, nosebleeds, fevers, headaches, rheumatism. It was once thought to help cramps, expel worms, and act as a nerve "tonic." Historically this plant was considered a substitute for Lobelia or Indian-tobacco (*L. inflata*, p. 207), but with weaker effects. It was seldom, if ever, used. **WARNING:** Potentially toxic; degree of toxicity unknown.

4–5 PETALS; FRUITS UPTURNED; "STORK'S BILLS"

FIREWEED
Epilobium angustifolium L.

Leaves, root
Evening-primrose Family

Perennial; 1–7 ft. Leaves lance-shaped. Flowers rose-pink; July–Sept. Fireweed has *4 rounded petals; drooping buds.* **WHERE FOUND:** This common weed is invasive in burned areas and land that has been recently cleared. It occurs throughout northern temperate regions and is used as a traditional medicine by native

(Left) *Fireweed* (Epilobium angustifolium) *is often invasive after burning.* (Above) *Stork's Bill, Alfileria* (Erodium cicutarium) *produces fernlike leaves. Photo by Curtis C. Freeman.*

peoples of North America, Europe, and Asia. Subarctic to Ga. mountains; Ind. to Iowa. **USES:** American Indians poulticed peeled root for burns, skin sores, swelling, boils, carbuncles. Leaf and root tea a folk remedy for dysentery, abdominal cramps, "summer bowel troubles." Leaf poultice used for mouth ulcers. Leaves used in Russia as "kaporie" tea (10 percent tannin). Leaf extract is antibacterial; shown to reduce inflammation.

STORK'S BILL, ALFILERIA   Leaves
Erodium cicutarium (L.) L'Her. ex Ait.   Geranium Family

Winter annual or biennial; 3–12 in. Leaves fernlike, twice pinnate, often in a basal rosette. Flowers pinkish, 5-petaled; less than ¼ in. long; Apr.–Oct.; blooms most of the year in the South. Seeds smooth, elongate, sharp—like a stork's bill. **WHERE FOUND:** Waste places. Much of our area. Alien. **USES:** Leaf tea a folk medicine used to induce sweating, allay uterine hemorrhage; diuretic. Seed poultice used for gouty tophus. Source of vitamin K. Leaves soaked in bath water for rheumatic patients.

WILD OR SPOTTED GERANIUM   Root
Geranium maculatum L.   Geranium Family

Perennial; 1–2 ft. Leaves *broad, deeply 5-parted*; segments toothed. Flowers pink to lavender (rarely white), 5-petaled; Apr.–June. Distinct "crane's bill" in center of flower enlarges into a seedpod. **WHERE FOUND:** Woods. Me. to Ga.; Ark., Kans. to Man.

Wild or Spotted Geranium (Geranium maculatum) is an early spring woodland wildflower.

Herb Robert (Geranium robertianum) has smaller flowers than the spotted geranium. Photo by Alan Detrick.

USES: Tannin-rich (10–20 percent) root is highly astringent, styptic; once used to stop bleeding, diarrhea, dysentery, relieve piles, gum diseases, kidney and stomach ailments; diuretic. Powdered root applied to canker sores. Externally used as a folk cancer remedy.

HERB ROBERT **Leaves**
Geranium robertianum L. Geranium Family
Perennial; 6–18 in. Stems often reddish, scent bitter-aromatic. Leaves pinnate, with 3–5 toothed segments; end segment *long-stalked.* Flowers pinkish, usually in pairs; *petals not notched;* May–Oct. **WHERE FOUND:** Rocky woods. Nfld. to Md., Ohio, Ill. to Man. **USES:** Leaf tea formerly used for malaria, tuberculosis, stomach and intestinal ailments, jaundice, kidney infections; to stop bleeding; gargled for sore throats. Fresh herb extract active against vesicular stomatitis virus. Ethanolic extracts are antibacterial. Externally, wash or poultice used to relieve pain of swollen breasts; folk cancer remedy; applied externally to fistulas, tumors, and ulcers. Fresh leaves chewed for stomatitis.

CORN-COCKLE
Seeds

Agrostemma githago L.
Pink Family

Silky annual or biennial; 1–3 ft. Leaves lance-shaped. Petals deep pink, veined. Calyx inflated; *strongly 10-ribbed*. Hairy, linear sepals extend beyond petals. Flowers June–Sept. **WHERE FOUND:** Noxious weed of grain fields, waste places. Throughout our area. Alien. **USES:** Minute amounts of powdered seeds once taken in honey as a diuretic, expectorant, vermifuge (dewormer); used for jaundice, dropsy, gastritis. European folk use for cancers, warts, hard swellings in uterus. **WARNING:** Seeds toxic, especially when broken; dangerous saponins are concentrated in seed embryo.

BOUNCING BET, SOAPWORT
Leaves, roots

Saponaria officinalis L.
Pink Family

Stem *thick-jointed*; smoothish perennial; 1–2 ft. Leaves opposite, oval to lance-shaped. Flowers white or rose, 1 in. across; July–Sept. Petals *reflexed, notched.* **WHERE FOUND:** Throughout our area. Alien. **USES:** Crushed leaves and roots make lather when mixed with water. American Indians poulticed leaves for spleen pain, boils. In European tradition, plant tea is used as a diuretic, laxative, expectorant, poulticed on acne, boils, eczema, psoriasis, Poison Ivy rash. Root tea used as above; also for lung disease, asthma, gall disease, and jaundice. A ribosome-activating protein

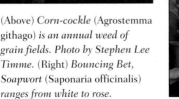

(Above) *Corn-cockle* (Agrostemma githago) *is an annual weed of grain fields. Photo by Stephen Lee Timme.* (Right) *Bouncing Bet, Soapwort* (Saponaria officinalis) *ranges from white to rose.*

(Above) *Fire Pink* (Silene virginica) *has notched petals.* (Right) *Pink-root* (Spigelia marilandica) *is easily recognized by its bicolored flowers, which are cream-colored within the throat.*

called saporin 6 inhibits the growth of breast cancer cells in laboratory experiments. Another component, quillaiac acid, provides diuretic activity. Considered expectorant (by irritating gastric mucosa). Root approved in Germany to treat catarrhs of the upper respiratory tract. **WARNING:** Contains saponins. Large doses may cause poisoning (toxic to cells). Causes rare stomach irritation in small doses (1.5 g per day).

FIRE PINK   Root
Silene virginica L.   Pink Family

Perennial; 8–20 in. Leaves *opposite,* in 2–6 pairs on stems. Flowers brilliant scarlet; 5 petals, *notched at tips;* Apr.–June. **WHERE FOUND:** Rocky woods. S. Ont. to Ga. Ark., Okla. to Minn. **USES:** Unconfirmed historical reports speak of worm-expellent properties. **WARNING:** Reports state American Indians considered the plant **poisonous.** It might have been confused with *Spigelia* (see below).

PINK-ROOT   Root
Spigelia marilandica (L.) L.   Logania Family

Perennial; 12–24 in. Leaves opposite, united by stipules; ovate to lance-shaped. Flowers *scarlet,* 5-lobed flaring trumpets, with a *cream-yellow interior;* May–June. **WHERE FOUND:** Rich woods, openings. Md. to Fla.; Texas. e. Okla. to Mo., Ind. **USES:** American Indians used root tea as a worm expellent. This plant was also once used by physicians for worms, especially in children. In the nine-teenth century, it was heavily harvested and became threatened. **WARNING:** Side effects include increased heart action, vertigo, convulsions, and possibly death.

FLOWERS WITH 5 SHOWY PETALS; MALLOWS

MARSHMALLOW
Althaea officinalis L.

Leaves, root
Mallow Family

Erect, branched, perennial; 2–5 ft. tall. Leaves velvety, mostly 3-lobed, margins serrated. Flowers in clusters from upper leaf axils, typically pale pink, to 1½ in. across; June–Sept. **WHERE FOUND:** Moist soils, naturalized in salt marshes along Mid-Atlantic States (Mass. to Va.). Alien from Europe. **USES:** Marshmallow roots and leaves traditionally used in tea for sore throat and expectorant in bronchitis. Externally poulticed for bruises, sprains, aching muscles, and inflammations. Root (up to 30 percent) and leaves (up to 16 percent) high in mucilagin, responsible for demulcent or soothing effect to irritated mucous membranes and skin. Has im-

Marshmallow (Althaea officinalis).

Hollyhock (Alcea rosea) is used similarly to the Marshmallow (Althaea officinalis), though its roots are considered an adulterant to Marshmallow root.

muno-stimulating activity. The German health authorities allow use of the leaf and root preparations to relieve local irritation (such as digestive-tract inflammatory conditions) and to soothe mucous membrane irritation, such as a sore throat accompanied by dry cough. **WARNING:** Root is high in sugar compounds; diabetics should avoid it. Like other mucilagin-containing plants, when taken internally, Marshmallow may hamper absorption of other drugs. **RELATED SPECIES:** The common Hollyhock, *Alcea rosea* L., used similarly, though roots are higher in tannins. In Europe, considered an adulterant to Marshmallow root.

PURPLE POPPY-MALLOW   Root
Callirhoe involucrata (Torr. & Gray) Gray   Mallow Family

Creeping herb. Leaves palmate, divided into 5–7 parts with pointed toothed lobes (especially lower leaves). Flowers *poppy-like,* reddish purple; May–Aug. **WHERE FOUND:** Prairies. S. Mo. to Texas; N.D. west to Utah, Wyo. **USES:** The Teton Dakotas crushed the dried root, burned it, and inhaled the smoke to treat head colds. Aching limbs were exposed to the smoke to reduce pain. Root boiled, then tea drunk for pains. One Dakota name for the plant means "smoke-treatment medicine."

COMMON MALLOW, CHEESES   Leaves, root
Malva neglecta Wallr.   Mallow Family

Deep-rooted herb; to 1 ft. Stems trailing. Leaves rounded, toothed; *slightly 5- to 7-lobed.* Flowers pale rose-lavender to

(Left) *Purple Poppy-mallow* (Callirhoe involucrata) *has poppylike flowers.* (Above) *Common mallow* (Malva neglecta) *is a common weed.*

whitish, in axils; Apr.–Oct. Petals *notched* (heart-shaped) on ends; *pistils smoothish, not veined.* The common name "Cheeses" is derived from the similarity of the shape of the flat, rounded fruits to a "round" of cheese. **WHERE FOUND:** Yards. Throughout our area. Alien. **USES:** Leaves edible, highly nutritious. Used as a soup base in China. As with Okra, also of the Mallow family, the mucilaginous properties tend to thicken soup. Leaf or root tea of this mallow soothing to irritated membranes, especially of digestive system. Tea also used for angina, coughs, bronchitis, stomachaches; anti-inflammatory, mildly astringent. Poulticed on wounds and tumors. Root extracts show activity against tuberculosis. The leaves of Common Mallow and High Mallow are approved in Germany for treatment of irritations of the mouth and throat associated with irritating, dry cough.

HIGH MALLOW
Malva sylvestris L.

Leaves, flowers, root
Mallow Family

Erect, hairy biennial; 8–36 in. Leaves long-stalked; rounded, with 5–7 *distinct lobes.* Flowers rose-purple, with darker veins; *pistils wrinkle-veined.* Flowers May–July. **WHERE FOUND:** Waste places. Frequently cultivated, then escaped, but not considered naturalized. Scattered over much of our area. Alien. **USES:** Leaves edible. Leaf or root tea soothing to irritated membranes, especially of digestive system; also used for coughs, bronchitis, stomachaches; anti-inflammatory, mildly astringent. In China the leaves and flowers have been used as an expectorant, a gargle for sore throats, and a mouthwash. Diuretic properties are also attributed to the plant, and it is said to be good for the stomach and spleen. Use of flowers (and leaves) approved in Germany to treat irritation of the mouth and throat, with associated dry cough. Other *Malva* species are used similarly.

High Mallow (Malva sylvestris) *produces striped flowers.*

SPREADING DOGBANE
Root

Apocynum androsaemifolium L.   Dogbane Family

Shrublike; 1–4 ft. *Milky latex within.* Leaves oval, opposite; smooth above. Flowers are drooping pink bells, *rose-striped within*; in leaf axils *and* terminal; June–July. **WHERE FOUND:** Scattered throughout our area. Fields, roadsides. Absent from Kans., south of N.C. highlands. **USES:** American Indians used root of this plant for many ailments. Induces sweating and vomiting; laxative. Used in headaches with sluggish bowels, liver disease, indigestion, rheumatism, and syphilis. **WARNING: Poisonous.** Cymarin, a cardioactive glycoside, poisons cattle. Nonetheless, the plant has shown antitumor activity. **RELATED SPECIES:** Indian Hemp (*A. cannabinum*), a close relative, is also used medicinally but is also considered poisonous.

TWINFLOWER
Whole plant

Linnaea borealis L.   Honeysuckle Family

Delicate creeper; 3–5 in. Leaves *paired*. Flowers fragrant, *nodding bells, in pairs* on a slender stalk; June–July. **WHERE FOUND:** Cold,

The flower of Spreading Dogbane (Apocynum androsaemifolium) has rose stripes within.

Twinflower (Linnaea borealis) with "twin" drooping flowers. Photo by Doug Elliott.

moist woods. Canada to L.I.; W. Va. mountains, Ohio to n. Ind. Locally too rare for harvest. **USES:** Algonquins used plant tea as a tonic for pregnancy and in difficult or painful menstruation; also for children's cramps, fevers. Historical use only.

HEART-LEAVED FOUR O'CLOCK
Root, leaves

Mirabilis nyctaginea (Michx.) MacM.   Four O'Clock Family

Perennial; 1–5 ft. Leaves opposite, heart-shaped. Pink to purple flowers *atop a 5-lobed, green, veiny cup or bracts*; June–Oct. **WHERE FOUND:** Prairies, rich soil. Wisc. to Ala.; Texas to Mont.; escaped and weedy eastward. **USES:** American Indians used root tea for burns, fevers, and to expel worms; externally, root poulticed for sprains, burns, sores, and swellings. Leaf (or root) tea used for bladder ailments. **WARNING:** Considered **poisonous.**

TOBACCO
Leaves

Nicotiana tabacum L.   Nightshade Family

Acrid, rank, clammy-hairy, large annual; 3–9 ft. Leaves lance-shaped to oval. Funnel-shaped flowers, to 3 in. long; greenish to pink, 5-parted; Aug.–Sept. **WHERE FOUND:** Escaped from recent culti-

Heart-leaved Four O'clock (Mirabilis nyctaginea). Note its heart-shaped leaves. Photo by Stephen Lee Timme.

Tobacco (Nicotiana tabacum) is cultivated in the Southeast.

vation. Alien (from tropical America). **USES:** Well-known addictive narcotic. American Indians employed it in rituals; leaf tea diuretic, emetic, strongly laxative, worm expellent, anodyne; used for cramps, sharp pains, toothaches, dizziness, dropsy, colic. Poulticed for boils, snakebites, insect stings. **WARNING:** Hazards of Tobacco use are well known. Still, the toxic insecticidal alkaloid, nicotine, is offered in pills and in skin patches to help curb the nicotine habit.

FLOWERS IN DOMED CLUSTERS; MILKWEEDS

SWAMP MILKWEED **Root**
Asclepias incarnata L. Milkweed Family
Strongly branched, smooth perennial; 2–4 ft. Leaves numerous, *opposite; narrowly lance-shaped* or oblanceolate (wider at base), veins ascending; soft-hairy, especially beneath; when broken, leaves exude small amounts of milky latex. Flower clusters in branched, flat-topped groupings (corymb). Flowers reddish to deep rose, in small umbels; June–Sept. **WHERE FOUND:** Wet areas, marshes, stream banks, and moist meadows. Scattered throughout our area. **USES:** Root tea used in "tonic" bath for weak patients. Root tea diuretic, carminative, strongly laxative; induces vomiting. American colonists used it for asthma, rheumatism, syphilis, worms, and as a heart tonic. **WARNING:** Potentially **toxic.**

Swamp Milkweed (Asclepias incarnata) *is found near wet habitats.*

Four-leaved Milkweed (Asclepias quadrifolia) *is usually white to pink. Photo by Stephen Lee Timme.*

FOUR-LEAVED MILKWEED · Root
Asclepias quadrifolia Jacq. · Milkweed Family

Perennial; stems solitary, 1–2¼ ft. Leaves ovate-elliptical; upper- and lowermost ones paired. Largest middle pair of leaves appears to be in a *whorl of 4*. Flowers pale pink to lavender, whitish, or greenish; in sparse umbels. May–July. **WHERE FOUND:** Open, deciduous woods and forest margins. N.H. to S.C., Ala. Ark., Kans. to Minn. **USES:** Cherokees used root tea as laxative, diuretic for "gravel" (kidney stones), dropsy. Leaves have been rubbed on warts to remove them. **WARNING:** Potentially **toxic.**

COMMON MILKWEED · Root, latex
Asclepias syriaca L. · Milkweed Family

Milky-juiced, *downy* perennial; 2–4 ft. Stems usually solitary. Leaves opposite, large, widely elliptical; to 8 in. long. Flowers pink-purple (variable), in globe-shaped (often drooping) clusters from leaf axils; June–Aug. Pods *warty*. **WHERE FOUND:** Fields, roadsides. S. Canada to Ga., Ala.; Okla., Kans. to N.D. The most common milkweed in the Northeast. **USES:** American Indians used root tea as a laxative and as a diuretic for "gravel" (kidney stones) and dropsy; applied milky latex to warts, moles, ringworm. Root tea expectorant, diuretic; induces sweating. Used by early American physicians for asthma, rheumatism. Latex is chewed as gum, a dangerous practice—see warning below. Silky seed tassels used in pillows, feather beds. Folk cancer remedy. One Mohawk antifertility concoction contained Milkweed and Jack-in-the-Pulpit (p. 228), both considered dangerous and contraceptive. **WARNING:** Potentially **toxic**—contains cardioactive compounds.

Common Milkweed (Asclepias syriaca) *is our most often seen milkweed.*

LOPSEED

Roots

Phryma leptostachya L.

Lopseed Family

Slender-branched perennial; 1–3 ft. Stems swollen for a short distance (1 in. or less) above each pair of leaves. Leaves opposite, oval, toothed. Leafstalks on middle leaf pairs longer than those on upper or lower leaves. Flowers small, purplish, snapdragon-like; in terminal spikes; July–Sept. **WHERE FOUND:** Woods, thickets. Throughout our area. **USES:** American Indians gargled root tea (or chewed root) for sore throats; drank root tea for rheumatism. Also found in e. Asia, where it is used for fevers, ulcers, ringworm, scabies, and insect bites. Root poulticed for boils, carbuncles, sores, and cancers. Also considered insecticidal.

EUROPEAN VERVAIN

Root, leaves

Verbena officinalis L.

Verbena Family

 Mostly smooth, loosely branched annual; 1–3 ft. Leaves paired, with deeply cut lobes and sharp teeth. Flowers tiny, purple to pinkish; in slender spikes; June–Oct. **WHERE FOUND:** Waste places. Escaped from gardens. Locally established. Alien. **USES:** In Europe,

Lopseed (Phryma leptostachya).
Photo by Martin Wall.

European Vervain (Verbena officinalis) *produces tiny flowers. Locally weedy.*

Purple or Spike Loosestrife (Lythrum salicaria). Despite its beauty, it is a rampant invasive alien.

plant tea used for obstructions of liver and spleen, headaches, and nervous disorders. Leaves considered diuretic, milk-inducing; extracts analgesic. Used experimentally in China to control malaria symptoms, kill blood flukes (parasites) and germs, stop pain and inflammation. Chinese studies suggest that herbage of this plant is synergistic with the prostaglandin E2. Russian studies show adaptogenic activity of the alcoholic extract or tincture. Said to be milder than Blue Vervain (*Verbena hastata*, p. 194) and other species. Animal studies have demonstrated anti-inflammatory, cough-suppressing, and milk-stimulating activity. **WARNING:** Plant suspected of poisoning cattle in Australia.

PURPLE OR SPIKE LOOSESTRIFE **Flowering plant**
Lythrum salicaria L. Loosestrife Family
  Downy perennial; 2–4 ft. Leaves whorled or opposite; *rounded or heart-shaped at base.* Purple-pink, *6-petaled* flowers, in spikes; June–Sept. **WHERE FOUND:** Invasive in swampy meadows, often forming large stands and blanketing moist meadows in a sea of color. New England to N.C.; Mo. to Minn. Alien. **USES:** Tea made from whole flowering plant, fresh or dried, is a European folk remedy (demulcent, astringent) for diarrhea, dysentery; used as a gargle for sore throats, a douche for leukorrhea, and a cleansing wash for wounds. Experimentally, plant extracts stop bleeding, kill some bacteria.

PEA-LIKE FLOWERS

GROUNDNUT **Root**
Apios americana Medik. Pea Family
  Twining vine. Leaves with 5–7 oval, sharp-pointed leaflets. *Sweetly fragrant maroon or purple-brown* flowers, in crowded

(Above) *Groundnut* (Apios americana). *Photo by Doug Elliot.*
(Right) *Naked-flowered Tick-trefoil* (Desmodium nudiflorum) *goes unnoticed until its seedpods stick to clothing. Photo by Stephen Lee Timme.*

clusters in leaf axils; July–Sept. **WHERE FOUND:** Rich, moist thickets. N.B. to Fla.; west to Texas, north to Minn., N.D. **USES:** Delicious tubers used as food by Pilgrims during first bleak winters. Favorite Indian food. With 3 times the protein of potatoes, each Groundnut plant, under cultivation, may produce 5 pounds of tubers. The plant has been suggested as a nitrogen-fixing edible ornamental for permaculturists. John Josselyn (1672) suggested a poultice of Groundnut root be used for cancerous conditions known as "proud flesh." Today we learn that, like many legumes, Groundnut contains estrogenic isoflavones (phytoestrogens) with anticancer activity, such as genistein, which can prevent the formation of blood vessels that nourish new tumors.

NAKED-FLOWERED TICK-TREFOIL   **Root**
Desmodium nudiflorum (L.) DC.   Pea Family
Perennial; 18–36 in. Leaves in whorls; 3 oval leaflets, the middle one on a longer stalk. *Leafstalk separate from flower stalk.* Pinkish red flowers on a *leafless stalk;* July–Aug. Pods jointed; "beggar's ticks" adhere to clothes. **WHERE FOUND:** Woods. Me. to Fla.; Texas to Minn. **USES:** Cherokees chewed the root for inflammation of the mouth, sore, bleeding gums, and periodontal diseases with pus discharge. Root tea was used as a wash for cramps.

RED CLOVER

Flowering tops

Trifolium pratense L.

Pea Family

⚠ Familiar biennial or short-lived perennial; to 18 in. Leaves divided into 3 oval leaflets; leaflets fine-toothed, with *prominent "V" marks*. Flowers pink to red, in rounded heads; May–Sept. **WHERE FOUND:** Fields, roadsides. Throughout our area. A weed. **USES:** Historically, flower tea has been used as an antispasmodic, expectorant, mild sedative, "blood purifier"; for asthma, bronchitis, spasmodic coughs; externally, a wash has been used as a folk cancer remedy, including the famous Hoxsey treatment, and for athlete's foot, sores, burns, and ulcers. Flowers formerly smoked in antiasthma cigarettes. Science has not confirmed traditional uses. However, Red Clover contains many biologically active compounds, including phytoestrogenic isoflavones, such as genistein, diadzen, formononetin, and biochanin A, among others. Phytoestrogens activate estrogen receptors in mammals. Epidemiological studies provide evidence that certain dietary components can have a significant effect on the incidence and location of cancers in humans. A laboratory study found that biochanin A inhibits the activation of cancer. Standardized extracts of Red Clover, produced in Australia, are now sold in the U.S. One tablet contains 40 mg of phytoestrogens, 8 times the amount consumed in the typical American diet. **WARNING:** Fall or late-cut hay in large doses can cause frothing, diarrhea, dermatitis, and decreased milk production in cattle. Diseased clover, externally showing no symptoms, may contain the indolizidine alkaloid slaframine, which is much more poisonous than castanospermine, now being studied for anti-AIDS and antidiabetic activity.

Red Clover (Trifolium pratense) *is a familiar weed.*

(Left) *Pennsylvania Smartweed* (Polygonum pensylvanicum) *is a highly variable annual. Photo by Stephen Lee Timme.* (Above) *Lady's Thumb, Heart's Ease* (P. persicaria) *has a purplish triangular blotch in the middle of leaf. Photo by Alan Detrick.*

PENNSYLVANIA SMARTWEED
Polygonum pensylvanicum L.

Leaves, tops
Buckwheat Family

Erect or sprawling annual; 1–5 ft. Leaves lance-shaped; sheaths *not fringed* (see Lady's Thumb, below). Flowers rose-pink (or white); in crowded, elongate clusters, July–Nov. Flower stalks often have *minute glandular hairs* near top. Highly variable. **WHERE FOUND:** Waste ground. Throughout our area. **USES:** American Indians used tea made from whole plant for diarrhea; poulticed leaves for piles. Bitter leaf tea used to stop bleeding from mouth. Tops were used in tea for epilepsy. **WARNING:** Fresh juice is acrid; may cause irritation.

LADY'S THUMB, HEART'S EASE
Polygonum persicaria L.

Leaves
Buckwheat Family

Reddish-stemmed, sprawling perennial; 6–24 in. Leaves lance-shaped, often with a purplish triangular blotch in the middle of leaf; papery sheath at leaf nodes has *fringes*. Pinkish flowers in elongate clusters; June–Oct. **WHERE FOUND:** Waste places. Throughout our area. Alien (Europe). **USES:** American Indians adopted the leaf tea for heart troubles, stomachaches, and as a diuretic for "gravel" (kidney stones). The whole herb was poulticed for pain,

Salad Burnet (Sanguisorba sp.). Asian, North American, and European species have highly astringent leaves.

rubbed on Poison Ivy rash, and rubbed on horses' backs to keep flies away. Leaf tea used as a foot soak for rheumatic pains of the legs and feet. In European tradition, leaf tea was used for inflammation, stomachaches, and sore throats. **WARNING:** Fresh juice may cause irritation. **RELATED SPECIES:** Other *Polygonum* species in our range, many naturalized from Europe, have been used similarly.

SALAD BURNET
Sanguisorba officinalis L.

Leaves, root
Rose Family

Perennial; 1–5 ft. Leaves compound; leaflets 7–15, *toothed*. Tiny, purplish red flowers, in oval or thickly rounded heads; May–Oct. **WHERE FOUND:** Me. to Minn. Escaped elsewhere. Alien. Mostly cultivated in herb gardens. **USES:** In Europe, leaf tea was used for fevers and as a styptic. American soldiers drank tea before battles in the Revolutionary War to prevent bleeding if wounded. Root tea is astringent, allays menstrual bleeding. In China the root tea is used to stop bleeding, "cool" blood; taken for piles, uterine bleeding, dysentery; externally for sores, swelling, burns. Experimentally, the plant is antibacterial (in China); stops bleeding and vomiting. Powdered root used clinically for second- and third-degree burns. **WARNING:** Contains tannins, contraindicated for burns in Western medicine, though many tannin-containing herbs, rightly or wrongly, have been recommended for burns in numerous folk traditions.

SQUARE-STEMMED PLANTS WITH LIPPED FLOWERS

AMERICAN DITTANY
Cunila origanoides (L.) Britton

Leaves
Mint Family

Wiry-stemmed, branched perennial; 1–2 ft. Leaves oval, to 1 in.; toothed, *oregano-scented*. Small, violet to white flowers, in clus-

(Above, Right) *American Dittany*
(Cunila origanoides) *blooms in au-*
tumn. It produces "frost flowers"
from root during the first freezes.

ters. July–Oct. 2 *stamens; hairy throat.* **WHERE FOUND:** Dry woods,
thickets. Se. N.Y. to Fla.; Texas, Okla., Mo., Ill. **USES:** Leaf tea is a
folk remedy for colds, fevers, headaches, snakebites; thought to
induce perspiration and menstruation.

MOTHERWORT
Leonurus cardiaca L.

Leaves

Mint Family

Square-stemmed perennial; 3–5 ft. Leaves 3-lobed; lobes
toothed. Pinkish flowers in whorls in axils; May–Aug. *Upper lip*
furry. **WHERE FOUND:** Much of our area. Alien. A weed. **USES:** Traditionally, leaf tea is used to promote menstruation, regulate menses,
aid in childbirth (hence the common name); also used for asthma
and heart palpitations. Said to be sedative; used for insomnia,
neuralgia, sciatica, spasms, fevers, and stomachaches. Scientists
have found extracts to have antispasmodic, hypotensive, sedative,
cardiotonic, diuretic, antioxidant, immuno-stimulating, and cancer-preventative activity. Extracts approved in Germany for nervous heart conditions and in the supportive treatment of hyperthyroidism. Experimentally, leonurine, a leaf constituent, is a
uterine tonic. **WARNING:** Rare cases of contact dermatitis reported.
Avoid use during pregnancy and lactation. **RELATED SPECIES:** Chinese
species, well documented with laboratory and clinical reports,
have been used similarly.

(Left) *Motherwort* (Leonurus cardiaca) *is often found around farmyards.* (Above) *Bee-balm, Oswego Tea* (Monarda didyma) *produces bright red flowers.*

BEE-BALM, OSWEGO TEA
Leaves

Monarda didyma L.
Mint Family

Perennial; 2–5 ft. Leaves paired. Flowers red, tubular, in crowded heads; June–Sept. Bracts often red or purplish. **WHERE FOUND:** Thickets, stream banks. N.Y. to Ga.; Tenn. to Mich. **USES:** American Indians used leaf tea for colic, gas, colds, fevers, stomachaches, nosebleeds, insomnia, heart trouble, measles, and to induce sweating. Believed to reduce muscle spasms, relieve digestive gas, and act as a diuretic. Poultice used for headaches. Historically, physicians used leaf to expel worms and gas.

Germander, Wood Sage, Wild Basil (Teucrium canadense), *a common adulterant to Skullcap. Sold as "pink skullcap."*

GERMANDER, WOOD SAGE, WILD BASIL

Leaves

Teucrium canadense L.   Mint Family

 Variable perennial; 1–3 ft. Leaves oval to lance-shaped, toothed, white-hairy beneath. Flowers purple, pink, or whitish; June–Sept. Calyx felty, *stamens protrude from cleft of upper lip.* **WHERE FOUND:** Woods, thickets. Throughout our area. **USES:** Leaf tea traditionally used to induce menstruation, urination, and sweating. Used like the bugleweeds or water horehounds *(Lycopus)* for lung ailments, worms, piles; externally, as a gargle and antiseptic dressing. Sold as "pink scullcap," it is a widespread adulterant to commercial supplies of true Skullcap *(Scutellaria lateriflora).* **WARNING:** Some species of *Teucrium* have proven to be highly toxic to the liver (resulting in fatalities). This species has not been studied.

COMPOSITES WITH FLAT-TOPPED FLOWER CLUSTERS

DAISY FLEABANE

Whole plant

Erigeron philadelphicus L.   Composite Family

Slender, hairy perennial; 1–3 ft. Basal leaves oblong; stem leaves smaller, *clasping at base.* Flowers less than 1 in. across., pinkish to magenta, with *numerous slender rays* and a yellow disk. Apr.–July. **WHERE FOUND:** Thickets. Most of our area. **USES:** Plant tea is used as a diuretic, astringent; a folk remedy for diarrhea, "gravel" (kidney stones), diabetes, painful urination; also used to stop hemorrhages of stomach, bowels, bladder, kidneys, and nose. Once used for fevers, bronchitis, tumors, piles, and coughs. **WARNING:** May cause contact dermatitis.

SPOTTED JOE-PYE-WEED

Leaves, root

Eupatorium maculatum L.   Composite Family

Perennial; 2–6 ft. Stem *purple or purple-spotted.* Leaves lance-shaped, in *whorls* of 4–5. Purple flowers in flat-topped clusters;

Daisy Fleabane (Erigeron philadelphicus) *produces white- to pink-violet-tinted ray flowers. Photo by Stephen Lee Timme.*

Spotted Joe-pye-weed (Eupatorium maculatum) *has spotted stems.*

Sweet Joe-pye-weed (Eupatorium purpureum) *has short leafstalks.*

July–Sept. **WHERE FOUND:** Wet meadows. N.S. to mountains of N.C.; Neb. to B.C. **USES:** American Indians used tea of whole herb as a diuretic for dropsy, painful urination, gout, kidney infections, rheumatism. Root tea once used for fevers, colds, chills, sore womb after childbirth, diarrhea, liver and kidney ailments; a wash for rheumatism. Its name is derived from "Joe Pye," a nineteenth-century Caucasian "Indian theme promoter" who used the root to induce sweating in typhus fever.

SWEET JOE-PYE-WEED, GRAVEL ROOT   **Leaves, root**
Eupatorium purpureum L.   Composite Family
Similar to *E. maculatum* (above). Perennial; to 12 ft. tall; stems green, purple at leaf nodes. Pale pink-purple flowers, in a somewhat rounded cluster; July–Sept. **WHERE FOUND:** Thickets. N.H. to Fla.; Ark., Okla., w. Neb. to Minn. **USES:** Leaf and root tea traditionally used to eliminate stones in urinary tract and to treat urinary incontinence in children, and dropsy; also for gout, rheumatism, impotence, uterine prolapse, asthma, chronic coughs. Homeopathically used for gallbladder and urinary ailments. **REMARKS:** Also known as Queen-of-the-Meadow, a name that is shared with a European species (*Spiraea ulmaria*—see p. 163).

RELATED SPECIES: German researchers report immunologically active polysaccharides from other *Eupatorium* species, both American and European.

THISTLE-LIKE, BRISTLY FLOWERS; BUR-DOCKS AND THISTLES

GREAT BURDOCK
Arctium lappa L.

Leaves, root, seeds
Composite Family

Biennial; 2–9 ft. Lower leaves *large, rhubarb-like*. Stalk solid, celerylike—*grooved* above. Reddish purple, thistle-like flowers, 1–1½ in. across; *long-stalked,* in flat-topped clusters; July–Oct. Seedpods (familiar "burs") stick to clothing. **WHERE FOUND:** Waste places. Canada south to Pa., N.C.; west to Ill., Mich. Local elsewhere. Alien. A widespread Eurasian weed used in traditional medicine in China, Japan, Europe, and N. America. **USES:** Traditionally, root tea (2 ounces dried root in 1 quart of water) used as a "blood purifier"; diuretic; stimulates bile secretion, digestion, and sweating; also used for gout, liver and kidney ailments, rheumatism, gonorrhea. Root is high in inulin (up to 50 percent); traditionally used for diabetes. Bitter compounds in roots, particularly artipicrin, are antibacterial; also explains use as digestive stimulant. In China, a tea of leafy branches is used for vertigo and rheumatism, and tea mixed with brown sugar is used for measles. Externally, used as a wash for hives, eczema, and other skin eruptions. Juice of fresh plant has been shown to protect against chromosome aberrations. Both flowers and leaves have antibacterial activity. Seeds diuretic; thought to be antiseptic. Seeds used for abscesses, sore throats, insect bites and snakebites, flu, constipa-

Burdock's leaves are large in the first year of growth.

Great Burdock (Arctium lappa) *flowers grow in a flat-topped cluster.*

(Above) *The hooked barbs on the fruit cling to clothing.* (Right) *The flowerheads of Common Burdock (Arctium minus) are arranged in a loose raceme.*

tion; once used to treat scarlet fever, smallpox, and scrofula. Crushed seeds poulticed on bruises. Leaves poulticed on burns, ulcers, sores. Japanese studies suggest that roots contain compounds that may curb mutations (and hence cancer?). **WARNING:** Leaf hairs may irritate skin. Do not confuse leaves with the toxic leaves of Rhubarb.

Canada Thistle (Cirsium arvense) is a rampant invasive weed (from Europe, not Canada).

COMMON BURDOCK
Root, seeds, leaves

Arctium minus Bernh.   Composite Family

Smaller than *A. lappa* (see above); 2–5 ft. Leaf stems *hollow, not furrowed.* Flowers smaller—to ¾ in. across, *without stalks or short-stalked;* July–Oct. **WHERE FOUND:** Waste places. Most of our area. Alien. **USES:** Same as for *A. lappa.* Used extensively by American Indians.

CANADA THISTLE
Leaves, root

Cirsium arvense (L.) Scop.   Composite Family

Perennial; 1–5 ft., with vigorous taproots; usually forms colonies. Stems smooth, leafy near top. Leaves oblong to lance-shaped, *margins very prickly.* Flowers small, pink to violet (rarely white), to 3–4 in. across; July–Sept. *Bracts strongly appressed.* **WHERE FOUND:** Fields, pastures, roadsides. Throughout our area. Serious alien weed from Europe. **USES:** Leaf tea "tonic" and diuretic. Once used for tuberculosis; externally, for skin eruptions, skin ulcers, and Poison Ivy rash. Root tea used for dysentery, diarrhea. American Indians used root tea as a bowel tonic and dewormer.

CRESTED DWARF IRIS

Root

Iris cristata Ait.

Iris Family

This diminutive iris of southern woods has yellow crests on the downward-curved blue sepals, hence the species name *cristata*. Spreading perennial; 4–8 in. Leaves *short*, lance-shaped; *sheathed* on stem. Blue (rarely white) flowers with yellow crests on down-curved sepals; Apr.–May. **WHERE FOUND:** Wet woods. Md. to N.C.; Miss., Ark., e. Okla. to Ind. **USES:** American Indians used root ointment (in animal fats or waxes) on cancerous ulcers. Root tea used for hepatitis. **WARNING:** Same as for Blue Flag.

BLUE FLAG

Root

Iris versicolor L.

Iris Family

Perennial; 1–2 ft. Leaves swordlike, similar to those of garden irises. Flowers violet-blue, sepals violet at outer edge; veins prominent; *sheaths papery.* Flowers May–July. **WHERE FOUND:** Wet meadows, moist soil. Lab. to Va.; Ohio, Wisc. to Minn., Man. **USES:** American Indians poulticed root on swellings, sores, bruises, rheumatism, analgesic agent; internally root tea used as strong

Crested Dwarf Iris (Iris cristata), *seen here growing among horsetail stems.*

Blue Flag (Iris versicolor) *is found near water.*

laxative, emetic, and to stimulate bile flow. Physicians formerly used root of this plant in small, frequent doses to "cleanse" blood and stimulate the bowels, kidneys, and liver. Homeopathically used for migraines and as a cathartic, diuretic, and emetic. Extracts reduced intake of food in rats. **WARNING:** Considered poisonous. Fresh root contains furfural, which may nauseate and irritate the gastrointestinal tract and eyes. Can cause headaches and inflammation of the eyes and throat. Iridin, another component, is toxic to humans and livestock. Avoid use during pregnancy and lactation.

SPIDERWORT

Leaves, root, whole plant

Tradescantia virginiana L. Spiderwort Family

Perennial; 1–3 ft. Leaves grass- or irislike; sheathing stem. Purple flowers in a terminal cluster; Apr.–June. 3 petals; many stamens, with *prominent, large-celled hairs.* (Individual stamen hair cells are so large they may be seen with naked eye.) **WHERE FOUND:** Me. to W. Va., Ky., Ga., Miss.; Ark. to Minn. **USES:** Root tea of this and other Spiderwort species used by American Indians for "female," kidney, and stomach ailments, and as a laxative. Smashed plant (leaf poultice) applied to insect bites, stings, and cancers.

ASIATIC DAYFLOWER

Leaves

Commelina communis L. Spiderwort Family

Sprawling perennial; 1–3 ft. Oval leaves, clasping stem. Flowers with 2 prominent, earlike blue petals and a smaller *whitish* petal

(Left) *Ohio Spiderwort* (Tradescantia ohiensis). (Above) *Dayflower* (Commelina erecta). *All dayflower species are used similarly.*

beneath; May–Oct. Each Dayflower blooms for only one day, hence the common name. **WHERE FOUND:** Waste places throughout our area. Troublesome weed. Alien (Asia). **USES:** In China, leaf tea gargled for sore throats; used for cooling, detoxifying, and diuretic properties in flu, acute tonsillitis, urinary infections, dysentery, and acute intestinal enteritis. Other *commelina* species used similarly.

MISCELLANEOUS NONWOODY VINES WITH VIOLET TO BLUE FLOWERS

PASSION-FLOWER, MAYPOP
Whole plant

Passiflora incarnata L.
Passion-flower Family

Climbing vine; to 30 ft. Tendrils *springlike*. Leaves *cleft* with 2–3 slightly toothed lobes. Flowers large, showy, unique, whitish to purplish, with *numerous threads* radiating from center. Flowers July–Oct. Fruits fleshy, egg-shaped; Aug.–Nov. **WHERE FOUND:** Sandy soil. Pa. to Fla.; e. Texas to s. Mo. **USES:** American Indians poulticed root for boils, cuts, earaches, and inflammation. Whole plant has traditionally been used in tea as an antispasmodic, and a sedative for neuralgia, epilepsy, restlessness, painful menses, insomnia, tension headaches. Research shows plant extracts are mildly sedative, slightly reduce blood pressure, increase respiratory rate, and decrease motor activity. Contains several compounds shown to contribute to sedative activity. Approved in Germany for nervous restlessness, nervous tension; considered

(Left) *Passion-flower* (Passiflora incarnata). (Above) *Passion-flower's egg-shaped fruits.*

especially useful in sleep disturbances or anxiety arising from restlessness. Fruits edible, delicious. **WARNING:** Potentially harmful in large amounts.

KUDZU   **Root, flowers, seeds, stems, root starch**
Pueraria montana var. *lobata* (Willd.) Maesen & S. Almeida
[*Pueraria lobata* (Willd.) Ohwi]   Pea Family

Noxious, robust, trailing or climbing vine. Leaves *palmate, 3-parted;* leaflets entire or palmately lobed. Flowers reddish purple, *grape-scented;* in a loose raceme. July–Sept. **WHERE FOUND:** Waste ground. Pa. to Fla.; Texas to Kans. Asian alien. **USES:** In China, root tea used for headaches, diarrhea, dysentery, acute intestinal obstruction, gastroenteritis, deafness; to promote measles eruptions, induce sweating. Experimentally, plant extracts lower blood sugar and blood pressure. Flower tea used for stomach acidity; "awakens the spleen," "expels drunkenness." Seeds used for dysentery. Root, flowers, and seeds used in China to treat drunkenness or sober an intoxicated person. Stem poulticed for sores, swellings, mastitis; tea gargled for sore throats. Root starch (used to stimulate production of body fluids) eaten as food. Roots are richer in estrogenic isoflavones, daidzein, and genistein than soybeans. Genistein may prevent development of tumors by preventing the formation of new blood vessels that nourish the tumors. Daidzein and daidzin have been shown to inhibit the desire for alcohol and to reduce blood pressure and venous obstruction. An

(Left, Above) *Kudzu* (Pueraria montana *var.* lobata) *produces large, three-divided leaves. Kudzu blankets millions of acres in the Southeast.*

extract of the root was found to have 1oo times the antioxidant activity of vitamin E. Kudzu extracts have also been found to stimulate regeneration of liver tissue while protecting against liver toxins.

MISCELLANEOUS PLANTS WITH SHOWY FLOWER SPIKES

TALL BELLFLOWER
Campanulastrum americanum (L.) Small
[*Campanula americana* L.]

Leaves
Bellflower Family

Annual; to 6 ft. Leaves lance-shaped to oblong-ovate (3–6 in.). Blue flowers in terminal spikes; July–Sept. Star-shaped petals are fused together. Note *long, curved style*. **WHERE FOUND:** Moist woods, stream banks. Ont. to Fla.; Texas to Minn. **USES:** American Indians used leaf tea for coughs and tuberculosis. Crushed root was used for whooping cough.

FOXGLOVE
Digitalis purpurea L.

Leaves
Figwort Family

Biennial; 3–6 ft. Leaves in a basal rosette, ovate to lance-shaped, soft-hairy, toothed; to 1 ft. long. Flowers purple to white, *spotted*

Tall Bellflower (Campanulastrum americanum) *is often found at the edge of woods.*

Foxglove (Digitalis purpurea) *is commonly cultivated.*

thimbles, 1 ¼ in. long, on spikes; *in summer of second year.* **WHERE FOUND:** Garden escape. New England. Alien. A biennial from Europe that is often cultivated as an ornamental for its showy purple or white flowers, Foxglove has become naturalized in some areas. **USES:** Dried leaves a source of heart-tonic glycosides. Used in modern medicine to increase force of systolic contractions in congestive heart failure; lowers venous pressure in hypertensive heart ailments; elevates blood pressure in weak heart; diuretic, reduces edema. **WARNING: Lethally toxic.** First year's leaf growth (rosette) has been mistaken for leaves of Comfrey (*Symphytum*—see p. 204), with fatal results. Therapeutic dose of *Digitalis* is dangerously close to lethal dose. For use by physicians only.

BLUE VERVAIN   **Leaves, root**
Verbena hastata L.   Verbena Family
Perennial; 2–4 ft. Stem 4-angled, grooved. Leaves mostly lance-shaped, sharp-toothed; base sometimes lobed. Flowers blue-violet, tops branched in *pencil-like* spikes; July–Sept. **WHERE FOUND:** Fields, thickets. Most of our area. **USES:** American Indians used leaf tea as a "female tonic"; also for colds, coughs, fevers, bowel complaints, dysentery, stomach cramps; emetic in large doses.

Blue Vervain (Verbena hastata)
blooms in late summer.

Purple or Spike Loosestrife
(Lythrum salicaria) *is a rampant
invasive weed.*

Root considered more active than leaves. Used similarly by nineteenth-century physicians.

PURPLE OR SPIKE LOOSESTRIFE

Lythrum salicaria L.

Flowering plant
Loosestrife Family

Downy perennial; 2–4 ft. Leaves whorled or opposite, *rounded or heart-shaped at base*. Flowers purple-pink, *6-petaled*; in spikes; June–Sept. **WHERE FOUND:** New England to N.C.; Mo. to Minn. Alien. Serious invasive weed in swampy meadows. **USES:** Tea made from whole flowering plant (fresh or dried) is a European folk remedy (demulcent, astringent) for diarrhea, dysentery; a gargle for sore throats; a douche for leukorrhea, a cleansing wash for wounds. Experimentally, stops bleeding, antibacterial, and anti-inflammatory. Contains tannins and other components, with bactericidal activity in the gastrointestinal tract.

COMMON LOW-GROWING WILDFLOWERS; PETALS IN 4'S OR 5'S

BLUETS

Houstonia caerulea L. [*Hedyotis caerulea* (L.) Hook.]

Flowering plant
Madder Family

Small perennial; 2–8 in. Leaves narrow, opposite; to ½ in. long. Flowers sky blue to white; *4-parted*, with *a yellow center*; March–July. **WHERE FOUND:** Fields, yards. N.S. to Ga.; Ark. to Wisc. **USES:** Cherokees used leaf tea to stop bed-wetting.

(Above) *Bluets* (Houstonia caerulea). (Right) *Speedwells* (Veronica *sp.*) *are used similarly.*

COMMON SPEEDWELL
Veronica officinalis L.

Leaves, root
Figwort Family

⚠ Creeping, hairy herb; to 7 in. Leaves elliptical, narrow at base; evenly toothed. Blue-violet flowers in *glandular-haired racemes*; May–Aug. **WHERE FOUND:** Waste places. Much of our area. Alien. Of the more than twenty *Veronica* species that occur in our range, almost all of them are naturalized weeds from European and Asia. They are often found growing on lawns in N. America. **USES:** In Europe, astringent root or leaf lea traditionally used to promote urination, sweating, and menstruation; "blood purifier" also used for skin and kidney ailments, coughs, asthma, lung diseases, gout, rheumatism, and jaundice. Considered expectorant, diuretic, tonic. Extracts found to prevent and speed healing of ulcers in experiments on animals. **WARNING:** One component, aucubin, though liver-protective, antioxidant, and antiseptic, can be **toxic** to grazing animals.

THYME-LEAVED SPEEDWELL
Veronica serpyllifolia L.

Leaves
Figwort Family

Creeping, much-branched, *smooth* perennial; 2–8 in. Leaves *oval to oblong; short-stalked.* Flowers small, violet-blue (to whitish); 4 petals with pale blue and dark stripes. Apr.–Sept. **WHERE FOUND:** Lawns, roadsides. Nfld. to Ga., Ark. to Minn. Alien. **USES:** Leaf juice used by American Indians for earaches, leaves poulticed for boils; tea used for chills and coughs.

JOHNNY-JUMP-UP, HEART'S EASE
Viola tricolor L.

Leaves
Violet Family

Angled-stemmed annual; 4–12 in. Leaves toothed, roundish on lower part of plant, oblong above; stipules large, leaflike; *strongly divided.* Pansylike flowers in patterns of purple, white, and yellow; May–Sept. **WHERE FOUND:** Escaped from gardens. Alien. Field weed.

USES: In Europe, leaf tea is a folk medicine for fevers; mild laxative; gargle for sore throats; considered diuretic, expectorant, mild sedative, "blood purifier"; used for asthma, heart

Johnny-jump-up, Heart's Ease (Viola tricolor).

palpitations, and skin eruptions, such as eczema. Rat experiments confirm possible use for skin eruptions. Approved for external use in Germany in treatment of mild seborrhea and related skin disorders. **WARNING:** Contains saponins; may be toxic in larger doses.

LOW-GROWING PLANTS WITH SHOWY FLOWERS; 5 OR MORE PETALS

PASQUEFLOWER

Whole plant

Pulsatilla patens ssp. *patens* (L.) P. Mill.
[*Anemone patens* L.]

Buttercup Family

Perennial; 2–16 in. Leaves arising from root; *silky, dissected into linear segments*. Showy flowers, 1½ in. wide; March–June. "Petals" (sepals) purple or white, in a *cup-shaped receptacle*. Seeds with *feathery plumes*. **WHERE FOUND:** Moist meadows, prairies, woods. Iowa to Colo., Wash., Alaska. **USES:** As few as 5 drops of highly diluted tincture in water used in homeopathic practice for eye ailments, skin eruptions, rheumatism, leukorrhea, obstructed menses, bronchitis, coughs, asthma. **WARNING: Poisonous.** Extremely irritating. Both external and internal use should be avoided. **REMARKS:** The homeopathic doses reported here and elsewhere in this plant identification guide are so dilute as to be harmless (i.e., without side effects), if not biologically inactive, by the medical establishment's standards. **RELATED SPECIES:** A European species, *Pulsatilla pratensis* (L.) Miller, has been used in German phytomedicine for inflammatory and infectious disease of the skin and mucous membranes, gastrointestinal and urinary tract disorders, migraines, neuralgia, and general restlessness. However, current use is prohibited because the risks outweigh the benefits.

Pasqueflower (Pulsatilla patens) *produces pale violet or white flower petals.*

SHARP-LOBED HEPATICA, LIVERLEAF   Leaves
Hepatica nobilis var. *acuta* (Pursh) Steyermak   Buttercup Family
[*Hepatica acutiloba* DC.]

⚠ Perennial; 4–8 in. Leaves usually evergreen, *3-lobed*; lobes *pointed*. Flowers lavender, blue, white, or pink; Feb.–June. "Petals" (6–10) are actually sepals. **WHERE FOUND:** Rich woods. W. Me. to Ga.; La., Ark., Mo. to Minn. **USES:** American Indians used leaf tea for liver ailments, poor digestion, laxative; externally, as a wash for swollen breasts. In folk tradition, tea used for fevers, liver ailments, coughs. Thought to be mildly astringent, demulcent, diuretic. A "liver tonic" boom resulted in the consumption of 450,000 pounds of the dried leaves (domestic and imported) in 1883 alone. Once used in European herbal medicine for liver disorders, as a general appetite stimulant, a tonic, to increase circulation, and many other uses. Not allowed for use in Germany because of potential risks and lack of scientific substantiation of claimed uses. **WARNING:** Contains irritating compounds (like many other members of the Buttercup family).

ROUND-LOBED HEPATICA   Leaves
Hepatica nobilis var. *obtusa* (Pursh) Steyermark   Buttercup Family
[*Hepatica americana* (DC.) Ker.]

Similar to *H. acutiloba,* but leaf lobes are *rounded*. Flowers March–June. **WHERE FOUND:** Dry woods. N.S. to Ga., Ala.; Mo. to Man. **USES:** Same as for *H. acutiloba* (see above).

(Above, Left) *Sharp-lobed Hepatica* (Hepatica nobilis) *has pointed leaf tips and white to violet flowers.*

(Above) *Round-lobed Hepatica* (Hepatica americana) *leaves have rounded leaf tips.* (Right) *Blue-eyed Grass* (Sisyrinchium sp.) *is not a grass but an iris.*

BLUE-EYED GRASS
Root, leaves
Sisyrinchium angustifolium P. Mill.
Iris Family

Perennial; 4–18 in. Differs from the other 10 or so *Sisyrinchium* species in our range in that the leaves are narrow (¼ in. wide), much flattened, and deep green. Flowers at tip of *long, flat stalk;* May–July. **WHERE FOUND:** Meadows. Most of our area. **USES:** American Indians used root tea for diarrhea (in children); plant tea for worms, stomachaches. Several species were used as laxatives.

MISCELLANEOUS FLOWERS WITH 5 PETALS

BORAGE
Leaves, flowers, seeds
Borago officinalis L.
Borage Family

Coarse annual; 1–4 ft. Stems succulent, hollow. Leaves with cucumber fragrance when crushed, rough-hairy, lower leaves broadly ovate and stalked, upper leaves sessile, clasping, 2–5 in. long. Flowers are brilliant blue stars with prominent black anthers forming a conelike structure in the center, to 1 in. across; drooping downward; June–Sept. **WHERE FOUND:** Near gardens, sometimes escaped casual weed. Alien from Europe. Occasional in our range. **USES:** Leaf tea historically used for fevers, jaundice, rheumatism. Considered cooling and diuretic. Externally, a poultice used for wounds; anti-inflammatory. Flowers edible. Seed oil is a rich source of gamma-linolenic acid (GLA). GLA-rich seed oils are said to alleviate imbalances and abnormalities of essential fatty acids in prostaglandin production. Most research on sources

Borage (Borago officinalis) *is usually found in gardens.*

Stiff Gentian, Ague-weed (Gentianella quinquefolia). *Photo by Harry Ellis.*

of GLA has involved Evening-primrose (p. 106). A small clinical study showed Borage seed oil reduced stress by lowering systolic blood pressure and heart rate. **WARNING:** Like Comfrey leaves, Borage leaves contain potentially liver-toxic and carcinogenic pyrrolizidine alkaloids. Risk of leaf use outweighs benefits.

STIFF GENTIAN, AGUE-WEED   Roots
Gentianella quinquefolia ssp. *quinquefolia* (L.) Small
[*Gentiana quinquefolia* L.]   Gentian Family
Perennial; 6–30 in. *Stem 4-ridged.* Leaves oval, clasping. Tubular flowers, in *tight, often 5-flowered clusters;* Aug–Oct. **WHERE FOUND:** Rich woods, moist fields. **USES:** Tea or root tincture was once used as bitter tonic to stimulate digestion, weak appetite. Also used for headaches, hepatitis, jaundice, constipation.

VIRGINIA WATERLEAF   Whole plant, root
Hydrophyllum virginianum L.   Waterleaf Family
Perennial; 1–3 ft. Leaves *deeply divided,* with *5–7 lobes;* lower segments 2-parted, with marks like water stains. Flowers bell-like with *protruding stamens;* violet to whitish; May–Aug. **WHERE FOUND:** Rich woods. Que. and w. New England to Va.; Tenn., n. Ark., e. Kans. to Man. **USES:** American Indians used root tea as an astrin-

Virginia Waterleaf (Hydrophyllum virginianum). *Note the protruding stamens.*

Flax (Linum usitatissimum) *has slightly overlapping petals.*

gent for diarrhea, dysentery. Tea (or roots chewed) for cracked lips, mouth sores.

FLAX   **Seeds**
Linum usitatissimum L.   Flax Family
 Delicate annual; 8–22 in. Leaves linear, 3-veined. Flowers with 5 *slightly overlapping* blue petals (½–¾ in. across); June–Sept. **WHERE FOUND:** Waste places. Throughout our area. Alien. **USES:** Source of linseed oil and linen. Said to be soothing and softening to irritated membranes. Seeds once used for skin and mouth cancers, colds, coughs, lung and urinary ailments, fevers; laxative poulticed (mixed with lime water) to relieve pain of burns, gout, inflammation, rheumatism, boils. Seeds used in European phytomedicine as a mild, lubricating laxative in constipation, for irritable bowel syndrome, diverticulitis, and for relief of gastritis and enteritis. Flaxseed is also used to correct problems caused from abuse of stimulant laxatives. Oil is a folk remedy used for pleurisy and pneumonia, high in omega-3 fatty acids. A folk cancer remedy, possibly containing some antitumor compounds found in Mayapple (p. 52). Flaxseed has been suggested as a possible preventative for colon cancer. **WARNING:** Contains a cyanide-like compound. Oil may be emetic and purgative.

Greek Valerian, Jacob's Ladder (Polemonium reptans) with "ladderlike" leaves.

GREEK VALERIAN, JACOB'S LADDER
Root
Polemonium reptans L.
Phlox Family
Perennial; 8–24 in. Leaves paired; sessile. The name "Jacob's Ladder" refers to the ladderlike arrangement of the leaves. Flowers are loose clusters of violet-blue bells; *stamens not protruding;* Apr.–June. **WHERE FOUND:** Moist bottoms. N.Y. to Ga., Miss., Okla. to Minn. **USES:** American Indians used root in prescriptions for piles, to induce vomiting, treat eczema, enhance action of Mayapple (p. 52). The Indian name for this plant, which translates as "smells like pine," refers to the root fragrance. Root tea once used to induce sweating, astringent; for pleurisy, fevers, scrofula, snakebites, bowel complaints, and bronchial afflictions. **RELATED SPECIES:** *P. vanbruntia* (not shown) is larger and has protruding stamens.

FLOWERS WITH 5 PETALS; CURLED CLUSTERS

HOUND'S TONGUE
Leaves, root
Cynoglossum officinale L.
Forget-me-not Family
Downy biennial; 1–3 ft., with a mousy odor. Leaves lance-shaped. Flowers purplish, enclosed by a soft-hairy calyx; Aug–Sept. Flat fruits covered with soft spines. **WHERE FOUND:** Roadsides, pastures. Much of our area. Alien. **USES:** Leaf and root tea once used to soothe coughs, colds, irritated membranes; astringent in diar-

Hound's Tongue (Cynoglossum of-ficinale) *has lance-shaped leaves. Photo by Stephen Lee Timme.*

Wild Comfrey (Cynoglossum vir-ginianum). *The stem leaves clasp the stem.*

rhea, dysentery. Leaf poultice used for insect bites, piles. **WARNING:** Contains the potentially carcinogenic alkaloids cynoglossine and consolidine, both CNS-depressant. May cause dermatitis.

WILD COMFREY   Leaves, root
Cynoglossum virginianum L.   Forget-me-not Family
Rough, hairy perennial; 1–2 ft. Basal leaves in a rosette; stalked stem leaves clasping. Violet-blue flowers on spreading racemes; May–June. Flowers are somewhat like those of Borage. **WHERE FOUND:** Open woods. Sw. Conn.; N.J.; Pa. to Fla.; Texas to Mo.; s. Ill. **USES:** Cherokees used root tea for "bad memory," cancer, itching of genitals, milky urine. In nineteenth-century texts, authors suggest use as a substitute for Comfrey (*Symphytum officinale*); leaves smoked like Tobacco. **WARNING:** Do not confuse the leaves of either Comfrey with those of Foxglove (*Digitalis*, p. 193); fatal poisoning may result.

VIPER'S BUGLOSS   Whole plant, root
Echium vulgare L.   Forget-me-not Family
Bristly biennial; 1–2½ ft. Leaves lance-shaped. Flowers violet-blue on curled branches. *One flower blooms at a time* on each curled branch; June–Sept. Upper lip longer than lower; stamens

Viper's Bugloss (Echium vulgare) *is extremely bristly; its hairs can irritate human skin.*

Comfrey (Symphytum *sp.*). *Often persistent in old garden sites.*

 red, protruding. **WHERE FOUND:** Waste places. Much of our area. Alien. **USES:** Leaf tea is a folk medicine, used to promote sweating, diuretic, expectorant, soothing; used for fevers, headaches, nervous conditions, and pain from inflammation. Root contains healing allantoin. **WARNING:** Contains a **toxic** alkaloid. Hairs may cause rash.

COMFREY   **Leaves, root**
Symphytum officinale L.   Borage Family

Large-rooted perennial; 1–3 ft. Leaves large, *rough-hairy;* broadly oval to lance-shaped. Bell-like flowers in furled clusters; purple-blue, pink, or white; May–Sept. **WHERE FOUND:** Escaped. Alien. Often cultivated. **USES:** While *Symphytum officinale* is listed as the species used in most herb books, a number of the 25 species of Comfrey (*Symphytum*) are cultivated in American gardens. Extremely popular in the 1970s and early '80s, studies showing toxic pyrrolizidine alkaloids, especially in the root, have halted the Comfrey love affair. Recent studies show that leaves harvested during the blooming period are very low in alkaloid content. Root tea and weaker leaf tea considered tonic, astringent, demulcent, for diarrhea, dysentery, bronchial irritation, coughs, vomiting of blood, "female maladies"; leaves and root poulticed to "knit bones," promote healing of bruises, wounds, ulcers, sore breasts. Contains allantoin, which promotes healing. In Germany, external application of the leaf is approved for the treatment of bruises and sprains; root poultice approved for bruising, pulled muscles and ligaments, and sprains. **WARNING:** Root use is discouraged because of high levels of liver-toxic (or cancer-causing) pyrrolizidine alkaloids. Certain types of leaf tea, although less carcinogenic than beer, were recently banned in Canada. In Germany, external use of the leaf is limited to 4 to 6 weeks each year. There is also a danger that the leaves of Comfrey (*Symphytum*) may be confused with the first-year leaf rosettes of Foxglove (*Digitalis*), with **fatal results.** Consult an expert on identification first. **RELATED SPECIES:** The most widely grown species is Russian Comfrey, S x *uplandicum,* a hybrid bred as a fodder crop.

5-PARTED FLOWERS; NIGHTSHADE FAMILY

JIMSONWEED	Leaves, root, seed
Datura stramonium L.	Nightshade Family

Annual; 2–5 ft. Leaves coarse-toothed. Flowers white to pale violet 3–5 in.; *trumpet-shaped;* May–Sept. Seedpods shiny, chambered, with *prickles;* seeds lentil-shaped. **WHERE FOUND:** Waste places. Throughout our area. **USES:** Whole plant contains atropine and other alkaloids, used in eye diseases (to dilate pupils); causes dry mouth, depresses action of bladder muscles, impedes action of parasympathetic nerves; used in Parkinson's disease; also contains scopolamine, used in patches behind ear for vertigo. Leaves once smoked as antispasmodic for asthma. Folk cancer remedy. **WARNING: Violently toxic.** Causes severe hallucinations. Many fatalities recorded. Those who collect this plant may end up with swollen eyelids. Licorice (*Glycyrrhiza*) has been suggested as an antidote.

Jimsonweed (Datura sp.). *Pictured here is* D. metel, *also with white to pale violet flowers.*

HORSE-NETTLE

Solanum carolinense L.   Nightshade Family

 Perennial; 1–4 ft. Stems *sharp-spined*. Leaves oval to elliptical; lobed to coarse-toothed. Flowers violet to white stars; May–Oct. Fruits orange-yellow; Aug.–Sept. **WHERE FOUND:** Sandy soil. Old fields, farmlands, waste places. New England to Fla.; Texas to s. S.D. **USES:** Properly administered, berries were once used for epilepsy; diuretic, painkiller, antispasmodic, aphrodisiac. Berries fried in grease were used as an ointment for dog's mange. American Indians gargled wilted leaf tea for sore throats; poulticed leaves for Poison Ivy rash; drank tea for worms. **WARNING: Toxic.** Fatalities reported in children from ingesting berries.

WOODY NIGHTSHADE, BITTERSWEET   Leaves, stems, berries

Solanum dulcamara L.   Nightshade Family

 A woody, climbing vine. Leaves oval, often with 1 or 2 *prominent lobes at base.* Flowers violet (or rarely white) stars with yellow protrusions (stamens); petals curved back; May–Sept. Fruits ovoid, red; Sept.–Nov. **WHERE FOUND:** Waste places. Throughout our area. Alien. **USES:** Externally, plant used as a folk remedy for felons, warts, and tumors. Science confirms significant anticancer activ-

Horse-nettle (Solanum carolinense). *Shown with white flowers. Its flowers are occasionally violet.*

Woody Nightshade, Bittersweet (Solanum dulcamara) *with violet blooms (rarely white).*

ity. Used as a starting material for steroids. Formerly used as narcotic, diuretic sweat inducer; used for skin eruptions, rheumatism, gout, bronchitis, whooping cough. In Germany, relatively nonpoisonous stems have been approved for use in supportive treatment of acne, eczema, furuncles, and warts. Stems contain significantly lower amounts of toxic alkaloids than other parts of the plant. **WARNING: Toxic.** Contains steroids, toxic alkaloids, and glucosides. Will cause vomiting, vertigo, convulsions, weakened heart, paralysis. Green berries can cause diarrhea, dilated pupils, nausea, and vomiting. Lethal dose is estimated to be 200 berries.

LIPPED FLOWERS WITH SPLIT COROLLAS; LOBELIAS

LOBELIA, INDIAN-TOBACCO
Lobelia inflata L.

Whole plant
Bluebell Family

Hairy annual; 6–18 in. Leaves oval, toothed; *hairy beneath*. Inconspicuous white to pale blue flowers, in racemes, to ¼ in., June–Oct. Seed pods *inflated*. **WHERE FOUND:** Fields, waste places, open woods. N.S. to Ga.; La., Ark., e. Kans. to Sask. **USES:** American Indians smoked leaves for asthma, bronchitis, sore throats, coughs. One of the most widely used herbs in nineteenth-century America. Traditionally used to induce vomiting (hence the nickname "pukeweed") and sweating; sedative; used for asthma, whooping cough, fevers, to enhance or direct action of other

(Above, right) *Lobelia* (Lobelia inflata), *with pale violet flowers. Note inflated seedpods.*

herbs. Lobeline, a chemical cousin of nicotine, one of 14 alkaloids in the plant, until recently was used in the U.S. in commercial "quit smoking" lozenges, patches, and chewing gums—said to appease physical need for nicotine without addictive effects. Still used in other countries. Also produces dilation of the bronchioles and increased respiration. **WARNING:** Considered **toxic** because of its strong emetic, expectorant, and sedative effects. This plant has rightly or wrongly been implicated in deaths from improper use as a home remedy.

GREAT LOBELIA
Lobelia siphilitica L.

Leaves, roots
Bluebell Family

Perennial; 1–5 ft. Leaves oval, toothed. Blue-lavender flowers. Corolla throat *white-striped*. Aug.–Oct. **WHERE FOUND:** Moist soil, stream banks. Me. to N.C.; Miss., Ark., e. Kans. to Minn. Often found growing with Cardinal Flower, this is a common fall wildflower along southern streams, but occurs as far north as Minnesota and Maine (where it is rare). **USES:** Early medical writers thought that American Indians primarily used the root to treat syphilis, hence the species name *siphilitica*. American Indians used root tea for syphilis, leaf tea for colds, fevers, "stomach troubles," worms, croup, nosebleeds; gargled leaf tea for coughs;

Great Lobelia (Lobelia siphilitica),
a showy autumn wildflower.

Pale-spike Lobelia (L. spicata).
Flowers are whitish to pale blue.

leaves poulticed for headaches, hard-to-heal sores. Formerly used to induce sweating and urination. Considered similar to, but weaker than, *L. inflata*. **WARNING**: Potentially **poisonous.**

PALE-SPIKE LOBELIA
Lobelia spicata Lam.

Leaves
Bluebell Family

Perennial; 2–4 ft. Stem *smooth* above, *densely hairy* at base. Leaves lance-shaped to slightly oval, barely toothed or without teeth. Flowers pale blue or whitish; June–Aug. **WHERE FOUND**: Fields, glades, meadows, thickets. Most of our area. **USES**: American Indians used a tea of the plant as an emetic. A wash made from the stalks was used for "bad blood" and neck and jaw sores. The root tea was used to treat trembling by applying the tea to scratches made in the affected limb. **WARNING**: Toxicity unknown. May have poisonous attributes.

MISCELLANEOUS MINT RELATIVES WITH SQUARE STEMS AND PAIRED LEAVES

WILD BERGAMOT, PURPLE BEE-BALM
Monarda fistulosa L.

Leaves
Mint Family

Perennial; 2–3 ft. Leaves paired; triangular to oval or lance-shaped. Flowers lavender; *narrow, lipped tubes* in *crowded heads;* May–Sept. Bracts slightly purple-tinged. **WHERE FOUND**: Dry wood edges, thickets. Que. to Ga.; La., e. Texas, Okla. to N.D., Minn. **USES**: American Indians used leaf tea for colic, flatulence, colds, fevers, stomachaches, nose-bleeds, insomnia, heart trouble; in measles to induce sweating; poulticed leaves for headaches. Historically, physicians used leaf tea to expel worms and gas. Essential oil is high in carvacrol, with anesthetic, worm-expelling, anti-inflammatory, antioxidant, and diuretic activity.

Wild Bergamot, Purple Bee-balm (Monarda fistulosa) *is relished by butterflies.*

(Above) *Perilla* (Perilla frutescens) *is an aggressive annual Asian weed.* (Right) *Mad-dog Skullcap* (Scutellaria lateriflora) *is usually found in small populations.*

PERILLA
Leaves, seeds
Perilla frutescens (L.) Britt.
Mint Family

Annual; 1–3 ft. Leaves oval, *wrinkled, long-toothed*; often *purplish,* with a *peculiar* fragrance. Flowers whitish to lavender or pale violet in axillary and terminal clusters; July–Sept. **WHERE FOUND:** Moist, open woods. Mass. to Fla.; Texas to Iowa. This Asian alien has become an invasive weed in the South. In the Ozarks it is called Rattlesnake Weed because the dried seed cases (the calyx) rattle as one walks by. **USES:** Leaf tea used in Asian traditional medicine for abdominal pains, diarrhea, vomiting, coughs, to "quiet a restless fetus," relieve morning sickness, irritability during pregnancy, fevers, colds. Considered diaphoretic, sedative, and spasmolytic. Dried leaves used in China to treat bronchitis. One Chinese clinical study found application of the fresh leaves (rubbing on infection) for ten to fifteen minutes a day made warts disappear in two to six days. A favorite culinary herb of some Asian cultures. Seed oil a rich source of alpha-linolenic acid, an omega-3 essential fatty acid. **WARNING:** Avoid during pregnancy. A component in the leaves was found to induce severe lung lesions in mice, rats, and sheep. Cattle have contracted acute pulmonary emphysema from eating the plant. Use in human foods and medicine has been questioned. Once used as a fish poison, antidote.

MAD-DOG SKULLCAP
Scutellaria lateriflora L.

Leaves

Mint Family

Perennial; 1–3 ft. Leaves opposite; oval to lance-shaped, toothed. Flowers violet-blue, *hooded,* lipped; May–Sept. Easily distinguished from other *Scutellaria* species—flowers are in 1-sided *racemes from leaf axils.* **WHERE FOUND:** Rich woods, moist thickets. Much of our area. **USES:** Known as Mad-dog Skullcap because tea was once used as a folk remedy for rabies. A strong tea was traditionally used as a sedative, nerve tonic, and antispasmodic for all types of nervous conditions, including epilepsy, insomnia, anxiety, and neuralgia. Scutellarin, a flavonoid compound in the plant, has confirmed sedative and antispasmodic qualities. Other *Scutellaria* species may have similar properties. **WARNING:** Large doses are of unknown toxicity. Native Germander or Wood Sage (*Teucrium canadensis*) is a widespread adulterant to commercial supplies of Skullcap. Reports of liver toxicity related to Skullcap may actually involve Wood Sage, which is traded under the name "pink skullcap." Two cases of "Skullcap" poisoning, including one fatality, might have involved Wood Sage.

STRONGLY SCENTED MINTS; SQUARE STEMS, PAIRED LEAVES

CANADIAN MINT
Mentha canadensis L. [*Mentha aquatica* L.]

Leaves

Mint Family

Perennial; to 2 ft. Leaves opposite, round to oval; *hairs curved.* Pale lavender flowers in *crowded globular terminal clusters* (or 1–3 clusters below); calyx hairy. Flowers Aug.–Oct. **WHERE FOUND:** Wet ground. N.S. to Del. Alien. **USES:** Leaf tea traditionally used for fevers, stomachaches, headaches, and other minor ailments. **WARNING:** Essential oil of this mint, probably like all essential oils, is antiseptic, but can be toxic to humans in a concentrated form.

PEPPERMINT
Mentha x piperita L. (pro sp.)

Leaves

Mint Family

Perennial; 12–36 in. *Stem* purplish (not greenish, as in Spearmint); smooth, with *few* hairs. Leaves opposite, stalked; distinct *odor of peppermint.* Flowers pale violet; in *loose, interrupted terminal spikes;* June–frost. Peppermint is a hybrid between Spearmint (*M. spicata*) and Watermint (*M. aquatica*). Native to Europe, it was first grown commercially in England about 1750. **WHERE FOUND:** Wet places. Escaped from cultivation. Throughout. European alien. **USES:** Leaf tea traditionally used for colds, fevers, indigestion, gas, stomachaches, headaches, nervous tension, insomnia. Extracts experimentally effective against herpes simplex,

Canadian Mint (Mentha canadensis) *is found in moist habitats.*

Peppermint (Mentha x piperita). *Leaves have a peppermint fragrance, and there is usually more red in the leaf veins.*

Newcastle disease, and other viruses. The oil stops spasms of smooth muscles. Animal experiments show that azulene, a minor component of distilled Peppermint oil residues, is anti-inflammatory and has anti-ulcer activity. Enteric-coated Peppermint capsules are used in Europe for irritable bowel syndrome. Peppermint leaf is approved in Germany for use in muscle spasms of the gastrointestinal tract, as well as spasms of the gallbladder and bile ducts. The essential oil is used externally to treat neuralgia and myalgia. Menthol is an approved ingredient in cough drops. **WARNING:** Oil is **toxic** if taken internally; causes dermatitis. Menthol, the major chemical component of Peppermint oil, may cause allergic reactions. Infants should never be exposed to menthol-containing products, as they can cause the lungs to collapse. Use should be avoided in cases of gallbladder or bile duct obstruction.

SPEARMINT
Mentha spicata L

Leaves
Mint Family

Creeping perennial; 6–36 in. Leaves opposite; without stalks (or with very short stalks); with a distinct *odor of spearmint.* Flowers pale pink-violet; in slender, elongated spikes; June–frost. **WHERE FOUND:** Wet soil. Much of our area. Escaped. European alien. **USES:**

Spearmint (Mentha spicata).
Leaves have a spearmint fragrance.

Spearmint and Spearmint oil are used as carminatives (to relieve gas), and primarily to disguise the flavor of other medicines. Spearmint has been traditionally valued as a stomachic, antiseptic, and antispasmodic. The leaf tea has been used for stomachaches, diarrhea, nausea, colds, headaches, cramps, fevers, and is a folk cancer remedy. **WARNING:** Oil is **toxic** if taken internally; causes dermatitis.

SQUARE-STEMMED PLANTS; LEAVES PAIRED; STRONGLY AROMATIC; NOT MINTY

BLUE GIANT HYSSOP, ANISE-HYSSOP

Leaves, roots

Agastache foeniculum (Pursh) O. Kuntze — Mint Family

Perennial; to 3 ft. Smooth-stemmed, branched above. Leaves *strongly anise-scented*, minute downy beneath. Bluish flowers in tight whorls; June–Sept. Stamens in 2 *protruding pairs*; pairs *crossing*. **WHERE FOUND:** Prairies, dry thickets. Ont. south to Ill., Iowa; west to Colo., S.D., Wash. Cultivated; escaped eastward. **USES:** Leaf tea used for fevers, colds, coughs; induces sweating, strengthens weak heart. **RELATED SPECIES:** The Chinese use *A. rugosa* leaf tea for angina pains. Root tea used for coughs, lung ailments.

AMERICAN PENNYROYAL

Leaves

Hedeoma pulegioides (L.) Pers. — Mint Family

Aromatic, soft-hairy annual; 6–18 in. Leaves small, lance-shaped; toothed or entire. Bluish flowers in leaf axils; July–Oct. Calyx 2-lipped, with 3 short and 2 longer teeth. **WHERE FOUND:** Dry woods. Que. to Ga.; Ala. to Okla.; Neb. to Mich. **USES:** Leaf tea traditionally used for colds, fevers, coughs, indigestion, kidney and liver ailments, headaches; to promote sweating, induce menstruation, expectorant; insect repellent. **WARNING:** Pulegone, the active insect repellent compound in essential oil, is absorbed through the skin and converted into a dangerous liver cancer–inducing compound. Ingesting essential oil can be **lethal;** contact with essential oil (a popular insect repellant) can cause dermatitis. Components of essential oil may be particularly dangerous to epileptics.

(Above left) *Blue Giant Hyssop, Anise-hyssop* (Agastache foeniculum) *has an anise scent.*
(Above right) *American Pennyroyal* (Hedeoma pulegioides) *has a distinct, vinyl-like fragrance.*
(Right) *Hyssop* (Hyssopus officinalis) *is mostly cultivated, locally naturalized.*

HYSSOP

Hyssopus officinalis L.

Leaves

Mint Family

Bushy, aromatic perennial; 1–2 ft. Leaves opposite; *lance-shaped to linear; stalkless, entire* (not toothed). Purple, bluish, or pink flowers in whorls of leaf axils, forming small spikes; June–Oct. **WHERE FOUND:** Dry soils. Locally abundant. Alien. **USES:** Traditionally, leaf tea was gargled for sore throats. Tea thought to relieve gas, stomachaches, loosen phlegm; used with Horehound (p. 82) for bronchitis, coughs, and asthma. The herb has been used externally to treat rheumatism, muscle aches, wounds, and sprains.

Experimentally, extracts are useful against herpes simplex; anti-inflammatory. Contains at least 8 antiviral compounds. In 1990 researchers found that a Hyssop extract inhibited replication of human immunodeficiency virus. A polysaccharide was identified in 1995 that inhibited the SF strain of HIV-1 (dose-dependent), preventing replication of the virus. Hyssop contains antioxidant components, such as rosmarinic acid and other compounds, that are associated with antiviral, anti-inflammatory, and antioxidant activity. Therapeutic claims are not permitted in Germany because traditional uses are not substantially researched.

CALAMINT
Calamintha arkansana (Nutt.) Shinners
[*Satureja arkansana* (Nutt.) Briq.]

Leaves
Mint Family

Creeping perennial; 4–8 in. Leaves oval at base of plant; stem leaves linear. Leaves *strongly pennyroyal-scented*. Flowers purplish, 2-lipped; Apr.–July. **WHERE FOUND:** Rocky glades. W. N.Y. to Ark., Texas; north to Ill., Ind. **USES:** Used as a substitute for American Pennyroyal (see above). **WARNING:** Contains pulegone in essential oil. The same warning applies as for American and European Pennyroyal.

(Left) *Calamint* (Calamintha arkansana) *has a pennyroyal fragrance.* (Above) *Note the glandular dots on its flower.*

DOWNY WOODMINT

Leaves

Blephila ciliata (L.) Bentham

Mint Family

Perennial; 10–26 in. Leaves oblong-oval to lance-shaped, *downy beneath*; stalkless, on flowering stems. Flowers pale bluish purple, in terminal and axillary whorls; June–Aug. Calyx 2-lipped, with bristly teeth; lower lip of corolla narrower than lateral lobes. **WHERE FOUND:** Dry woods, clearings. Vt. to Ga.; e. Texas to Minn. **USES:** Cherokees used poultice of fresh leaves for headaches.

GROUND IVY, GILL-OVER-THE-GROUND

Leaves

Glechoma hederacea L.

Mint Family

⚠ Creeping, ivy-like perennial. Leaves scallop-edged, round to kidney-shaped; sometimes tinged with purple. Two-lipped violet flowers, in whorls of leaf axils; March–July. **WHERE FOUND:** Roadsides, lawns. Throughout our area. Alien. **USES:** Traditionally, leaf tea used for lung ailments, asthma, jaundice, kidney ailments, "blood purifier." Externally, a folk remedy for cancer, backaches, bruises, piles. Alcohol extracts are anti-inflammatory and reduce edema. Two components in the plant were found to protect mice from ulcers. Ursolic acid in leaves experimentally anticancer against lymphocytic leukemia and human lung carcinoma. **WARNING:** Reportedly **toxic** to horses, causing throat irritation and labored breathing. Also reported in humans. In one case the fresh

(Above) *Downy Woodmint* (Blephila ciliata) *has pale bluish purple flowers.* (Right) *Ground Ivy* (Glechoma hederacea) *has rounded leaves with scalloped edges.*

leaves were steeped in ¼ cup of hot water for ten minutes and then drunk. Within five minutes tea produced swelling of throat and labored breath, and resulted in difficulty sleeping that night. Symptoms abated in 24 hours.

HEAL-ALL, SELF-HEAL
Prunella vulgaris L.

Whole plant
Mint Family

Low perennial; to 1 ft. Leaves oval to lance-shaped; mostly smooth; opposite, on a weakly squared stem. Purple flowers crowded on a terminal head; hooded, with a fringed lower lip; May–Sept. **WHERE FOUND:** Waste places, lawns. Throughout our area. Eurasian alien. **USES:** Traditionally, leaf tea was used as a gargle for sore throats and mouth sores, also for fevers, diarrhea; externally, for ulcers, wounds, bruises, sores. In China, a tea made from the flowering plant is considered cooling. The plant was also used in China to treat heat in the liver and aid in circulation; used for conjunctivitis, boils, and scrofula; diuretic for kidney ailments. Research suggests the plant possesses antibiotic, hypotensive, and antimutagenic qualities. Contains the antitumor and diuretic compound ursolic acid. Also rich in natural antioxidant components, containing more rosmarinic acid than Rosemary itself.

Heal-all, Self-heal (Prunella vulgaris) *is a common weed on lawns.*

Lyre-leaved Sage, Cancerweed (Salvia lyrata) *blooms in spring. Leaves are lyre-shaped, hence the name.*

LYRE-LEAVED SAGE, CANCERWEED

Roots, leaves

Salvia lyrata L.

Mint Family

Perennial; to 1 ft. Leaves mostly basal, oblong, cleft (dandelion-like); edges rounded. Purple-blue flowers, to 1 in., in whorled spikes; Apr.–June. **WHERE FOUND:** Sandy soils, lawns. Pa. to Fla.; Texas to se. Kans., Ill. **USES:** American Indians used root in salve for sores. Whole-plant tea used for colds, coughs, nervous debility; with honey for asthma; mildly laxative and diaphoretic. Folk remedy for cancer and warts.

LEGUMES (PEA FAMILY)

PURPLE PRAIRIE-CLOVER

Leaves, root

Dalea purpurea Vent.

Pea Family

[*Petalostemon purpureus* (Vent.) Rydb.]

Perennial; 1–2 feet. Leaves numerous, densely crowded on stems; 3–7 (usually 5) leaflets. Flowers purple, tiny, densely crowded on a conelike or cylindrical head. **WHERE FOUND:** Dry prairies, glades. Ind., Ky., Ark.; Texas west to N.M. **USES:** American Indian groups of the prairies used the whole plant in flower to treat heart problems. The root was used to treat measles and pneumonia and as a general preventative to disease. Strongly antibacterial.

Purple Prairie-clover (Dalea purpurea) *has thimblelike flowerheads.*

Alfalfa (Medicago sativa) *is often
found near cultivated fields.*

ALFALFA
Medicago sativa L.

Flowering plant
Pea Family

⚠ Deep-rooted perennial; 1–3 ft. Leaves cloverlike, but leaflets elongate. Violet-blue flowers in loose heads ¼–⅓ in. long; Apr.–Oct. Pods loosely spiral-twisted. **WHERE FOUND:** Fields, roadsides. Throughout our area. Often cultivated, escaped. Alien. **USES:** Nutritious fresh- or dried-leaf tea traditionally used to promote appetite, weight gain; diuretic; stops bleeding. Experimentally, antifungal and estrogenic. Unsubstantiated claims include use for cancer, diabetes, alcoholism, and arthritis. A source of commercial chlorophyll and carotene, both with valid health claims. Contains the antioxidant tricin. **WARNING:** Consuming large quantities of Alfalfa saponins may cause breakdown of red blood cells, causing bloating in livestock. Recent reports suggest that Alfalfa sprouts (or the canavanine therein, especially in seeds) may be associated with lupus (systemic lupus erythematosus), causing recurrence in patients in which the disease had become dormant.

BLUE FALSE INDIGO
Baptisia australis (L.) R. Br. ex Ait. f.

Root
Pea Family

⚠ Smooth perennial; 3–5 ft. Leaves thrice-divided, cloverlike; leaflets obovate (wider at tips). Deep blue to violet flowers, to 1

Blue False Indigo (Baptisia australis), *with brilliant blue-violet flowers.*

A cultivated Lupine species, with characteristic flower spikes and leaves.

in. long, on erect racemes; Apr.–June. **WHERE FOUND:** Open woods, forest margins, thickets. Pa. to Ga.; Texas to Okla., Neb., s. Ind. **USES:** American Indians used the root tea as an emetic and purgative; cold tea given to stop vomiting. Root poulticed as an anti-inflammatory. Held in mouth to treat toothaches. Like other *Baptisia* species, *B. australis* is currently under investigation as a potential stimulant of the immune system. **WARNING:** Considered potentially toxic.

WILD LUPINE
Leaves
Lupinus perennis L.
Pea Family

 Perennial; 1–2 ft. Leaves long-stalked; divided into 7–11 oblong, lance-shaped segments. Flowers blue, *pea-like*; in a showy raceme; Apr.–July. **WHERE FOUND:** Dry soils, open woods. Sw. Me., N.Y. to Fla.; W. Va., Ohio, Ind., Ill. **USES:** American Indians drank cold leaf tea to treat nausea and internal hemorrhaging. A fodder used to fatten horses and make them "spirited and full of fire." **WARNING:** Seeds are poisonous. Some lupines are toxic, others are not. Even botanists may have difficulty distinguishing between toxic and nontoxic species.

FLAT-TOPPED CLUSTERS OR SPIKES; COMPOSITE FAMILY

WILD LETTUCE
Leaves
Lactuca biennis (Moench) Fernald
Composite Family

Smooth biennial; 2–15 ft. Leaves irregularly divided; coarsely toothed. Flowers bluish to creamy white (rarely yellow); July–Sept. **WHERE FOUND:** Damp thickets. Nfld. to Va. mountains; Tenn. to Iowa and westward. **USES:** American Indians used root tea for diarrhea, heart and lung ailments; for bleeding, nausea, pains. Milky stem juice used for skin erup-

Wild Lettuce (Lactuca biennis).
Photo by Doug Elliott.

A Rough Blazing-star (Liatris aspera) *flower.*

Rough Blazing-star (L. aspera) *is often found in dramatic colonies.*

tions. Leaves applied to stings; tea sedative, nerve tonic, diuretic. **WARNING:** May cause dermatitis or internal poisoning. **REMARKS:** Variable genus; highly technical taxonomy.

ROUGH BLAZING-STAR
Root

Liatris aspera Michx.
Composite Family

Perennial; 6–30 in. Leaves alternate, linear. Rose-purple flowers with 25–30 florets, in crowded, *sessile or short-stalked* heads on a *crowded spike;* Aug.–Sept. Note wide, rounded bracts. **WHERE FOUND:** Dry soils, prairies. Ohio to N.C.; La., Texas to N.D. **USES:** Root tea of most *Liatris* species was used as a folk remedy for kidney and bladder ailments, gonorrhea, colic, painful or delayed menses; gargled for sore throats; root used externally in poultice for snakebites. Thought to be diuretic, tonic.

DEER'S TONGUE
Leaves

Carphephorus odoratissimus (J. F. Gmel.) Herbert   Composite Family
[*Trilisa odoratissima* (Walter ex J. F. Gmel.) Cass.]

Smooth perennial; 2–5 ft. Leaves elliptic, to 1 ft.; toothed or entire; *vanilla-scented when dry.* Flowers lavender or pink; July–Oct. **WHERE FOUND:** Pine barrens. N.C. to Fla., Ala., Miss. **USES:** Folk remedy for coughs, malaria, neuroses; induces sweating; diuretic, tonic, demulcent. Each year, 1 million pounds are used to flavor tobacco products. High in coumarins, experimentally effective for

Deer's Tongue (Carphephorus odoratissimus). *Photo by Doug Elliott.*

Ironweed (Vernonia spp.) are used interchangeably for medicinal purposes.

high-protein edema. **WARNING:** Coumarins are implicated in liver disease and hemorrhage. However, recent evidence suggests a lack of significant coumarin toxicity in humans, even though coumarin was banned as a food additive by the Food and Drug Administration in 1954. Compounds responsible for blood-thinning activity are related to coumarin. A recent study found coumarin not to be mutagenic or carcinogenic in rodents, and failed to produce sensitization reactions in 25 human volunteers.

IRONWEED   Root
Vernonia glauca (L.) Willd.   Composite Family
Blue-green perennial; 2–5 ft. Leaves on stem only (not at base); *oval* to *lance-shaped; narrowly sharp-pointed* at tip and base. Flowers July–Oct. Seed crowns *yellowish* (brown-purple in other *Vernonia*s). **WHERE FOUND:** Rich woods. N.J. to Ga.; Ala. to Pa. **USES:** American Indians used the root as a "blood tonic," to regulate menses, relieve pain after childbirth; also for bleeding, stomachaches. **RELATED SPECIES:** Other *Vernonia*s have been used similarly.

DAISYLIKE FLOWERS OR THISTLES

NEW ENGLAND ASTER
Root

Aster novae-angliae L. Composite Family

Hairy-stemmed perennial; 3–7 ft. The *most showy wild aster in our area.* Leaves *lance-shaped,* without teeth; clasping stem. Flowers *deeper violet* than most asters, with up to 100 rays; Aug.–Oct. Bracts sticky. **WHERE FOUND:** Moist meadows, thickets. S. Canada, Me. to uplands of N.C., Ark., Kans.; Colo. to N.D. **USES:** American Indians used root tea for diarrhea, fevers.

CHICORY
Roots, leaves

Cichorium intybus L. Composite Family

Biennial or perennial; 2–4 ft. Basal leaves dandelion-like; upper ones reduced. Flowers blue (rarely white or pink), *stalkless;* rays square-tipped; June–Oct. **WHERE FOUND:** Roadsides. Throughout our area. Alien. **USES:** 1 ounce root in 1 pint of water used as a diuretic, laxative. Folk use in jaundice, skin eruptions, fevers. Extract diuretic, cardiotonic; lowers blood sugar, slightly sedative, and mildly laxative. Homeopathically used for liver and gallbladder ailments. Leaf extracts weaker than root extracts. Experimentally,

New England Aster (Aster novae-angliae). Photo by Harry Ellis.

Chicory (Cichorium intybus) has sky blue to violet flowers (rarely white).

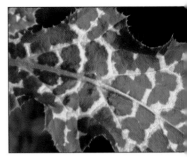

(Left) *Milk Thistle* (Silybum marianum) *is widely naturalized in California.* (Above) *Note the milky veins in its leaves.*

root extracts are antibacterial. In experiments, animals given chicory root extracts exhibit a slower and weaker heart rate (pulse). Root extracts in alcohol solutions have proven anti-inflammatory effects. Root and leaves approved in Germany for treatment of loss of appetite and dyspepsia. **WARNING:** May cause rare allergic reactions.

MILK THISTLE
Silybum marianum (L.) Gaertn.

Seeds, whole plant

Composite Family

Annual or biennial thistle; to 6 ft. Leaves *mottled* or *streaked with white veins; sharp-spined,* clasping. Flowers purple tufts; receptacle densely bristle-spined. Flowers June–Sept. **WHERE FOUND:** Escaped from cultivation, common in Calif. Alien (Europe). **USES:** Young leaves (with spines removed) eaten as a vegetable. Traditionally, tea made from whole plant used to improve appetite, allay indigestion, and restore liver function. Used for cirrhosis, jaundice, hepatitis, and liver poisoning from chemicals or drug and alcohol abuse. Silymarin, a seed extract, dramatically improves liver regeneration in hepatitis, cirrhosis, mushroom poisoning, and other liver diseases. In the form of an intravenous preparation, silybin, a flavonoid component of the seed, is clinically useful in treating severe *Amanita* mushroom poisoning in Germany. While used clinically in Europe, its use in the U.S. is not well known. Oral commercial preparations of the seed extracts are manufactured in Europe and now widely available in the U.S. Approved in Germany and other countries for the supportive treatment of chronic inflammatory liver disorders such as hepatitis, cirrhosis, and fatty infiltration caused by alcohol or other toxins. In addition to treating liver disease, it also has a preventative effect, helping to prevent liver damage from exposure to toxic chemicals.

PURPLE CONEFLOWERS

NARROW-LEAVED PURPLE CONEFLOWER

Root, whole plant

Echinacea angustifolia DC.　　　　　　　　Composite Family

Tap-rooted perennial; 6–20 in. Leaves lance-shaped, stiff-hairy. Flowers with prominent cone-shaped disk surrounded by pale to deep purple spreading rays; June–Sept. *Rays about as long as width of disk* (to 1 ¼ in.) **WHERE FOUND:** Prairies. Texas, w. Okla., w. Kans., Neb.; west to e. Colo., e. Mont., N.D., Man., Sask. **USES:** Plains Indians are said to have used *Echinacea* for more medicinal purposes than any other plant group. Root (chewed, or in tea) used for snakebites, spider bites, cancers, toothaches, burns, hard-to-heal sores and wounds, colds, and the flu. Science confirms many traditional uses, plus cortisone-like activity and insecticidal, bactericidal, and immuno-stimulant activities. Considered a nonspecific immune system stimulant. More than 300 pharmaceutical preparations are made from *Echinacea* plants in

(Left) *Narrow-leaved Purple Coneflower* (Echinacea angustifolia) *produces short ray flowers.*
(Above) *Pale Purple Coneflower* (Echinacea pallida). *Its ray flowers grow to 4 in. long.*

Germany, including extracts, salves, and tinctures; used for wounds, herpes sores, canker sores, throat infections; preventative for influenza, colds. A folk remedy for brown recluse spider bites. **REMARKS:** Hybrids occur where the range of this species overlaps that of Pale Purple Coneflower (*E. pallida*, below), though not necessarily hybrids between *E. angustifolia* and *E. pallida*.

PALE PURPLE CONEFLOWER
Echinacea pallida Nutt.

Root

Composite Family

Similar to *E. angustifolia* (above), but larger—to 40 in. Rays strongly drooping, to 4 in. long. Flowers May–Aug. **WHERE FOUND:** Prairies, glades. Ark. to Wisc., Minn.; e. Okla., Kans., Neb. **USES:** Same as for *E. angustifolia,* though some consider this plant less active. Ironically, the root of *E. pallida* is approved for use in Germany as an immuno-stimulant for preventing and reducing cold and flu symptoms, while *E. angustifolia* is unapproved. It appears that most chemical and pharmacological studies thought to be conducted on *E. angustifolia* prior to 1988 were actually conducted on *E. pallida,* emphasizing the importance of proper identification of plant material used in scientific research.

*Purple Coneflower (*Echinacea purpurea*) produces orange-tipped spines in the flowerhead.*

*The leaves of the Purple Coneflower (*E. purpurea*) are oval-toothed.*

PURPLE CONEFLOWER
Echinacea purpurea (L.) Moench.

Root, whole flowering plant
Composite Family

Perennial; 2–3 ft. Leaves oval, *coarsely toothed*. Bristle tips of flower disks *orange*. Rays typically purple (sometimes white). Flowers June–Sept. **WHERE FOUND:** Open woods, thickets; cultivated in gardens. Mich., Ohio to La., e. Texas, Okla. Widely grown as a flower garden perennial. **USES:** Same as for *E. angustifolia*. Widely used in Europe, but not native there. Most commercial German *Echinacea* preparations utilize extracts of above-ground parts and/or roots of *E. purpurea*. Extracts enhance particle ingestion capacity of white blood cells and other specialized immune system cells, increasing their ability to attack foreign particles, such as cold or flu viruses. German studies showed significant immune-system stimulating activity with orally administered extracts of *E. purpurea, E. angustifolia,* and *E. pallida*, both in mice and laboratory experiments. Several clinical studies have revealed that *E. purpurea* reduces severity and duration of cold and flu symptoms. However, recent clinical studies found that ethanolic extracts of *E. angustifolia* and *E. purpurea* did not *prevent* colds and flu. Different preparations (water versus alcoholic extracts) may have different active components. Cichoric acid, polysaccharides, alkylamides, and other compounds have attributed immuno-stimulating activity. Tops (not roots) approved in Germany as an immuno-stimulant for colds and flu; externally for hard-to-heal wounds and sores. In topical preparations, echinacoside has antioxidant activity, reducing degradation of skin when exposed to sunlight. **WARNING:** *Echinacea* and other immuno-stimulants are not used in cases of autoimmune disease or impaired immune response, including tuberculosis, multiple sclerosis, and HIV infection. Rare allergic reactions have been reported from *Echinacea* use. There is contraindication to the use of *Echinacea* in fighting HIV because it appears to increase tumor-necrosis factor, which is associated with a poorer prognosis for AIDS patients. **REMARKS:** Wild Quinine root (*Parthenium integrifolium*) is often used as an adulterant to the root (sold in dried form) of Purple Coneflower (*E. purpurea*). See p. 90.

PLANTS WITH GREEN HOODLIKE FLOWERS

DRAGON OR GREEN ARUM
Arisaema dracontium (L.) Schott

Root
Arum Family

⚠ Perennial; 1–3 ft. Leaf solitary; divided into 5–15 lance-shaped leaflets along a horseshoe-shaped frond. Spathe sheathlike, *narrow; spadix much longer.* Flowers May–July. **WHERE FOUND:** Rich, moist woods. Sw. Que., Vt., s. N.H. to Fla.; Texas, e. Kans., Neb., Wisc., Mich. **USES:** American Indians used dried, aged root for "female disorders." Root considered edible once it has been dried, aged, and elaborately processed. **WARNING:** Whole fresh plant contains intensely burning, irritating calcium oxalate crystals. **RELATED SPECIES:** The Chinese use related *Arisaema* species for epilepsy, hemiplegia (paralysis); externally, as a local anesthetic or in ointment for swellings and small tumors.

JACK-IN-THE-PULPIT
Arisaema triphyllum (L.) Schott

Root
Arum Family

⚠ Perennial; 1–2 ft. 1–2 leaves, 3 leaflets each; green beneath. Spathe *cuplike, with a curving flap;* green to purplish brown, often striped. Flowers Apr.–early July. Berries clustered, scarlet. **WHERE FOUND:** Moist woods. Most of our area. **USES:** American In-

The leaves of the Dragon or Green Arum (Arisaema dracontium) *grow in a horseshoe pattern.*

Dragon or Green Arum (A. dracontium) *has a long green flower spathe.*

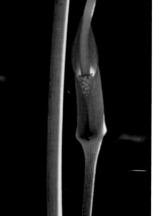

Jack-in-the-pulpit (Arisaema triphyllum) *is easily identified when in bloom.*

dians used the dried, aged root for colds and dry coughs, and to build blood. Externally, the root was poulticed for rheumatism, scrofulous sores, boils, abscesses, and ringworm. Dried-root tea traditionally considered expectorant, diaphoretic, and purgative. Historically used for asthma, bronchitis, colds, cough, laryngitis, and headaches. Externally for rheumatism, boils, and swelling from snakebites. **WARNING:** Intensely irritating. Calcium oxalate crystals found in whole fresh herb. **RELATED SPECIES:** *A. atrorubens* (not shown) is generally larger; leaves grayish green beneath. Both species are treated as one by most modern authorities. The Chinese used related species to treat snakebites.

SKUNK CABBAGE   Root
Symplocarpus foetidus (L.) Salisb. ex Nutt.   Arum Family

⚠   Strongly skunk-scented perennial; 1–2 ft. Leaves broad, oval. Flowers appear before leaves, Feb.–May; greenish to purple,

Skunk Cabbage (Symplocarpus foetidus) *produces large, cabbage-like leaves.*

Skunk Cabbage (S. foetidus). *Its unique flowers range from green to red.*

hooded, *sheathing spathe*, with a *clublike* organ within. **WHERE FOUND:** Wet, rich woods. N.S. to Ga.; Tenn.; Ill. to Iowa. One of the first spring wildflowers, it often grows in melting snow because of the thermogenesis of salicylic acid and salicylates in the flower. Temperature within the flower spathe is often 60°F higher than the ambient air. **USES:** American Indians used root for cramps, convulsions, whooping cough, toothaches; root poulticed for wounds, underarm deodorant. Leaf poulticed to reduce swelling, ate dried root to stop epileptic seizures. Subsequently used by physicians as antispasmodic for epilepsy, spasmodic coughs, asthma; used externally in lotions for itching, rheumatism; diuretic; emetic in large doses. Micmac Indians sniff the root to relieve migraines. **WARNING:** Eating leaves causes burning, inflammation. Roots considered toxic.

MISCELLANEOUS GREEN-FLOWERED VINES

WILD YAM   **Roots**
Dioscorea villosa L.   Yam Family

Perennial twining vine; *stem smooth*. Leaves *alternate* (lower ones in whorls of 3–8), heart-shaped, hairy beneath; veins conspicuous. Flowers not showy; male and female flowers separate; May–Aug. **WHERE FOUND:** Wet woods. Conn. to Tenn.; Texas to Minn. **USES:** American Indians used root tea to relieve labor pains. Fresh dried root (tea) formerly used by physicians for colic, gastrointestinal irritations, morning sickness, asthma, spasmodic hiccough, rheumatism, and "chronic gastritis of drunkards." Contains diosgenin, used to manufacture progesterone and other steroid drugs. Of all plant genera, there is perhaps none with greater impact on modern life but whose dramatic story is as little known as *Dioscorea*. Most of the steroid hormones used in modern medicine, especially those in contraceptives, were developed from elaborately processed chemical components derived from yams. Drugs made with yam-derived components (diosgenins) relieve asthma, arthritis, eczema; they also regulate metabolism and control fertility. Synthetic products manufactured from diosgenins include human sex hormones (contraceptive pills), drugs to treat menopause, dysmenorrhea, premenstrual syndrome, testicular deficiency, impotency, prostate hypertrophy, and psychosexual problems, as well as high blood pressure, arterial spasms, migraines, and other ailments. Widely prescribed cortisones and hydrocortisones were indirect products of the genus *Dioscorea*. They are used for Addison's disease, some allergies, bursitis, contact dermatitis, psoriasis, rheumatoid arthritis, sciatica, brown recluse spider bites, insect stings, and other diseases and ail-

Wild Yam (Dioscorea villosa) *leaves have conspicuous veins.*

Hops (Humulus lupulus). *Note the three-lobed leaves.*

Hops (H. lupulus) *can become weedy.*

Hops (H. lupulus). *Its fruiting bodies, or strobiles, produce a yellow crystalline resin within.*

ments. Wild yam has appeared in the American market in recent years as a "source" of estrogen or progesterone, prompting some to call this marketing effort the "wild yam scam," since the root does not contain human sex hormones. **WARNING:** Fresh plant may induce vomiting and other undesirable side effects.

HOPS   **Fruits (strobiles)**
Humulus lupulus L.   Hemp Family
Rough-prickly, twining perennial. Leaves mostly with 3–5 lobes; *sinuses (notches) rounded;* yellow resinous granules beneath. Male and female flowers on separate plants; July–Aug. Fruits (strobiles) inflated. **WHERE FOUND:** Waste places. Throughout our area. Alien. **USES:** Tea of fruits (strobiles) traditionally used as sedative, antispasmodic, diuretic; for insomnia, cramps, coughs, fevers; externally, for bruises, boils, inflammation, rheumatism. Experimentally antimicrobial, relieves spasms of smooth muscles, acts as sedative (disputed). Hops contains several sedative and pain-relieving components. Hops-picker fatigue is a condition believed to result from release of the essential oil during harvest. Used to relieve mood disturbances, nervous tension, anxiety, and unrest. Approved in Germany to treat discomfort from restlessness or anxiety and sleep disturbances. Considered calming and helpful in promoting sleep. **WARNING:** Handling plant often causes dermatitis. Dislodged hairs may irritate eyes. Crystalline resin in fruits causes rare allergic reactions. **RELATED SPECIES:** Japanese hops, *Humulus japonicus,* is a weedy annual with 5–9 leaf lobes. Leaves much rougher than common hops. Naturalized from N.E. to N.C. west to Kans.

MISCELLANEOUS PLANTS WITH GREEN FLOWERS

CANNABIS, HEMP, MARIJUANA   **Leaves, seeds, flowering tops**
Cannabis sativa L.   Hemp Family
Annual weed; 5–14 ft. Leaves *palmate, with 5–7 lobes.* Leaflets lance-shaped, toothed. Flowers greenish, sticky; Aug.–Sept. **WHERE FOUND:** Escaped or cultivated (illegally) throughout our area. Alien. **USES:** Leaves smoked; illegal intoxicant. Legitimate use of chemical components to treat glaucoma; also relieves nausea following chemotherapy. Antibiotic for gram-positive bacteria. Many folk uses. Much maligned, but potentially a very useful medicinal plant. We are jointly convinced that the whole leaf is better than the sum of its parts—that whole marijuana is, through synergy, safer, more effective, and cheaper than its isolated silver bullet active compound, THC. Further, we believe that legalized mari-

(Left) *Cannabis, Hemp, Marijuana* (Cannabis sativa). *Its palmate leaves represent a counterculture symbol.* (Above) *Blue Cohosh* (Caulophyllum thalictroides) *produces inedible blueberry-like fruits.*

juana would generate more funds for the government and less organized crime. Considered pain-relieving, anticonvulsant; relieves nausea. A legitimate fiber (hemp) and oil-seed plant in many other countries. **WARNING:** Not accepted socially or legally.

BLUE COHOSH Root
Caulophyllum thalictroides (L.) Michx. Barberry Family

⚠ Perennial; 1–2 ft. Smooth-stemmed; stem and leaves covered with *bluish film.* Leaves divided into 3 (occasionally 5) *leaflets with 2–3 lobes.* Flowers greenish yellow, in terminal clusters; Apr.–June, before leaves expand. **WHERE FOUND:** Moist, rich woods. N.B. to S.C.; Ark., N.D. to Man. Like Black Cohosh, coming under increasing collecting pressures. **USES:** Root tea used extensively by American Indians to aid labor, treat profuse menstruation, abdominal cramps, urinary tract infections, lung ailments, fevers; emetic. A folk remedy for rheumatism, cramps, epilepsy, and inflammation of the uterus. Historically prescribed by physicians for chronic uterine diseases. Said to cause abortion by stimulating uterine contractions. Roots possess estrogenic activity and check muscle spasms. Studies by scientists in India suggest the root may possess some contraceptive potential. Extracts shown to be anti-inflammatory (in rats). An alkaloid in the root, methylcytisine, has effects similar to those of nicotine, increasing blood pressure, stimulating the small intestine, and causing hyper-

Wild Ipecac (Euphorbia ipecacuanhae) *has green to purple leaves. Photo by Doug Elliott.*

glycemia. It also contains glycosides, which are believed to be responsible for its uterine-stimulant activity and to constrict coronary blood vessels. **WARNING:** Root powder strongly irritating to mucous membranes. Avoid during pregnancy.

WILD IPECAC
Leaves, root

Euphorbia ipecacuanhae L. Spurge Family

Large-rooted perennial with underground stems; 3–12 in. tall. Stems smooth, succulent. Leaves inserted at joints; rounded to linear, green to purple. Solitary flowers on long stalks; "cups" have 5 glands, with narrow white, yellow, green, or purple appendages. Flowers Apr.–May. **WHERE FOUND:** Sandy soil. Mostly coastal. N.J. to Fla. **USES:** American Indians used leaf tea for diabetes; root tea as a strong laxative and emetic, for pinworms, rheumatism; poulticed root on snakebites. **WARNING:** Extremely strong laxative. Juice from fresh plant may cause blistering.

LARGE PLANTS; LEAVES TO 1 FT. LONG OR MORE

CASTOR-OIL-PLANT, CASTOR BEAN
Seed oil

Ricinus communis L. Spurge Family

Large annual or perennial (in South); 5–12 ft. Leaves large, palmate with 5–11 lobes. Flowers in clusters—female ones above, male ones below; July–Sept. Seed capsule with soft spines. **WHERE FOUND:** Escaped exotic cultivar, alien. **USES:** Seed oil famous since

Castor-oil-plant, Castor Bean (Ricinus communis) *is a large-leaved tropical annual with green to red seed capsules.*

Castor Bean (R. communis) *seeds are mottled with brown streaks and are highly toxic.*

ancient Egyptian time as a purgative or laxative, folk remedy used to induce labor. Nauseous taste may induce vomiting. Oil used as a laxative in food poisoning or before X-ray diagnosis of bowels. Used externally for ringworm, itch, piles, sores, abscesses, and hairwash for dandruff. Oil even suggested as a renewable energy resource. Poulticed boiled leaves a folk remedy to produce milk flow. Jim Duke wishes his mother had heeded the warning "not to be administered to children under twelve years." His mother believed that castor oil cut with orange juice was a panacea. Ricin, the deadly poison found in the seeds, can be bioengineered to attach to monoclonal antibodies that attack only cancer cells, a technique reportedly tried in 1,000 cancer patients. The AIDS virus can infect an immune cell by locking on to its cell receptor protein, CD4. By genetically affixing the deadly poison ricin to genetically engineered CD4 proteins, one obtains CD4-ricin, which will lock on the external viruses of infected cells 1,000 times more often than on healthy cells. Using such techniques, one might possibly kill enough infected cells to prevent the disease from spreading and causing life-threatening symptoms. Ricinoleic acid has served as a component in contraceptive jellies. In some African countries, seed is used as a contraceptive. **WARNING: Seeds are a deadly poison**—1 seed may be fatal to a child. After oil is squeezed from seeds, the toxic protein ricin, which is deadly, remains in seed cake. Oil is used in industrial lubricants, varnishes, and plastics. May induce dermatitis. Judi DuCellier, Jim Duke's assistant, took some castor bean seeds home to poison some mice. Judi's grandson chewed on one of the seeds and was given ipecac immediately.

Colombo Root (Frasera spp.) produces distinctive purple-spotted flowers with a green gland.

American White or False Hellebore (Veratrum viride) produces greenish flowers and pleated leaves.

COLUMBO ROOT

Root

Frasera caroliniensis Walt.
[*Swertia caroliniensis* (Walt.) Ktze.]

Gentian Family

Smooth biennial; 3–8 ft. Leaves in *4's; large,* lance-shaped or oblong. Flowers greenish yellow with *brown-purple dots;* 4-parted, with a *large, glandular, greenish dot on each division.* Flowers June–July. **WHERE FOUND:** Limey slopes, rich woods. N.Y. to Ga.; La. to Wisc. **USES:** Root tea formerly used for colic, cramps, dysentery, diarrhea, stomachaches, lack of appetite, nausea; general tonic. **RELATED SPECIES:** Asian species have been used similarly.

AMERICAN WHITE OR FALSE HELLEBORE

Root

Veratrum viride Ait.

Lily Family

Perennial; 2–8 ft. Leaves large, broadly oval, *strongly ribbed.* Flowers yellowish, turning dull green; small, *star-shaped,* in a many-flowered panicle; Apr.–July. **WHERE FOUND:** Wet wood edges, swamps. New England to Ga. mountains. Tenn. to Wisc. **USES:** Historically valued as an analgesic for pain, epilepsy, convulsions, pneumonia, heart sedative; weak tea for sore throats, tonsillitis. Used in pharmaceutical drugs to slow heart rate, lower blood pressure; for arteriosclerosis forms of nephritis. Powdered root used in insecticides. **WARNING: All parts, especially root, are highly or fatally toxic.** Leaves have been mistaken for Pokeweed (p. 65) or Marsh-marigold (p. 101) and eaten, with fatal results.

FLOWERS IN SLENDER TERMINAL CLUSTERS

HORSEWEED. CANADA FLEABANE

Whole plant
Composite Family

Conyza canadensis (L.) Cronq.
[*Erigeron canadensis* L.]

Bristly annual or biennial weed; 1–7 ft. Leaves numerous, lance-shaped. Tiny (to ¼ in.) greenish white flowers on many branches from leaf axils; disk yellow, with short rays. Flowers July–Nov. **WHERE FOUND:** Waste places, roadsides. Throughout our area; has become a weed on other continents. **USES:** Plant tea used as a folk diuretic, astringent for diarrhea, "gravel" (kidney stones), diabetes, painful urination, hemorrhages of stomach, bowels, bladder, and kidneys; also used for nosebleeds, fevers, bronchitis, tumors, piles, coughs. Africans used it for eczema and ringworm. Essential oil traditionally used for bronchial ailments and cystitis. Contains pain-relieving, antioxidant, spasm-relieving, antibacte-

Horseweed (Conyza canadensis) *is weedy with greenish flowers. Photo by Stephen Lee Timme.*

Alumroot (Heuchera americana) *produces small, greenish white flowers. Photo by Martin Wall.*

rial, antifungal, and anticancer components. **WARNING:** May cause contact dermatitis.

ALUMROOT

Root, leaves

Heuchera americana L.

Saxifrage Family

Variable perennial; 1–2 ft. Leaves toothed, roundish to somewhat maple-shaped; base heart-shaped. Flowers small, greenish white; on short stalks; Apr.–June. **WHERE FOUND:** Woods, shaded rocks. S. Ont.; Conn. to Ga.; Okla. to Mich. **USES:** Similar to those of alum; styptic, astringent. Leaf tea used for diarrhea, dysentery, piles; gargled for sore throats. Root poulticed on wounds, sores, abrasions. Other *Heucheras* are used similarly.

DITCH STONECROP

Seeds, whole plant

Penthorum sedoides L.

Saxifrage Family

Perennial; 1–3 ft. Leaves lance-shaped, finely toothed. Yellowish green flowers on 2–3 spreading, terminal stalks; July–Sept. **WHERE FOUND:** Muddy soil. Most of our area. **USES:** American Indians used seeds in cough syrups. Historically, plant tincture was used as a

Ditch Stonecrop (Penthorum sedoides) *is found in muddy soils. Note the spreading inflorescence with white to greenish flowers. Photo by Stephen Lee Timme.*

Figworts (Scrophularia *sp.*) *produce tiny flowers that have a protruding upper petal.*

demulcent, laxative, and tonic, for mucous membrane irritations, vaginitis, diarrhea, dysentery, pharyngitis, tonsillitis, piles, chronic bronchitis, and nervous indigestion.

FIGWORT
Leaves, root
Scrophularia marilandica L.
Figwort Family

Perennial; 3–6 ft. Stems angled, grooved. Leaves are oval, rounded, or heart-shaped at base; toothed. Flowers like a *miniature scoop,* 4 stamens, with an additional wide, sterile, *purple* stamen (yellow in *S. lanceolata* not shown). Flowers June–Oct. **WHERE FOUND:** Rich woods. Sw. Me. to n. Ga.; La.; Okla. to Minn. **USES:** American Indians used root tea for irregular menses, fevers, piles; diuretic, tonic. Poultice a folk cancer remedy. Folk remedy to allay restlessness, anxiety, sleeplessness in pregnant women. Other species used similarly. **WARNING:** Of unknown toxicity.

FLOWERS IN AXILS; PLANTS WITH STINGING OR BRISTLY HAIRS

STINGING NETTLE
Whole plant
Urtica dioica L.
Nettle Family

Perennial; 12–50 in. *Stiff, stinging hairs.* Leaves mostly oval; bases barely *heart-shaped.* Flowers greenish, in branched clusters; June–Sept. Male and female flowers on separate plants or branches. The N. American genetic material, designated *U. dioica* spp. *gracilis* (Ait.) Seland., with 6 varieties, differs from the European *U. dioica* spp. *dioica* in that the European material has male and female flowers on separate plants. **WHERE FOUND:** Waste places, moist soils. Most of N. America; Lab. to Alaska and southward. European subspecies occasionally naturalized in our range. **USES:** Traditionally, leaf tea used in Europe as a "blood purifier," "blood builder," diuretic, astringent; for anemia, gout, glandular diseases, rheumatism, poor circulation, enlarged spleen, mucous discharges of lungs, internal bleeding, diarrhea, dysentery. Its effect involves the action of white blood cells, aiding coagulation and formation of hemoglobin in red blood corpuscles. Iron-rich leaves have been cooked as a potherb. Studies suggest CNS-depressant, antibacterial, and mitogenic activity; inhibits effects of adrenaline. This plant should be studied further for possible uses against kidney and urinary system ailments. Recently, Germans have been using the root in treatments for prostate cancer. Russians are using the leaves in alcohol for cholecystitis (inflammation of the gallbladder) and hepatitis. Some people keep potted Stinging Nettle in the kitchen window, alongside an aloe plant, in the belief that an occasional sting alleviates arthritis. Leaves ap-

Stinging Nettle (Urtica dioica) *is seldom noticed until the plant is touched.*

Cocklebur (Xanthium sp.) *produce familiar characteristic burrs.*

proved in Germany for supportive treatment of rheumatism and kidney infections. Root preparations approved for symptomatic relief of urinary difficulties associated with early stages of benign prostatic hyperplasia, which affects a majority of men over 50 years of age. **WARNING:** Fresh plants **sting.** Dried plant (used in tea) does not sting. One fatality has been attributed, rightly or wrongly, to the sting of a larger tropical nettle. Histamine, acetylcholine, 5-hydroxy-tryptamine, small amounts of formic acid, leukotrienes, and other unknown compounds act together to produce the sting. Some of these compounds are neurotransmitters in the human brain. **RELATED SPECIES:** Other *Urtica* species occurring in N. America are said to be used interchangeably.

COCKLEBUR
Leaves, root

Xanthium strumarium L.   Composite Family

⚠ Variable weedy annual; to 5 ft. Leaves oval to heart-shaped, somewhat lobed or toothed, on long stalks. Flowers inconspicuous, green. Fruits oval, with *crowded, hooked prickles;* Sept.–Nov. **WHERE FOUND:** Waste places. Scattered. **USES:** Root historically used for scrofulous tumors (strumae—hence the species name). This plant and the related species *X. spinosum* L. (not shown) were formerly used for rabies, fevers, malaria; considered diuretic, fever-reducing, sedative. American Indians used leaf tea for kidney disease, rheumatism, tuberculosis, and diarrhea; also as a blood tonic. Chinese used it similarly. **WARNING:** Most Cocklebur species are **toxic** to grazing animals, and are usually avoided by them. Seeds contain toxins, but seed oil has served as lamp fuel. **REMARKS:** Taxonomy confusing.

SLENDER, MOSTLY TERMINAL FLOWER CLUSTERS; BUCKWHEAT FAMILY

COMMON SMARTWEED, MILD WATER PEPPER
Polygonum hydropiper L.

Leaves

Buckwheat Family

Reddish-stemmed annual; to 2 ft. Leaves lance-shaped, lacking sheath bristle; very *acrid* and *peppery to taste;* margin wavy. Greenish flowers in arching clusters (most *Polygonums* have pink flowers); June–Nov. **WHERE FOUND:** Moist soils, shores. Much of our area. **USES:** American Indians used leaf tea as a diuretic for painful or bloody urination, fevers, chills; poulticed leaves for pain, piles; rubbed them on a child's thumb to prevent sucking. Leaf tea a folk remedy for internal bleeding and menstrual or uterine disorders. Leaves contain rutin, which helps strengthen fragile capillaries and thus helps prevent bleeding. Contains pain-relieving compounds and spilanthin, which numbs a toothache. Also contains hot pungent compounds, which may explain the name "smartweed." **WARNING:** Plant can irritate skin. **RELATED SPECIES:** Many other *Polygonums* have been used in American, European, and Asian folk or traditional medicine.

Smartweed, Water Pepper (Polygonum spp.). Often separated on highly technical characteristics.

Sheep-sorrel (Rumex acetosella) *produces reddish fruits and often covers infertile fields.*

SHEEP-SORREL
Leaves, root

Rumex acetosella L.
Buckwheat Family

 Slender, smooth, *sour-tasting* perennial; 4–12 in. Leaves *arrow-shaped*. Tiny flowers in green heads, interrupted on stalk; turning reddish or yellowish; Apr.–Sept. **WHERE FOUND:** Acid soils. Throughout our area. **USES:** Leaf tea of this common European alien traditionally used for fevers, inflammation, scurvy. Fresh leaves considered cooling, diuretic; leaves poulticed (after roasting) for tumors, wens (sebaceous cysts); folk cancer remedy. Root tea used for diarrhea, excessive menstrual bleeding. Has become popular in recent years as a component of the reputedly anticancer Essiac formula and Ojibwa teas. Sheep sorrel is rich in cancer-preventative vitamins; also includes four antimutagenic and four antioxidant compounds, perhaps laying the foundation for reported anticancer (or cancer-preventing) folk uses. **WARNING: May cause poisoning** in large doses, due to high oxalic acid and tannin content.

YELLOW OR CURLY DOCK
Roots, leaves

Rumex crispus L.
Buckwheat Family

 Perennial; 1–5 ft. Leaves large, lance-shaped; *margins distinctly wavy.* Flowers green, on spikes; May–Sept. Winged, heart-shaped seeds; June–Sept. Roots yellowish in cross-section. **WHERE FOUND:** Waste ground. Throughout our area. **USES:** Herbalists consider dried-root tea an excellent "blood purifier." Used to treat "bad

(Left) *The leaves of Yellow or Curly Dock* (Rumex crispus) *have prominently wavy margins.*
(Above) *"Yellow" refers to the interior color of the root.*

blood," chronic skin diseases, chronic enlarged lymph glands, skin sores, rheumatism, liver ailments, sore throats. May cause or relieve diarrhea, depending on dose, harvest time, and concentrations of anthraquinones (laxative) and/or tannins (antidiarrheal). Anthraquinones can arrest growth of ringworm and other fungi. **WARNING:** Large doses may cause gastric disturbance, nausea, and diarrhea.

FLOWERS IN TERMINAL CLUSTERS AND IN UPPER AXILS: AMARANTH AND GOOSEFOOT FAMILIES

SMOOTH PIGWEED (NOT SHOWN) Leaves
Amaranthus hybridus L. Amaranth Family

Smooth-stemmed annual; 1–6 ft. Leaves to 6 in. long, hairy. Flower spikes green (or red-tinged); *lateral spikes erect or ascending*; Aug.–Oct. **WHERE FOUND:** Throughout our area. Alien weed. **USES:** Leaf tea astringent, stops bleeding; used in dysentery, diarrhea, ulcers, intestinal bleeding. Reduces swelling. Many members of the Pigweed (Amaranth) family and Goosefoot family serve as potherbs and/or cereal grains. The National Academy of Sciences is vigorously investigating both grain amaranths and the goosefoot relatives as food crops.

Green Amaranth, Pigweed (Amaranthus retroflexus). *Photo by Stephen L. Timme.*

Spiny Amaranth (Amaranthus spinosus). *Note spines in leaf axils.*

GREEN AMARANTH, PIGWEED
Leaves
Amaranthus retroflexus L.
Amaranth Family

Grayish, downy annual; 6–24 in. Leaves oval, stout-stalked. Flower spikes to 2½ in. long; blunt, chaffy, interspersed with bristly bracts; Aug.–Oct. **WHERE FOUND:** Throughout our area. Alien weed. **USES:** Astringent. Used for diarrhea, excessive menstrual flow, hemorrhages, hoarseness.

SPINY AMARANTH
Leaves
Amaranthus spinosus L.
Herb

Branched, erect annual to 3 ft. tall. Leaves ovate to lance-ovate, 1¼–2½ in. long, with a pair of curved spines in the leaf axils. Flower spikes numerous, 2–6 in. long; rough and spongy toward top. June–August. **WHERE FOUND:** Waste places, fields. N.Y. to Mo. southward. Weed found throughout the tropics, spreading into N. America. Probably originating from S. America. **USES:** Leaves astringent. Adopted by American Indian groups for the treatment of profuse menstruation. Many Amaranth species valued for astringency; most often used to stop bleeding, both internal and external.

LAMB-QUARTERS, PIGWEED
Leaves

Chenopodium album L.
Goosefoot Family

Annual weed; 1–3 ft. Stem *often mealy, red-streaked*. Leaves somewhat diamond-shaped, coarsely toothed; mealy white beneath. Flowers greenish, inconspicuous; in clusters; June–Oct. **WHERE FOUND:** Gardens, fields, waste places. Throughout our area. Alien. **USES:** American Indians ate leaves to treat stomachaches and prevent scurvy. Cold tea used for diarrhea; leaf poultice used for burns. A folk remedy for vitiligo, a skin disorder. Leaves considered edible.

MEXICAN TEA, AMERICAN WORMSEED
Seeds, essential oil

Chenopodium ambrosioides L.
Goosefoot Family

Stout, *aromatic* herb; 3–5 ft. Leaves *wavy-toothed*. Flowers greenish in spikes, among leaves; Aug.–Nov. Seeds *glandular-dotted*. **WHERE FOUND:** Waste places. Throughout our area. **USES:** Until recently, the essential oil distilled from flowering and fruiting plant was used against roundworms, hookworms, dwarf (not large) tapeworms, intestinal amoeba. Now largely replaced by synthetics. **WARNING:** Oil is **highly toxic.** Still, a dash of the leaves is added

The leaves of Lamb-quarters, Pigweed (Chenopodium album) *have a mealy surface.*

Mexican Tea, American Wormseed (Chenopodium ambrosioides). *Its deeply lobed leaves are strongly aromatic.*

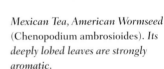

as a culinary herb to Mexican bean dishes in the belief that it may reduce gas. May cause dermatitis or an allergic reaction. Steven Foster has experienced vertigo from contact with essential oil released during harvest. Ingesting just 10 ml of the essential oil has proven fatal (much less in children).

NODDING, INCONSPICUOUS FLOWERS WITH YELLOW POLLEN; RAGWEEDS

COMMON RAGWEED
Ambrosia artemisiifolia L.

Leaves, root
Composite Family

Annual; 1–5 ft. Leaves dissected, artemisia-like; highly variable— *as a rule alternate*, but opposite as well. Drooping, *inconspicuous green flowerheads on conspicuous erect spikes*; July–Oct. **WHERE FOUND:** Waste ground throughout our area. Noxious weed. **USES:** American Indians rubbed leaves on insect bites, infected toes, minor skin eruptions, and hives. Tea used for fevers, nausea, mucous discharges, intestinal cramping; very astringent, emetic. Root tea used for menstrual problems and stroke. **WARNING:** Pollen causes allergies. Ingesting or touching plant may cause allergic reactions. Pollen from the genus *Ambrosia* is responsible for approximately 90 percent of pollen-induced allergies in the U.S.

Common Ragweed (Ambrosia artemisiifolia) *is a major culprit of summer allergies.*

Giant Ragweed (Ambrosia trifida). *Note its large, three-lobed leaves.*

Goldenrods (*Solidago* species) are often pointed to as the source of late-summer allergies, but at the same time the showy goldenrods are blooming, the inconspicuous flowers of ragweeds are really guilty.

GIANT RAGWEED
Ambrosia trifida L.

Leaves, root
Composite Family

Annual; to 6–15 ft. Stems and leaves with stiff hairs, rough to the touch. Leaves opposite, deeply 3-lobed (sometimes 5-lobed or without lobes); tips pointed. Lower leaves are most uniform in appearance. Flowers similar to those of Common Ragweed. **WHERE FOUND:** Alluvial waste places, sometimes forming vast, pure, pollen-producing stands. Much of our area. **USES:** Astringent; stops bleeding. Leaf tea formerly used for prolapsed uterus, leukorrhea, fevers, diarrhea, dysentery, nosebleeds; gargled for mouth sores. American Indians used the crushed leaves on insect bites. The root was chewed to allay fear at night. The pollen of both this and Common Ragweed are harvested commercially, then manufactured into pharmaceutical preparations for the treatment of Ragweed allergies. **WARNING:** Pollen causes allergies. Ingesting or touching plant may cause allergic reactions. The Composite family, to which the ragweeds and the allergy-inducing artemisias (see following pages) belong, is the worst family as far as pollenosis is concerned.

FLOWERS IN TERMINAL CLUSTERS; LEAVES SILVER-HAIRY, AT LEAST BENEATH; ARTEMISIAS

WORMWOOD
Artemisia absinthium L.

Leaves
Composite Family

Aromatic perennial; 1–4 ft. Leaves silver-green, strongly divided; *segments blunt*, with *silky silver hairs on both sides*. Flowers are tiny, drooping; July–Sept. **WHERE FOUND:** Waste ground. Escaped from cultivation in n. U.S. Alien. **USES:** Extremely bitter leaves are nibbled to stimulate appetite. Tea is a folk remedy for delayed menses, fevers, worm expellent, and liver and gallbladder ailments. Formerly used for flavoring absinthe liqueurs. Contains the toxic principle thujone, which occurs only in minute amounts in water extracts (such as teas). Intoxication from absinthe liqueurs has been likened to that induced by marijuana. It is theorized that the active component of both plants may react with the same receptors of the central nervous system. Despite potential toxicity, the herb is approved in Germany to stimulate appetite and dyspepsia. **WARNING:** Relatively small doses may cause nervous disorders, convulsions, insomnia, nightmares, and other symp-

Wormwood (Artemisia absinthium) *produces extremely bitter leaves.*

Western Mugwort, White Sage, Cudweed (Artemisia ludoviciana). *Photo by Martin Wall.*

toms. Flowers of artemisias may induce allergic reactions. Approved as a food additive (flavoring) with thujone removed.

WESTERN MUGWORT, WHITE SAGE, CUDWEED
Leaves

Artemisia ludoviciana Nutt. Composite Family

Highly variable aromatic perennial; to 3 ft. Leaves *white-felty beneath*; lance-shaped, entire. Flowers in dense panicles; July–Sept. **WHERE FOUND:** Waste ground. Mich. to s. Ill., Texas; north to Mont. and westward. Naturalized east to New England. A weed. **USES:** Much used by American Indians as an astringent, to induce sweating, curb pain and diarrhea. Weak tea used for stomachaches, menstrual disorders. Leaf snuff used for sinus ailments, headaches, nosebleeds. Externally, wash used for itching, rashes, skin eruptions, swelling, boils, sores. Compress for fevers. Used in steam baths for rheumatism, fevers, colds, and flu. **WARNING:** May cause allergies.

MUGWORT
Leaves

Artemisia vulgaris L. Composite Family

Aromatic; 2–4 ft. Leaves *deeply cut, silvery-woolly beneath*. Flowerheads erect; July–Aug. **WHERE FOUND:** Waste ground. S. Canada to Ga.; Kans., Mich.; occasional westward. Alien weed. **USES:** Leaf tea diuretic, induces sweating; checks menstrual irregularity, promotes appetite, "tonic" to nerves. Used for bronchitis, colds, colic, epilepsy, fevers, kidney ailments, sciatica. Experimentally, lowers blood sugar. Components have antibacterial and antifungal activity. Dried leaves used as "burning stick" (moxa), famous in Chinese medicine to stimulate acupuncture points and treat

Mugwort (Artemisia vulgaris) has become a rampant weed.

rheumatism. Clinically proven to lower incidence of breached birth presentations. **WARNING:** May cause dermatitis. Reported to cause abortion and allergic reactions.

FLOWERS IN TERMINAL CLUSTERS; LEAVES NOT SILVER-HAIRY; ARTEMISIAS

ANNUAL WORMWOOD, SWEET ANNIE
Leaves, seeds

Artemisia annua L. — Composite Family

Sweet-scented, bushy annual; 1–9 ft. Leaves thrice-divided, *fernlike* segments oblong to lance-shaped, sharp-toothed or cleft. Tiny green-yellow flowers, in clusters; July–Oct. **WHERE FOUND:** Waste ground. Throughout our area; becoming much more common, escaping from cultivation. Alien. **USES:** Leaf tea (gather before flowering) used for colds, flu, malarial fevers, dysentery, diarrhea. Externally, pouticed on abscesses and boils. For quinine-

(Left) *Annual Wormwood, Sweet Annie (Artemisia annua) with finely divided aromatic leaves.* (Above) *It is a coarse annual in flower.*

and/or chlorquinine-resistant malaria (of interest to U.S. Army); clinical use of derivative compounds in China (tested with 8,000 patients) shows near 100 percent efficacy. Seeds used for night sweats, indigestion, flatulence. The compound responsible for the antimalarial activity also demonstrates marked herbicidal activity. Contains six or more antiviral compounds, some proven synergetic. Jim Duke's assistant is allergic to nonflowering material, even in a sealed envelope. **WARNING:** May cause allergic reactions or dermatitis.

TALL WORMWOOD, WESTERN SAGEBRUSH (NOT SHOWN)
Leaves

Artemisia campestris spp. *caudata* (Michx.) Hall & Clements
[*Artemisia caudata* Michx.]   Composite Family

Smooth-stemmed biennial; 2–6 ft. Leaves divided into *linear segments, not toothed.* Flower stalks *very leafy.* Flowers tiny, greenish yellow, in *drooping clusters;* July–Oct. **WHERE FOUND:** Sands. Me. to Fla.; Texas, N.D., and westward. **USES:** American Indians used leaf tea for colds, coughs, tuberculosis. Externally, poultice of steamed herb used for bruises and sores. **WARNING:** Allergic reactions may result from use.

WILD OR RUSSIAN TARRAGON
Leaves, roots

Artemisia dracunculus L.   Composite Family
[*A. redowskii* Led., *A. glauca* var. *draculina* (S. Wat.) Fern.]

Variable—aromatic to odorless. To 5 ft. Leaves lance-shaped to linear (sometimes divided), without teeth. Whitish green flowers

in loose, spreading clusters; July–Oct. **WHERE FOUND:** Prairies, dry soil. Wisc., Mo., Texas, and westward. Rare eastward to New England. **USES:** American Indians used leaf or root tea for colds, dysentery, diarrhea, headaches, difficult childbirth. Promotes appetite. Leaves poulticed for wounds, bruises.

Wild or Russian Tarragon
(Artemisia dracunculus).

Sometimes substituted for the cooking herb French Tarragon, which must be propagated vegetatively; it does not produce viable seed. French Tarragon smells strongly of anise; Wild Tarragon may be odorless and flavorless. **WARNING:** Allergic reactions may result from use.

MISCELLANEOUS PLANTS WITH GREEN-BROWN FLOWERS

VIRGINIA SNAKEROOT   **Root**
Aristolochia serpentaria L.   Birthwort Family

Delicate; 8–20 in. Leaves elongate, *strongly arrow-shaped.* Flowers *calabash-pipelike,* purplish brown; *at base of plant,* often under leaf litter; May–July. **WHERE FOUND:** Woods. Sw. Conn. to Fla.; Texas to Mo.; Ohio. Too rare to harvest. **USES:** Aromatic root nibbled (in minute doses) or in weak tea (1 teaspoon dried root in 1 cup of water) promotes sweating, appetite; expectorant. Used for fevers, stomachaches, indigestion, suppressed menses, and snakebites. Tea gargled for sore throats. **WARNING:** Irritating in large doses. **REMARKS:** Recent high prices following increasing demand and decreasing supplies may suggest this as a prospect for cultivation in the forest—further justification for saving our forests.

(Above) *Virginia Snakeroot* (Aristolochia serpentaria) *is a small plant with a camphorous root. Flower is beneath leaf litter.* (Right) *Dutchman's-pipe* (A. tomentosa) *produces a woody, twining vine.*

DUTCHMAN'S-PIPE
Aristolochia tomentosa Sims

Leaves

Birthwort Family

A climbing, woody vine. Leaves *heart-shaped*; blunt-tipped lower surface has *dense, soft white hairs*. Flowers *pipe-shaped*; calyx yellowish; May–June. **WHERE FOUND:** Rich riverbanks. N.C., Fla., and Texas; north to e. Kans., Mo., s. Ill., to s. Ind. **USES:** Like those of *A. serpentaria* (above), but much weaker in effect. Little used. **WARNING:** Potentially irritating in large doses. **RELATED SPECIES:** *A. macrophylla* (not shown) has nearly smooth, sharp-pointed leaves. Flowers brown-purple. Ironically, Virginia farmers spray *A. macrophylla* as a weed. It contains the antiseptic, antitumor compound aristolochic acid.

BEECH-DROPS
Epifagus virginiana (L.) W. Barton

Whole plant

Broomrape Family

A chlorophyll-lacking parasite found under Beech trees. Brownish, cream-colored, yellowish, or reddish. Leaves scalelike. Flowers whitish; Aug.–Oct. **WHERE FOUND:** Ont. to Fla.; Miss., La., Ark. and northward. **USES:** The highly astringent tea of the whole fresh plant (loses strength upon drying) was once used for diarrhea, dysentery, mouth sores, "obstinate ulcers" (external), cold sores.

Beech-drops (Epifagus virginiana) *is brown. Photo by Martin Wall.*

Skunk Cabbage (Symplocarpus foetidus) *with dark red to brown flowers.*

Folk cancer remedy; also known as "cancer root." Recent scientific investigations for antitumor activity proved negative.

SKUNK CABBAGE
Root

Symplocarpus foetidus (L.) Salisb. ex Nutt.   Arum Family

⚠ Strongly skunk-scented perennial. Flowers appear before leaves, Feb.–May. Greenish to purple, hooded, *sheathing spathe* with a *clublike* organ within. Root toxic. See p. 229.

EVERGREEN SHRUBS

COMMON JUNIPER

Fruits

Juniperus communis L.

Pine Family

⚠ Shrub or small tree; 2–20 ft. Bark reddish brown, shredding off in papery peels. Leaves (needles) taper to a spiny tip, in *whorls* of 3's with 2 *white bands above* (or 1 white band sometimes divided by a green midrib, broader than green margin). Fruits on short stalk; round to broadly oval, bluish black, usually with 3 seeds. **WHERE FOUND:** Rocky, infertile soils. Canada to Alaska, south to mountains of Ga.; e. Tenn. north to Ill.; Minn. west to N.M., Calif.; N. America, Europe, and Asia. N. American forms are small and shrublike, whereas European forms are more treelike. **USES:** Fruits used to flavor gin and other alcoholic beverages. also used commercially in some diuretic and laxative products. Juniper berries are one of the most widely used herbal diuretics. Approved in Germany in teas for stomach complaints and to simulate appetite. Science confirms anti-inflammatory and spasm-reducing activity, which may contribute to diuretic activity. Fruits eaten raw or in tea are a folk remedy used as a diuretic and urinary antiseptic for cystitis, carminative for flatulence, antiseptic for intestinal infections; once used for colic, coughs, stomachaches, colds, and bronchitis. Externally, used for sores, aches, rheumatism, arthritis, snakebites, and cancer. Volatile oil is responsible for diuretic and intestinal antiseptic activity. Diuretic activity results from irritation of renal tissue. **WARNING:** Potentially toxic. Large or frequent doses cause kidney failure, convulsions, and digestive irritation. In Germany, use limited to four weeks. Avoid during pregnancy. Oil may cause blistering.

Common Juniper (Juniperus communis).

Common Juniper (J. communis), *as found in commerce.*

English Yew (Taxus baccata) *is commonly cultivated.*

ENGLISH YEW
Leaves (needles), bark

Taxus baccata L.
Yew Family

Often grown as ornamental shrub, but the tree will grow to 40 ft. Bark is red-brown, peeling in plates. Leaves arranged in spirals—narrow, glossy, dark green above, lighter beneath, to 1¼ in. long. Fruit (aril), globose, red, to ½ in. in diameter. **WHERE FOUND:** Sometimes naturalized near old plantings; widely cultivated as an ornamental evergreen shrub or hedge throughout, represented by more than 250 cultivated varieties. **USES:** Yew toxins were used in Old World cultures as poison arrow tips to kill fish and animals. The pitch of yew trees was mixed with clarified butter and used for the treatment of cancer, a portend to the use by modern Western societies. The bark and leaves contain paclitaxel (once popularly called taxol, which is now a registered trademark of Bristol-Myers). Paclitaxel was first isolated in 1969, and its structure determined by 1971. The name was first applied by its discoverer, Monroe Wall. At first commercially derived from the bark of the Pacific Yew *Taxus brevifolia* Nutt., most supply now comes from *T. baccata* and its relatives in Europe and India. Today it is used in chemotherapy for the treatment of certain forms of breast cancer and ovarian cancer. Sales of the drug are expected to pass $1 billion per year, making it one of the most important natural products ever. **WARNING:** All plant parts (except perhaps the red aril) of this and other yews contain highly toxic components and are considered **poisonous,** possibly fatally so.

AMERICAN YEW (NOT SHOWN)
Leaves (needles)

Taxus canadensis Marsh.
Yew Family

Straggling evergreen shrub; rarely to 7 ft. Twigs *smooth*, green; reddish brown on older branches. Needles 2-ranked, ⅜–1 in. long, narrowing into abrupt fine points. Needles are *green on both sides* and with light green bands below; they often develop a reddish tint in winter. Female plants produce juicy, *cuplike, red arils* (pulp) surrounding ½ in. fruits. Seeds stony. **WHERE FOUND:** Rich woods. Nfld. to w. Va.; ne. Ky. to Iowa; Man. **USES:** American Indians used minute amounts of toxic leaf tea internally and externally for rheumatism, bowel ailments, fevers, colds, scurvy; to expel afterbirth, dispel clots; diuretic; twigs used as fumigant in steam baths for rheumatism. Leaves (needles) said to be antirheumatic and hypotensive. Yew sap was used by Celts to produce poison arrows. A component of the plant is under investigation for anticancer activity. **WARNING:** All plant parts (except perhaps the red aril) of this and other yews contain highly toxic components and are considered **poisonous.** Ingesting as few as 50 leaves (needles) has resulted in fatalities.

EVERGREEN SHRUBS WITH SWORDLIKE LEAVES; PALMS AND YUCCAS

SAW PALMETTO
Serenoa repens (Bartr.) Small

Fruits
Palm Family

⚠ Shrub; to 6 ft., with horizontal creeping stems above ground. Leafstalks armed with *sawlike teeth*. Leaves fanlike, with sword-shaped leaf blades *radiating from a central point*. Flowers whitish green, with 3–5 petals, May– July. Fruits black, fleshy, 1 in. long,

Saw Palmetto (Serenoa repens) *covers millions of acres in Florida.*

Saw Palmetto (S. repens) *with frond of ripening fruits.*

Saw Palmetto (S. repens). *Freshly harvested fruits.*

surrounding 1 large seed; in large, branched clusters; Oct.–Nov. **WHERE FOUND:** Low pine woods, savannas, thickets. S.C., Ga., Fla. to Ala., Miss. **USES:** Fruits once used as a staple food of Indian groups of Flor-ida. Early European settlers found it less palatable; one described their flavor as that of "rotten cheese steeped in tobacco juice." Fruit extracts, tablets, and tincture traditionally used to treat prostate enlargement and inflammation. Also used for colds, coughs, irritated mucous membranes, tickling feeling in throat, asthma, chronic bronchitis, head colds, and migraine. A suppository of the powdered fruits in cocoa butter was used as a uterine and vaginal tonic. Considered expectorant, sedative, diuretic. Pharmacological and clinical studies show that the fruits are useful in the treatment of prostate disorders. In the 1990s, saw palmetto berry extracts have emerged as the most important natural treatment for benign prostatic hyperplasia, a nonmalignant enlargement of the prostate that affects a majority of men over 50 years of age. Evaluated in several thousand men in more then two dozen controlled clinical trials, alone or in comparison with a conventional drug, saw palmetto preparations have been found equally effective as the conventional drug in relieving symptoms of benign prostatic hyperplasia while producing fewer side effects. Saw palmetto fruit preparations are approved in Germany, France, Italy, and other countries for treatment of symptoms related to benign prostatic hyperplasia. **WARNING:** Benign prostatic hyperplasia can be diagnosed only by a physician.

YUCCA, ADAM'S NEEDLES
Roots
Yucca filamentosa L.
Lily Family

Perennial; to 9 ft. in flower. Leaves in a rosette; stiff, spine-tipped, oblong to lance-shaped, with *fraying twisted threads on margins*. Flowers whitish green bells, on *smooth*, branched stalks; June–Sept. **WHERE FOUND:** Sandy soils. S. N.J. to Ga. **USES:** American Indians used root in salves or poultices for sores, skin diseases, and sprains. Pounded roots were put in water to stupefy corralled fish so they would float to the surface for easy harvest. Could be used as yet another starting material for steroids. **WARNING:** Root compounds **toxic** to lower life forms. See photo on p. 22.

YUCCA, SOAPWEED
Roots

Yucca glauca Nutt.
Lily Family

Blue-green perennial; 2–4 ft. Leaves in a rosette; stiff, swordlike; rounded on back, margins rolled in. Flowers are whitish bells; May–July. **WHERE FOUND:** Dry soils. Iowa, N.D. to Mo., Texas. **USES:** American Indians poulticed root on inflammations, used it to stop bleeding, in steam baths for sprains and broken limbs, and as a hairwash for dandruff and baldness. In experiments with mice, water extracts have shown antitumor activity against B16 melanoma. One human clinical study suggests that saponin extracts of root were effective in the treatment of arthritis (findings disputed). **WARNING:** See *Y. filamentosa* (above). See photo on p. 22.

EVERGREEN SHRUBS WITH 5-PARTED FLOWERS; HEATH FAMILY

SHEEP LAUREL, LAMBKILL
Twigs, leaves, flowers

Kalmia angustifolia L.
Heath Family

Slender shrub; 3–5 ft. Leaves opposite, leathery, elliptical to lance-shaped. Flowers deep rose-pink (or white) to ¼ in. across in *clusters on sides of twigs*; May–July. **WHERE FOUND:** Dry soils. Nfld. to Va., Ga. mountains; north to Mich. **USES:** American Indians used

(Left) *Sheep Laurel* (Kalmia angustifolia). *Note flowers in leaf axils.* (Above) *Mountain Laurel* (Kalmia latifolia). *Flowers terminal.*

minute amounts of flower, leaf, and twig tea for bowel ailments. Tiny amounts of leaf tea used for colds, backaches, stomach ailments; externally, for swelling, pain, and sprains. **WARNING: Highly toxic. Do not ingest.**

MOUNTAIN LAUREL
Leaves

Kalmia latifolia L.
Heath Family

Shrub or small tree; 5–30 ft. Leaves evergreen, leathery, ovate, without teeth. Flowers pink (rose or white), about 1 in. wide; in *terminal clusters;* May–July. **WHERE FOUND:** Rocky woods, clearings. New England; N.Y. to Fla., La. to Ohio, Ind. **USES:** American Indians used leaf tea as an external wash for pain, rheumatism, in liniments for vermin. Historically, herbalists used minute doses to treat syphilis, fever, jaundice, heart conditions, neuralgia, and inflammation. **WARNING:** Plant is **highly toxic;** even the honey from flowers is reportedly toxic. **Avoid use.**

LABRADOR TEA
Leaves

Ledum groenlandicum Oeder
Heath Family

Shrub; to 3 ft. Leaves fragrant, oblong or linear-oblong, *white to rusty-woolly* beneath; *edges turned under.* Small white flowers in terminal clusters; May–July. **WHERE FOUND:** Peat soils, bogs. Lab. to N.J., Pa., Ohio, Mich., Wisc., Minn., across Canada to Alaska. **USES:** American Indians used leaf tea for asthma, colds, stomachaches, kidney ailments, scurvy, fevers, rheumatism; "blood pu-

(Left) *Labrador Tea* (Ledum groenlandicum). *Like its relatives, it can be toxic.* (Above) *Great Rhododendron* (Rhododendron maximum). *A showy native shrub.*

rifier"; externally, as a wash for burns, ulcers, stings, chafing, Poison Ivy rash. Folk remedy for coughs, lung ailments, dysentery, indigestion; used externally for leprosy, itching, and to kill lice.

GREAT RHODODENDRON
Rhododendron maximum L.

Leaves
Heath Family

Thicket-forming evergreen shrub or small tree; 10–14 ft. Leaves large, *leathery*, without teeth, edges *rolled under*. Rose pink (white) spotted flowers in very showy clusters; June–July. **WHERE FOUND:** Damp woods. S. Me. to Ga.; Ala. to Ohio. **USES:** American Indians poulticed leaves to relieve arthritis pain, headaches; taken internally in controlled dosage for heart ailments. **WARNING:** Leaves toxic. Ingestion may cause convulsions and coma. **Avoid use.**

SEMI-EVERGREEN SHRUBS; LEAVES LEATHERY

YAUPON HOLLY
Ilex vomitoria Ait.

Leaves, berries
Holly Family

Evergreen shrub or small tree; 6–15 ft. Leaves to 2 in. long; elliptical, leathery, round-toothed. Berries in clusters, red (rarely yellow); Sept.–Nov. Calyx segments rounded, with few hairs on margins. **WHERE FOUND:** Sandy woods. Se. Va. to Fla.; Texas, Ark. **USES:** American Indians used a very strong leaf tea as a ceremonial cleansing beverage, drinking large amounts to induce vomiting or act as purgative. This may be the only caffeine-containing plant native to N. America, although presence of caffeine is disputed. **WARNING:** Many hollies are considered potentially toxic.

Yaupon Holly (Ilex vomitoria).   *Thyme* (Thymus vulgaris).

THYME
Leaves
Thymus vulgaris L. — Mint Family

⚠ Prostrate perennial subshrub; to 6 in. Short-stalked; leaves small (to ⅜ in. long), oval, entire (not toothed). Flowers small, purple, or (rarely) white; clustered at ends of branches; July–Aug. **WHERE FOUND:** Scattered to rare. N.S. to N.C.; Ohio to Ind. European alien; escaped from cultivation. **USES:** In European folk tradition, Thyme leaf tea has been used for nervous disorders, angina pectoris, flu, coughs, stomachaches; "blood purifier"; also to relieve cramps. Widely used in modern European herbal medicine to treat spasmodic coughs, bronchitis, whooping cough, emphysema, and asthma. Experimentally, oil of Thyme is antispasmodic, expectorant, antimicrobial, lowers arterial pressure, increases heart rhythms, respiratory volume; lowers blood pressure, alleviates toothaches. Eriodicytol, a flavonoid component of the leaf, is strongly antioxidant. Approved in Germany for the treatment of bronchitis, whooping cough, and inflammation of the upper respiratory tract. **WARNING:** Oil is **toxic** and highly irritating to skin.

BEARBERRY, UVA-URSI
Leaves
Arctostaphylos uva-ursi (L.) Spreng — Heath Family

Trailing shrub; to 1 ft. Bark finely hairy. Leaves *shiny, leathery, spatula-shaped.* Flowers white, urn-shaped; May–July. Fruit is a dry red berry. **WHERE FOUND:** Sandy soil, rocks. Arctic to n. U.S. See p. 29.

WINTERGREEN, TEABERRY
Leaves
Gaultheria procumbens L. — Heath Family

Wintergreen-scented; to 6 in. Leaves oval, glossy. Flowers waxy, drooping bells; July–Aug. Fruit is a dry berry. See p. 30.

Bearberry, Uva-ursi (Arctostaphylos uva-ursi).

Wintergreen, Teaberry (Gaultheria procumbens).

PARTRIDGEBERRY, SQUAW VINE
Leaves

Mitchella repens L. — Madder Family

Leaves opposite, rounded. Flowers white (or pink), 4-parted; terminal, paired; May–July. Each flower produces a single dry red berry, lasting over the winter. See p. 31.

CRANBERRY
Fruits

Vaccinium macrocarpon Aiton — Heath Family

Trailing evergreen shrub with slender stems, to 6 in. tall. Leaves leathery, somewhat spatula-shaped, rounded at end, stalkless, ¼ to ½ in. long. Flowers, 3–6 in clusters in leaf axils, white to pink, to ½ in. long with 4 reflexed lobes; June–Aug. Fruits are the familiar red, tart berries of cranberry sauce. **WHERE FOUND:** Bogs. Nfld. to Man., south to Va.; Ohio south to mountains of N.C. and Tenn. **USES:** American Indians used the fruits as food; given to early European sailors to treat scurvy and dysentery. Regarded as a urinary antiseptic throughout the twentieth century. Contrary to popular belief, Cranberry does not serve as a urinary antiseptic by acidifying the urine. Recent studies show that Cranberry contains compounds that prevent the adhesion of bacteria to linings of the bladder and gut, therefore preventing infection. Recent clinical studies have shown that cranberry juice cocktail and dried cranberry juice extracts prevent urinary tract infections and act as a urinary deodorant. **RELATED SPECIES:** Small Cranberry *Vaccinium oxycoccos* L. (not shown) occurs throughout boreal regions of the Northern Hemisphere (south to N.J., Minn., and n. Ind. in the U.S.). In Europe, used as a Cranberry source.

(Above) *Partridgeberry, Squaw Vine* (Mitchella repens).
(Right) *Cranberry* (Vaccinium macrocarpon).

SHRUBS WITH WHITE, 5-PETALED FLOWERS; ROSE FAMILY

NINEBARK   Bark
Physocarpus opulifolius (L.) Maxim.   Rose Family

⚠ Shrub; to 9 ft. *Bark peels in thin strips* or layers. Leaves oval to obovate; irregularly toothed, with star-shaped hairs. Flowers white, May–July. Seedpods inflated, 2-valved; usually 3 pods per cluster. **WHERE FOUND:** Stream banks. Que. to S.C.; Ala., Ark. to Minn. Often cultivated and then escaped, the bark on older branches separates, peeling into several layers, hence the common name Ninebark. The species name *opulifolius* refers to the resemblance of the leaves to those of Crampbark, *Viburnum opulus*. **USES:** American Indians used inner-bark tea for "female maladies," gonorrhea, tuberculosis; to enhance fertility; emetic, laxative. **WARNING:** Potentially **toxic.**

LARGE-HIP, RUGOSA OR WRINKLED ROSE   Fruit, flowers
Rosa rugosa Thunb.   Rose Family

Coarse, *bristly stemmed* shrub; 2–6 ft. Leaves *strongly wrinkled*; 5–9 leaflets. Large, rose (or white) flowers to 3¼ in. across, June–Sept. Fruits (hips) red, to 1 in., crowned with sepals. **WHERE**

Ninebark (*Physocarpus opulifolius*) *has delicate, fragrant flowerheads.*

Large-hip, Rugosa or Wrinkled Rose (*Rosa rugosa*) *flowers.*

Large-hip, Rugosa or Wrinkled Rose (R. rugosa), *our largest rose hip.*

Red Raspberry (Rubus idaeus) *leaves are used in herbal medicines.*

FOUND: Seaside, sand dunes. Northern U.S., Canada. Asian alien. Common, often in large thickets along coastal beaches and dunes, this Asian introduction has larger fruits (rose hips) than any of our native roses. **USES:** The Chinese use flower tea to "regulate vital energy," promote blood circulation; also for stomachaches, liver pains, mastitis, dysentery, leukorrhea, rheumatic pains; also thought to "soothe a restless fetus." Fruits (rose hips) make a pleasant, somewhat tart tea. High in vitamin C, the fruits have been used to treat scurvy (a disease caused by deficiency of vitamin C).

RED RASPBERRY
Rubus idaeus L.

Leaves, root, fruits
Rose Family

Upright shrub; canes do not root at tips. Smooth bristly stem, with or without hooked prickles; 3–7 oval leaflets. Flowers white, June–Oct. *Drupelets not separated by bands of hairs.* **WHERE FOUND:** Cultivated throughout our area. European alien. **USES:** Astringent leaf tea a folk remedy for diarrhea, dysentery; used to strengthen pregnant women, aid in childbirth. Root also used. Animal studies suggest efficacy in childbirth, painful menstrual cramps. Therapeutic use not approved in Germany because of lack of scientific support of claimed activities as a uterine tonic. Active compound relaxes and stimulates the uterus. Fruit syrup (juice boiled in sugar) gargled for inflamed tonsils.

BLACK RASPBERRY
Rubus occidentalis L.

Root, leaves, fruits
Rose Family

Shrub with *arching canes* that *root at tips. Stem glaucous* with *curved prickles.* Leaves whitened beneath; sharply double-

(Above) *Red Raspberry* (R. idaeus) *fruits*. (Right) *Black Raspberry* (Rubus occidentalis). *The roots are the primary herbal ingredient.*

toothed. Flowers white; Apr.–July. Fruits *purple-black*; July–Sept. *Rows of white hairs between drupelets.* **WHERE FOUND:** Throughout our area. Alien. **USES:** Astringent root tea traditionally used for diarrhea, dysentery, stomach pain, gonorrhea, back pain; a "female tonic"; blood tonic for boils. Leaf tea a wash for sores, ulcers, boils. Leaf tea approved in Germany for treatment of diarrhea, and mild inflammation of the mouth and throat. It is astringent, because of the tannins in both leaf and root. **RELATED SPECIES:** The same parts of most Blackberry plants (other *Rubus* species) have been used similarly.

MISCELLANEOUS SHRUBS WITH THORNY BRANCHES

AMERICAN OR ALLEGHENY BARBERRY   Root bark
Berberis canadensis P. Mill. (NOT SHOWN)   Barberry Family

Shrub; 10–25 in. *Brownish to dull purple branches*; spines usually 3-parted. Leaves spatula-shaped, sparsely toothed; grayish white beneath, without prominent veins. Flowers bright yellow, 5–10 per raceme; May. *Petals notched.* Berries red, *round.* **WHERE FOUND:** Rocky woods. Mountains. Va. to Ga., Ala.; Mo. to Ind. **USES:** Root tea used for fevers. A Cherokee remedy for diarrhea. See Common Barberry (p. 266).

(Above) Berberis vulgaris. (Right) *Common Barberry* (Berberis vulgaris). *Its fruits turn bright red when they ripen.*

COMMON BARBERRY

Root bark

Berberis vulgaris L.

Barberry Family

⚠ Branching shrub; to 9 ft. *Grayish branches;* spines 3-parted. Leaves alternate or in rosettes from previous year's leaf axils, spatula-shaped, with numerous *spiny teeth; veins beneath prominent.* Flowers 10–20 per raceme; Apr.–June. Petals not notched. Fruits red, *elliptical.* Root bark yellow. **WHERE FOUND:** Widely planted and escaped; gone wild in s. New England. Alien. **USES:** Berry tea used to promote appetite, diuretic, expectorant, laxative; also relieves itching. Root-bark tea promotes sweating; astringent, antiseptic, "blood purifier"; used for jaundice, hepatitis (stimulates bile production), fevers, hemorrhage, diarrhea. Leaf tea for coughs. Root-bark tincture used for arthritis, rheumatism, sciatica. Contains berberine, which has a wide spectrum of biological activity, including antibacterial activity; useful against infection. Contains berbamine, which increases white blood cell and platelet counts. Barberry is used in Traditional Chinese Medicine for treating lowered white blood cell counts following chemotherapy or radiation therapy in cancer patients. **WARNING: Large doses harmful.**

HAWTHORNS

Flowers, fruits

Crataegus species

Rose Family

Very complex group; 100–1,000 species in N. America. Highly variable; hybridize readily — species identification is difficult even for the specialist. Spiny shrubs. Leaves simple, toothed; cut or

Hawthorns (Crataegus sp.), a highly variable plant group.

lobed. Flowers mostly white, usually with 5 petals; calyx tube bell-shaped, 5-parted. Flowers spring–early summer. Fruits are dry red berries; each berry has 1–5 hard seeds. **WHERE FOUND:** Most abundant in e. and cen. U.S. **USES:** Fruits and flowers famous in herbal folk medicine (American Indian, Chinese, European) as a heart tonic. Studies confirm use in hypertension with weak heart, angina pectoris, arteriosclerosis. Dilates coronary vessels, reducing blood pressure; acts as direct and mild heart tonic. Prolonged use necessary for efficacy. Tea or tincture used. Hawthorn products are very popular in Europe and China. Hawthorn leaf and flower (though not the fruits) are approved in Germany for treating early stages of congestive heart failure, characterized by diminished cardiac function, a sensation of pressure or anxiety in the heart area, age-related heart disorders that do not require digitalis, and mild arrhythmias. Use confirmed by at least 14 controlled clinical studies. **WARNING:** Eye scratches from thorns can cause blindness. Contains heart-affecting compounds that may affect blood pressure and heart rate.

SHRUBS OR SMALL TREES WITH COMPOUND LEAVES; BRANCHES OR TRUNKS ARMED WITH SHORT SPINES

DEVIL'S-WALKING STICK, ANGELICA TREE   Root, berries
Aralia spinosa L.   Ginseng Family

Woody; 6–30 ft. Main stem and leafstalks with many sharp (*often stout*) *spines.* Leaves large (to 6 ft. long), twice-divided; leaflets numerous, oval, toothed. Tiny white flowers in umbels, in a very large panicle; July–Sept. **WHERE FOUND:** Rich woods, alluvial soils. S. New England (cultivated) to Fla.; Texas north to Mich. **USES:** In folk tradition, fresh bark strongly emetic, purgative; thought to cause salivation. Tincture of berries used for toothaches, rheumatic pain. Root poulticed for boils, skin eruptions, swelling. Diabetic Koreans in the Washington, D.C., area take the plant to lower their insulin requirements. **WARNING:** Handling roots may cause dermatitis. Large amount of berries poisonous.

Devil's-walking Stick, Angelica Tree (Aralia spinosa) *in fruit.*

Northern Prickly-ash (Zanthoxylum americanum) *leaves.*

NORTHERN PRICKLY-ASH
Bark, berries

Zanthoxylum americanum P. Mill.
[*Xanthoxylum americanum*]
Rue Family

Aromatic shrub with *paired short spines.* Compound leaves with 5–11 leaflets; oval, toothed, *lemon-scented* when crushed. Tiny green-yellow flowers; Apr.–May, before leaves. Fruits are red-greenish berries covered with lemon-scented dots; Aug.–Oct. **WHERE FOUND:** Moist woods, thickets. Que. to Fla.; Okla. to Minn. **USES:** Bark tea or tincture historically used by American Indians and herbalists for chronic rheumatism, dyspepsia, dysentery, kidney trouble, heart trouble, colds, coughs, lung ailments, uterine cramps, and nervous debility. When chewed, bark induces copious salivation. Once popular to stimulate mucous surfaces, bile, and pancreas activity. Bark chewed for toothaches. Berry tea used for sore throats, tonsillitis; also used as a diuretic.

SOUTHERN PRICKLY-ASH
Bark, berries

Zanthoxylum clava-herculis L.
Rue Family

Small tree or shrub; larger than Z. *americanum*—to 30 ft. Bark with large, *triangular,* corky knobs. Fruits Aug.–Oct. **WHERE FOUND:** Poor soils. S. Va. to Fla.; Texas to s. Ark., se. Okla. **USES:** Similar as for Z. *americanum;* also a folk cancer remedy. Contains the alkaloid chelerythrine, with antibacterial and anti-inflammatory activity. Affects muscle contractility by blocking or stimulating neuromuscular transmissions, rather than through a direct effect on smooth muscle tissue. Used in European herbal medicine for treating rheumatic conditions, Raynaud's disease, and as a circulatory stimulant in intermittent claudication. An alkylamide, neoherculin, produces a localized numbing effect. Most research on the genus relates to Asian or African species.

Northern Prickly-ash (Z. americanum). *Note spines on branches.*

Southern Prickly-ash (Zanthoxylum clava-herculis), *with large triangular spikes on trunk.*

COMPOUND LEAVES;
SHRUBS WITHOUT SPINES

ELDERBERRY   **Flowers, berries, inner bark, leaves**
Sambucus canadensis L.   Honeysuckle Family

Shrub; 3–12 ft. Stem with *white pith*. Leaves opposite (paired), compound, with 5–11 elliptical to lance-shaped leaflets, sharply toothed. Fragrant white flowers in flat, umbrella-like clusters, June–July. Fruits purplish black; July–Sept. **WHERE FOUND:** Rich soils. N.S. to Ga., Texas to Man. **USES:** American Indians used inner-bark tea as a diuretic, strong laxative, emetic; poulticed on cuts, sore or swollen limbs, newborn's navel, and boils to relieve pain and swelling; also for headaches. Leaves poulticed on bruises and on cuts to stop bleeding. Bark tea was formerly used as a wash for eczema, old ulcers, skin eruptions. A tea with Peppermint (see p. 211) in water is a folk remedy for colds; induces sweating and nausea. Considered a mild stimulant, carminative, and diaphoretic. In West Virginia, concentrated fruit syrup is made as a wintertime remedy for colds and flu. An Israeli research group has conducted clinical studies on the use of a fruit extract of European Elder (*Sambucus nigra*) with positive results for colds and flu. Flowers approved in Germany for use in treating colds, as they reduce fever while increasing bronchial secretions.

(Left) *Elderberry* (Sambucus canadensis) *in flower.* (Above) *Elderberry* (S. canadensis) *in fruit.*

WARNING: Bark, root, leaves, and unripe berries **toxic;** said to cause cyanide poisoning, severe diarrhea. Fruits edible when cooked. Flowers not thought to be toxic; eaten in pancakes and fritters.

CHASTE TREE
Fruits

Vitex agnus-castus L.
Verbena Family

 Aromatic shrub or low tree; 3–15 ft. Twigs with dense short hairs, resinous. Leaves palmate; 5–9 (rarely 3), narrowly elliptical leaflets, pointed on both ends; to 4½ in. long, ½–¾ in. wide, entire or wavy margined, densely white hairy beneath, slightly hairy above. Leaflets unequal in size; *only the three largest with leafstalks.* Flowers small lavender to lilac (rarely white), tubular, five-lobed, ¼ in. long; mostly in terminal, large, pyramid-shaped panicles to 1 ft. tall; Apr.–Oct. **WHERE FOUND:** Dry to moist soils. Alien. Native to w. Asia and sw. Europe. Widely naturalized in the South; Md. to Fla; west to Texas, Okla. **USES:** Seeds (fruits) used for more than 2,500 years for menstrual difficulties. In medieval Europe, seeds were thought to allay sexual desire, hence the names Chaste Tree and Monk's Pepper. In the late nineteenth century, American physicians used tincture to increase milk secretion and treat menstrual irregularities. Today it is widely prescribed by European gynecologists for treatment of premenstrual syndrome, heavy or too frequent periods, acyclic bleeding, infertility, suppressed menses, and to stimulate milk flow. Fruit preparations approved in Germany for menstrual disorders, pressure

Chaste Tree (Vitex agnus-castus) *produces showy flowers.*

Yellowroot (Xanthorhiza simplicis-sima) *has a bright yellow root.*

and swelling in the breasts, and premenstrual syndrome. **WARNING.** May cause rare dermatitis. Avoid during pregnancy or hormone replacement therapy.

YELLOWROOT   **Root**
Xanthorhiza simplicissima March.   Buttercup Family
Small shrub; 1–3 ft. Thick, deep yellow root with yellowish bark. The erect, unbranched woody stem, usually 2–3 ft. high, bears leaves and flowers only on the upper portion, which is marked with the scars of the previous year's leaves. Leaves usually divided into 5 *leaflets,* on long stalks; leaflets cleft, toothed. Flowers small, *brown-purple* in drooping racemes, Apr.–May. 5 petals, 2-lobed, with glandlike organs on a short claw. **WHERE FOUND:** Moist woods, thickets, and stream banks. N.Y. to Fla.; Ala. to Ky. **USES:** American Indians used root tea for stomach ulcers, colds, jaundice, cramps, sore mouth or throat, menstrual disorders; blood tonic, astringent; externally for piles, cancer. A folk remedy used in the South for diabetes and hypertension. Contains berberine —anti-inflammatory, astringent, hemostatic, antimicrobial, anti-convulsant, immuno-stimulant, uterotonic; also produces a transient drop in blood pressure. Berberine stimulates the secretion of bile and bilirubin and may be useful in correcting high tyramine levels in patients with liver cirrhosis. Yellowroot was for-

merly used as an adulterant to or substitute for Goldenseal (p. 57), though nineteenth-century physicians believed its medicinal action was quite different than that of Goldenseal. An Alabama herbalist, the late Tommie Bass, used to sell "sticks" of the root for smokers to chew on in efforts to quit smoking. Root use as a substitute for Goldenseal. **WARNING:** Yellowroot is potentially **toxic** in large doses.

LEAVES OPPOSITE; FLOWERS SHOWY; MIS-CELLANEOUS SHRUBS

CAROLINA ALLSPICE
Root, bark

Calycanthus floridus L. — Calycanthus Family

⚠ Aromatic shrub; 3–9 ft. Leaves oval, opposite, entire (not toothed), *with soft fuzz beneath.* Flowers terminal, maroon-brown, about 2 in. *across;* on an urn-shaped receptacle, Apr.–Aug. Flowers have a *strong, strawberry-like fragrance when crushed.* **WHERE FOUND:** Rich woods. Va. to Fla., Ala. to W. Va. **USES:** Cherokees used root or bark tea as a strong emetic, diuretic for kidney and bladder ailments. Cold tea used as eye drops for failing sight. Settlers used tea as a calming tonic for malaria. **WARNING:** Grazing cattle have been reported to have a toxic reaction to eating this plant.

BUTTONBUSH
Bark

Cephalanthus occidentalis L. — Madder Family

⚠ Shrub; 9–20 ft. Leaves *oblong-ovate;* essentially smooth. *White* flowers in a *globe-shaped cluster;* July–Aug. *Stamens strongly protruding.* **WHERE FOUND:** Stream banks, moist soils. N.B.; New Eng-

Carolina Allspice (Calycanthus floridus). *Note its deep maroon flowers.*

Buttonbush (Cephalanthus occidentalis) *has a spherical flowerhead.*

land to Fla. and Mexico; north to Wisc. and west to Calif. **USES:** American Indians chewed inner bark for toothaches, bark tea used as a wash for eye inflammation; also emetic, stops bleeding. Leaf tea was drunk to check menstrual flow. Thought to be tonic, diuretic, astringent; promotes sweating. Leaf tea once used for fevers, coughs, "gravel" (kidney stones), malaria, palsy, pleurisy, and toothaches. Interestingly, this plant, which superficially resembles a diminutive Cinchona bush (source of quinine), belongs to the same plant family and has a folk reputation, as Dogwood does, for relieving fever and malaria. **WARNING:** Contains the glucosides cephalanthin and cephalin. The leaves have caused poisoning in grazing animals.

WILD HYDRANGEA

Root, bark

Hydrangea arborescens L.　　　　　　　　　　Saxifrage Family

⚠ Shrub; to 9 ft. Leaves opposite, mostly *ovate*; toothed, pointed. Flowers in flat to round clusters, often with *papery, white, sterile, petal-like calyx lobes on outer edge*; June–Aug. Like cultivated hydrangeas, the flower head of our native Wild Hydrangea is surrounded by sterile, papery, white, flowerlike structures that attract pollinators to the inconspicuous (tiny) fertile blooms. **WHERE FOUND:** Rich woods. N.Y. to n. Fla., La.; Okla. to Ind., Ohio. **USES:** American Indians used root tea as diuretic, cathartic, emetic; scraped bark poulticed on wounds, burns, sore muscles, sprains, tumors; bark chewed for stomach problems, heart trouble. Root traditionally used for kidney stones, mucous irritation of bladder, bronchial afflictions. The root bark was formerly marketed under the name Gravel Root, referring to its use for kidney stones. Compounds in plant have anti-inflammatory and diuretic activity; inhibit tumor formation. **WARNING:** Experimentally, causes bloody diarrhea, painful gastroenteritis, cyanide-like **poisoning.**

Wild Hydrangea (Hydrangea arborescens) *is common in rich woods.*

AMERICAN BEAUTY BUSH, FRENCH MULBERRY

Leaves, roots, berries

Callicarpa americana L.   Verbena Family

Shrub; 3–6 ft. Leaves ovate-oblong, toothed; *woolly beneath.* Tiny whitish blue flowers in whorl-like cymes; June–Aug. *Rich blue-violet berries* in clusters, in leaf axils; Oct.–Nov. **WHERE FOUND:** Rich thickets. N. Md. to Fla.; north to Ark., Okla. Occurring only in the southern part of our range (to n. Ark.), though Asian species of this genus are grown as ornamentals as far north as Boston. Easily recognized by the sticky, aromatic, opposite leaves and whorls of magenta fruits. **USES:** American Indians used root and leaf tea in steam baths for rheumatism, fevers, and malaria. Root tea used for dysentery, stomachaches. Root and berry tea used for colic. Formerly used in the South for dropsy and as a "blood purifier" in skin diseases. **RELATED SPECIES:** The Chinese use the leaves of a related *Callicarpa* species as a vulnerary (to stop bleeding of wounds). It is also used to treat flu in children, and menstrual disorders.

American Beauty Bush, French Mulberry (Callicarpa americana) with purplish berries in leaf axils.

Strawberry Bush (Euonymus americanus). Note its warty fruit.

STRAWBERRY BUSH
Stem and root bark, seeds

Euonymus americanus L.

Staff-tree Family

Erect or straggling, deciduous or nearly evergreen shrub; 3–6 ft. Stalks green, 4-angled. Leaves rather thick, lustrous, sessile; tips sharp-pointed. Flowers greenish purple; *petals stalked.* Flowers May–June. Fruits *scarlet, warty.* **WHERE FOUND:** Rich woods. Se. N.Y., Pa. to Fla.; Texas, Okla. to Ill. **USES:** American Indians used root tea for uterine prolapse, vomiting of blood, stomachaches, painful urination; wash for swellings. Bark formerly used by physicians as tonic, laxative, diuretic, and expectorant. Tea used for malaria, indigestion, liver congestion, constipation, lung afflictions. Powdered bark applied to scalp was thought to eliminate dandruff. Seeds strongly laxative. **WARNING:** Fruit, seeds, and bark may be **poisonous.** Do not ingest—fruits may cause vomiting, diarrhea, and unconsciousness.

WAHOO
Stem and root bark, seeds

Euonymus atropurpureus Jacq.

Staff-tree Family

Shrub or small tree; 6–25 ft. *Leaves hairy beneath,* oblong-oval, stalked. Flowers purplish; June–July. Fruits purplish, *smooth;* seeds covered with *scarlet* pulp. **WHERE FOUND:** Rich woods. Ont. to Tenn., Ala. Ark., Okla. to N.D. **USES:** Essentially the same as for *E. americanus* (see above). Historically, the bark was considered tonic, laxative, diuretic, and expectorant. Extracts, syrups, or tea were used for fevers, upset stomach, constipation, dropsy, lung ailments, liver congestion, and heart medicines. The seeds were considered emetic and strongly laxative. Bark and root contain digitalis-like compounds. **WARNING:** Fruit, seeds, and bark are considered **poisonous.**

Wahoo (Euonymus atropurpureus) *fruit is smooth.*

POSSUMHAW, SOUTHERN WILD-RAISIN Bark
Viburnum nudum L.   Honeysuckle Family

Deciduous shrub; to 12 ft. Leaves *glossy, leathery;* oval, wavy-edged, or slightly toothed; those below flowers wedgelike, widest near middle. Small white flowers in flat clusters; Apr.–June. **WHERE FOUND:** Bogs, low woods. Md. to Fla.; Ark. to Ky. **USES:** American Indians used bark tea as a diuretic, tonic, uterine sedative, antispasmodic; for diabetes. According to Ed Croom, Lumbees boiled bark for 12 hours to reduce liquid to ⅓ original amount. A 1-ounce dose was taken 3 times per day for 4 days, then dosage was reduced to ½ ounce, taken twice a day.

CRAMPBARK, GUELDER ROSE, HIGHBUSH CRANBERRY Bark
Viburnum opulus L.   Honeysuckle Family

Shrub; to 12 ft. Leaves maplelike, with 3–5 lobes; *hairy beneath.* Leafstalks with a narrow groove, and a disk-shaped gland. White flowers in a rounded head, to 4 in. across; Apr.–June. Berries red. **WHERE FOUND:** Ornamental from Europe. Sometimes escaped. **USES:** In Europe, bark tea has been used to relieve all types of spasms, including menstrual cramps; astringent, uterine sedative. Science confirms antispasmodic activity. In China, leaves and fruit are used as an emetic, laxative, and antiscorbutic. **WARNING:** Berries are considered potentially **poisonous**; they contain chlorogenic acid, betasitosterol, and ursolic acid, at least when they are unripe.

Possumhaw, Southern Wild-raisin (Viburnum nudum) *has glossy, leathery leaves. Note raisinlike fruits. Photo by Doug Elliot.*

Crampbark, Guelder Rose, Highbush Cranberry (Viburnum opulus) *produces maplelike leaves and bright red fruits.*

Blackhaw (Viburnum pruni-folium). *Most of the dozen or so species in our range are used similarly.*

BLACKHAW
Bark

Viburnum prunifolium L.
Honeysuckle Family

⚠ Large shrub to small tree; 6–30 ft. Leaves elliptic to ovate. Finely toothed; mostly smooth, dull (not shiny). White flowers in flat clusters; March–May. Fruits black (bluish at first). **WHERE FOUND:** Bogs, low woods. Conn. to Fla.; Texas to e. Kans. **USES:** Root- or stem-bark tea used by American Indians, then adopted by Europeans for painful menses, to prevent miscarriage, relieve spasms after childbirth. Considered uterine tonic, sedative, antispasmodic, and nervine. Also used for asthma. Research has confirmed uterine-sedative, pain-relieving (like willows, it contains salicin), anti-inflammatory, and spasm-reducing, properties. **WARNING:** Berries may produce nausea and other discomforting symptoms.

MISCELLANEOUS SHRUBS WITH ALTERNATE LEAVES

NEW JERSEY TEA, RED ROOT
Leaves, root

Ceanothus americanus L.
Buckthorn Family

Shrub; 1–2 ft. Leaves oval, toothed, to 2 in. long, with 3 *prominent parallel veins*. White flowers in showy, puffy clusters on herbaceous *(nonwoody) flower stalks*; Apr.–Sept. **WHERE FOUND:** Dry, gravelly banks, open woods. Me. to Fla.; Okla. to Minn. **USES:** Leaf tea once a popular beverage. American Indians used root tea for

New Jersey Tea, Red Root (Ceanothus americanus).

Currants (Ribes sp). *The seeds of Ribes nigra have become a commercial seed oil source.*

colds, fevers, snakebites, stomachaches, lung ailments; laxative, blood tonic. Root strongly astringent (8 percent tannin content), expectorant, sedative. Tannin content could explain many of the indications. Root tea was once used for dysentery, asthma, sore throats, bronchitis, whooping cough, and spleen inflammation or pain. Alkaloid in root is mildly hypotensive (lowers blood pressure).

BLACK CURRANT   Root bark
Ribes americanum P. Mill.   Saxifrage Family
   Thornless shrub, to 5 ft. Leaves maplelike, both sides with yellow *glandular dots* (use hand lens). Flowers large, tubular to bell-shaped, yellow-white, in a drooping raceme; Apr.–June. Fruits black, smooth. **WHERE FOUND:** Rich thickets. N.B. to W. Va., Md.; Mo. to Sask. **USES:** American Indians used root-bark tea to expel worms and for kidney ailments; poulticed root bark for swelling. **RELATED SPECIES:** Seeds of other *Ribes* species (e.g., another Black Currant, *R. nigrum*) contain gamma-linolenic acid (see p. 106).

STEEPLEBUSH, HARDHACK   Leaves, flowers
Spiraea tomentosa L.   Rose Family
   Small shrub; 2–4 ft. Stems woolly. Leaves *very white or tawny-woolly* beneath; oval-oblong, saw-toothed. Flowers rose (or

Steeplebush, Hardhack (Spiraea tomentosa) *produces woolly stems and leaves that have tawny-woolly undersides.*

white), in a *steeple-shaped* raceme; July–Sept. **WHERE FOUND:** Fields, pastures. N.S. to N.C.; Ark. to Ont. **USES:** American Indians used leaf tea for diarrhea, dysentery; flower and leaf tea for morning sickness. Leaves and flowers were once used to stop bleeding; also for leukorrhea. Other *Spireas* were used similarly.

LATE LOWBUSH BLUEBERRY
Leaves
Vaccinium angustifolium Ait.   Heath Family
Shrub; 3–24 in. Leaves narrowly *lance-shaped*, with tiny stiff teeth that are green and hairless on both sides. Flowers white (or pink-tinged); urn-shaped, 5-lobed. Flowers May–June. Fruits (blueberries) Aug.–Sept. **WHERE FOUND:** Sandy or acid soils. Nfld. to Md.; n. Iowa to Minn. **USES:** American Indians used leaf tea as a

Late Lowbush Blueberry (Vaccinium angustifolium), *our most common blueberry. Note its serrated leaves.*

Late Lowbush Blueberry (V. angustifolium). *Its fruits are familiar to all.*

"blood purifier"; also used for colic, labor pains, and as a tonic after miscarriage; fumes of burning dried flowers were inhaled for madness.

SHRUBS WITH ALTERNATE COMPOUND LEAVES; SUMACS

FRAGRANT OR STINKING SUMAC
All parts
Rhus aromatica Ait.
Cashew Family

Bush or shrub; 2–7 ft. Leaves 3-parted, *fragrant*, blunt-toothed; end leaflet *not stalked*. Flowers small. Fruits *very oily to touch; hairy, red*; May–Aug. Highly variable. **WHERE FOUND:** Dry soil. W. Vt. to nw. Fla.; Texas to S.D. and westward. **USES:** American Indians used leaves for colds, bleeding; chewed leaves for stomachaches; diuretic. The patient chewed the bark for colds and slowly swallowed juice. Fruits chewed for toothaches, stomachaches, and grippe. Physicians formerly used astringent root bark to treat irritated urethra, leukorrhea, diarrhea, dysentery, bronchitis, laryngitis, and bed-wetting in children and elderly. Contraindicated if inflammation is present. **WARNING:** May cause dermatitis.

WINGED OR DWARF SUMAC
Berries, bark, leaves
Rhus copallina L.
Cashew Family

Shrub or small tree; to 30 ft. Leaves divided into 9–31 *shiny, mostly toothless* leaflets, with a prominent *wing* along midrib.

(Above) *Fragrant or Stinking Sumac* (Rhus aromatica) *produces fragrant leaves and oily, hairy fruits.* (Right) *Winged or Dwarf Sumac* (Rhus copallina). *Note wings on stems.*

Fruits red, short-hairy, Oct.–Nov. **WHERE FOUND:** Dry woods, clearings. S. Me. to Fla.; e. Texas to n. Ill. **USES:** American Indians used bark tea to stimulate milk flow; wash for blisters. Berries chewed to treat bed-wetting and mouth sores. Root tea used for dysentery.

SMOOTH SUMAC
Rhus glabra L.

Fruits, bark, leaves
Cashew Family

Shrub; 3–20 ft. Twigs and leafstalks *smooth, without hairs.* Leaves with 11–31 *toothed* leaflets. Fruits red, with short, appressed hairs; June–Oct. **WHERE FOUND:** Fields and openings. Throughout our area. **USES:** American Indians used berries to stop bed-wetting. Leaves smoked for asthma; leaf tea used for asthma, diarrhea, stomatosis (mouth diseases), dysentery. Root tea emetic, diuretic. Bark tea formerly used for diarrhea, dysentery, fevers, scrofula, general debility from sweating; also for mouth or throat ulcers, leukorrhea, and anal and uterine prolapse; astringent, tonic, antiseptic. Of 100 medicinal plants screened for antibiotic activity, this species was most active, attributed to content of gallic acid, 4-methoxygallic acid, and methyl gallate. Alcoholic extracts had the strongest activity. **WARNING:** Do not confuse this sumac with Poison Sumac, which has white fruits and toothless leaves and grows in or near swamps.

STAGHORN SUMAC
Rhus hirta (L.) Sudworth [*Rhus typhina* L.]

Leaves, berries, bark, root
Cashew Family

Shrub or small tree; 4–15 ft. Similar to *R. glabra* (above), but twigs and leafstalks *strongly hairy.* Fruits long-hairy; June–Sept.

(Left) *Smooth Sumac* (Rhus glabra) *has smooth leaves and stems.* (Above) *Staghorn sumac* (Rhus hirta) *has strongly hairy leaves and twigs.*

WHERE FOUND: Dry, rocky soil. N.S. to N.C., S.C., Ga.; Ill. to Minn. **USES:** Similar to those for *R. glabra*. American Indians used berries in cough syrups. Berry tea used for "female disorders," lung ailments. Gargled for sore throats, worms. Leaf tea used for sore throats, tonsillitis. Root or bark tea astringent; used for bleeding.

SHRUBS WITH SIMPLE ALTERNATE LEAVES; NOT TOOTHED

LEATHERWOOD   Bark
Dirca palustris L.   Leatherwood Family

Branched shrub; 1 –9 ft. Branchlets *pliable,* smooth, jointed; bark very tough. Leaves oval to obovate, on short stalks. Yellowish, bell-like flowers appear before leaves, Apr.–May. **WHERE FOUND:** Rich woods, along streams. N.B. to Fla.; La. to Minn. **USES:** American Indians used bark tea as a laxative. Minute doses cause burning of tongue, salivation. Folk remedy for toothaches, facial neuralgia, paralysis of tongue. **WARNING: Poisonous.** Causes severe dermatitis, with redness, blistering, and sores.

SPICEBUSH   Leaves, bark, berries, twigs
Lindera benzoin (L.) Blume   Laurel Family
Shrub; 4–15 ft. Leaves aromatic, ovate, without teeth. Tiny yellow flowers in axillary clusters *appear before leaves,* March–Apr.. Fruits highly aromatic, glossy, scarlet, with a single large seed;

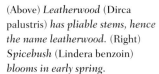

(Above) *Leatherwood* (Dirca palustris) *has pliable stems, hence the name leatherwood.* (Right) *Spicebush* (Lindera benzoin) *blooms in early spring.*

Spicebush (Lindera benzoin) *has bright red, spicy-aromatic berries that remain after leaves drop.*

Staggerbush (Lyonia mariana) *is a poisonous shrub. Photo by Pamela Harper.*

Sept.–Nov. **WHERE FOUND:** Moist, rich soils. Common along stream banks in rich, moist woods from Me. to Fla., Texas to Mich. The scarlet, strongly spice-scented berries and the pleasant-scented, entire (without teeth) leaves distinguish this plant. The berries often persist on branches after leaves drop in autumn. **USES:** American Indians used berry tea for coughs, cramps, delayed menses, croup, measles; bark tea used as a "blood purifier" and for sweating, colds, rheumatism, anemia. Settlers used berries as an All-spice substitute. Medicinally, the berries were used as a carminative for flatulence and colic. The oil from the fruits was applied to bruises and muscles or joints (for chronic rheumatism). Twig tea was popular for colds, fevers, worms, gas, and colic. The bark tea was once used to expel worms, for typhoid fevers, and as a diaphoretic for other forms of fevers. An extract of the stem bark has been found to strongly inhibit yeast (*Candida albicans*), much better than any of the other 53 species studied.

STAGGERBUSH Leaves

Lyonia mariana (L.) D. Don. Heath Family

 Slender, deciduous shrub; to 7 ft. Leaves thin, oblong to oval. White or pinkish flowers in *umberlike racemes, in clusters on old leafless branches;* Apr.–June. **WHERE FOUND:** Sandy, acid pine thickets. Southern R.I., Conn., N.Y. to Fla.; e. Texas to Ark. **USES:** Cherokees used leaf tea externally for itching, ulcers. Benjamin Smith Barton, in his classic *Essay Towards a Materia Medica of the United States* (1801), wrote that leaf tea was used as a wash for "disagreeable ulceration of the feet, which is not uncommon among the slave, & c., in the southern states." **WARNING: Poisonous;** produces "staggers" in livestock, hence the common name.

SWEETFERN
Comptonia peregrina (L.) Coult.

Leaves
Wax-myrtle Family

Strongly aromatic, deciduous shrub; 2–5 ft. Leaves soft-hairy, lance-shaped; 3–6 in. long, with *prominent rounded teeth.* Flowers inconspicuous. Fruits *burlike*; Sept.–Oct. **WHERE FOUND:** Dry soil. N.S. to Va., Ga. mountains; Ohio, Neb., Ill. to Minn., Man. The distinctly shaped, leathery, aromatic leaves of *Comptonia* give the plant a feathery or fernlike appearance. While often found in infertile soils near shores, it is a common weedy shrub of dry roadsides, gravel banks, and woodland clearings. The species name *peregrina* means "foreign." This is a misnomer from an American perspective—it was foreign to the European botanist who first named it. **USES:** Leaf tea astringent; folk remedy for diarrhea, dysentery, leukorrhea, rheumatism, vomiting of blood. American Indians used leaf tea as a beverage; wash for Poison Ivy rash, bleeding.

WAX-MYRTLE, CANDLEBERRY
Myrica cerifera L.

Leaves, fruit, root bark
Wax-myrtle Family

Coarse shrub or small tree; to 26 ft. Young branchlets *waxy.* Leaves oblong to lance-shaped; leathery, evergreen, with waxy globules. Fruits ⅛ in. across; March–June. The hard seeds are covered in a white or gray wax, long used in candle-making. **WHERE**

(Above) *Sweetfern* (Comptonia peregrina) *leaves, suggestive of fern leaves, are sweetly fragrant.* (Right) *Wax-myrtle, Candleberry* (Myrica cerifera) *can grow into a small tree.*

FOUND: Swamp thickets. S. N.J. to Fla.; Texas to Ark. **USES:** Candle wax is produced from fruits. Root bark formerly used in tea as an astringent and emetic for chronic gastritis, diarrhea, dysentery, leukorrhea, "catarrhal states of the alimentary tracts," jaundice, scrofula, and indolent (hard to heal) ulcers. Leaf tea was used for fevers, externally as a wash for itching. Powdered root bark was an ingredient in "composition powder," once a widely used home remedy for colds and chills. One component in the plant, myricitrin, has anti-inflammatory, antimutagenic, diuretic, and antibacterial activity. **WARNING:** Wax is irritating. Constituents of the wax are reportedly carcinogenic.

SWEET GALE
Myrica gale L.

Berries, root bark, leaves
Wax-myrtle Family

Fragrant deciduous shrub; 2–6 ft. Leaves gray; oblong to lance-shaped. Flowers in clusters, at ends of previous year's branchlets; Apr.–June. Fruit with 2 winglike bracts; July–Aug. **WHERE FOUND:** Swamps, shallow water. Nfld. to mountains of N.C., Tenn. to Mich.; Wisc., Minn. **USES:** Similar to those for *Myrica cerifera* (above). Branch tea once used as a diuretic for gonorrhea. This plant, like legumes, takes nitrogen from the atmosphere and locks it into the soils as a natural fertilizer. Myrigalone-B, an extract from the fruit exudates, is a potent antioxidant that inhibits free radical damage from the liver, therefore possibly having liver protectant activity. Antiviral activity has been reported for aqueous

(Above) *Sweet Gale* (Myrica gale). *Note its grayish leaves. Photo by Martin Wall.* (Right) *Bayberry* (Myrica pensylvanica) *fruits are often used to scent candle wax.*

extracts of the fresh plant. **WARNING:** Essential oil is reportedly toxic; inhibits growth of various bacteria.

BAYBERRY
Myrica pensylvanica Loisel.

Leaves, bark, fruits
Wax-myrtle Family

⚠ Stout shrub; 3–12 ft. *Branches grayish white.* Leaves elliptic to obovate (widened at tips). Flowers in clusters *below leafy tips;* Apr.–July. Young fruits very hairy. **WHERE FOUND:** Sterile soils near coast. Canadian coast to Va., N.C. (rare). **USES:** Same as for *Myrica cerifera* (above). Micmac used leaf snuff for headaches, leaf tea as a stimulant; poulticed root bark for inflammation. **WARNING:** Wax is considered **toxic.**

ALTERNATE, TOOTHED, OVAL LEAVES

SMOOTH ALDER
Alnus serrulata (Ait.) Willd.

Stem bark
Hazelnut Family

Shrub; to 15 ft. Leaves wedge-shaped, or only slightly rounded at base, *broadest above middle;* toothed, wavy-edged. Bark dark, *with few speckles.* Male catkins *abruptly bent.* Flowers (catkins) Feb.–May. "Cones" woody, erect, persistent. **WHERE FOUND:** Forms thickets along waterways. Me. to n. Fla.; se. Okla., Mo., Ill., Ind. **USES:** American Indians used bark tea for diarrhea, pain of childbirth, coughs, toothaches, sore mouth, and as a "blood purifier"; diuretic, purgative, emetic, externally, as an eyewash, and a wash for hives, Poison Ivy rash, piles, swellings, and sprains. Used in 1800s for malaria and syphilis. **RELATED SPECIES:** Indians across N. America used other alders similarly.

Smooth Alder (Alnus serrulata). Photo by Craig C. Freeman.

American Hazelnut (Corylus americana) *produces distinctive fringed fruit.*

AMERICAN HAZELNUT

Inner bark, twig hairs

Corylus americana Walt.

Hazelnut Family

Shrub; to 10 ft. Stems and leafstalks with *stiff hairs*. Leaves *heart-shaped, double-toothed*, to 5 in. long. Flowers Apr.–May. Fruits with edible nuts encased in beaked, toothed bracts. **WHERE FOUND:** Thickets. Me. to Ga.; Mo., Okla. to Sask. **USES:** American Indians drank bark tea for hives, fevers; astringent. Bark poultice used to close cuts and wounds and to treat tumors, old sores, and skin cancers. Twig hairs were used by American Indians and historically by physicians to expel worms.

HOP-HORNBEAM

Bark

Ostrya virginiana (Miller) K. Koch.

Birch Family

Small tree often shrublike, usually to 20 ft. (rarely to 60 ft.). Leaves narrow to broad ovate of oblong, margins sharply (often double) serrated, 3–5 in. long. Catkins are short, cylindrical, producing flattened oval seed to 1 in. across, with bristly hairs at base. **WHERE FOUND:** Moist and dry woods, stream banks. N.S. to Fla., west to Texas, north to Man. **USES:** American Indians used bark decoction as blood builder, to bathe sore muscles, rheumatism, and as a treatment for rectal cancer. Inner bark used historically to treat fevers, as a tonic, and blood purifier for malaria, nervous conditions, and dyspepsia.

WITCH-HAZEL

Bark, leaves

Hamamelis virginiana L.

Witch-hazel Family

Deciduous *shrub* or small tree; to 15 ft. Leaves obovate, scalloped margins (large wavy teeth), with uneven, wedge-shaped bases;

Hop-hornbeam (Ostrya virginiana) *fruits superficially resemble hops.*

Witch-hazel (Hamamelis virginiana) *usually flowers after leaves drop.*

end buds distinctly scalpel-shaped. Flowers yellow, in axillary clusters; petals *very slender,* to 1 in. Flowers *bloom after leaves drop,* Sept.–Dec. **WHERE FOUND:** Woods. N.S., Que. to Fla.; Texas to Minn. **USES:** American Indians took leaf tea for colds, sore throats. Twig tea rubbed on athletes' legs to keep muscles limber, relieve lameness; tea drunk for bloody dysentery, cholera, cough, and asthma. Astringent bark tea taken internally for lung ailments; used externally for bruises and sore muscles. Widely used today (in distilled extracts, ointments, eyewashes) as an astringent for piles, toning skin, suppressing profuse menstrual flow, eye ailments. Used commercially in preparations to treat hemorrhoids, irritations, minor pain, and itching. Tannins (hamamelitannin and proanthocyanidins) in the leaves and bark are thought to be responsible for astringent and hemostatic properties, antioxidant activity. In the U.S., approved as a nonprescription drug for use in external analgesic and skin protectant products, and as an external anorectal, primarily used for symptomatic relief of hemorrhoids, irritation, minor pain, and itching. Products are available in every pharmacy. Approved in Germany for treatment of burns, dermatitis, piles, local inflammation of mucous membranes, minor skin injuries, varicose veins and venous conditions, among others. Bottled Witch-hazel water, widely available, is a steam distillate that does not contain the astringent tannins of the shrub. **RELATED SPECIES:** Vernal Witch Hazel *H. vernalis,* with a range centered in the Ozarks, blooms from Dec.–March. Leaves and bark indiscriminately harvested as Witch-hazel, without distinguishing species. More than five *Hamamelis* species also occur in Japan and China.

BALSAM FIR

Resin, leaves

Abies balsamea (L.) Mill
Pine Family

Spire-shaped tree; to 60 ft. Flattish needles, to 1 ¼ in. long, in flattened sprays; stalkless. Needles *rounded at base,* each with 2 *white lines beneath.* Cones 1–4 in. long, *erect;* purple to green, *scales mostly twice as long as broad.* Bark smooth, with *numerous* resin pockets. **WHERE FOUND:** Moist woods. Canada, south through New England and along mountains to Va. and W. Va.; west through n. Ohio to ne. Iowa, Mich. **USES:** Canada Balsam, an oleoresin, is collected by cutting bark blisters or pockets in wood, July–Aug. Used as an antiseptic, in creams and ointments for piles, and as a root-canal sealer. Diuretic (may irritate mucous membranes). American Indians applied resin as an analgesic for burns, sores, bruises, and wounds. Leaf tea used for colds, coughs, and asthma. The oleoresin is pale yellow to greenish yellow; transparent and pleasantly scented. Its primary commercial application has been as a sealing agent for mounted microscope slides. **WARNING:** Resin may cause dermatitis in some individuals.

Balsam Fir (Abies balsamea).

Fraser Fir, She Balsam (Abies fraseri) *is commonly used as a Christmas tree. Photo by Harry Ellis.*

Eastern Hemlock (Tsuga canadensis) *needles are dark green above, silvery beneath.*

FRASER FIR, SHE BALSAM
Resin

Abies fraseri (Pursh) Poiret — Pine Family

Similar to *A. balsamea* (above), but needles and cones are generally smaller; cone-scale *margins toothed or jagged.* **WHERE FOUND:** Isolated to mountains. Va., N.C., Tenn. **USES:** Cherokees used resin for chest ailments, coughs, sore throat, urinary tract infections, and wounds.

EASTERN HEMLOCK
Leaves, bark

Tsuga canadensis (L.) Carr. — Pine Family

Evergreen tree, 50–90 ft. Needles flat, ⁵⁄₁₆–⁹⁄₁₆ in. long, on short *slender stalks.* Needles bright green above, *silvery whitish beneath.* Cones drooping, to 1 in. long, with few scales; scales rounded. **WHERE FOUND:** Hills in rocky woods. N.S. to Md., Ga. mountains; Ala. to Ky., Ind., e. Minn. **USES:** American Indians used tea made from leafy twig tips for kidney ailments, in steam baths for rheumatism, colds, and coughs, and to induce sweating. Innerbark tea used for colds, fevers, diarrhea, coughs, "stomach troubles," and scurvy. Tannins explain many of the indications. All green leaves, even hemlock leaves, contain some vitamin C, which explains use in treating scurvy. Externally, used as a wash for rheumatism and to stop bleeding. Bark is very astringent; formerly used as poultice for bleeding wounds, and in tanning leathers. The oleoresin derived from the bark is dark reddish brown, opaque, and has a characteristic turpentine-like fragrance.

NEEDLES MORE THAN 1 IN. LONG, IN CLUSTERS

Tamarack, Black Larch (Larix laricina) has deciduous leaves in whorls.

TAMARACK, BLACK LARCH
Larix laricina (DuRoi) K. Koch

Bark, gum

Pine Family

Coniferous tree; to 100 ft. Deciduous needles, to 1 in. long, in *circular clusters*. Cones oval, to ¾ in. long; scales few, rounded. **WHERE FOUND:** Swamps, wet soils. Lab. to W. Va.; n. Ill.; across s. Canada to Alaska. **USES:** Bark tea traditionally used as a laxative, tonic, and diuretic for jaundice, rheumatism, and skin ailments. Gargled for sore throats. Poulticed on sores, swellings, and burns. Leaf tea astringent; used for piles, diarrhea, dysentery, and dropsy; poulticed for burns and headaches. Gum chewed for indigestion. **WARNING:** Sawdust can cause dermatitis.

SHORTLEAF PINE, YELLOW OR HARD PINE
Pinus echinata P. Mill.

Inner bark, buds, pitch

Pine Family

Straight evergreen tree; to 120 ft. Slender needles 3–5 in. long; in 2's or 3's. Cones oval; each *scale tipped with a short* prickle. **WHERE FOUND:** Dry woods. Se. N.Y., Ohio to Fla.; Texas to s. Ill. **USES:** American Indians used inner bark in tea to induce vomiting. Cold tea of buds once used as a worm expellent. Pitch tea used as laxative and for tuberculosis; also for kidney ailments causing backaches. **WARNING:** Wood, sawdust, balsam, and turpentine of various pines may cause dermatitis in sensitive individuals.

LONGLEAF PINE
Pinus palustris P. Mill.

Pitch, turpentine

Pine Family

Evergreen tree; to 90 ft. Needles in 3's; very long—7–12 (occasionally 18) in. Cones cylindrical, 6–10 in. long; each scale with a short, curved spine. **WHERE FOUND:** Sandy soil, coastal plains. Se. Va. to Fla.; Texas. **USES:** Turpentine, derived from sap, formerly used

Shortleaf Pine, Yellow or Hard Pine (Pinus echinata) is one of the most common pines of the South.

Longleaf pine (Pinus palustris) produces needles that grow to a foot long.

for colic, chronic diarrhea, worms, to arrest bleeding from tooth sockets, rubefacient (local irritant to skin); folk remedy for abdominal tumors. **WARNING:** Considered potentially toxic.

WHITE PINE
Pinus strobus L.

Twigs, bark, leaves, pitch
Pine Family

Evergreen tree, to at least 150 ft. Needles in 5's; slender, pale green, glaucous. Cones cylindrical; to 8 in. long. **WHERE FOUND:** Common in East from Canada to Ga. mountains; west to n. Ill., c. Iowa. **USES:** Used extensively by American Indians; pitch poulticed to "draw out" boils, abscesses; also used for rheumatism, broken bones, cuts, bruises, sores, felons, and inflammation. Twig tea

White Pine (Pinus strobus), a majestic evergreen of the northeast.

White pine (P. strobus) needles have a whitish caste.

used for kidney and lung ailments; emetic. Bark and/or leaf tea used for colds, coughs, grippe, sore throats, lung ailments; poulticed for headaches and backaches. Inner bark formerly used in cough syrups.

MISCELLANEOUS CONIFERS

EASTERN RED CEDAR
Fruits, leaves
Juniperus virginiana L.
Pine Family

Spire-shaped; 10–50 ft. Leaves *scalelike, overlapping;* twigs 4-sided. Fruits hard, round, dry, blue-green. **WHERE FOUND:** Infertile soils, old pastures. Canada, Me. to Ga.; Texas to Minn., Mich. **USES:** American Indians used fruit tea for colds, worms, rheumatism, coughs, and to induce sweating. Chewed fruit for canker sores. Leaf smoke or steam inhaled for colds, bronchitis, rheumatism, and purification rituals. Said to contain the antitumor compound podophyllotoxin, best known from Mayapple (p. 52). **WARNING:** All parts may be **toxic.**

BLACK SPRUCE (NOT SHOWN)
Inner bark, resin
Picea mariana (P. Mill.) B. S. P.
Pine Family

Evergreen tree; 10–90 ft. Needles stiff, crowded, 4-angled, dark-green, *mostly glaucous.* Cones are short-oval to rounded; dull gray-brown. **WHERE FOUND:** Woods. Canada to Pa., Va. mountains; Wisc. **USES:** American Indians poulticed inner bark on inflamma-

(Below) *Eastern Red Cedar* (Juniperus virginiana). *Note its overlapping, scalelike leaves.* (Right) *It is a medium-sized tree in the South.*

(Left) *Eastern Red Cedar* (J. virginiana *var.* cerebra) *is common east of the Mississippi River.* (*Above*) *Red Spruce* (Picea rubens) *produces hairy branchlets and yellowish needles.*

tions. Inner-bark tea a folk medicine for kidney stones, stomach problems, rheumatism. Resin was poulticed on sores to promote healing; needles were used to make a beer that was drunk for scurvy. **WARNING:** Sawdust, balsam (resin), and even the needles may produce dermatitis.

RED SPRUCE   **Boughs, pitch**
Picea rubens Sarg.   Pine Family

Evergreen tree; to 100 ft., with *hairy* branchlets. Needles slender; yellowish, *not glaucous.* Cones *elongate-oval; brown to red-tinged brown.* **WHERE FOUND:** Woods. Canada; New England to N.C., Tenn., Ohio. **USES:** American Indians used tea of boughs for colds and to "break out" measles. Pitch formerly poulticed on rheumatic joints, chest, and stomach to relieve congestion and pain. **WARNING:** See under Black Spruce (above).

NORTHERN WHITE CEDAR   **Leaves, inner bark, leaf oil**
Thuja occidentalis L.   Cypress Family

Evergreen tree; to 60 ft. Leaves in *flattened sprays*; small, *appressed, overlapping.* Cones *bell-shaped,* with *loose scales.* **WHERE FOUND:** Swamps; cool, rocky woods. N.S. to Ga. mountains; n. Ill. to Minn. **USES:** American Indians used leaf tea for headaches, colds; also in cough syrups; in steam baths for rheumatism, arthritis, colds, congestion, headaches, gout; externally, as a wash for swollen feet, and burns. Inner-bark tea used for congestion

Northern White Cedar (Thuja occidentalis) *leaves appear in flattened sprays.*

and coughs. Physicians once used leaf tincture externally on warts, venereal warts, piles, ulcers, bed sores, and fungus infections. Internally, leaf tincture is used for bronchitis, asthma, pulmonary disease, enlarged prostate with urinary incontinence. Folk cancer remedy. Experimentally, leaf oil is antiseptic, expectorant, counterirritant; extracts have shown antiviral properties against herpes simplex. **WARNING:** Leaf oil is **toxic,** causing hypotension, convulsions. Fatalities have been reported.

BROAD LEAVES; EVERGREENS

AMERICAN HOLLY
Ilex opaca Ait.

Leaves, bark, berries
Holly Family

Evergreen tree; to 90 ft. Leaves, smooth, leathery; with few to many *spine-tipped teeth.* Fruits red or orange (rarely yellow); Sept.–Oct. Sprigs a familiar Christmas decoration. **WHERE FOUND:** Mixed woods. E. Mass. to Fla.; Texas, Okla. to Ill. **USES:** American Indians chewed berries for colic, indigestion. Leaf tea for measles, colds, flu, pneumonia; drops for sore eyes; externally, for sores, itching. Thick syrup of berries formerly used to treat children's diarrhea. Chewing only 10–12 berries acts as strong laxative, emetic, and diuretic. Bark tea once used in malaria and epilepsy. **WARNING:** Fruits considered **poisonous,** inducing violent vomiting.

American Holly (Ilex opaca) *has distinctive leathery, spine-tipped leaves. The holly of Christmas.*

(Left) *Bull-bay, Southern Magnolia* (Magnolia grandiflora) *is our largest evergreen magnolia, with petals to 5 in. long.* (Above) *Sweetbay* (Magnolia virginiana) *is evergreen with petals to 2 in. long.*

BULL-BAY, SOUTHERN MAGNOLIA
Magnolia grandiflora L.

Bark, leaves, seeds
Magnolia Family

Our largest Magnolia, to 90 ft. Leaves, leathery, evergreen, elliptical, to 10 in. long, 5 in. wide. Smooth above, rusty-hairy beneath. Flowers creamy white, cup-shaped, large, to 9 in. across; Apr.–July. **WHERE FOUND:** Rich woods, moist bottomlands. Se. Va., south to Fla., west to Texas. Widely grown for its beautiful evergreen foliage and dramatic flowers. **USES:** American Indians used a wash of the bark to treat prickly-heat itching and a wash for sores. Crushed bark used in steam baths to treat water retention. In nineteenth-century America, bark used to treat malaria, and for rheumatism. Fruits used as a digestive tonic, for dyspepsia, and general debility. Seeds used in Mexican traditions for antispasmodic activity. Also used for high blood pressure, heart problems, abdominal discomfort, muscle spasms, infertility, and epilepsy. Contains magnolol and honokiol, with antispasmodic activity. Science confirms sedative activity of seed. **WARNING:** Leaves have caused severe contact dermatitis.

SWEETBAY
Magnolia virginiana L.

Bark, leaves
Magnolia Family

Small tree or shrub; to 30 ft. Leaves leathery, evergreen (deciduous in North); 3–6 in. long. Flowers white, cup-shaped, *very fragrant*; petals to 2 in. Flowers Apr.–July. **WHERE FOUND:** Low woods. Mass.; Pa. to Fla.; Miss. north to Tenn. **USES:** American Indians used leaf tea to "warm blood," "cure" colds. Traditionally, bark was used like that of *M. acuminata* (see above). Bark also used for rheumatism, malaria, epilepsy.

DECIDUOUS TREES WITH OPPOSITE, COMPOUND LEAVES

OHIO BUCKEYE
Nuts
Aesculus glabra Willd.
Horsechestnut Family

Small tree; 20–40 ft. Leaflets 5 (rarely 4–7); toothed, 4–15 in. long. Twigs *foul-smelling* when broken. Buds not sticky; scales at tips *strongly ridged.* Bark rough-scaly. Flowers yellow; Apr.–May. Fruit husk with *weak prickles;* Sept.–Oct. **WHERE FOUND:** Rich, moist woods. W. Pa., W. Va., e. Tenn., c. Ala., c. Okla. to Neb., Iowa. **USES:** Traditionally, powdered nut (minute dose) used for spasmodic cough, asthma (with tight chest), intestinal irritations. Externally, tea or ointment used for rheumatism and piles. American Indians put ground nuts in streams to stupefy fish, which floated to the surface for easy harvest. **WARNING:** Nuts **toxic,** causing severe gastric irritation. Still, Indians made food from them after elaborate processing.

HORSECHESTNUT
Nuts, leaves, flowers, bark
Aesculus hippocastanum L.
Horsechestnut Family

To 100 ft. Leaflets 5–7; to 12 in. long; without stalks, toothed. Buds large, *very sticky.* Broken twigs *not foul-smelling* as in Ohio Buckeye (above). Flowers white (mottled red and yellow); May. Fruits *spiny or warty;* Sept.–Oct. **WHERE FOUND:** Planted in towns.

Ohio Buckeye (Aesculus glabra) has smooth leaves and yellow flowers.

Horsechestnut (Aesculus hippocastanum) is often grown as a shade tree.

Naturalized. **USES:** As in *A. glabra* (see above); also, peeled, roasted nuts of this tree were brewed for diarrhea, prostate ailments. Leaf tea tonic; used for fevers. Flower tincture used on rheumatic joints. Bark tea astringent, used in malaria, dysentery; externally, for lupus and skin ulcers. Horsechestnut seed extracts widely prescribed orally in European phytomedicine for edema with venous insufficiency, for varicose veins and to improve vascular tone, help to strengthen weak veins and arteries in reducing leg edema, nighttime calf muscle spasms, thrombosis, and hemorrhoids; uses backed by clinical studies. Contains aescin, which reduces capillary wall permeability, lessening diameter and number of capillary wall openings, regulating the flow of fluids to surrounding tissue; increases blood circulation. Also used in gastritis and gastroenteritis. Topically, aescin-containing gels or creams widely used to allay swelling and pain in bruising, sprains, and contusions. Injectable forms of aescin used in European trauma centers to help stabilize brain-trauma patients. Only chemically well-defined products are used; not the crude drug. **WARNING:** Outer husks **poisonous; all parts can be toxic.** Fatalities reported. Seeds (nuts) contain 30–60 percent starch, but can be used as a foodstuff only after the toxins have been removed.

RED BUCKEYE   **Nuts, bark**
Aesculus pavia L.   Horsechestnut Family
Small tree or shrub; to 15 ft. Leaflets 5, oblong to oblanceolate, smooth above. Flowers *red* (rarely yellow) on reddish stalks; petals with glandular hairs on the margins. Apr.–May. Fruits with smooth thick leathery cover, nuts about an inch in diameter. Sept.–Oct. **WHERE FOUND:** Rich moist woods. Ill. to N.C. south to Fla, west to Texas, s. Mo. **USES:** American Indian groups used the nuts as a talisman (carried in pocket) to ward off rheumatism and piles, and for good luck. Externally, poultice of crushed nut used for cancers, sores, infections. Bark tea used to treat bleeding after childbirth. **WARNING:** All parts potentially **toxic.** Avoid use.

WHITE OR AMERICAN ASH   **Bark, leaves**
Fraxinus americana L.   Olive Family
To 100 ft. Twigs hairless. Leaves opposite, pinnate, with 5–9 leaflets oval, slightly toothed or entire; *white* or pale beneath. Flowers Apr.–June. Fruits narrow, winged; Oct.–Nov. **WHERE FOUND:** Woods. N.S. to Fla.; Texas, Neb. to Minn. **USES:** American Indians used inner-bark tea as an emetic or strong laxative, to remove bile from intestines, as a "tonic" after childbirth and to relieve stomach cramps, fevers; diuretic, promotes sweating; wash used for sores, itching, lice, snakebites. Inner bark chewed and applied as a poultice to sores. Seeds thought to be aphrodisiac.

(Left) *Red Buckeye* (Aesculus pavia) *produces red flowers.* (Above) *White or American Ash* (Fraxinus americana) *produces winged, maplelike seeds.*

LARGE HEART-SHAPED LEAVES; OPPOSITE, OR WITH 3 LEAVES AT EACH NODE

COMMON CATALPA

Catalpa bignonioides Walt.

Bark, leaves, seeds, pods
Bignonia Family

Ornamental tree; to 45 ft. Leaves opposite, or in 3's from each node, large—to 10 in. long and 7 in. wide; oval to heart-shaped, with an *abruptly pointed apex*; not toothed. Leaves foul-odored when bruised. Flowers whitish, marked with 2 orange stripes and numerous *purple spots* within; thimblelike, with 5 unequal, wavy-edged lobes. Flowers in large, upright, showy clusters; June–July. Seedpods long, cigar-shaped; seeds have 2 papery wings. **WHERE FOUND:** Waste

Common Catalpa (Catalpa bignonioides) *is one of our showiest spring-flowering trees.*

ground; a street tree. Fla., Ala., Miss., La. Naturalized north to New England; N.Y., Ohio, and westward. **USES:** Bark tea formerly used as an antiseptic, snakebite antidote, laxative, sedative, worm expellent (a Chinese species is also used against worms). Leaves poulticed on wounds, abrasions. Seed tea used for asthma, bronchitis; externally, for wounds. Pods sedative; thought to possess cardioactive properties. **RELATED SPECIES: Northern** or **Hardy Catalpa** (*Catalpa speciosa,* not shown) is a larger tree; leaves have a long, pointed tip, flowers have fewer spots. Original range is unclear—perhaps native from Ind. to e. Ark. Now commonly naturalized in se. U.S.

PRINCESS-TREE, PAULOWNIA **All parts**

Paulownia tomentosa (Thunb.) Sieb. & Zucc. ex Steub.   Figwort Family
Medium-sized, thick-branched tree; 30–60 ft. Leaves *heart-shaped*, pointed at tip; large—to 12 in. long and broad (sometimes larger); velvety beneath; leafstalks to 8 in. long. Flowers fragrant, hairy, with purple thimbles, to 2 in. long; with 5 flared, *unequal lobes*; in large, candelabra-like clusters. Apr.–May. Fruits upright; hollow hulls are filled with tiny winged seeds; hulls split in two, suggesting hickory fruits in shape; persist through winter.

Princess-tree, Paulownia (Paulownia tomentosa) *is easily identified when flowering.*

Princess-tree, Paulownia (P. tomentosa). *Note the thimblelike blooms with densely hairy calyx.*

WHERE FOUND: Occurs from N.Y. to Fla. and westward. Asian alien, introduced as an ornamental in the U.S. by 1843. Another Chinese native introduced as an ornamental that has made itself quite at home, especially in the American South. The wood is highly valued by the Japanese and is exported at a high price. **USES:** In China, a wash of the leaves and capsules was used in daily applications to promote the growth of hair and prevent graying. Leaf tea was used as a foot bath for swollen feet. Inner-bark tincture (soaked in 2 parts whisky) given for fevers and delirium. Leaves or ground bark were fried in vinegar, poulticed on bruises. Flowers were mixed with other herbs to treat liver ailments. In Japan the leaf juice is used to treat warts. **WARNING:** Contains potentially **toxic** compounds.

OPPOSITE LEAVES; MAPLES

BOX-ELDER, ASHLEAF MAPLE
Acer negundo L.

Inner bark
Maple Family

Tree; 40–70 ft. *Twigs glossy green. Leaflets 3–5 (occasionally 7); similar to those of Poison Ivy,* but Box-elder leaves are *opposite,* not

Box-elder, Ashleaf Maple (Acer negundo) *leaves resemble those of Poison Ivy.*

Striped Maple (Acer pensylvanicum) *leaves have three large lobes on the upper half. Note the striped bark.*

alternate; coarsely toothed (or without teeth); end leaflet often 3–lobed, broader than lateral leaflets. Fruits are paired, maple-type "keys"; seed itself is longer and narrower than in most maple species. **WHERE FOUND:** Riverbanks, fertile woods. N.S. to Fla., Texas; n. to cen. Man., s. Alta.; also in Calif. **USES:** American Indians used the inner-bark tea as an emetic (induces vomiting). Sap boiled down as a sugar source.

STRIPED MAPLE
Acer pensylvanicum L.

Inner bark, leaves, twigs
Maple Family

Slender tree; to 15 ft. *Bark greenish,* with *vertical white stripes.* Leaves 3-lobed, finely double-toothed; to 8 in. wide. Small, greenish flowers, in long clusters; May–June. Fruits ("keys") with paired winged seeds, usually set widely apart; June–Sept. **WHERE FOUND:** Woods. N.S. and south through New England, mountains of Pa., Ohio to Tenn., N.C., n. Ga.; west to Mich. **USES:** American Indians used inner-bark tea for colds, coughs, bronchitis, kidney infections, gonorrhea, spitting up of blood; wash used for swollen limbs and paralysis. Historically, bark tea was used as a folk remedy for skin eruptions, taken internally and applied as an external wash. Leaf and twig tea used both to allay or induce nausea, and induce vomiting, depending on dosage. **RELATED SPECIES:** Bark from a closely related Asian species has shown significant anti-inflammatory activity.

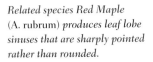

Sugar Maple (Acer saccharum). *Note the rounded sinuses between lobes.*

Related species Red Maple (A. rubrum) *produces leaf lobe sinuses that are sharply pointed rather than rounded.*

SUGAR MAPLE

Inner bark, sap

Acer saccharum Marsh.

Maple Family

Large tree; 60–130 ft. Leaves *green on both sides.* Leaves 5-lobed; *lobes not drooping, notches between lobes rounded.* Twigs glossy. Fruits paired, maplelike "keys." **WHERE FOUND:** Rich, hilly woods, fields. Nfld. to n. Ga., e. Texas; north to Minn. **USES:** American Indians used inner bark in tea for coughs, diarrhea; diuretic, expectorant, "blood purifier." Maple syrup said to be a liver tonic and kidney cleanser, and used in cough syrups. During the maple sap-gathering process in spring, New Englanders once drank the sap collected in buckets as a spring tonic. **RELATED SPECIES:** **Red Maple** (*A. rubrum*) has red flowers and reddish branches. The leaf lobes are sharply pointed rather than rounded. Range is similar.

TREES WITH OPPOSITE LEAVES; SHOWY WHITE SPRING FLOWERS

FRINGETREE

Root bark, trunk bark

Chionanthus virginica L.

Olive Family

⚠ Shrub or small tree; 6–20 ft. Leaves opposite, oval, 3–8 in. long; mostly smooth. Flowers white, *in drooping clusters;* May–June. Petals slender. Fruits bluish black, resembling small olives. **WHERE FOUND:** Dry slopes. N.J. to Fla.; Texas, e. Okla. north to Mo., s.

(Left) *Fringetree* (Chionanthus virginica) *produces beautiful strap-like flowers.* (Above) *Flowering Dogwood* (Cornus florida) *is a familiar spring-flowering tree of the East.*

(Left) *Flowering Dogwood*
(C. florida) *can easily be identified by its distinctive bark.* (Above) *It produces extremely bitter, inedible red fruits.*

Ohio. **USES:** Physicians formerly used 10 drops (every 3 hours) of tincture (1 part bark by weight in 5 parts 50 percent grain alcohol and water) for jaundice. In the late nineteenth century, Fringetree bark tincture was widely employed by physicians who thought it relieved congestion of glandular organs and the venous system. It was employed for hypertrophy of the liver, wounds, nephritis, and rheumatism. Once considered diuretic, alterative, cholagogue, and a useful tonic. American Indians used the root-bark tea to wash inflammations, sores, cuts, and infections. **WARNING:** Overdoses cause vomiting, frontal headaches, slow pulse. **RELATED SPECIES:** Leaves of the Chinese species *C. retusus* have been used in Asia as a tea substitute.

FLOWERING DOGWOOD   **Inner bark, berries, twigs**
Cornus florida L.   Dogwood Family
⚠ Our most showy deciduous tree, 10–30 ft. Leaves ovate; *latex threads appear at veins when leaves are split apart.* Flowers in clusters; Apr.–May; *4 showy white (or pink) bracts* surround the true flowers. Fruits scarlet, dry, inedible, very bitter. **WHERE FOUND:** Understory tree of dry woods. Me. to Fla.; Texas to Kans. Widely cultivated in natural range and elsewhere as an ornamental. **USES:** Astringent root-bark tea or tincture widely used in South, especially during the Civil War, for malarial fevers (substitute for quinine); also for chronic diarrhea. Root bark also poulticed onto external ulcers. Scarlet berries soaked in brandy as a bitter digestive tonic

and for acid stomach. Twigs used as "chewing sticks"—forerunners of modern toothbrushes. An 1830 herbal reported that the Indians and captive Africans in Virginia were remarkable for the whiteness of their teeth, and attributed it to the use of Dogwood chewing sticks. Once chewed for a few minutes, the tough fibers at the ends of twigs split into a fine soft "brush." Contains verbenalin, which has reported pain-reducing, anti-inflammatory, cough suppressant, uterotonic, and laxative qualities. **WARNING:** As with hard toothbrushes, Dogwood chewing sticks can cause receding gums.

MISCELLANEOUS TREES WITH COMPOUND LEAVES

TREE-OF-HEAVEN, STINKTREE   Bark, root bark
Ailanthus altissima (P. Mill.) Swingle   Quassia Family

Smooth-barked tree; 20–100 ft. Leaves compound, similar to those of sumacs; crushed leaves *smell like peanuts.* Each leaflet has 2 *glandular-tipped teeth at base* (on underside). Flowers small, yellow; June–July. Male flowers *foul-smelling.* Fruits look like winged "keys," persisting through winter. **WHERE FOUND:** Waste places. Throughout our area. This Chinese native was introduced in the late nineteenth century as an ornamental. It quickly established itself. In cities like New York and Boston, it grows in harsh conditions where no other plants seem able to survive. Considered a weed tree in many American cities. **USES:** Two ounces bark infused in 1 quart water, given in teaspoonfuls for diarrhea, dysentery, leukorrhea, tapeworm; used in Traditional Chinese

Tree-of-heaven, Stinktree (Ailanthus altissima). Note the gland at base of leaf lobe.

Silk Tree, Mimosa (Albizia julibrissin) produces showy pink flowers and feathery leaves.

Medicine. National Cancer Institute researchers have reported several antimalarial compounds, five of which are more potent than the standard antimalarial drug, chloroquine. **WARNING:** Large doses potentially **poisonous.** Gardeners who cut the tree may suffer from rashes.

SILK TREE, MIMOSA
Albizia julibrissin Durazz.

Bark, Flowers
Mimosa Family

Fast-growing, broad-crowned, short-trunked tree; to 30 ft. Leaves with a graceful, feathery appearance, doubly compound, with 2–30 pairs of oblong leaflets (pinnules) to 1 in. long, *one side distinctly longer than the other;* sensitive to touch, folding up at night. Flowers pink (rarely white), silky, fluffy blooms. May–August. Flat, brown, dry, papery, pea-like pod to 6 in. long. **WHERE FOUND:** Dry soils. Alien from tropical Asia, introduced by 1785. N.Y. southward and west. Commonly naturalized throughout the South. **USES:** In Traditional Chinese Medicine, bark *(he-huan-pi)* and the flowers *(he-huan-hua)* are still in use. Bark is used in tea (mostly in combination with other herbs) for depression, restlessness, and insomnia caused by anxiety. Externally, poultice is used for traumatic injuries. Flowers are used as sedative for insomnia.

Kentucky Coffee-tree (Gymnocladus dioicus). *Note the compound leaves with 7–13 leaflets.*

Hoptree, Wafer Ash (Ptelea trifoliata) *produces three leaflets and waferlike fruits.*

KENTUCKY COFFEE-TREE
Bark, pods
Gymnocladus dioicus (L.) K. Koch
Pea Family

To 50–60 ft. Compound leaves with 7–13 leaflets. Whitish flowers in axillary wands; May–June. Hard, flat pods to 10 in. (2½ in. wide), pulpy within; seeds large, hard. **WHERE FOUND:** Rich woods. Cen. N.Y. to Tenn.; Ark. to S.D. **USES:** Caramel-like pod pulp used by American Indians to treat "lunacy." Leaf and pulp tea formerly employed for reflex troubles, and as a laxative. Root-bark tea used for coughs caused by inflamed mucous membranes; diuretic; given to aid childbirth in protracted labor, stops bleeding; used in enemas for constipation. **WARNING: Toxic** to grazing animals. Leaves are a fly poison. Seeds contain toxic saponins.

HOPTREE, WAFER ASH
Root bark, young leaves and shoots, fruits
Ptelea trifoliata L.
Rue Family

Small tree; 10–20 ft. Leaves palmately divided into 3 *parts or leaflets,* mostly without teeth; black-dotted (use lens). Flowers small, greenish; May–July. Fruits round, 2-seeded "wafers"; July–Sept. Each seed pair is surrounded by a papery wing. **WHERE FOUND:** Rocky woods, outcrops. Sw. Que., N.Y. to Fla.; Texas (Colo., N.M.) to n. Kans., Mo. **USES:** American Indians added root to strengthen other medicine. Historically used by physicians as a tonic ("surpassed only by Goldenseal") for asthmatic breathing, fevers, poor appetite, gastroenteritis, irritated mucous membranes. A tea of the young leaves and shoots was once considered useful as a worm expellant. The bitter, slightly aromatic fruits were once thought to be a useful substitute to hops in the manufacture of beer. Contains antibacterial, antifungal, and anticandida components. **WARNING:** Do not confuse leaves of this small tree with Poison Ivy leaves. Coumarins in the leaves can induce photodermatitis.

TREES WITH COMPOUND LEAVES; TRUNK AND BRANCHES USUALLY THORNY

HONEY LOCUST
Pods, inner bark
Gleditsia triacanthos L.
Pea Family

To 80 ft. This tree is usually armed with large, often compound thorns (except in form *inermis,* which lacks thorns). Leaves feathery-compound; leaflets lance-shaped to oblong, barely toothed. Flowers greenish, clustered; May–July. Fruits flat, pods twisted; 8–18 in. **WHERE FOUND:** Dry woods, openings. N.S. to Fla.; Texas, w. Okla. to S.D. **USES:** Pods formerly made into tea for indigestion, measles, catarrh of lungs. Inner-bark tea (with Sycamore bark) was once used for hoarseness, sore throats. Juice of pods antisep-

(Above) *Honey Locust* (Gleditsia triacanthos) *leaves are feathery, compound.* (Right) *It is one of our most heavily armed trees.*

tic. Russian researchers are studying compounds from leaves to retard certain types of cancer. **RELATED SPECIES:** The seedpods of a Chinese species, *G. sinensis,* are used in Chinese medicine for sore throats, asthmatic coughs, swellings, and stroke. Experimentally, these seedpods cause the breakdown of red blood cells, are strongly antibacterial, antifungal, and act as an expectorant, aiding in the expulsion of phlegm and secretions of the respiratory tract. Minute amounts of the seeds are taken in powder for constipation. The spines constitute another drug used in Traditional Chinese Medicine; they are used as a wash to reduce swelling and disperse toxic matter in the treatment of carbuncles and lesions. Early reports of cocaine in the plant have been discredited. **WARNING:** All plant parts of both species contain potentially toxic compounds.

BLACK LOCUST   **Root bark, flowers**
Robinia pseudoacacia L.   Pea Family

To 70–90 ft.; armed with stout *paired thorns,* ½–1 in. long. Leaves *pinnately compound;* 7–21 elliptic to oval leaflets. Fragrant white flowers in racemes. May–June. Pods *smooth,* flat; 2–6 in. **WHERE FOUND:** Dry woods. Pa. to Ga.; La., Okla. to Iowa; planted elsewhere. **USES:** American Indians chewed root bark to induce vomiting, held bark in mouth to allay toothaches. A folk tonic, purgative, emetic. Flower tea used for rheumatism. In China the root bark is also considered purgative and emetic, and the flowers are

Black Locust (Robinia pseudoacacia) *in flower. The strong-smelling flowers can induce nausea and headaches.*

considered diuretic. Flowers contain a glycoside, robinin, which is experimentally diuretic. **WARNING:** All parts are potentially toxic. The strong odor of the flowers has been reported to cause nausea and headaches in some persons.

TREES WITH ALTERNATE COMPOUND LEAVES; WALNUTS, MOUNTAIN ASH

BUTTERNUT
Inner bark, nut oil
Juglans cinerea L.
Walnut Family

To 80 ft. Stem pith *dark brown.* Leaves pinnate, with 7–17 leaflets; leaflets are *opposite, rounded at base,* with *minute clusters of downy hairs beneath.* Flowers Apr.–June. Fruits egg-shaped; sticky on outer surface. Nuts rough and deeply furrowed. **WHERE FOUND:** Rich woods. N.B. to Ga.; west to Ark., N.D. **USES:** Inner-bark tea or extract a popular early American laxative; thought to be effective in small doses,

Butternut (Juglans cinerea). *Note the terminal leaflet.*

without causing griping (cramps). American Indians used bark in tea for rheumatism, headaches, toothaches; strong warm tea for wounds to stop bleeding, promote healing. Oil from nuts used for tapeworms, fungal infections. Juglone, a component, is antiseptic and herbicidal; some antitumor activity has also been reported.

BLACK WALNUT
Juglans nigra L.

Inner bark, fruit husks, leaves
Walnut Family

To 120 ft. Stem pith *light brown.* Leaves pinnate, with 12–23 leaflets; leaflets *slightly alternate, heart-shaped,* or *uneven at base.* Leafstalks and leaf undersides slightly hairy; hairs solitary or in pairs, not in clusters. Fruits rounded; Oct.–Nov. **WHERE FOUND:** Rich woods. W. Mass. to Fla., Texas to Minn. **USES:** American Indians used inner-bark tea as an emetic, laxative; bark chewed for toothaches. Fruit-husk juice used on ringworm; husk chewed for colic, poulticed for inflammation. Leaf tea astringent, insecticidal against bedbugs. Walnut leaves and hulls have traditionally been used for their astringent activity against diarrhea. They have also been valued as a tonic and strong antifungal. Recent scientific studies have found that the leaf extracts have strong antiviral activity against vesicular stomatitis, a protective effect on the vascu-

Black Walnut (Juglans nigra). *Note that there is not a terminal leaflet.*

Black Walnut (J. nigra) *fruit husks drying on black plastic.*

(Above) *Black Walnut* (J. nigra) *dried fruit husks.* (Right) *Mountain Ash* (Sorbus sp.), *with showy fruit clusters.*

lar system, and an inhibitory effect on certain kinds of tumors. A recent animal study suggests that juglone, a growth inhibitor in the leaves, possesses sedative activity comparable with diazepam (the prescription drug Valium). **WARNING:** Fruit husks and leaves can cause contact dermatitis.

AMERICAN MOUNTAIN ASH

Fruits, bark

Sorbus americana Marsh.

Rose Family

[*Pyrus americana* (Marsh.) DC.]

Shrub or small tree; to 40 ft., with *red, gummy* buds. Leaves compound with 11–17 leaflets; leaflets toothed, *long-pointed,* narrow —3 times longer than broad. Flowers in clusters. Fruits in clusters, *red,* about ¼ in.; Aug.–March. **WHERE FOUND:** Woods, openings. Nfld. to N.C. mountains; Ill. to Man. **USES:** American Indians used tea from ripe fruit for scurvy, worms; tea made from inner bark or buds for colds, debility, boils, diarrhea, tonsillitis; also as a "blood purifier," appetite stimulant; astringent, tonic. **RELATED SPECIES:** Fruits of the **European Mountain Ash** (*S. aucuparia*) have been used similarly, for piles, urinary difficulty, indigestion, gallbladder ailments, angina, and other coronary problems.

GINKGO
Seeds, Leaves

Ginkgo biloba L.
Ginkgo Family

Large deciduous tree to 100 ft.; a living fossil surviving over 200 millions years. Leaves alternate or in fascicles; *fan-shaped, 2-lobed,* broader than long; 1–3½ in. wide, with parallel veins. Male and female flowers on separate trees; females producing oval, fleshy, foul-smelling fruit with hard-coated, oval to elliptical seed. **WHERE FOUND:** Widely cultivated shade tree, adaptable to soil type, survives in cities where other trees do poorly. Alien. China. Throughout, near dwellings; though rarely naturalized, survives in cultivation. **USES:** Seeds (after removal of toxic flesh with obnoxious odor), cooked, are used in Traditional Chinese Medicine for treatment of lung ailments. Leaves rarely used historically for cough, asthma, and diarrhea. Externally, as a wash for skin sores and to remove freckles. Today, complex, highly processed, concentrated Ginkgo leaf extracts (calibrated to 24 percent flavonoids; 6 percent ginkgolides, with toxic components removed) are the best-selling herbal preparation in Europe. The subject of hundreds of scientific studies, Ginkgo leaf extracts increase circulation and improve oxygen metabolism to the extremities and the brain; antioxidant. Clinically shown to improve short-term memory, attention span, and mood in early stages of Alzheimer's. Extract approved in Germany for memory deficits, poor concentration, peripheral arterial occlusive disease (improv-

ing pain-free walking distance), and for vertigo and ringing in the ears (tinnitus) caused by vascular disturbances. However, the crude leaf does not carry therapeutic claims, only the complex extract does. **WARNING:** Leaf extracts may cause relatively rare gastrointestinal upset, headaches, or skin allergies. Fleshy seed coat causes severe contact dermatitis (like Poison Ivy). Fruits and seeds are handled with rubber gloves.

Ginkgo (Ginkgo biloba) *produces unique fan-shaped leaves.*

(Above) *Tuliptree* (Liriodendron tulipifera) *with four-lobed leaves.* (Right) *Its flowers resemble a tulip.*

TULIPTREE
Bark, leaves, buds

Liriodendron tulipifera L.　　　　　　　　Magnolia Family

To 100 ft. Leaves *spicy; 4-lobed, apex notched.* Flowers to 2 in. long; *tuliplike,* green to greenish yellow or yellow-orange. Flowers May–June. **WHERE FOUND:** Moist soil. Mass. to Fla.; La., e. Ark., Ill. to Mich. **USES:** American Indians used bark tea for indigestion, dysentery, rheumatism, pinworms, fevers, and in cough syrups; externally, as a wash on fractured limbs, wounds, boils, snakebites. Green bark chewed as an aphrodisiac, stimulant. Bark tea a folk remedy for malaria, toothaches, ointment from buds used for burns, inflammation. Crushed leaves poulticed for headaches.

WHITE OAK
Bark

Quercus alba L.　　　　　　　　　　　Beech Family

⚠ Tall tree, 60–120 ft. Bark light, flaky; flat-ridged. Leaves with *evenly rounded lobes,* without bristle tips; glabrous and whitened beneath when mature. Bowl-shaped cup covers ⅓ or less of acorn. **WHERE FOUND:** Dry woods. Me. to n. Fla.; e. Texas to Minn. **USES:** Astringent inner-bark tea once used for chronic diarrhea, dysentery, chronic mucous discharge, bleeding, anal prolapse, piles; as a gargle for sore throat and a wash for skin eruptions, Poison Ivy rash, burns; hemostatic. Folk cancer remedy. Contains tannins. Experimentally, tannic acid is antiviral, antiseptic, cavity stabilizing, growth depressant, antitumor, and carcinogenic. In Germany, a related species, English Oak, *Quercus robur,* is approved

(Above) *White Oak* (Quercus alba). *Oaks in this group have rounded lobes.* (Right) *Sassafras* (Sassafras albidum). *Its aromatic leaves are mitten-shaped.*

for external use for the treatment of inflammatory skin diseases. **WARNING:** Tannic acid is potentially **toxic.**

SASSAFRAS   **Leaves, twig pith, root bark**
Sassafras albidum (Nutt.) Nees.   Laurel Family
Tree; 10–100 ft. Leaves in 3 *shapes: oval, mitten-lobed, or 3-lobed*; fragrant, mucilaginous. Yellow flowers in clusters appear before leaves; Apr.–May. Fruits blue-black, 1-seeded. **WHERE FOUND:** Poor soils. S. Me. to Fla.; Texas to e. Kans. **USES:** In the early days of European settlement, Sassafras was a major export. In fact, the Plymouth colonies were in part founded on speculation of Sassafras exports. Root-bark tea was a famous spring blood tonic and "blood purifier"; also a folk remedy for stomachaches, gout, arthritis, high blood pressure, rheumatism, kidney ailments, colds, fevers, and skin eruptions. The mucilaginous twig pith has been used as a wash or poultice for eye ailments, also taken internally, in tea, for chest, bowel, kidney, and liver ailments. Leaves mucilaginous, once used to treat stomachaches; widely used as a base for soup stocks. **WARNING:** Safrole (found in oil of Sassafras) reportedly is carcinogenic; it is banned by the FDA. However, the safrole in a 12-ounce can of old-fashioned root beer is not as carcinogenic as the alcohol (ethanol) in a can of beer.

Sweetgum (Liquidambar styraciflua). *Its leaves are aromatic and
usually 5-lobed.*

Sweetgum (L. styraciflua) *produces spiny, globular fruit.*

SWEETGUM

Inner bark, gum

Liquidambar styraciflua L.

Witch-hazel Family

Tree; to 125 ft. Outer branches often corky-winged. Leaves shiny, star-shaped or maplelike, with 5–7 lobes, lobes pointed, toothed leaves pine-scented when rubbed or crushed. Fruits spherical (to 1¼ in.), with projecting points. **WHERE FOUND:** Moist woods, bottomland; usually along streams, riverbanks. Often invasive in old fields and in areas that have been recently logged. Mo. to Ill., se. Conn. to Fla., Texas, Mexico, Cen. America. Common in the South. The "gum" produced in pockets in the bark is used medicinally. The hard, spiny, 1-in.-diameter fruits make this tree a poor choice for lawn plantings, though the inherent ornamental value of the brilliant autumn leaves offsets this slight negative aspect. **USES:** The "gum" produced in pockets in the bark after bruised or incised is used medicinally. Gum or balsam (resin) was traditionally chewed for sore throats, coughs, colds, diarrhea, dysentery, ringworm; used externally for sores, skin ailments, wounds, piles. An ingredient in "compound tincture of benzoin," it is available from pharmacies. Considered expectorant, antiseptic, antimicrobial, anti-inflammatory. Children sometimes chew the gum in place of commercial chewing gum. The mildly astringent inner bark was used as a folk remedy, boiled in milk for diarrhea and cholera infantum. The essential oil of the leaf contains similar components to Australian Tee Tree (*Melaleuca alternifolia*), well known for its antimicrobial activity.

Northern Red Oak (Quercus rubra). *Oaks in the red or black oak group have pointed lobes.*

NORTHERN RED OAK

Inner bark

Quercus rubra L.

Beech Family

 To 60–120 ft. Bark dark, smoother than White Oak bark. Leaves hairless, thin, dull, with 7–11 *bristle-tipped* lobes; leaves 5–9 in. long, 3–6 in. wide. Cup covers ⅓ of acorn. **WHERE FOUND:** Woods. N.S. to n. Ga.; se. Okla. to Minn. **USES:** Considered similar to but weaker than White Oak (p. 313). Astringent inner-bark tea once used for chronic diarrhea, dysentery, chronic mucous discharge, bleeding, anal prolapse, piles; gargle for sore throats; wash for

Sycamore (Platanus occidentalis) *with its multicolored, peeling bark.*

Sycamore (P. occidentalis) *leaves are broadly oval with 5–7 toothed lobes.*

skin eruptions, Poison Ivy rash, burns; hemostatic. Folk cancer remedy. Contains tannins; experimentally, tannic acid has been shown to be antiviral, antiseptic, anticancer, *and* carcinogenic. **WARNING:** Tannic acid is potentially **toxic.**

SYCAMORE Inner bark
Platanus occidentalis L. Plane-tree Family
Large tree; to 150 ft. Bark mottled, multicolored, *peeling*. Leaves broadly oval, with 3–5 lobes; 5–8 in. Long and wide, with round, shallow sinuses. Fruits globular; to 2 in. across. Without seeing leaf or fruit, it is often easy to identify this tree by its multicolored peeling bark, smooth and light-colored, especially on upper portions of the trunk. **WHERE FOUND:** Moist soils, swamps, lake edges, and stream banks. S. New England to Fla.; Texas to N.M., north to c. Iowa, Neb. **USES:** American Indians used inner-bark tea for dysentery, colds, lung ailments, measles, coughs; also as a "blood purifier" and emetic (to induce vomiting), laxative. Bark once suggested for rheumatism and scurvy. Efficacy unconfirmed.

LEAVES TOOTHLESS; INEDIBLE FRUIT

OSAGE-ORANGE Root, fruit
Maclura pomifera (Raf.) Schneid. Mulberry Family
Small tree; 30–60 ft. Branches armed with short spines. Leaves lustrous, oval or oblong to lance-shaped. Fruit large (to 6 in.), round, fleshy; surface *brainlike*. Fruits Oct.–Nov. **WHERE FOUND:**

(Left) *Osage-orange* (Maclura pomifera). *Its inedible fruits are softball-sized.* (Above) Cucumber Magnolia (Magnolia acuminata) *with greenish flower petals. Photo by Doug Elliott.*

Roadsides, clearings. Mostly spread from cultivation. Originally, Ark. to Texas. **USES:** American Indians used root tea as a wash for sore eyes. Fruit sections used in Md. and Pa. as a cockroach repellent. Inedible fruits contain antioxidant and fungicidal compounds. **WARNING:** Milk (latex or sap) may cause dermatitis.

CUCUMBER MAGNOLIA
Bark, fruits
Magnolia acuminata (L.) L.
Magnolia Family

A *deciduous* magnolia; to 80 ft. Leaves large; oblong to lance-shaped. Greenish, cup-shaped flowers appear as leaves unfold, Apr.–June. Fruits resemble small cucumbers. **WHERE FOUND:** Rich woods. W. N.Y. to Ga.; Ala., Ark. to s. Ill.; Ont. **USES:** Bark tea historically used in place of Cinchona (source of quinine) for malarial and typhoid fevers, also for indigestion, rheumatism, worms, toothaches. Bark chewed to break tobacco habit. Fruit tea a tonic for general debility; formerly esteemed for stomach ailments.

CAROLINA BUCKTHORN
Bark
Frangula caroliniana (Walt.) Gray
Buckthorn Family
[*Rhamnus caroliniana* Walt.]

 Small tree; 10–30 ft. Leaves elliptic to oval, scarcely fine-toothed, usually smooth beneath when mature, but velvety in var. *mollis*. Flowers *perfect* (each one includes petals, sepals, and both male and female parts). Fruits black; 3-seeded, *not grooved on back.* **WHERE FOUND:** Rich woods. Va. to Fla.; Texas to Neb. **USES:** American Indians used bark tea to induce vomiting; also a strong laxative. Still used for constipation with nervous or muscular atony of intestines. **RELATED SPECIES:** The European species *R. cathartica* L., becoming increasingly naturalized in the eastern U.S., and the West Coast species *F. purshiana* (DC.) Cooper (*Rhamnus purshiana* DC., Cascara Sagrada) have been used similarly as official drugs for their laxative effects. Some botanists separate the 125 species of *Rhamnus* (5 petals, and bisexual) from *Frangula* (4 petals, with male and female flower separate). **WARNING:** Fruits and bark of all 3 species will cause diarrhea, vomiting.

Carolina Buckthorn (Frangula caroliniana) *is the most common eastern buckthorn.*

(Left) *Common Pawpaw* (Asimina triloba) *produces large, oblong leaves.* (Above) *It has a deep maroon flower.*

COMMON PAWPAW
Fruits, leaves, seeds

Asimina triloba (L.) Dunal.   Custard-apple Family

Small tree or shrub; 9–30 ft. Leaves oblong to lance-shaped (wider above); *large*—to 1 ft. long. Flowers *dull purple, drooping; petals curved backward;* Apr.–May. Fruits slightly curved, elongate; green to brown; edible (except seeds)—flavor and texture likened to that of bananas. Seeds *toxic; large, lima bean–like.* **WHERE FOUND:** Rich, moist woods. N.J. to Fla.; Texas; se. Neb. to Mich. **USES:** Fruit edible, delicious; also a laxative. Leaves insecticidal, diuretic; applied to abscesses. Seeds emetic, narcotic (produce stupor). The powdered seeds, formerly applied to the heads of children to control lice, have insecticidal properties. **WARNING:** Seeds **toxic.** Seeds and probably the leaves and bark contain potentially useful (anticancer), yet potentially toxic, acetogenins. More than one USDA chemist working with the acetogenins has experienced visual problems, which were corrected after they ceased working with the material. Leaves may cause rash.

REDBUD
Bark, flowers

Cercis canadensis L.   Pea Family

Small tree with a rounded crown; to 40 ft. Leaves heart-shaped, entire (toothless); 3–6 in. long and wide. Flowers red-purple, pea-

The pink, pea-like flowers of the Redbud (Cercis canadensis) *appear before the leaves do.*

like; on long stalks; *in showy clusters before leaves appear;* March–May. Fruit a flat, pea pod–shaped, dry, inedible legume; Aug.–Nov. **WHERE FOUND:** Rich woods, roadsides. S. Conn., s. N.Y. to Fla.; Texas to Wisc. Often planted as an ornamental. **USES:** Inner-bark tea highly astringent. An obscure medicinal agent once used for diarrhea and dysentery; also as a folk cancer remedy for leukemia. Flowers edible.

COMMON PERSIMMON   Bark, fruits
Diospyros virginiana L.   Ebony Family

⚠ To 15–50 ft. Leaves shiny, elliptic; to 5 in. long. Flowers greenish yellow, thickish, lobed, urn-shaped. May–June. Fruits plumlike, 1–2 in. across; with 6–8 compressed seeds. **WHERE FOUND:** Dry woods. S. New England to Fla.; Texas e. Kans. **USES:** Inner-bark tea highly astringent. In folk use, gargled for sore throats and thrush. Bark tea once used as a folk remedy for stomachaches, heartburn, diarrhea, dysentery, and uterine hemorrhage. The bark tea was

(Left, Above) *Common Persimmon* (Diospyros virginiana) *has plumlike fruits.*

used as a wash or poulticed for warts and cancers. Fruits edible, but astringent before ripening; best after frost. Seed oil is suggestive of peanut oil in flavor. **WARNING:** Contains tannins; potentially **toxic** in large amounts.

MISCELLANEOUS TREES WITH ALTERNATE, TOOTHED LEAVES

SOURWOOD, SORREL-TREE
Oxydendrum arboreum (L.) DC.

Leaves, twigs
Heath Family

Deciduous tree; to 80 ft. Leaves finely toothed, wide, lance-shaped; to 6 in. Leaf flavor acrid, sour—hence the common name. Flowers are white urns, resembling Lily-of-the-Valley flowers, in drooping panicles to 10 in. long; May–June. Fruits egg-shaped, *upturned*; about ⅜ in. long. **WHERE FOUND:** Rich woods. Pa. to Fla.; La. to s. Ind., Ohio. Cultivated as an ornamental elsewhere. **USES:** American Indians chewed bark for mouth ulcers. Leaf tea used for "nerves," asthma, diarrhea, indigestion, and to check excessive menstrual bleeding. Leaf tea is a Kentucky folk remedy for kidney and bladder ailments (diuretic), fevers, diarrhea, and dysentery. Flowers yield the famous Sourwood honey.

WHITE WILLOW (NOT SHOWN)
Salix alba L.

Bark
Willow Family

To 90 ft. Branchlets pliable, *not brittle at base; silky.* Leaves lance-shaped, mostly without stipules; *white-hairy above and beneath*

(Above) *Sourwood* (Oxydendrum arboreum) *produces white, urn-shaped flowers.* (Right) *The heavily drooping branches of the Weeping Willow* (Salix babylonica).

(use lens). **WHERE FOUND:** Naturalized; in moist woods, along stream edges. Throughout. Alien (Europe). **USES:** The bark of this willow, and the very bitter and astringent bark of other willows, has traditionally been used for diarrhea, fevers, pain, arthritis, rheumatism; poultice or wash used for corns, cuts, cancers, ulcers, and Poison Ivy rashes. Salicylic acid, derived from salicin (found in bark), is a precursor to the most widely used semisynthetic drug, acetyl-salicylic acid (aspirin), which reduces pain, inflammation, and fever. Aspirin reduces risk of heart disease in males; experimentally, delays cataract formation. In the intestines, compounds in the bark are transformed to saligenin, which is oxidized in the liver and blood to produce salicylic acid. Pain is reduced by inhibition of prostaglandin synthesis in sensory nerves. Use of bark is approved in Germany for fever, rheumatic complaints, and headaches. In short, used similarly to aspirin as an antipyretic, antiphlogistic, and analgesic. **RELATED SPECIES:** While many herb books list White Willow as the most common *Salix* species used, many *Salix* species are involved in the commercial supply of willow bark. In fact, other species contain ten times as much active constituents as White Willow. Crack Willow (*S. fragilis* L.) and Basket Willow or Purple Osier (*S. purpurea* L.) are native to Europe and cultivated and escaped in our range. Both are higher in salicin than White Willow and are used as official sources of Willow bark in Europe.

WEEPING WILLOW   **Bark, leaves**
Salix babylonica L.   Willow Family
  Perhaps the best-known willow species, Weeping Willow is a medium-sized tree to 40 ft. with long, pendulous (weeping) branches. Leaves are lance-linear, to 6 in. Catkins appear at same time as leaves. **WHERE FOUND:** Moist soils. Alien. Native to China. Often grown as an ornamental tree; occasionally naturalized. **USES:** Traditionally used in Europe for tonic, antiseptic, fever-reducing, and astringent qualities. Bark used for at least 2,000 years in China for rheumatoid arthritis, jaundice, and fevers. Leaves used in China to reduce heat (fevers), treat skin eruptions, regulate urination, and as a blood purifier. Used in the treatment of mastitis, toothache, scalds, and other conditions. Like most willows, contains salicin and tannins.

COASTAL PLAIN WILLOW, CAROLINA WILLOW   **Bark**
Salix caroliniana Michx.,   Willow Family
[*S. amphibia*, Michx., *S. longipes*, Shuttlw. ex. Anderss.]
  Shrubby or tree to 30 ft., trunk to 1 ft. in diameter. Leaves spreading, lanceolate, to 6 in. long (5 to 10 times longer than wide), gray-green, *strongly glaucous (and gray powdery) beneath*, with

Coastal Plain Willow, Carolina Willow (Salix caroliniana) *is typically shrublike, on gravel bars. Note stipules at leaf base.*

Black willow (Salix nigra), *one of our largest willows.*

long, sharp tip, toothed. *Stipules well developed and persistent, broadly kidney-shaped and toothed.* **WHERE FOUND:** Flood plains, along rivers, creek beds, wet or low habitats. Del., Md., south to Cuba and Guatemala, west to e. Kans. and Okla. **USES:** Widely used by American Indians across its range. Root-bark tea used to thin blood, to alleviate fevers, stiff neck, backaches, rheumatism, headaches, diarrhea; to induce vomiting.

BLACK WILLOW   **Bark, leaves**
Salix nigra Marshall.   Willow Family
Tree to 100 ft. or more, sometimes shrublike, trunks often leaning, twigs yellowish brown, mostly hairless. Leaves often drooping, lance-linear to lanceolate, finely sharp-toothed, to 6 in. long, ¾ in. wide, dark green above, lighter (not glaucous beneath). Male and female flowers on separate trees, with drooping catkins about 2 in. long. **WHERE FOUND:** Wet soils, flooded areas, along streams, ponds, and moist depressions. Throughout. Perhaps our most common willow. **USES:** American Indians used bark tea for diarrhea, headaches, fevers, dyspepsia; as a tonic, blood thinner, and as a wash to stimulate hair growth; externally, leaves poulticed on sprains, bruises, and sores. See White Willow (p. 321) for modern use. Used similarly.

MISCELLANEOUS TREES WITH ALTERNATE, TOOTHED LEAVES

(Left) The American Beech (Fagus grandifolia) has smooth, light gray bark. (Above) *Its leaves are persistent in winter.*

AMERICAN BEECH
Nuts, bark, leaves

Fagus grandifolia Ehrh.   Beech Family

Large tree; to 80 ft. (occasionally 120 ft.). *Smooth gray bark.* Leaves oval, *sharp-toothed,* yellow-green, persistent in winter; *veins silky beneath.* Flowers Apr.–May. Fruits are edible; *triangular nuts;* Sept.–Oct. **WHERE FOUND:** Rich woods. P.E.I. to Fla.; Texas to Ill., Ont. **USES:** American Indians chewed nuts as a worm expellent. Bark tea used for lung ailments. Leaf tea a wash for burns, frostbite, Poison Ivy rash (1 ounce to 1 pint of salt water).

RED MULBERRY
Root, fruit

Morus rubra L.   Mulberry Family

Small tree; 20–60 ft. Leaves heart-shaped, toothed, often lobed; *sandpapery above, downy beneath.* Flowers in tight, drooping clusters. Fruits like a thin blackberry; red, white, or black; June–July. **WHERE FOUND:** Rich woods. Sw. Vt., N.Y. to Fla.; Texas, Okla. to S.D. **USES:** American Indians drank root tea for weakness, difficult urination, dysentery, tapeworms; panacea; externally, sap used for ringworm. Nutritious fruits used for lowering fever. **WARNING:** Large doses cause vomiting.

Red Mulberry (Morus rubra) *produces elongated fruit that is relished by birds.*

WHITE MULBERRY (NOT SHOWN)
Morus alba L.

Leaves, inner bark
Mulberry Family

Similar to Red Mulberry (above), but leaves are *less hairy* and coarsely toothed, often with 3–5 lobes. Fruits whitish to purple. **WHERE FOUND:** Planted and naturalized in much of our range. Asian alien, introduced for silkworm production. **USES:** In China, leaf tea used for headaches, hyperemia (congestion of blood), thirst, coughs; "liver cleanser." Experimentally, leaf extracts are antibacterial. Young-twig tea used for arthralgia, edema. Fruits eaten for blood deficiency, to improve vision and circulation, and for diabetes. Inner-bark tea used for lung ailments, asthma, coughs, and edema.

AMERICAN BASSWOOD, LINDEN
Tilia americana L.

Flowers, bark
Basswood Family

 Deciduous tree, 60–80 (occasionally 120) ft. Leaves *finely sharp-toothed; heart-shaped,* base uneven; to 10 in. long. Flowers yellow, *fragrant;* from an *unusual winged stalk;* June–Aug. Where found: Rich woods. N.B. to Fla., Texas to Man. **USES:** American Indians used inner-bark tea for lung ailments, heartburn, weak stomach; bark poultice to draw out boils. Leaves, flower and bud tea, or tincture traditionally used for nervous headaches restlessness, painful digestion. **WARNING:** Frequent consumption of flower tea may cause heart damage. **RELATED SPECIES:** Small-leaved European Linden *T. cordata* P. Mill., and Large-leaved European Linden *T. platyphyllos* Scop., both cultivated and sometimes naturalized in N. America, are used in European herbal medicine. In Germany, the flowers are approved for treatment of colds and cold-related coughs. Primarily used as a diaphoretic. Preparations of the leaves and wood, also traditionally used for fevers and cellulitis, are not approved because claimed applications are not scientifically evaluated. Despite lack of scientific proof, the leaves are widely used in herbal products for colds and coughs.

(Left) *Basswood, Linden (Tilia sp.), with an uneven, heart-shaped base.* (Above) *Dried flowers and the prominent winged stalk are used commercially.*

TREES WITH ALTERNATE, TOOTHED LEAVES; ROSE FAMILY: CHERRIES, SERVICEBERRY

SERVICEBERRY
Amelanchier canadensis (L.) Medik.

Root, bark
Rose Family

Small tree; to 24 ft. Leaves fine-toothed, oblong, tip rounded; *veins in 10–15 main pairs, fading at edges.* Flowers white, in drooping clusters; late March–June. Fruits black. **WHERE FOUND:** In clumps. Moist thickets. S. Que., Me. to Ga., Miss. **USES:** Chippewas used root-bark tea (with other herbs) as a tonic for excessive menstrual bleeding, "female tonic," and to treat diarrhea. Cherokees used in herb combinations as a digestive tonic. Bath of bark tea used on children with worms. **RELATED SPECIES:** American Indians and Chinese used bark tea of other *Amelanchier* species to expel worms.

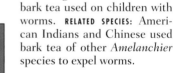

Serviceberry (Amelanchier sp.). The ten or more species in our range are the showiest early-spring-flowering trees.

BLACK OR WILD CHERRY
Prunus serotina Ehrh.

Bark, fruits
Rose Family

⚠ Tree; 40–90 ft. Bark rough, dark, reddish beneath. Leaves oval to lance-shaped, blunt-toothed; smooth above, pale beneath, with *whitish brown hairs on prominent midrib.* Flowers in drooping slender racemes; Apr.–June. Fruits nearly black cherries. **WHERE FOUND:** Dry woods. N.S. to Fla.; Texas to N.D. **USES:** *Aromatic* inner bark traditionally used in tea or syrup for coughs, "blood tonic," fevers, colds, sore throats, diarrhea, lung ailments, bronchitis, pneumonia, inflammatory fever diseases, and dyspepsia. Useful for general debility with persistent cough, poor circulation, lack of appetite; mild sedative, expectorant. Fruits used as "poor man's" cherry substitute. **WARNING:** Bark, leaves, and seeds contain a cyanide-like glycoside, prunasin, which converts (when digested) to the **highly toxic** hydrocyanic acid. Toxins are most abundant in bark harvested in fall.

CHOKECHERRY
Prunus virginiana L.

Bark, fruits
Rose Family

⚠ Shrub or small tree; to 20 ft. Smaller than Black Cherry. Leaves oval, *sharp-toothed,* midrib *hairless.* Flowers white in a thicker

Black or Wild Cherry (Prunus serotina) flowers grow in a drooping raceme.

Chokecherry (Prunus virginiana). Photo by Harry Ellis.

raceme Apr.–July. Fruits reddish. **WHERE FOUND:** Thickets. Nfld. to N.C. Mo., Kans. to Sask. **USES:** *Nonaromatic* bark, similar to that of Black Cherry. Externally, used for wounds. Dried powdered berries once used to stimulate appetite, treat diarrhea, bloody discharge of bowels. **WARNING:** As with Black Cherry, seeds, bark, and leaves may cause cyanide poisoning.

TREES WITH ALTERNATE, TOOTHED LEAVES; STALKS MOSTLY FLATTENED; POPLARS

BALSAM POPLAR, BALM-OF-GILEAD, TACAMAHAC

Populus balsamifera L.

Leaf buds, root, bark
Willow Family

To 30–90 ft. Winter buds *yellowish, gummy, strongly fragrant*; end buds more than ¼ in. long. Leaves broadly oval, with *fine wavy teeth*; leafstalks mostly rounded (rather them flat). **WHERE FOUND:** Moist soils. Lab. to Alaska; south to n. New England, Wisc., Minn., Iowa to Colo. **USES:** Buds boiled to separate resin, then dissolved in alcohol, once used as preservative in ointments. Folk remedy (balm) used for sores; tincture for toothaches, rheumatism, diarrhea, wounds; tea used as a wash for inflammation, frostbite, sprains, and muscle strain. Internally, bud tea used for cough, lung ailments (expectorant). Inner-bark tea used for scurvy, also as an eyewash, "blood tonic." Root tea used as a wash for headaches. Probably contains salicin, explaining its aspirin-like qualities. Dried, unopened leaf buds approved in Germany for treatment of skin injuries, for hemorrhoids, frostbite, and sunburn. Extracts are antibacterial and stimulate wound healing.

Balsam Poplar, Balm-of-Gilead, Tacamahac (Populus balsamifera). *Sticky leaf buds are used in herbal medicine.*

COTTONWOOD
Bark

Populus deltoides Bartr. ex Marsh.
Willow Family

   Large tree; to 150 ft. Leaves broadly oval, coarsely toothed; stalks *flattened* with *2–3 glands at top of each stalk* (use lens). Seeds dispersed by cottony "parachutes." **WHERE FOUND:** Along streams and rivers. S. Que., w. New England to Fla.; Texas to Man. and westward. **USES:** Inner-bark tea used for scurvy, and as a female tonic. Tree held sacred by American Indians of the prairies. Bark contains the aspirinlike compound salicin.

QUAKING ASPEN
Root, bark, leaf buds

Populus tremuloides Michx.
Willow Family

   To 60 ft. Bark smooth, greenish to gray-white. Leaves roundish to broadly oval, smooth, *fine-toothed;* leafstalks *flattened.* Branches and leaves *sway restlessly in breeze.* **WHERE FOUND:** Widely distributed in n. U.S.; absent south of n. Mo., Tenn.; found again in highlands of w. Texas, s. Calif. **USES:** American Indians used root-bark tea for excessive menstrual bleeding; poulticed root for cuts, wounds. Inner-bark tea used for stomach pain, venereal disease, urinary ailments, worms, colds, fevers, and as an appetite stimulant. Leaf buds used in a salve for colds, coughs, irritated nostrils. Bark tincture (contains salicin) a folk remedy used for fevers, rheumatism, arthritis, colds, worms, urinary infections, and diarrhea. Bark contains aspirinlike salicin, which is anti-inflammatory, analgesic; reduces fevers.

(Above) *Cottonwood* (Populus deltoides). *Photo by Stephen Lee Timme.* (Right) *Quaking Aspen* (Populus tremuloides). *Photo by Martin Wall.*

SWEET OR BLACK BIRCH
Betula lenta L.

Bark, twigs, essential oil
Birch Family

To 50–70 ft. Nonpeeling, *sweet, aromatic, black bark,* often ⚠ smooth, like that of our more familiar white birches, but black and not papery. Leaves oval, toothed; to 6 in. long. Buds and leaves *hairless.* Broken twigs and, to a lesser extent, the leaves, have a strong *wintergreen fragrance.* Inconspicuous, separate male and female flowers in catkins, early spring. Fruits are oblong, upright, ¾–1¼ in. long. **WHERE FOUND:** Rich woods. S. Que., sw. Me. to n. Ga., Ala.; north to e. Ohio. **USES:** Our most fragrant birch was widely used by American Indians, in bark tea for fevers, stomachaches, lung ailments, twig tea for fever. Essential oil (methyl salicylate) distilled from bark was used for rheumatism, gout, scrofula, bladder infection, neuralgia; anti-inflammatory, analgesic. To alleviate pain or sore muscles, the oil has been applied as a counterirritant. Essential oil was formerly produced in Appalachia. But now, methyl salicylate is produced synthetically, using menthol as the precursor. **WARNING:** Essential oil **toxic.** Easily absorbed through skin. Fatalities reported.

Sweet or Black Birch (Betula lenta) gets its name from its black bark, which emits a strong wintergreen fragrance.

Paper (American White) Birch (Betula papyrifera) is easily recognized by its white bark.

PAPER (AMERICAN WHITE) BIRCH
Bark, twigs

Betula papyrifera Marsh.
Birch Family

Small to medium tree; 50–70 ft. Bark *white, peeling;* one of the easiest trees to identify from bark. Leaves are oval with acute tips, 2–3 in. long, ½–2 in. wide; base wedge- or heart-shaped; margins doubly serrated; prominent raised midrib is yellow; marked by black glandular dots. Above, the leaves are dark green and shiny, beneath, yellowish. Male flowers appear before leaves in early spring in long clusters or pairs; 3–4 in. long. Female catkins are 1–1½ in. long, with pale green lance-shaped scales. **WHERE FOUND:** Rich, moist woods, streams, and lake banks from Lab. to Long Island and n. Penn. Iowa to Mich., Neb., S.D., Mont. to w. Wash. **USES:** Famous as the material of birch-bark canoes. American Indians used an infusion of the inner bark as an enema for constipation; root bark for diarrhea; in tea to disguise the flavor of other medicines; with maple sugar to make a syrup for stomach cramps. Sap suggested by Colonists against scurvy, as a diuretic and laxative. Externally the leaves and bark poulticed for "hard tumors." Betulinic acid from many species, including birches, is a promising anticancer compound (against melanomas); also anti-inflammatory and antiviral. Betulin, contained in bark, has anticancer, antiviral, and anti-inflammatory activity. Chagga (*Inonotus*), a black fungus on white birch, has a folk reputation against skin and internal cancers. It is said to take up betulin from birches.

AMERICAN ELM
Inner bark

Ulmus americana L.
Elm Family

Our largest elm, decimated by Dutch elm disease, often with drooping or arching branches, to 120 ft. tall. Leaves oval; 3–6 in. long, to 2¼ in. wide; smooth or only somewhat rough above, sharply double-toothed. Papery, winged, to ¼ in. long; tips incurved (often overlapping), with prominent hairs along margins. March–May. **WHERE FOUND:** Moist to dry soils. N.S. to Fla, west to Texas, north to Sask. **USES:** Bark sometimes an adulterant to Slippery Elm bark. Seldom used except by American Indians who used the bark tea for colds, severe coughs, menstrual cramps, diarrhea, internal hemorrhage, hemorrhoids, and as a folk cancer remedy.

American Elm (Ulmus americana) *leaves are smooth above.*

SLIPPERY ELM
Ulmus rubra Muhl.
[*Ulmus fulva* Michx.]

Inner bark
Elm Family

To 40–60 ft., with large, *rust-hairy* buds. White, mildly scented, inner bark is very mucilaginous (slippery). Leaves oval; 3–7 in. long, to 3 in. wide; sides of base distinctly unequal. Leaves *sandpapery above*, soft-hairy below, *sharply double-toothed*. Papery, winged, yellowish green, 1-seeded fruits, about ¼ in. wide, *without hairs on margins*; March–May. **WHERE FOUND:** Moist woods. Me. to Fla.; Texas to N.D. **USES:** The Osage applied bark poultices to extract thorns and gunshot balls. American Revolution surgeons used bark poultice as primary treatment for gunshot wounds. Three tablespoons of inner bark in a cup of hot water makes a thick, mucilaginous tea, traditionally used for sore throats, upset stomach, indigestion, digestive irritation, stomach ulcers, coughs, pleurisy; said to help in diarrhea and dysentery. Inner bark considered edible. Once used as a nutritive broth for children, the elderly, and convalescing patients who had difficulty consuming or digesting food. Externally, the thick tea, made from powdered inner bark, was applied to fresh wounds, ulcers, burns, scalds. Science confirms tea is soothing to mucous membranes and softens hardened tissue. Despite few scientific studies, approved by the Food and Drug Administration as a nonprescription demulcent for use in throat lozenges. Bark once used as an antioxidant to prevent rancidity of fat. Slivers of inner bark once used—dangerously—as a mechanical abortifacient.

(Above) *Slippery Elm* (Ulmus rubra) *leaves are sandpapery above.* (Right) *Its fruits mature before leaves appear in spring.*

BARK GREEN; LEAVES SIMPLE, SHINY; VINES AND MISTLETOE

SUPPLEJACK, RATTAN VINE
Leaf, bark

Berchemia scandens (Hill) K. Koch.   Buckthorn Family

High-climbing, twining woody vine; stems *smooth, green.* Alternate oval leaves with *conspicuous parallel veins;* no teeth. Tiny white flowers in panicles; May. Dark blue fruit in clusters; Sept.–Oct. **WHERE FOUND:** Moist woods, thickets. Se. Va. to Fla., Texas; north to s. Ill. **USES:** American Indians used bark or leaf tea as a "blood purifier" and to restore youthful vigor and sexual vitality. Tea of burned stems used for coughs.

MISTLETOE
Leafy branches

Phoradendronleucarpum (Raf.) Reveal & M. C. Johnston
[*P. serotinum* (Raf.) M. C. Johnston, *P. flavescens* (Pursh) Nutt.]

Mistletoe Family

Parasitic, thick-branched perennial; semi-evergreen. Leaves oblong to obovate; to 3 in. long. Flowers small. Fruits *translucent white.* **WHERE FOUND:** On trees. N.J. to Fla.; Mo. north to Ohio, Minn. **USES:** American Indians used tea for epilepsy, "fits," headaches, hypertension, lung ailments, debility, paralysis, also as oral contraceptive. Formerly used to stop bleeding after childbirth. **WARNING:** Often considered **poisonous.** Unconfirmed reports of deaths have been attributed to eating berries. May cause dermatitis.

Supplejack, Rattan Vine (Berchemia scandens) *bark is typically smooth and olive green.*

Mistletoe (Phoradendron leucarpum), *a parasite, is easy to spot after leaves drop from trees.*

Smilax *spp. There are six or more woody catbriers or greenbriers in our range.*

SAWBRIER, WILD SARSAPARILLA
Smilax glauca L.

Root
Lily Family

Entangling, climbing shrub, with stiff prickles. Leaves with a *whitish film*; oval, base rounded or heart-shaped; *white beneath*. Flowers not showy. Berries blue to black; July–winter. **WHERE FOUND:** Thickets. S. New England to Fla.; Texas to Okla., Ind. **USES:** American Indians rubbed stem prickles on skin as a counterirritant to relieve localized pains, muscle cramps, twitching; leaf and stem tea used for rheumatism, stomach troubles. Wilted leaves poulticed on boils. Root tea taken to help expel afterbirth. Some *Smilax* spp. contain diosgenin, which can be converted (by chemists —not in the human body) to testosterone and other steroidal compounds. Science confirms anti-inflammatory, estrogenic, cholesterol-lowering, and anti-stress activity of various *Smilax* species.

GREENBRIER, CATBRIER
Smilax rotundifolia L.

Leaves, stems, roots
Lily Family

Green, stout-thorny, climbing shrub. Leaves leathery, round, shiny; base mostly heart-shaped. Fruits blue-black; July–Nov. **WHERE FOUND:** Thickets. Weedy. N.S. to Fla., e. Texas to s. Ill. **USES:** Same as for *S. glauca* (above). Most of our *Smilax* species are used similarly.

LEAVES SIMPLE; BARK NOT GREEN

AMERICAN BITTERSWEET
Celastrus scandens L.

Root bark, fruits
Staff-tree Family

⚠ Climbing, twining shrub, to 50 ft. Leaves *ovate to oblong*, sharp-pointed, fine-toothed. Flowers greenish, in clusters, May–June. Fruit capsule scarlet to orange, *splitting*, to reveal *scarlet* seeds. **WHERE FOUND:** Rich thickets. Que. to Ga., Ala. Okla. to N.D. **USES:**

Root-bark tea induces sweating; diuretic; emetic. Folk remedy for chronic liver and skin ailments, rheumatism, leukorrhea, suppressed menses. Externally, bark used in ointment for burns, scrapes, skin eruptions. American Indians used this plant as above, also used astringent leaf tea for diarrhea, dysentery. Root-bark tea used for pain of childbirth. Bark extracts thought to be cardioactive. **RELATED SPECIES:** Oriental Bittersweet (*C. orbiculatus*), an Asian species naturalized in many areas, differs in that the flowers occur in groups of 1–3, in axillary cymes. Uncommon, but a serious weed in some areas. Uses in Asia similar to those for the American species. **WARNING:** Fruit **toxic. All parts potentially toxic.**

YELLOW JESSAMINE
Gelsemium sempervirens St.-Hil.

Roots
Logania Family

Twining, tangling evergreen shrub. Leaves lance-shaped to oval; shiny. Flowers yellow, shaped like an open trumpet with 5 *rounded petal lobes* that are *notched at end;* sweetly fragrant. Feb.–June. **WHERE FOUND:** Dry or wet woods, thickets. Se. Va. to Fla.;

Bittersweet (Celastrus sp.). The two species in our range produce red-orange fruit that splits when mature.

Yellow Jessamine (Gelsemium sempervirens).

Texas to Ark. **USES:** Root preparations were once used as a powerful CNS-depressant, deadening pain, reducing spasms. Externally, a folk cancer remedy. **WARNING: Deadly poison.** Eating a single flower has resulted in death. Can also cause contact dermatitis.

JAPANESE HONEYSUCKLE
Lonicera japonica Thunb.

Bark, flowers, leaves
Honeysuckle Family

Evergreen trailing, twining vine. Leaves oval, entire (not toothed). Flowers white or buff; lobes strongly spreading from throat, stamens protruding; Apr.–July. The flowers are white, but quickly fade yellow, earning it the name Gold and Silver Flower in China. **WHERE FOUND:** Noxious weed in much of the South; north to Mass., Ind. Alien. **USES:** Leaves and flowers a beverage tea (Japan). Flowers traditionally used (in e. Asia) in tea for bacterial dysentery, enteritis, laryngitis, colds, fevers, flu; externally, as a wash for rheumatism, sores, tumors (especially breast cancer), infected boils, scabies, swelling. Stem tea is weaker. Experimentally, flower extracts lower cholesterol; also antiviral, antibacterial, tuberculostatic. Widely used in prescriptions and patent medicines in Traditional Chinese Medicine to treat colds and flu. Pills are made from floral concentrates. Both authors have used such preparations for bronchitis, colds, and flu. When Echinacea or Garlic have failed against flu, Jim Duke has used the plant as a last resort. Flowers contain at least a dozen antiviral compounds. With the rapid evolution of viruses, synergistic combinations of phytochemicals, such as those found in Japanese Honeysuckle, are less liable to lead to resistant viral strains than solitary chemical compounds. This serious weed might be managed by using it for proven medicinal purposes.

Japanese Honeysuckle (Lonicera japonica) *is called "Gold and Silver Flower" in China.*

LEAVES 3-PARTED OR LOBED

KUDZU
Root, flowers, seeds, stems, root starch

Pueraria montana var. *lobata*
Pea Family
(Willd.) Maesen & S. Almeida [*Pueraria lobata* (Willd.) Ohwi]

Noxious, robust, trailing, climbing vine. Leaves *palmate, 3-parted;* leaflets entire or palmately lobed. Flowers reddish purple, *grape-scented;* in a loose raceme; July–Sept. **WHERE FOUND:** Waste ground. Pa. to Fla.; Texas to Kans. Asian alien. Perhaps this pernicious invasive weed of the South could best be controlled by harvesting its economic and medicinal potential. **USES:** In China, root tea used for headaches, diarrhea, dysentery, acute intestinal obstruction, gastroenteritis, deafness; to promote measles eruptions, induce sweating. Experimentally, lowers blood sugar and blood pressure. Flower tea used for stomach acidity, "awakens the spleen," "expels drunkenness." Seeds used for dysentery and also to expel drunkenness. Stem poulticed for sores, swellings, mastitis; tea gargled for sore throats. Root starch (used to stimulate production of body fluids) eaten as food.

POISON IVY
Leaf preparations

Toxicodendron radicans (L.) Kuntze [*Rhus radicans* L.]
Cashew Family

Highly variable—grows as a trailing or climbing vine or an erect shrub. Leaves on long, glossy to hairy stalks; 3 highly variable leaflets, outer one on a longer stalk. Flowers whitish; berries

(Left) *Kudzu* (Pueraria montana) *is one of our most rampant weeds.* (Above) *Poison Ivy* (Toxicodendron radicans) *is a highly variable species. Note both entire and strongly toothed leaves.*

white. Fruits Aug.–Nov. **WHERE FOUND:** Woods, thickets. Most of our area. **USES:** Once used by physicians for paralytic and liver disorders. Fighting fire with fire, American Indians rubbed leaves on Poison Ivy rash as a treatment. Jim Duke does not recommend the Indian approach (rubbing Poison Ivy on Poison Ivy), eating tiny amounts of the leaves to prevent Poison Ivy rash, or drinking milk from goats who have eaten Poison Ivy (did not work for his goat-tending sister-in-law). Micro doses are used homeopathically to treat Poison Ivy rash. Duke has received numerous unsolicited favorable comments on using homeopathic "Rhus tox" to immune oneself from Poison Ivy. Smoke from burning weeds (which included Poison Ivy) next door put Duke's father-in-law in the hospital with an internal case of Poison Ivy. Crushed Jewelweed, or Touch-me-not, is also rubbed on skin to prevent or relieve outbreak of rash. **WARNING:** If human skin comes in contact with Poison Ivy, severe dermatitis often results. Internal consumption of Poison Ivy may cause severe effects, necessitating steroid or other therapies. Dried plant specimens more than 100 years old can still cause dermatitis, as can the smoke from a burning plant. Ironically, the active ingredient, urushiol, inhibits prostaglandin synthesis.

DOMESTIC GRAPE   Leaves, berries, seeds
Vitis vinifera L. (and related species)   Grape Family
A high-climbing liana vine. At least 10 native species found in our range. Leaves simple, lobed or rounded in outline, with tendrils opposite leaves (rarely absent). Flowers in cymose panicles, fruits a juicy berry, with 4 or fewer ovoid seeds. A familiar species is the common domestic grape, *Vitis vinifera*. Grown for thousands of years, more than 8,000 varieties have been described, 20 percent of which are still grown. Fruits are purple-black, amber, white, or red grapes in a cluster; Sept.–Oct. **WHERE FOUND:** Cultivated throughout. Native *Vitis* species found in thickets, woods, fence rows. **USES:** American Indians used leaf tea for diarrhea, hepatitis, stomachaches, thrush; externally, poulticed wilted leaves for sore breasts; also poulticed leaves for rheumatism, headaches, fevers. Other *Vitis* species have been used similarly. Vines, when cut in summer, yield potable water, possibly purer than today's acid rainwater. Seeds contain compounds known as oligomeric procyanidins (OPCs), from which commercial extracts are made; valued for antioxidant activity. Ten to a hundred times more of the compounds have been found in the leaves (not used commercially in products) compared to fruits or wine. Grape-seed extracts have been scientifically evaluated (with positive results) for microcirculatory disorders, such as a tendency toward bruising (particu-

Domestic grape (Vitis vinifera) is becoming increasingly recognized for its health benefits.

Domestic grape (V. vinifera) leaves.

larly in the elderly) and varicose veins, as well as circulatory problems. **WARNING:** Do not confuse this with Canada Moonseed, which is considered **toxic.**

MISCELLANEOUS WOODY VINES

DUTCHMAN'S-PIPE
Aristolochia tomentosa Sims

Leaves
Birthwort Family

Climbing woody vine. Leaves *heart-shaped,* blunt-tipped; lower surface *densely covered with soft white hairs.* Flowers *pipelike;* calyx yellowish; May–June. **WHERE FOUND:** Rich riverbanks. N.C., Fla., Texas; north to e. Kans., Mo., s. Ill., s. Ind. **USES:** Similar to but much weaker in effect than Virginia Snakeroot (*A. serpentaria,* p. 251). Aromatic weak tea promotes sweating, appetite; expectorant. Used for fevers, stomachaches, indigestion, suppressed menses, snakebites. Little used. **WARNING:** Potentially irritating in large doses. **RELATED SPECIES:** *A. macrophylla* (not shown) differs in that it produces nearly smooth, sharp-pointed leaves. Flowers brown-purple. Ironically, Virginia farmers spray *A. macrophylla* as a weed. It contains the antiseptic antitumor compound aristolochic acid.

Dutchman's-pipe (Aristolochia tomentosa) *is a woody, twining vine.
Flowers are shaped like a pipe.*

Canada Moonseed (Menispermum
canadense). *Note the stalk attached at base of leaf. Photo by
Stephen Lee Timme.*

CANADA MOONSEED
Menispermum canadense L.

Leaves, root
Moonseed Family

Climbing woody vine; 8–12 ft. Root bright yellow within. Leaves
smooth, with *3–7 angles or lobes; stalk attached above base.* Flowers small, whitish, in loose clusters. June–Aug. **WHERE FOUND:** Rich,
moist thickets. Que., w. New England south to Ga.; Ark., Okla.
USES: American Indians used root tea for indigestion, arthritis,
bowel disorders, also as a "blood cleanser" and "female tonic"; externally, salve used for chronic sores. Historically, physicians used
root (tincture) as a laxative, diuretic; for indigestion, rheumatism,
arthritis, syphilis, general debility, and chronic skin infections.
WARNING: Poisonous. Fatalities have been reported from children
eating seeds and fruits. Some people reportedly confuse this plant
with edible wild grapes. **RELATED SPECIES:** The Asian species *M.
dahurica* has been used similarly; also for cervical and esophageal
cancers.

VIRGINIA CREEPER
Parthenocissus quinquefolia (L.) Planchon

Root, leaves
Grape Family

Climbing (or creeping) vine with *adhesive disks on much-
branched tendrils.* Leaves divided into 5 *leaflets;* elliptical to oval,
sharply toothed. Small flowers in terminal groups; June. **WHERE
FOUND:** Thickets. Weedy. Me. to Fla.; Texas to Kans., Minn. **USES:**
American Indians used plant tea for jaundice; root tea for gonorrhea, diarrhea. Leaf tea used to wash swellings and poison-sumac

(Above) *Virginia Creeper*
(Parthenocissus quinquefolia).
*Note the five leaflets radiating
from a single point.* (Right) *It often climbs and covers tree trunks.*

rash; mixed with vinegar for wounds and lockjaw; astringent and diuretic. **WARNING:** Berries reportedly **toxic.** Leaves **toxic;** touching autumn foliage may cause dermatitis on human skin.

FIELD HORSETAIL

Equisetum arvense L.

Whole plant
Horsetail Family

⚠ Stiff-stemmed, apparently leafless herb; to 1 ft. Internodes elongate; sheaths of nodes with 8–12 distinct teeth (the leaves). Branchlets *radiating upward from nodes*. Fertile stalks without branches to 18 in. Variable. **WHERE FOUND:** Damp sandy soil. Most of our area. **USES:** American Indians used plant tea for kidney and bladder ailments, constipation. Asian Indians consider the Field Horsetail diuretic, hemostatic. Root given to teething babies. Folk remedy for bloody urine, gout, gonorrhea, stomach disorders. Poultice used for wounds. High silica content. Also once used in tea for tubercular lung lesions. Shown to be valuable against inflammation, though scientific validity in question. Approved in Germany for treatment of posttraumatic edema; irrigation therapy for bacterial and inflammatory diseases of the lower urinary tract and kidney and bladder gravel; externally for wounds, burns. **WARNING: Toxic** to livestock; questionable for humans—may disturb thiamine metabolism.

SCOURING RUSH, GREATER HORSETAIL

Equisetum hyemale L.

Whole plant
Horsetail Family

⚠ Evergreen, hollow-stemmed, rough-surfaced, jointed primitive perennial; to 5 ft. Variable. The jointed, apparently leafless,

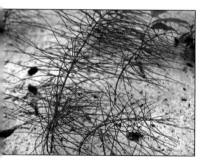

(Left) *Field Horsetail* (Equisetum arvense) *grows in moist soils. Note its branched stems.* (Right) *Scouring Rush, Greater Horsetail* (Equisetum hyemale) *has ribbed stems, apparently leafless.*

rough, finely ribbed, nonbranching stems make it easy to distinguish from other species of horsetail in our range. **WHERE FOUND:** Found in moist sandy soils, along stream banks, moist depressions, and pond edges throughout our range and beyond. **USES:** Essentially the same as for *E. arvense* (above), though this species is considered stronger by some authors. A folk remedy used throughout the Northern Hemisphere. Rough stems are used like sandpaper to give a very fine, satiny finish to wood. Early settlers used the stems to scour pots and pans. Homeopathically used for cystitis, bladder ailments, urinary incontinence, urethritis. Contains up to 15 percent silica, consisting of silicic acids and silicates, available in tea as water-soluble components (up to 80 percent). A number of flavonoids in the plant may contribute to diuretic activity. Externally, strengthens and regenerates connective tissue (due to the silica content). **WARNING:** Toxic to livestock; questionable for humans — may disturb thiamine metabolism.

COMMON OR RUNNING CLUBMOSS, GROUND PINE
Leaves, spores

Lycopodium clavatum L. Clubmoss Family

Mosslike evergreen; 3–15 in., with long, creeping runners. Tiny linear leaves, *tipped with soft, hairlike bristles.* Spores on leafy-bracted stalk, with 1–6 strobiles. **WHERE FOUND:** Dry woods. Canada south to N.Y., N.C. mountains; west to Wisc., Wash. **USES:** American Indians used plant tea for postpartum pains, fever, weakness. In folk medicine, spores used for diarrhea, dysentery, rheumatism; also as diuretic, gastric sedative, aphrodisiac, styptic; externally, in powders for a baby's chafing, tangled or matted hair with vermin, herpes, eczema, dermatitis in folds of skin, erysipelas. Spores, called vegetable sulphur, formerly used to coat pills and sup-

Common or Running Clubmoss (Lycopodium clavatum). Note the linear leaves tipped with soft, hairlike bristles.

positories. A related Chinese species in the Clubmoss family is being researched as a potential treatment for Alzheimer's disease. **WARNING:** This clubmoss (*L. clavatum*) contains a **toxic** alkaloid.

EVERGREEN FERNS

RESURRECTION FERN
Leaves, stems
Pleopeltis polypodioides ssp. *polypodioides* (L.) Andrews & Windham
[*Polypodium polypodioides* (L.) D. Watt.]   Fern Family

Small evergreen fern; to 8 in. Shrivels when dry, unfurls and turns green after rain. Leaves *leathery, blunt-lobed*; smooth above, densely scaly below. **WHERE FOUND:** Shaded rocks, trees (epiphytic), stumps. N.J. to Fla., Texas, and Cen. America.; north to Kans., Iowa. **USES:** American Indians used ointment of heated stem and leaves for sores, ulcers. Leaf tea used for headaches, dizziness, thrush, sore mouth, and bleeding gums.

COMMON POLYPODY
Root, whole fern
Polypodium virginianum L. [*Polypodium vulgare* L.]   Fern Family

Vigorous, evergreen mat-forming fern; to 12 in. Leaves leathery; deep green above, *smooth below*; 10–20 leaflet pairs; veins obvious, variable. **WHERE FOUND:** Shaded, rich, shallow soils or among rocks. Nfld. to Ga. mountains; Ark. to e. S.D., Minn. **USES:** American Indians used root tea for pleurisy, hives, sore throats, stomachaches; poulticed root for inflammations. Historically, root steeped in milk as laxative for children. Once considered valuable for lung ailments and liver disease. Tea or syrup of whole plant used for liver ailments, pleurisy, worms. Like Male Fern (p. 348), this fern was believed to be toxic to tapeworms. The root has a unique, rather unpleasant odor, and a sweet (cloying) flavor at first, but then quickly becomes nauseating. Root contains fructose, glucose, and sucrose, plus methyl salicylate (wintergreen flavor—see p. 30); it may also contain glycyrrhizin, the sweetener found in Licorice root (*Glycyrrhiza* species), but reports to that effect have not been confirmed. Root contains up to 2 percent insect-regulating "hormones." Resins active against worms. **WARNING:** Of unknown toxicity.

CHRISTMAS FERN
Root
Polystichum acrostichoides (Michx.) Schott.   Fern Family

Shiny evergreen fern; 1–3 ft. Leaves lustrous, leathery, tapering, leaflets *bristle-tipped, strongly eared*; teeth incurved. **WHERE FOUND:** Rich wooded slopes. N.B. to n. Fla.; e. Texas to Kans., Wisc. **USES:** American Indians used root tea for chills, fevers, stomachaches (to induce vomiting), pneumonia, poulticed root for rheumatism. **WARNING:** Of unknown toxicity.

(Left top) *Resurrection Fern* (Pleopeltis polypodioides) *completely wilts when dry, then is revitalized after a rain. Photo by Doug Elliot.* (Above) *Common Polypody* (Polypodium virginianum) *is an evergreen mat-forming fern. Photo by Craig C. Freeman.* (Left bottom) *Christmas Fern* (Polystichum acrostichoides). *Note lobe at base of leaflet.*

MAIDENHAIRS AND BRACKEN FERN

VENUS MAIDENHAIR FERN
Adiantum capillus-veneris L.

Whole fern
Fern Family

Fronds to 20 in.; oblong in outline, mostly twice-compound. Leaflets very thin; wedge-shaped, lobed at apex. Stalks delicate, brittle; shiny, dark, scaly at base. **WHERE FOUND:** Wet limestone rocks, waterfalls bluffs, usually in shaded areas. Va. to Fla., Texas, and Calif.; north through Utah, Colo. to Mo., S.D. Introduced as a curio farther north. Found throughout many parts of the world. **USES:** In folk tradition, a handful of dried leaves are steeped to make a tea drink as an expectorant, astringent, and tonic for coughs, throat afflictions, and bronchitis. Used as a hair wash for dandruff and to promote hair growth. In Traditional Chinese

Venus Maidenhair Fern (Adiantum capillus-veneris). *Note black stems and triangular leaf pattern.*

Venus Maidenhair Fern (A. capillus-veneris) *on a moist rock outcrop, surrounding Wild Hydrangea* (Hydrangea arborescens).

Medicine, the leaves are similarly used for bronchial diseases and as an expectorant. This fern has also been used as a worm expellent, an emetic, and an agent to reduce fevers. Externally, it has been poulticed on snakebites, and used as a treatment for impetigo.

MAIDENHAIR FERN
Whole fern

Adiantum pedatum L.
Fern Family

One of the ferns easiest to recognize, given the arrangement of the wedge-shaped leaflets in a horseshoe-like frond atop shiny ebony-colored stems. A distinctive fern; to 1 ft. Leaflets long, fan-shaped, lobed on upper side; alternate. **WHERE FOUND:** Rich woods, moist limestone ravines. Me. south to Ga., La.; west to Okla., north to Minn. and westward. **USES:** Considered expectorant, cooling, and antirheumatic. Tea or syrup used for nasal congestion, asthma, sore throats, hoarseness, colds, fevers, flu, and pleurisy. This fern was highly valued as a medicinal plant by some nineteenth-century medical practitioners, suggesting that its efficacy should be investigated by science. Stems were used by Indians throughout N. America as a hair wash to make the hair shiny.

Maidenhair Fern (Adiantum peda-tum) *leaves grow in a horseshoe pattern.*

Bracken Fern (Pteridium aquil-inum). *Note the lateral, thrice-divided leaves.*

BRACKEN FERN
Root

Pteridium aquilinum (L.) Kuhn
Fern Family

Our most common fern; 3–6 ft. tall, forming large colonies. Leaves triangular, divided into 3 parts; leaflets blunt-tipped; upper ones not cut to midrib. Variable. **WHERE FOUND:** Barren soils. Much of our area; mostly absent from Great Plains. **USES:** American Indians used root tea for stomach cramps, diarrhea; smoke for headaches; poulticed root for burns and sores, caked breasts; wash to promote hair growth; astringent, tonic. Historically, root tea used for worms. **WARNING: Poisonous** in excess doses—disturbs thiamine metabolism. Recently reported to cause cancer in grazing animals; contains at least 3 carcinogens.

MISCELLANEOUS FERNS

LADY FERN
Root (rhizome)

Athyrium filix-femina (L.) Roth.
Fern Family

"Discouragingly variable" (*Gray's Manual*, 5th ed.). Fern; to 3 ft. Stems *smooth*, with a *few pale scales*. Grows in circular clumps from horizontal rootstock. Leaves (fronds) broad, lance-shaped; mostly twice-divided, lacy-cut; *tips drooping. Leaflets toothed.* **WHERE FOUND:** Moist, shaded areas. Much of our area. **USES:** American Indians used root tea as a diuretic, to stop breast pains caused by childbirth, induce milk in caked breasts. Stem tea taken to ease labor. Like many ferns, this one was traditionally used to eliminate worms. Dried powdered root used externally for sores. **RELATED SPECIES:** Japanese researchers found anti-gout potential in the related fern *A. mersosorum.*

(Above) *Lady Fern* (Athyrium filix-femina). *Photo by Harry Ellis.*
(Right) *Rattlesnake Fern*
(Botrychium virginianum) *unfurls in late winter or early spring.*

RATTLESNAKE FERN

Root

Botrychium virginianum (L.) Swartz

Adder's-tongue Family

The largest *Botrychium* in our area. Delicate, lacy, nonleathery, broadly triangular leaf (sterile frond); to 10 in. long, 12 in. wide. Fertile frond on a much longer stalk, bearing bright yellow spores. **WHERE FOUND:** Rich, moist, or dry woods. P.E.I., Minn. to Fla.; Calif., B.C. Unfurls before other *Botrychiums*. **USES:** American Indians used root poultice or lotion for snakebites, bruises, cuts, sores. In folk medicine, root tea emetic, induces sweating; also an expectorant, used for lung ailments.

CRESTED WOOD FERN

Root

Dryopteris cristata (L.) Gray

Fern Family

Ladderlike, blue-green fern. Leaves 30 in. long, to 5 in. wide (widest above middle), with 20 or so *horizontal* leaflet pairs. Spore-bearing areas (sori) kidney-shaped, halfway between margin and midvein (leaf underside). **WHERE FOUND:** Damp woods. Nfld. to Tenn., n. La.; Neb. to N.D. **USES:** Root tea traditionally used to induce sweating, clear chest congestion, expel intestinal worms.

MALE FERN

Roots

Dryopteris filix-mas (L.) Schott

Fern Family

⚠ Yellow-green, leathery, semi-evergreen fern; 7–20 in., with blackish thick-wiry roots. Leaves divided into about 20 lance-shaped, pointed leaflets; leaflets narrow, oblong, cut nearly to midrib,

(Above) *Crested Wood Fern (Dry-opteris cristata). Photo by Harry Ellis.* (Right) *Male Fern (Dry-opteris filix-mas) root was formerly used to expel worms*

with rounded lobes or subleaflets, or slightly toothed. **WHERE FOUND:** Rocky woods. Me., Vt., N.Y. to Mich. **USES:** An oleoresin extracted from the roots has been used as a worm expellent. It is toxic to tapeworms. **WARNING: Toxic** poison and skin irritant.

LARGE GRASSES OR GRASSLIKE PLANTS

SWEETFLAG, CALAMUS
Rootstock

Acorus americanus L. — Arum Family

⚠ Strongly aromatic perennial; 1–4 ft. Root jointed. *Cattail-like leaves*, with a *vertical midrib*. Flowers tightly packed on a finger-like spadix, jutting *at an angle* from leaflike stalk. Flowers May–Aug. **WHERE FOUND:** Pond edges, wet fields. Most of our area. **USES:** See p. 99.

GIANT CANE
Root

Arundinaria gigantea (Walt.) Muhl. — Grass Family

⚠ Bamboo-like, woody-stemmed grass; to 10 ft. Lance-shaped leaves, in fanlike clusters. Flowers in racemes, on leafy branches. **WHERE FOUND:** Among our largest native grasses, this distinctly bamboo-like perennial forms large thickets along rivers, creeks, and moist soils south of Delaware. S. Del. to Fla.; Texas to Ill. **USES:** Houma Indians used root decoction (see p. 6) to stimulate kidneys. **WARNING:** Ergot, a highly **toxic** fungus, occasionally replaces the large seeds of Giant Cane. Do not collect or use any specimens from areas with diseased plants.

COMMON CATTAIL
Root, seed down

Typha latifolia L. — Cattail Family

⚠ Perennial; 4–8 ft., forming thick stands. Leaves *swordlike*. Stiff, erect flowering stalks, topped with yellow, pollen-laden *male flow-*

(Above) *Sweetflag, Calamus* (Acorus americanus) *produces a fingerlike flower spathe.* (Right) *Giant Cane* (Arundinaria gigantea) *has a bamboo-like stalk.*

ers above *hot dog–shaped, brown female flowerheads.* May–July. **WHERE FOUND:** Fresh marshes, ponds. Throughout our area. **USES:** American Indians poulticed jelly-like pounded roots on wounds, sores, boils, carbuncles, inflammations, burns, and scalds. Fuzz from mature female flowerheads applied to scalds, burns, and to prevent chafing in babies. Young flowerheads eaten for diarrhea. Root is infused in milk to cure dysentery and diarrhea. Anthers, pollen, rhizomes, and shoots have all served as human food. Pulp can be converted to rayon. **WARNING:** Though it is widely eaten by human foragers, Cattail is suspected of being **poisonous** to grazing animals. **RELATED SPECIES:** Root tea of **Narrowleaf Cattail** (*T. angustifolia,* not shown) has been used for "gravel" (kidney stones).

CORN
Zea mays L.

Whole plant

Grass Family

So well known that a description is unnecessary. Introduced to the U.S. by American Indians centuries ago; cultivated throughout our area. **USES:** Corn "silk," a well-known herbal diuretic, was once used in tea for cystitis, gonorrhea, gout, and rheumatism. Recently, water-soluble components of corn silk (chitinases and glucanases) have been found to be antifungal, inhibiting infection from aflatoxin produced by *Aspergillus flavus.*; seeds contain al-

Common Cattail (Typha latifolia) *has an easily recognizable seed head.*

Corn (Zea mays) *is one of the most important food plants from the Americas.*

lantoin (best known from Comfrey, p. 204), a cell-proliferant, wound-healing substance. Science has confirmed diuretic, hypoglycemic, and hypotensive activity in animal experiments with corn extracts.

MISCELLANEOUS GRASSES

QUACK GRASS
Whole plant

Elytrigia repens var. *repens* (L.) Desv. Ex B. D. Jackson   Grass Family
[*Agropyron repens* (L.) Beauvois, *Elymus repens* (L.) Gould]
   Grass; to 3 ft. Spreads on creeping *yellow* rhizomes. Leaves soft, flat, somewhat drooping; *crowded with fine ribs.* Flower spike is *not square,* as in most *Agropyron* species; 2–9 flowered spikelets, bract below spikelets not stiff, with slender keel and ribs. **WHERE FOUND:** Fields, gardens. Troublesome weed throughout our area. Eurasian alien. **USES:** American Indians used tea as a diuretic for "gravel" (kidney stones) and urinary incontinence; worm expellent; wash for swollen limbs. Approved in Germany in irrigation therapy for inflammatory conditions of the urinary tract and prevention (not treatment) of kidney gravel. Also used for bronchitis, cold, cough, fever, infections, pharyngitis, and stomatitis. In times of famine, American Indians used the rhizomes to make

Quack Grass (Elytrigia repens) *is a troublesome weed throughout.*

Big Bluestem Grass (Andropogon gerardii) *produces bluish stems. A famous prairie grass.*

breadstuffs; also scorched as a coffee substitute. Roots sometimes chewed like licorice. Considered an antidote to arrow poisons in Africa. Essential oil in root is antimicrobial.

BIG BLUESTEM GRASS
Root, leaves

Andropogon gerardii Vitman.
Grass Family

Coarse grass; 4–7 ft. Large clumps. Stem bluish. Flowers in a purplish or bronze-green raceme. Bristlelike awn projects from stalkless flowers—*stiff, sharply bent, to ¾ in. long.* Awn absent on stalked flowers. **WHERE FOUND:** Prairies, open ground. Que., Me. to Fla., Texas; north to Minn., Wyo., Sask., Man. **USES:** Diuretic, analgesic. Chippewas used root decoction for stomachaches, gas. Omahas used leaf tea as an external wash to relieve fevers, general debility.

BROOMSEDGE
Leaves

Andropogon virginicus L.
Grass Family

Highly variable grass; 28–55 in. Bluish or green stem. Leaf sheath *overlapping, keeled,* and *strongly compressed.* Small flowers emerge from envelopes that are *not inflated;* racemes usually in pairs, with *silvery white* hairs. **WHERE FOUND:** Dry soil, open woods. Mass., N.Y. south to Fla.; west to Texas, Kans.; north to Ill., Ind., Ohio. **USES:** Catawbas used root decoction for backaches. Cherokees used leaf tea for diarrhea; externally, as a wash for frostbite, sores, and itching. Also used for piles and Poison Ivy rash.

WILD OATS
Stems, fruits

Avena fatua L.
Grass Family

⚠ Annual; coarse grass; 2–4 ft. tall. Leaves rough to soft-hairy. Flowers in a panicle with spreading branches. Spikelets mostly

Broomsedge (Andropogon virginicus).

Wild Oats (Avena fatua) produce nodding spikelets.

nodding, usually longer than 1 ¼ in. Bracts (glumes) *nearly as long as the flower spikelets;* rounded at back, with numerous veins. **WHERE FOUND:** Waste places, cultivated ground. Scattered throughout. Alien Europe. **RELATED SPECIES:** Oats (*Avena sativa* L., the common oats of commerce, derives from *A. fatua*). They differ on small technical characteristics. **USES:** A folk medicine used as a nerve tonic, diuretic, and antispasmodic. In modern herbal medicine, oat straw is commonly used for treatment of skin conditions characterized by inflammation and pustules (approved in Germany). Oats themselves are considered nutritive and demulcent; they lower cholesterol.

SWEET GRASS
Hierochloe odorata (L.) Beauv.

Leaves
Grass Family

Vanilla-scented grass; 10–24 in. Spreads on slender, creeping rhizomes. Leaf clumps arise from dead foliage of previous year and wither soon after flowering. Flowers in pyramid-shaped clusters. **WHERE FOUND:** Meadows. N.S. to Pa., Ohio, Iowa, S.D. Sweet Grass is threatened because of overcollection. **USES:** American Indians widely used Sweet Grass as incense for ceremonies. Tea used for coughs, sore throats, chafing, venereal infections; to stop vaginal bleeding, expel afterbirth. **WARNING:** Roots contain a coumarin, sometimes considered carcinogenic.

Sweet Grass (Hierochloe odorata) is growing increasingly rare because of overharvest.

GLOSSARY

REFERENCES

LIFE LIST

INDEX TO PLANTS

INDEX TO MEDICAL TOPICS

Glossary

ADAPTOGENIC: Helping the human organism adapt to stressful conditions.

ALKALOID: A large, varied group of complex nitrogen-containing compounds, usually alkaline, that react with acids to form soluble salts, many of which have physiological effects on humans. Includes nicotine, cocaine, caffeine, etc.

ALTERATIVE: A medicinal substance that gradually restores health.

ANALGESIC: A pain-relieving medicine.

ANODYNE: A pain-relieving medicine, milder than analgesic.

ANTI-ALLERGENIC: Reducing or relieving allergies.

ANTI-APHRODISIAC: Suppressing sexual desire.

ANTIBIOTIC: An agent that inhibits the growth or multiplication of, or kills, a living organism; usually used in reference to bacteria or other microorganisms.

ANTICONVULSANT: Reducing or relieving convulsions or cramps.

ANTIFUNGAL: An agent that inhibits the growth or multiplication of fungi, or kills them outright.

ANTIHISTAMINIC: Neutralizing the effect or inhibiting production of histamine.

ANTI-INFLAMMATORY: Reducing or neutralizing inflammation.

ANTIMICROBIAL: An agent that inhibits the growth or multiplication of microorganisms, or kills them.

ANTIOXIDANT: Preventing oxidation; a preservative.

ANTISCORBUTIC: An agent effective against scurvy.

ANTISEPTIC: Preventing sepsis, decay, putrification; also, an agent that kills germs, microbes.

ANTISPASMODIC: Preventing or relieving spasms or cramps.

ANTITUMOR: Preventing or effective against tumors (cancers).

ANTITUSSIVE: Preventing or relieving cough.

ANTIVIRAL: An agent that inhibits growth or multiplication of viruses, or kills them.

APHRODISIAC: Increasing or exciting sexual desire.

ASTRINGENT: An agent that causes tissue to contract.

BACTERICIDAL: An agent that kills bacteria.

CALMATIVE: An agent with mild sedative or calming effects.

CARDIOACTIVE: Affecting the heart.

CARMINATIVE: An agent that relieves and removes gas from the digestive system.

CATHARTIC: A powerful purgative or laxative, causing severe evacuation, with or without pain.

CHOLAGOGUE: An agent that increases bile flow to the intestines.

CNS: The central nervous system.

COUNTERIRRITANT: An agent that produces inflammation or irritation when applied locally to affect another, usually irritated surface to stimulate circulation. (Example: a mustard plaster or liniment.)

CYTOTOXIC: An agent that is toxic to certain organs, tissues, or cells.

DECOCTION: A preparation made by boiling a plant part in water. Compare with **INFUSION** (p. 359).

DEMULCENT: An agent that is locally soothing and softening.

DIAPHORETIC: An agent that induces sweating.

DIGESTIVE: An agent that promotes digestion.

DIURETIC: An agent that induces urination.

EMETIC: An agent that induces vomiting.

EMOLLIENT: An agent that softens and soothes the skin when applied locally.

ESTROGENIC: A substance that induces female hormonal activity.

EXPECTORANT: An agent that induces the removal (coughing-up) of mucous secretions from the lungs.

FUNGICIDAL: An agent that kills fungi.

HEMOSTATIC: An agent that checks bleeding.

HOMEOPATHIC: Relating to homeopathy, a system of medicine founded in the late 1700s by Samuel Hahnemann. The system is based on the principle that "like cures like." Practitioners believe that a substance that produces a set of symptoms in a well person will, in minute, "potentized" doses, cure those same symptoms in a diseased individual.

HYPERTENSIVE: Causing or marking a rise in blood pressure.

HYPOGLYCEMIC: Causing a lowering of blood sugar.

HYPOTENSIVE: Causing or marking a lowering of blood pressure.

IMMUNOSTIMULANT: Stimulating various functions or activities of the immune system.

INFUSION: A preparation made by soaking a plant part in hot water (or cold water, for a cold infusion); in essence, a "tea." Compare with **DECOCTION**.

LAXATIVE: A mild purgative.

MITOGENIC: An agent that affects cell division.

MOXA: A dried herb substance burned on or above the skin to stimulate an acupuncture point or serve as a counterirritant. A famous technique of Traditional Chinese Medicine, using dried pressed leaves of Mugwort (*Artemisia* vulgaris).

MUCILAGINOUS: Pertaining to, resembling, or containing mucilage; slimy.

NERVINE: An agent that affects, strengthens, or calms the nerves.

PANACEA: An agent good for what ails you, or what doesn't ail you.

POULTICE: A moist, usually warm or hot mass of plant material applied to the skin, or with cloth between the skin and plant material, to effect a medicinal action.

PURGATIVE: An agent that causes cleansing or watery evacuation of the bowels, usually with griping (painful cramps).

RUBEFACIENT: An agent that causes reddening or irritation when applied to the skin.

SAPONIN: A glycoside compound common in plants, which, when shaken with water, has a foaming or "soapy" action.

SPASMOLYTIC: Checking spasms or cramps.

STIMULANT: An agent that causes increased activity of another agent, cell, tissue, organ, or organism.

STYPTIC: Checking bleeding by contracting blood vessels.

TINCTURE: A diluted alcohol solution of plant parts.

TERATOGEN: A substance that can cause the deformity of a fetus.

TONIC: An ambiguous term referring to a substance thought to have an overall positive medicinal effect of an unspecified nature (see **ADAPTOGENIC**).

TUBERCULOSTATIC: Arresting the tubercle bacillus (the "germ responsible for causing tuberculosis").

UTEROTONIC: Having a positive effect of an unspecified nature on the uterus.

VASOCONSTRICTOR: An agent that causes blood vessels to constrict.
VASODILATOR: An agent that causes blood vessels to dilate.
VERMICIDAL: Having worm-killing properties; an agent that kills worms, a vermifuge.
VULNERARY: An agent used for healing wounds.

BOTANICAL TERMS

BASAL ROSETTE: Leaves radiating directly from the crown of the root.
BRACTS: The leaflike structures of a grouping or arrangement of flowers (inflorescence).

CALYX: The sepals collectively; the external floral envelope.

DECOMPOUND: Divided several or many times; compound with further subdivisions.

FLORET: A very small flower, especially one of the disk flowers of plants in the Composite family.

GLAUCOUS: Covered with a fine, white, often waxy film, which rubs off.

HERBACEOUS: Nonwoody.

LIANA: A vigorous woody vine (usually refers to tropical vines).

OBOVATE: Oval, but broader toward the apex; refers to leaf shape.
OVATE: Oval but broader toward the base; egg-shaped.

PALMATE: With 3 or more leaflets, nerves, or lobes radiating from a central point.
PANICLE: A branching flower grouping, with branches that are usually racemes (see below).
PERFECT (FLOWER): A flower that has a full complement of male and female parts as well as floral envelopes (petals *and* sepals).
PERFOLIATE: A leaf that appears to be perforated by the stem.
PINNATE: A featherlike arrangement; usually refers to a compound leaf with leaflets arranged on each side of a central axis.

RACEME: An unbranched, elongated flower grouping, with individual flowers on distinct stalks.

RAYS (RAY FLOWERS): The straplike, often sterile flowers (commonly called "petals") surrounding the flowerhead (disk) of a plant in the Composite family. (Examples: the yellow rays of sunflowers or the purple rays surrounding the cone of Purple Coneflower.)

RHIZOME: A creeping underground stem.

ROSETTE (BASAL): Leaves radiating directly from the crown of the root.

SAPROPHYTIC: A plant (usually lacking chlorophyll) that lives on dead organic matter.

SEPALS: The individual divisions of the calyx (outer floral envelope).

SESSILE: Lacking a stalk; such as a leaf or flower with no obvious stalk.

SILIQUE: A term applied to the peculiar seedpod structure of plants in the Mustard family.

SPADIX: A thick, fleshy flower spike (usually enveloped by a spathe) as in members of the Arum family (Skunk Cabbage, Jack-in-the-Pulpit, Dragon Arum, etc.).

SPATHE: A modified, leaflike structure surrounding a spadix, as in members of the Arum family (Skunk Cabbage, Jack-in-the-Pulpit, Dragon Arum, etc.).

SPIKE (FLOWER): An unbranched, elongated flower grouping in which the individual flowers are sessile (attached without stalks).

STAMENS: The pollen-bearing anthers with attached filaments (sometimes without filaments).

STIPULES: Appendages (resembling small or minute leaves) at the base of leaves of certain plants.

SUBSHRUB: Somewhat or slightly shrublike; usually a plant with a stem that is woody at the base, but mostly herbaceous.

TENDRILS: A modified leaf or branch structure, often coiled like a spring, used for clinging in plants that climb.

UMBELS: A flower grouping with individual flower stalks or floral groupings radiating from a central axis; often flat-topped and umbrella-like.

REFERENCES

TECHNICAL MANUALS

Bailey, Liberty Hyde, and Ethel Zoe Bailey. Revision by L. H. Bailey Hortorium Staff. 1976. *Hortus Third*, New York: Macmillan.

Barkley, T. M., ed. 1986. *Flora of the Great Plains*. Lawrence: University Press of Kansas.

Fernald, Merritt Lyndon. 1950. *Gray's Manual of Botany*. 8th ed. New York: Van Nostrand.

Gleason, Henry A., and Arthur Cronquist. 1991. *Manual of Vascular Plants of Northeastern United States and Adjacent Canada*. 2nd ed. New York: New York Botanical Garden.

Radford, Albert E., Harry E. Ahles, and C. Ritchie Bell. 1968. *Manual of the Vascular Flora of the Carolinas*. Chapel Hill: University of North Carolina Press.

POPULAR GUIDES

Cobb, Boughton. 1963. *A Field Guide to the Ferns*. Boston: Houghton Mifflin.

Dobells, Inge N., ed. 1986. *Magic and Medicine of Plants*. Pleasantville, N.Y.: The Reader's Digest Association.

Duke, James A. 1986. *Handbook of Northeastern Indian Medicinal Plants*. Lincoln, Mass.: Quarterman Publications.

———. 1997. *The Green Pharmacy*. Emmaus, Penn.: Rodale Press.

Foster, Steven. 1991. *Echinacea: Nature's Immune Enhancer*. Rochester, Vt.: Healing Arts Press.

———. 1993. *Herbal Renaissance—Understanding, Using and Growing Herbs in the Modern World*. Layton, Ut.: Gibbs Smith Publisher.

———. 1995. *Forest Pharmacy—Medicinal Plants in American Forests*. Durham, N.C.: Forest History Society.

————. 1996. *Herbs for Your Health*. Loveland, Colo.: Interweave Press.

————. 1998. *101 Medicinal Herbs*. Loveland, Colo.: Interweave Press.

Foster, Steven, and Varro E. Tyler. 1999. *Tyler's Honest Herbal*. 4th ed. Binghamton, N.Y.: Haworth Press.

Foster, Steven, and Yue Chongxi. 1992. *Herbal Emissaries—Bringing Chinese Herbs to the West*. Rochester, Vt.: Healing Arts Press.

Grieve, Maude. 1931. *A Modern Herbal*. 2 vols. Reprint ed. 1971. New York: Dover.

Millspaugh, Charles F. *American Medicinal Plants*. 1892. Reprint ed. 1974. New York: Dover.

Peterson, Lee Allen. 1977. *A Field Guide to Edible Wild Plants*. Boston: Houghton Mifflin.

Peterson, Roger Tory, and Margaret McKinney. 1968. *A Field Guide to Wildflowers*. Boston: Houghton Mifflin.

Petrides, George A. 1972. *A Field Guide to Trees and Shrubs*. 2nd ed. Boston: Houghton Mifflin.

SCHOLARLY WORKS

Beckstrom-Sternberg, Stephen, and James A. Duke. 1996. *Handbook of Mints (Aromathematics): Phytochemicals and Biological Activities*. Boca Raton, Fla.: CRC Press.

Blumenthal, Mark, ed. 1998. *The Complete German Commission E Monograph: Therapeutic Guide to Herbal Medicines*. Austin, Texas: American Botanical Council. Boston: Integrative Medicine.

Duke, James A. 1986. *Handbook of Medicinal Herbs*. Boca Raton, Fla.: CRC Press.

————. 1992. *CRC Handbook of Phytochemical Constituents in GRAS Herbs and other Economic Plants*. Boca Raton, Fla.: CRC Press.

————. 1992. *CRC Handbook of Biologically Active Phytochemicals and Their Activities*. Boca Raton, Fla.: CRC Press.

Felter, Harvey Wickes, and John Uri Lloyd. 1901. *King's American Dispensatory*. 18th ed. 2 vols. Reprint ed. 1983. Portland, Ore.: Eclectic Medical Publications.

Hardin, James W., and Jay M. Arena. 1974. *Human Poisoning from Native and Cultivated Plants*. 2nd ed. Durham: Duke University Press.

Kartesz, John. 1994. *A Synonymized Checklist of the Vascular Flora of the United States, Canada, and Greenland*. 2nd ed. Portland, Ore.: Timber Press.

Leung, Albert Y., and Steven Foster. 1996. *Encyclopedia of Common*

Natural Ingredients Used in Foods, Drugs, and Cosmetics. 2nd ed. New York: Wiley-Interscience.

Moerman, Daniel E. 1998. *Native American Ethnobotany.* Portland, Ore.: Timber Press.

Robbers, James E., Marilyn K. Speedie, and Varro E. Tyler. 1996. *Pharmacognosy and Pharmacobiotechnology.* Baltimore: Williams & Wilkins.

Schulz, Volker, Rudolf Hänsel, and Varro E. Tyler. 1998. *Rational Phytotherapy— A Physician's Guide to Herbal Medicines.* Berlin: Springer.

Weiss, Rudolf Fritz. 1988. *Herbal Medicine* (translated from 6th German ed. of *Lehrbuch der Phytotherepie* by A. R. Meuss). Beaconsfield, England: Beaconsfield Publishers, Ltd.

Witchl, M. 1994. *Herbal Drugs and Phytopharmaceuticals* (translated by Norman Grainger Bissett). Boca Raton, Fla.: CRC Press.

LIFE LIST

	FLOWERING OR FRUITING DATES
WHITE	
___PRICKLY POPPY, 15	_____to_____
___TURTLEHEAD, 15	_____to_____
___LILY-OF-THE-VALLEY, 16	_____to_____
___DUTCHMAN'S-BREECHES, 17	_____to_____
___WILD CALLA, 17	_____to_____
___BUCKBEAN, 18	_____to_____
___FRAGRANT WATER-LILY, 18	_____to_____
___LIZARD'S-TAIL, 18	_____to_____
___WATER-PLANTAIN, 19	_____to_____
___COMMON WATER-PLANTAIN, 21	_____to_____
___BROAD-LEAVED ARROWHEAD, 21	_____to_____
___RATTLESNAKE-MASTER, 21	_____to_____
___YUCCA (Y. FILAMENTOSA), 23	_____to_____
___YUCCA (Y. GLAUCA), 23	_____to_____
___FIELD BINDWEED, 23	_____to_____
___HEDGE BINDWEED, 23	_____to_____
___JIMSONWEED, 24	_____to_____
___WILD POTATO-VINE, 24	_____to_____
___VIRGIN'S BOWER, 25	_____to_____
___WILD CUCUMBER, 25	_____to_____
___PASSION-FLOWER, 27	_____to_____
___DOWNY RATTLESNAKE-PLANTAIN, 27	_____to_____
___NODDING LADIES' TRESSES, 29	_____to_____
___PINK LADY'S-SLIPPER, 29	_____to_____
___BEARBERRY, 29	_____to_____
___TRAILING ARBUTUS, 30	_____to_____
___WINTERGREEN, 30	_____to_____
___PARTRIDGEBERRY, 31	_____to_____
___ROUND-LEAVED SUNDEW 32	_____to_____
___INDIAN-PIPE, 32	_____to_____
___GIANT BIRD'S NEST, 33	_____to_____
___WILD LEEK, 34	_____to_____

BLUE/VIOLET

SHRUBS

___COMMON JUNIPER, 254   _____to_____
___ENGLISH YEW, 255   _____to_____
___AMERICAN YEW, 255   _____to_____
___SAW PALMETTO, 256   _____to_____
___YUCCA (Y. FILAMENTOSA), 257   _____to_____
___YUCCA (Y. GLAUCA), 258   _____to_____
___SHEEP LAUREL, 258   _____to_____
___MOUNTAIN LAUREL, 259   _____to_____
___LABRADOR TEA, 259   _____to_____
___GREAT RHODODENDRON, 260   _____to_____
___YAUPON HOLLY, 260   _____to_____
___THYME, 261   _____to_____
___BEARBERRY, 261   _____to_____
___WINTERGREEN, 261   _____to_____
___PARTRIDGEBERRY, 262   _____to_____
___CRANBERRY, 262   _____to_____
___NINEBARK, 263   _____to_____
___LARGE-HIP ROSE, 263   _____to_____
___RED RASPBERRY, 264   _____to_____
___BLACK RASPBERRY, 264   _____to_____
___AMERICAN BARBERRY, 265   _____to_____
___COMMON BARBERRY, 266   _____to_____
___HAWTHORNS, 266   _____to_____
___DEVIL'S-WALKING-STICK, 267   _____to_____
___NORTHERN PRICKLY-ASH, 268   _____to_____
___SOUTHERN PRICKLY-ASH, 268   _____to_____
___ELDERBERRY, 269   _____to_____
___CHASTE TREE, 270   _____to_____
___YELLOWROOT, 271   _____to_____
___CAROLINA ALLSPICE, 272   _____to_____
___BUTTONBUSH, 272   _____to_____
___WILD HYDRANGEA, 273   _____to_____
___AMERICAN BEAUTY BUSH, 274   _____to_____
___STRAWBERRY BUSH, 275   _____to_____
___WAHOO, 275   _____to_____
___POSSUMHAW, 276   _____to_____
___CRAMPBARK, 276   _____to_____
___BLACKHAW, 277   _____to_____
___NEW JERSEY TEA, 277   _____to_____
___BLACK CURRANT, 278   _____to_____
___STEEPLEBUSH, 278   _____to_____
___LATE LOWBUSH BLUEBERRY, 279   _____to_____
___FRAGRANT SUMAC, 280   _____to_____
___WINGED SUMAC, 280   _____to_____
___SMOOTH SUMAC, 281   _____to_____
___STAGHORN SUMAC, 281   _____to_____
___LEATHERWOOD, 282   _____to_____
___SPICEBUSH, 282   _____to_____
___STAGGERBUSH, 283   _____to_____

____MAINDENHAIR FERN, 346   _____to_____
____BRAKEN FERN, 347   _____to_____
____LADY FERN, 347   _____to_____
____RATTLESNAKE FERN, 348   _____to_____
____CRESTED WOOD FERN, 348   _____to_____
____MALE FERN, 348   _____to_____

GRASSES OR GRASSLIKE

____SWEETFLAG, 350   _____to_____
____GIANT CANE, 350   _____to_____
____COMMON CATTAIL, 350   _____to_____
____CORN, 51   _____to_____
____QUACK GRASS, 352   _____to_____
____BIG BLUESTEM GRASS, 353   _____to_____
____BROOMSEDGE, 353   _____to_____
____WILD OATS, 353   _____to_____
____SWEET GRASS, 353   _____to_____

INDEX TO PLANTS

Numbers in **bold** refer to the page numbers of photographs.

INDEX TO MEDICAL TOPICS

Caution: This field guide is a guide to the recognition of plants, not a prescriptor. Only your doctor or other health-care professional who is licensed to do so can prescribe medications for you. We cannot and do not prescribe herbal medication. This index simply serves as a guide to the listings of medicinal usage of the plants treated in this book. Qualified medical diagnosis is essential to the treatment of disease. See your health-care professional rather than attempting self-diagnosis, which may be unreliable or incorrect.

Anesthetic, 55, 209, 228, 241, 268, 336

Angina, 70, 73, 101, 171, 261, 267, 311

Antioxidant, 78, 87, 110, 126, 182, 193, 196, 209, 215, 217, 219, 227, 237, 242, 261, 285, 288, 312, 318, 338

Anodyne, *throughout*

Anorexia, 70, 74

Anthelmintic (intestinal dewormer),15, 18, 52, 69, 75, 98, 117, 118, 122, 128, 129, 135, 138, 140, 141, 142, 148, 164, 168, 169, 173, 174, 183, 184, 188, 199, 206, 208, 209, 245, 247, 278, 282, 283, 287, 291, 292, 293, 300, 305, 307, 310, 313, 324, 326, 344, 348, 349

Anti-adrenalinic, 239

Anti-AIDS, 66, 71, 179, 215, 227, 235

Anti-allergenic, 88, 97, 247

Anti-aphrodisiac, 69, 313, 343

Antibacterial, 32, 34, 41, 42, 50, 58, 67, 69, 77, 78, 88, 96, 97, 110, 115, 124, 125, 129, 130, 135, 137, 138, 151, 152, 160, 165, 166, 177, 181, 186, 195, 218, 224, 225, 238, 239, 248, 262, 266, 268, 285, 286, 307, 308, 325, 328, 336, 342

Antibiotic. *See* Antiseptic.

Anticancer, 15, 23, 24, 34, 36, 42, 43, 48, 52, 53, 55, 60, 66, 67, 68, 69, 71, 85, 87, 92, 97, 104, 105, 109, 134, 137, 138, 141, 151, 152, 155, 166, 167, 168, 175, 176, 178, 179, 182, 187, 189, 190, 201, 203, 205, 206, 213, 216, 218, 219, 225, 235, 238, 239, 242, 253, 254, 255, 256, 266, 268, 271, 287, 298, 307, 308, 325, 328, 336, 342

Anticoagulant, 86

Anticonvulsant, 25, 32, 58, 88, 99, 115, 119, 233, 236, 254, 271, 295

Antidiabetic, 64, 75, 81, 102, 106, 114, 138, 145, 148, 158, 170, 179, 184, 186, 219, 237, 267, 271, 276, 325

Antidiarrhetic. *See* Diarrhea.

Antidiuretic, 160, 303, 304, 307, 309, 319, 351, 352, 353, 354

Antidote, 101, 210, 235, 300, 353

Antifertility, 69, 175, 230, 270, 296

Antifungal, 23, 32, 34, 41, 97, 138, 151, 219, 238, 243, 248, 295, 307, 308, 310, 318, 351

Antihistamine, 78, 99, 146, 154, 240

Anti-inflammatory, *throughout*

Antilactagogue, 21

Antimicrobial. *See* Antiseptic.

Antimutagenic, 186, 187, 217, 242, 285

Antiphlogistic, 322

Antipyretic, 322

Antirheumatic. *See* Rheumatism.

Antiscorbutic, 276

Antiseptic, 18, 29, 30, 31, 40, 41, 50, 52, 55, 83, 85, 98, 99, 128, 130, 132, 140, 145, 177, 184, 186, 196, 211, 213, 217, 232, 252, 254, 261, 262, 266, 271, 281, 295, 300, 307, 308, 313, 315, 317, 322, 339, 353

Antismoking, 50, 174, 208, 318, 272

Antispasmodic, 24, 25, 27, 32, 42, 50, 52, 58, 67, 69, 70, 71, 78, 79, 83, 85, 89, 94, 96, 97, 99, 102, 105, 107, 123, 124, 125, 127, 130, 131, 132, 133, 137, 138, 139, 140, 146, 155, 160, 164, 165, 173, 174, 178, 179, 182, 183 191, 194, 205, 206, 210, 211, 212, 213, 230, 232, 233, 236, 238, 246, , 253, 261, 264, 268, 271, 276, 277, 283, 296, 297, 298, 310, 331, 334, 336, 347, 354

Antitumor, 23, 25, 27, 31, 41, 42, 48, 50, 60, 85, 101, 105, 113, 121, 122, 130, 140, 141, 144, 155, 158, 166, 172, 178, 184, 192, 201, 206, 227, 237, 240, 242, 252, 253, 258, 273, 287, 292, 293, 310, 311, 313, 331, 336, 339; *see also* Anticancer.

Antitussive, 21, 25, 32, 34, 37, 40, 42, 45, 49, 50, 52, 54, 57, 60, 63, 64, 67, 70, 71, 72, 77, 79, 80, 81, 82, 83, 85, 86, 88, 93, 94, 99, 101, 103, 108, 111, 117, 121, 130, 134, 137, 140, 144, 145, 146, 148, 151, 153, 155, 157, 161, 170, 171, 177, 179, 184, 185, 193, 194, 196, 197, 198, 201, 202, 204, 207, 208, 210, 212,

Edema, *(cont.)*
216, 222, 296, 298, 325, 342

Emetic, 15, 16, 21, 34, 43, 45, 52, 54, 66,
75, 85, 89, 101, 104, 113, 115, 129,
131, 141, 148, 160, 172, 174, 190,
194, 201, 202, 208, 209, 220, 230,
230, 233, 234, 235, 246, 260, 263,
267, 269, 272, 273, 275, 276, 281,
285, 286, 292, 295, 298, 302, 308,
310, 317, 319, 335, 346, 348,

Emmenagogue, 64, 65, 67, 70, 73, 76, 80,
83, 85, 96, 98, 109, 119, 125, 128,
135, 136, 140, 150, 152, 157, 160,
173, 181, 182, 184, 191, 196, 213,
221, 222, 230, 233, 239, 241, 242,
244, 246, 247, 248, 251, 263, 264,
270, 271, 274, 277, 283, 321, 326,
329, 331, 335, 339

Emollient, 115, 163, 201, 204, 205, 288,
332

Emphysema, 210

Enema, 307, 331

Energy, 60, 235, 264, 332

Enteritis. *See* Abdomen.

Enterorrhagia (intestinal bleeding), 74, 95,
184, 220, 237, 239, 288, 241, 243,
244, 328, 331

Enuresis, 112, 121, 185, 281, 295, 343,
352,

Epilepsy, 16, 27, 32, 50, 71, 119, 180,
191, 206, 211, 213, 228, 230, 233,
236, 248, ,295, 296, 297, 333

Epistaxis (nosebleed), 34, 38, 45, 164,
183, 184, 208, 209, 237, 247, 248

Eruptions, 18, 25, 34, 38, 39, 41, 45, 49,
50, 60, 66, 69, 72, 75, 83, 101, 104,
107, 120, 122, 123, 137, 143, 167,
186, 187, 192, 197, 202, 220, 223,
246, 248, 267, 269, 294, 302, 313,
314, 317, 322, 335, 337, 354

Erysipelas, 117, 322, 343

Esophagus, 47, 340

Estrogenic, 38, 87, 88, 114, 178, 179,
192, 219, 232, 233, 334

Expectorant, 25, 38, 40, 45, 49, 64, 66,
67, 72, 74, 82, 85, 93, 101, 115,
124, 138, 144, 145, 146, 154, 155,

167, 168, 169, 171, 175, 179, 196,
204, 208, 213, 229, 251, 257, 261,
266, 275, 278, 295, 303, 308, 315,
327, 328, 339, 345, 346

Eyes. *See* Ophthalmia.

Eyewash. *See* Collyrium.

Fainting, 62

Fatality, 24, 48, 69, 70, 90, 140, 163, 169,
184, 194, 203, 205, 206, 208, 211,
213, 235, 237, 240, 246, 255, 256,
295, 298, 330, 333, 336, 340

Fatigue, 60, 133, 134, 160

Fear, 221, 247

Feet, 113, 122, 179, 181, 283, 294, 300

Feline euphoria, 83, 160

Felons, 160, 206, 292

Female ailments, 21, 23, 27, 29, 31, 36,
37, 38, 43, 45, 64, 70, 76, 78, 80,
87, 92, 94, 95, 106, 109, 118, 119,
125, 132, 136, 152, 155, 156, 157,
160, 166, 167, 173, 177, 190, 194,
195, 197, 204, 213, 221, 228, 230,
233, 239, 241, 242, 244, 246, 247,
248, 251, 255, 257, 263, 264, 265,
270, 271, 274, 276, 277, 279, 280,
281, 282, 283, 284, 285, 305, 321,
326, 329, 334, 335, 339, 340, 347

Fertility, 230, 263, 270

Fetus, 210, 264

Fever, *throughout*

Fish poison, 23, 131, 134, 141, 210, 255,
257, 297

Fistula, 166

Fits, 42, 333

Flatulence. *See* Carminative.

Flu (influenza), 17, 53, 70, 71, 74, 89, 94,
97, 127, 130, 187, 191, 225, 226,
227, 248, 249, 261, 269, 274, 280,
293, 295, 336, 346

Flukes, 152, 177

Forgetfulness, 203

Fractures, 23, 89, 117, 204, 205, 257,
292, 313

Freckles, 18, 312

Frostbite, 324, 328, 353

Fumitory (steam or smoke inhalants), 36,

45, 90, 93, 113, 119, 132, 145, 150,
170, 179, 205, 207, 248, 256, 257,
274, 280, 281, 290, 293, 294, 296,
338, 347

Fungicide, 23, 32, 34, 97, 138, 151, 295,
318

Fungus, 23, 32, 34, 97, 138, 151, 219,
238, 243, 248, 295, 307, 308, 310,
318, 351 350

Furuncles, 207

Gall bladder, 24, 82, 106, 121, 145, 167,
185, 212, 223, 237, 239, 247,
311

Gall, 29, 167, 185

Gallstones, 29

Gangrene, 132

Gargle, 37, 39, 50, 52, 72, 113, 121, 132,
166, 171, 176, 177, 184, 191, 192,
195, 196, 206, 214, 217, 221, 238,
247, 264, 282, 291, 313, 316, 320,
337

Gas. *See* Carminative.

Gastritis (gastrosis), 34, 57, 60, 88, 97,
118, 120, 123, 124, 135, 138, 167,
168, 170, 171, 191, 192, 194, 195,
197, 201, 210, 212, 230, 285, 290,
312, 332, 243, 297, 298, 334, 337;
see also Abdomen.

Genital, 203

Geriatric, 267, 280, 332, 339

Gingivitis, 95

Glands, 18, 199, 200, 239, 243, 304

Glaucoma, 15, 55, 232

Gleet, 21

Glossitis (inflammation of the tongue), 49,
282

Goiter, 40, 81

Gonorrhea, 29, 43, 58, 91, 137, 148, 186,
221, 263, 265, 285, 302, 340, 342,
351

Gout, 34, 43, 62, 87, 89, 97, 99, 102, 121,
122, 135, 152, 165, 185, 186, 196,
201, 207, 239, 294, 314, 330, 342,
347, 351

Grave's Disease, 81

Gravel (kidney stones), 19, 30, 42, 43, 50,

52, 69, 90, 101, 102, 139, 158, 175,
180, 184, 185, 237, 273, 294, 342,
351, 352

Gray hair, 95, 300

Griping (intestinal cramp), 262, 310

Grippe, 17, 53, 70, 71, 74, 89, 94, 97,
127, 130, 187, 191, 225, 226, 227,
248, 249, 261, 269, 274, 280, 293,
295, 336, 346

Gums, 95, 96, 97, 101, 117, 166, 175,
178, 344

Hallucinogen, 24, 205

Head cold, 15, 27, 31, 32, 34, 39, 43, 57,
60, 70, 71, 74, 78, 79, 82, 83, 89,
93, 94, 95, 99, 108, 127, 135, 137,
139, 140, 141, 142, 150, 155, 158,
160, 164, 170, 183, 194, 201, 208,
209, 210, 211, 213, 218, 229, 248,
249, 250, 257, 278, 302, 311, 315,
317, 325, 327, 329, 336, 346, 352

Headache, 15, 25, 27, 29, 31, 34, 37, 39,
60, 62, 71, 77, 78, 79, 83, 95, 96,
97, 98, 104, 106, 109, 110, 113,
119, 131, 132, 134, 135, 140, 153,
156, 160, 164, 172, 177, 182, 183,
190, 191, 192, 197, 200, 204, 209,
211, 213, 216, 229, 230, 248, 250,
257, 260, 269, 286, 291, 293, 294,
304, 309, 310, 312, 313, 322, 323,
325, 328, 333, 337, 338, 344, 347

Heart rate (pulse), 119, 169, 200, 224,
236, 261, 267, 304

Heart. *See* Carditis.

Heartburn, 99, 320, 325

Heat, 152, 217, 296, 322

Hematemesis (vomiting of blood), 25, 144,
161, 162, 181, 204, 275, 284, 302

Hematonic, 27, 50, 108, 121, 222, 229,
239, 241, 243, 271, 278, 287, 327,
328, 340

Hematoptysis, 122

Hematuria (blood in urine), 83, 237, 241,
342

Hemiplegia (stroke, partial paralysis), 228,
246, 308

Hemorrhage, 17, 38, 74, 94, 110, 119,

Hemorrhage,(cont.)
132, 139, 144, 157, 160, 165, 184,
220, 222, 237, 241, 243, 244, 266,
321, 331

Hemorrhoids. *See* Piles.

Hemostat (stops bleeding), 17, 18, 23, 29,
30, 34, 38, 45, 50, 66, 74, 75, 94,
95, 110, 119, 121, 132, 135, 144,
157, 163, 165, 166, 177, 180, 181,
183, 184, 195, 219, 220, 237, 238,
239, 241, 243, 244, 247, 258, 269,
271, 273, 274, 279, 282, 288, 290,
292, 298, 307, 310, 313, 317, 331,
333, 342, 343, 354

Hepatitis, 15, 18, 19, 31, 43, 52, 62, 82,
89, 90, 96, 107, 122, 134, 145, 146,
150, 162, 172, 189, 190, 193, 198,
200, 204, 205, 211, 213, 217, 222,
223, 224, 225, 239, 243, 247, 264,
266, 275, 300, 314, 335, 338, 344

Hepato-protective, 160, 193, 196, 285

Herbicide, 83, 310

Herpes, 15, 53, 78, 117, 130, 134, 211,
215, 226, 252, 295, 343

Hiccoughs, 230

Hives, 31, 62, 106, 129, 186, 246, 286,
287, 344

Hoarseness, 39, 77, 146, 208, 244, 307,
346

Homeopathy, 45, 185, 190, 197, 223, 338,
343

Hookworm, 18, 52, 69, 98, 117, 118, 122,
125, 128, 129, 135, 138, 140, 141,
142, 148, 164, 168, 169, 173, 174,
183, 184, 188, 199, 206, 208, 245,
247, 278, 282, 283, 287, 291, 292,
293, 300, 307, 326, 348

Hormones, 114, 199, 230, 232, 233, 271,
334

Hoxsey treatment, 179

Hyperacidity, 192, 337

Hypercholesterolemia, 36, 83, 86, 99,
334, 336, 354

Hyperemia, 325

Hyperglycemia, 64, 75, 81, 102, 106, 114,
137, 148, 158, 170, 179, 186, 219,
233, 234, 237, 276, 325

Hypertension, 19, 27, 34, 38, 42, 58, 60,
69, 88, 99, 102, 105, 151, 194, 211,
230, 233, 267, 271, 314, 333

Hyperthyroidism, 81, 155, 812

Hypertrophy, 304

Hypochondria, 160

Hypoglycemia, 19, 64, 135, 138, 145, 192,
223, 248, 271, 337, 352

Hypotensive, 69, 83, 86, 102, 110, 119,
151, 182, 191, 192, 217, 236, 237,
256, 261, 267, 271, 278, 295,
296, 337, 352

Hypothermia, 325

Hysteria, 29, 109, 156

Immuno-active, 89, 91, 96, 131, 142, 170,
218, 220, 225, 226, 227, 235, 271

Impetigo, 346

Impotency, 101, 134, 185, 230

Inappetence, 15, 18, 38, 54, 82, 118, 136,
145, 186, 190, 198, 200, 219, 224,
236, 247, 248, 250, 251, 253, 266,
307, 311, 327, 328, 329, 339

Incontinence, 112, 121, 185, 281, 295,
343, 352; *see also* Bedwetting.

Indigestion. *See* Dyspepsia.

Infection, 41, 58, 63, 64, 88, 93, 109,
113, 114, 130, 166, 185, 191, 210,
226, 240, 246, 254, 262, 266, 290,
295, 298, 302, 304, 310, 329, 330,
336, 340, 351, 352, 354

Inflammation. *See* Anti-inflammatory.

Influenza. *See* Flu.

Insanity, 36

Insect repellent, 83, 99, 181, 213, 318

Insecticide, 83, 99, 119, 120, 132, 140,
141, 174, 176, 213, 225, 237, 307,
310, 319

Insomnia, 25, 27, 29, 37, 78, 83, 97, 109,
126, 156, 160, 182, 183, 191, 192,
209, 211, 217, 232, 306

Intestinal amoebas, 245

Intestines. *See* Abdomen.

Intoxication, 42, 101, 106, 192, 219, 224,
230, 232, 247, 337

Ipecac, 235

Irritable bowel syndrome, 201, 212

Irritant, irritation, *throughout*

Itch, 15, 25, 37, 49, 63, 87, 110, 139, 203, 230, 235, 248, 260, 266, 283, 285, 288, 295, 296, 298, 353

Jaundice, 15, 24, 38, 42, 43, 52, 58, 82, 96, 105, 120, 121, 135, 140, 152, 166, 167, 196, 198, 200, 216, 223, 224, 225, 243, 259, 266, 271, 285, 291, 300, 304, 322, 340, 344

Jaws, 209

Kidneys, effects on, 21, 27, 29, 30, 31, 37, 42, 43, 50, 62, 64, 73, 85, 91, 104, 106, 113, 119, 126, 129, 130, 137, 139, 140, 145, 158, 166, 175, 180, 184, 185, 190, 196, 213, 216, 217, 221, 237, 239, 240, 241, 248, 273, 294, 254, 259, 268, 272, 273, 278, 290, 291, 293, 303, 304, 314, 321, 342, 350, 352

Labor, 31, 38, 57, 60, 92, 110, 113, 136, 157, 162, 182, 230, 233, 235, 249, 250, 256, 264, 276, 280, 286, 307, 335, 347

Lactation (Galactagogue), 21, 67, 92, 124, 125, 135, 144, 177, 182, 190, 235, 270, 347

Lameness, 132, 154, 268, 288

Laryngitis, 54, 111, 126, 229, 280, 336

Lassitude, 29, 63

Laxative, 15, 23, 24, 25, 37, 43, 52, 67, 75, 83, 89, 99, 101, 117, 120, 124, 132, 133, 145, 154, 160, 162, 167, 172, 174, 175, 187, 190, 196, 198, 199, 200, 201, 218, 223, 234, 235, 239, 243, 254, 263, 266, 269, 275, 276, 278, 291, 295, 298, 300, 305, 307, 308, 309, 310, 317, 318, 319, 331, 340, 342, 344; *See also* Cathartic; Purgative.

Leaky Gut Syndrome, 138, 148

Leprosy, 134, 260

Lesions, 210, 308, 342

Lethargy, 40, 60

Leucorrhea, 45, 87, 94, 136, 152, 177, 195, 197, 247, 264, 279, 280, 281, 284, 285, 305, 335

Leukemia, 53, 71, 216, 320

Libido, 125, 270

Lice (vermin), 134, 153, 259, 260, 298, 319, 343

Ligaments, 205

Lipolytic, 19

Lips, 201

Liver, 18, 19, 31, 43, 52, 62, 82, 89, 90, 96, 107, 122, 134, 145, 146, 150, 162, 172, 177, 184, 185, 186, 189, 190, 193, 198, 200, 259, 264, 266, 271, 275, 285, 300, 302, 303, 314, 322, 325, 335, 338, 344; *See also* Cirrohsis; Hepatitis; Jaundice.

Lockjaw, 341

Love potion (philtre), 17, 27, 55, 153, 156, 163, 164

Lumbago, 21, 31, 62, 64

Lunacy, 307

Lungs, effects on, 18, 21, 32, 34, 37, 40, 41, 42, 43, 53, 64, 81, 85, 92, 93, 94, 102, 105, 111, 116, 136, 145, 146, 148, 150, 154, 157, 162, 163, 167, 184, 196, 201, 202, 210, 212, 213, 214, 216, 220, 233, 239, 260, 268, 273, 275, 278, 282, 288, 293, 295, 307, 312, 317, 324, 325, 327, 328, 330, 332, 333, 342, 343, 344, 346, 348

Lupus, 219, 298

Lymph nodes, swollen, 28, 113, 114, 187, 202, 217, 229, 240, 243, 281, 285

Lymph, 28, 113, 114, 187, 202, 216, 217, 229, 240, 243, 281, 285, 330

Madness, 36, 42 307

Malaria, 52, 53, 89, 91, 146, 166, 177, 221, 241, 249, 250, 272, 273, 274, 275, 286, 287, 295, 296, 297, 298, 304, 306, 313, 318

Mange, 203

Mastitis. *See* Breasts.

Measles, 140, 183, 186, 192, 209, 218, 283, 294, 295, 307, 317, 337

Melanoma, 200, 331

THE PETERSON SERIES®

PETERSON FIELD GUIDES®

BIRDS

ADVANCED BIRDING (39) North America 97500-X

BIRDS OF BRITAIN AND EUROPE (8) 66922-7

BIRDS OF TEXAS (13) Texas and adjacent states 92138-4

BIRDS OF THE WEST INDIES (18) 0-618-00210-3

EASTERN BIRDS (1) Eastern and central North America 91176-1

EASTERN BIRDS' NESTS (21) U.S. east of Mississippi River 93609-8

HAWKS (35) North America 93615-2

WESTERN BIRDS (2) North America west of 100th meridian and north of Mexico 91173-7

WESTERN BIRDS' NESTS (25) U.S. west of Mississippi River 47863-4

MEXICAN BIRDS (20) Mexico, Guatemala, Belize, El Salvador 97514-X

WARBLERS (49) North America 78321-6

FISH

PACIFIC COAST FISHES (28) Gulf of Alaska to Baja California 0-618-00212-X

ATLANTIC COAST FISHES (32) North American Atlantic coast 97515-8

FRESHWATER FISHES (42) North America north of Mexico 91091-9

INSECTS

INSECTS (19) North America north of Mexico 91170-2

BEETLES (29) North America 91089-7

EASTERN BUTTERFLIES (4) Eastern and central North America 90453-6

WESTERN BUTTERFLIES (33) U.S. and Canada west of 100th meridian, part of northern Mexico 79151-0

EASTERN MOTHS North America east of 100th meridian 36100-1

MAMMALS

MAMMALS (5) North America north of Mexico 91098-6

ANIMAL TRACKS (9) North America 91094-3

ECOLOGY

EASTERN FORESTS (37) Eastern North America 92895-8

CALIFORNIA AND PACIFIC NORTHWEST FORESTS (50) 92896-6

ROCKY MOUNTAIN AND SOUTHWEST FORESTS (51) 92897-4

VENOMOUS ANIMALS AND POISONOUS PLANTS (46) North America north of Mexico 93608-X

AUDIO AND VIDEO

EASTERN BIRDING BY EAR
cassettes 97523-9
CD 97524-7
WESTERN BIRDING BY EAR
cassettes 97526-3
CD 97525-5
EASTERN BIRD SONGS, Revised
cassettes 53150-0
CD 97522-0
WESTERN BIRD SONGS, Revised
cassettes 51746-X
CD 975190

PETERSON'S MULTIMEDIA GUIDES: NORTH AMERICAN BIRDS
(CD-ROM for Windows) 73056-2

PETERSON FLASHGUIDES™

ATLANTIC COASTAL BIRDS	79286-X
PACIFIC COASTAL BIRDS	79287-8
EASTERN TRAILSIDE BIRDS	79288-6
WESTERN TRAILSIDE BIRDS	79289-4
HAWKS	79291-6
BACKYARD BIRDS	79290-8
TREES	82998-4
MUSHROOMS	82999-2
ANIMAL TRACKS	82997-6
BUTTERFLIES	82996-8
ROADSIDE WILDFLOWERS	82995-X
BIRDS OF THE MIDWEST	86733-9
WATERFOWL	86734-7
FRESHWATER FISHES	86713-4

WORLD WIDE WEB: http://www.petersononline.com

PETERSON FIELD GUIDES can be purchased at your local bookstore
or by calling our toll-free number, (800) 225-3362.

When referring to title by corresponding ISBN number,
preface with 0-395, unless title is listed with 0-618.